NAVAL POWER IN THE TWENTIETH CENTURY

Naval Power in the Twentieth Century

Edited by

N. A. M. Rodger

Foreword by

Admiral of the Fleet Sir Julian Oswald, GCB

MACMILLAN

Selection and editorial matter © N. A. M. Rodger 1996
Foreword © Sir Julian Oswald 1996
The chapters © their authors 1996

All rights reserved. No reproduction, copy or transmission of
this publication may be made without written permission.

No paragraph of this publication may be reproduced, copied or
transmitted save with written permission or in accordance with
the provisions of the Copyright, Designs and Patents Act 1988,
or under the terms of any licence permitting limited copying
issued by the Copyright Licensing Agency, 90 Tottenham Court
Road, London W1P 9HE.

Any person who does any unauthorised act in relation to this
publication may be liable to criminal prosecution and civil
claims for damages.

First published 1996 by
MACMILLAN PRESS LTD
Houndmills, Basingstoke, Hampshire RG21 6XS
and London
Companies and representatives
throughout the world

ISBN 0-333-64413-1 hardcover

A catalogue record for this book is available
from the British Library.

10 9 8 7 6 5 4 3 2 1
05 04 03 02 01 00 99 98 97 96

Printed and bound in Great Britain by
Antony Rowe Ltd
Chippenham, Wiltshire

WORCESTERSHIRE COUNTY COUNCIL	
988	
Cypher	05.05.02
359.00904	£60.00

Contents

List of Abbreviations		vii
Foreword by Admiral of the Fleet Sir Julian Oswald		xi
Notes on the contributors		xiv
	Introduction *N. A. M. Rodger*	xvii
1	Parameters of Power: The US Navy in the Twentieth Century *George W. Baer*	1
2	Luxury Fleet? The Sea Power of (Soviet) Russia *Geoffrey Till*	14
3	Imperial Germany and the Importance of Sea Power *Michael Epkenhans*	27
4	The Opportunities of Technology: British and French Naval Strategies in the Pacific, 1905–1909 *Nicholas A. Lambert*	41
5	French Naval Strategy: A Naval Power in a Continental Environment *Hervé Coutau-Bégarie*	59
6	The Indispensable Navy: Italy as a Great Power, 1911–43 *James J. Sadkovich*	66
7	Japan and Sea Power *Ian Nish*	77
8	German Naval Power in the First and Second World Wars *Werner Rahn*	88
9	Confusions and Constraints: The Navy and British Defence Planning 1919–39 *Daniel A. Baugh*	101
10	The Influence of History upon Sea Power: The Royal Navy in the Second World War *Correlli Barnett*	120
11	Wings over the Sea: The Interaction of Air and Sea Power in the Mediterranean, 1940–42 *Michael Simpson*	134
12	Seizing the Initiative: The Arctic Convoys 1944–45 *Andrew D. Lambert*	151

13	Blockade and the Royal Navy *David Brown*	163
14	Decolonisation and Coastal Operations in the East Indies, 1945–50 *G. Teitler*	177
15	The Canadian Experience of Sea Power *Alec Douglas*	188
16	Imperial Jetsam or National Guardians? The Navies of the Indian Sub-continent, 1947–72. *James Goldrick*	200
17	British Naval Planning Post-1945 *J. R. Hill*	215
18	Patnership Spurned: The Royal Navy's Search for a Joint Maritime–Air Strategy East of Suez, 1961–63. *Eric Grove*	227
19	American Naval Strategy in the Era of the Third World War: An Inquiry into the Structure and Process of General War at Sea, 1945–90 *David Alan Rosenberg*	242
Index		255

List of Abbreviations

AA	Anti-Aircraft
AOC-in-C	Air Officer Commanding-in-Chief
ASW	Anti-Submarine Warfare
BA-MA	Bundesarchiv-Militärarchiv [Freiburg-im-Breisgau & Potsdam]
BL	British Library
CID	Committee of Imperial Defence
C-in-C	Commander-in-Chief
CNO	Chief of Naval Operations [of the USN]
CNS	Chief of Naval Staff
CSM	Comité Supérieure de la Marine
DF	Direction Finding
EEC	European Economic Community
FAA	Fleet Air Arm
HF/DF	High-Frequency Direction Finding
HMS	Her/His Majesty's Ship
IAF	Indian Air Force
IN	Indian Navy
IRBM	Inter-Regional Ballistic Missile
JCS	Joint Chiefs of Staff
MAS	Motoscafo Antisommergibile *or* Motoscafo Armato con Silurante
NATO	North Atlantic Treaty Organisation
NID	Naval Intelligence Division [of the British Naval Staff]
NRN	Netherlands Royal Navy
NSHQ	Naval Service Head Quarters [of Canada]
PN	Pakistan Navy
PRO	Public Record Office [London]
RAF	Royal Air Force
RAN	Royal Australian Navy
RCAF	Royal Canadian Air Force
RCN	Royal Canadian Navy
RIN	Royal Indian Navy
RN	Royal Navy
RPN	Royal Pakistan Navy
SEATO	South-East Asia Treaty Organisation
SHM	Service Historique de la Marine [Vincennes]

List of Abbreviations

SLOC	Sea Lines of Communication
SSBN	Nuclear submarine armed with ballistic missiles
SSN	Nuclear submarine
STOVL	Short Take-Off, Vertical Landing
UN	United Nations
USN	United States Navy
VSTOL	Vertical or Short Take-Off and Landing
WEU	Western European Union

Acknowledgements

This book prints the proceedings of a conference held at the University of Exeter in July 1994. It could not have happened without the support of the University, and the hard work of Dr Peter Morris who managed it. The organisers of the conference wish also to thank D. M. L. Plymouth for supporting the Conference and providing a visit to Devonport Dockyard, and the British Academy for a grant in aid.

Foreword
Julian Oswald

There could hardly have been a more auspicious or appropriate time to call a major international conference on the parameters of naval power; as the world, newly emerged from the dark shadows of the Cold War, opens its eyes to the stark reality that all is not sweetness and light, and that threats and challenges to peace and security abound. Sadly, aggression is alive and well. In *World Conflicts* (London, 1989), Patrick Brogan estimates that since 1945 at least 80 wars have resulted in the deaths of some 15 to 20 million people (the very imprecision is frightening). Not one of these deaths was directly caused by the superpowers' struggle.

So, although the focus of this historical conference was inevitably on past events, it had special relevance and importance in providing pointers for the future. Partially at least this is because there is a certain recurring continuity in the uses of and requirements for maritime power. To be more specific, the post Cold War challenges see the emphasis moving away from possible deep ocean or blue water operations, the main concern of the last 45 years, towards the coastal or littoral use of sea power, which featured so strongly in naval annals in previous centuries.

The question posed by strategists, analysts and planners to historians, therefore centres on how navies should be organised, equipped, trained, supported, deployed and employed in the light of the historians' views of current challenges to security world-wide. Historians cannot, of course, provide a complete answer to such questions; political, financial and technical factors are also relevant. But the historians can advise when, why and in what manner the tea leaves were misread in the past.

One oft-discussed aspect of sea power is whether it is or was being used offensively or defensively. Of course the two sides in a particular theatre may consider their stance to be quite different. In the Battle of the Atlantic, 1939–43, for example, German naval operations were clearly offensive, those of the Allies defensive. But the operations of Allied anti-submarine hunter-killer groups were at least tactically offensive too. Whether NATO Maritime force operations in the Adriatic in support of the United Nations in the former Yugoslavia are offensive or defensive is a moot point.

To what extent can maritime forces exert a decisive leverage on events ashore? Very little in the case of the Second World War German offensive against Russia; a great deal in the 1991 Gulf War. But as the range, striking power and accuracy of carrier-borne aircraft, and perhaps particularly of sea-launched cruise missiles, increase, we can I think expect to see maritime forces exerting influence in more and more cases. Not least this will be because of the inherent ability of navies to provide presence and punch without the political difficulties and uncertainties of stationing and committing land troops – involving potential embroilment.

I believe it is important to signal one particular potential trap. It is clearly the case that navies will carry a steadily increasing proportion of the world's declining nuclear arsenal. The United Kingdom's position – phasing out land based systems – is a plausible precedent. Even where other countries retain some land systems the number is likely to be sharply reduced. There must exist at least a slight danger that in such circumstances some strategists will try to extend the well-thought-through, well-understood concepts of nuclear deterrence to its conventional younger brother. This would be a serious mistake. Nuclear deterrence worked. Conventional deterrence has failed, not of course always, but on more than one occasion with serious results. We need look no further than the 1991 Gulf War to see that Saddam Hussein, faced by the military might of most of the rest of the world, was not deterred, even when the destruction of a large part of his strength was inescapable.

Another aspect of naval operations on which a historian's perspective is particularly helpful is the problem, for such it is for the commander at sea, of political control. Van Tromp, de Grasse, Hawke and Nelson knew or cared little about Rules of Engagement. Their unequivocal objective was the total destruction of the enemy. As late as the Second World War the concept of Rules of Engagement as such was virtually non-existent. Now, especially in lower-level confrontational situations, tight political control is crucial. Any suggestion that it is inadequate is very sensitive politically – but this inevitably results in lack of freedom of decision on the spot. The fact that a wrong move, sometimes even an inauspicious word, will be on the world's screens, courtesy of CNN, in minutes, has a very real and direct effect on the employment of force. Inevitably political vacillation and delay will make achievement of the military objective more difficult and less certain. We need, with the help of history, to understand this trend and anticipate its further development.

Some may feel that only the rich can play at sea-power and dismiss it as irrelevant, and therefore wasteful, for other countries. Others will argue that the leverage of sea power can be very great, and at modest cost – the whole sweep of British Naval history might be held to support this later view. Some components of sea power – super-carriers for example – are clearly well beyond the reach of almost all countries. But there are very much cheaper naval systems now freely available – small missile firing fast patrol boats, quiet modern conventional submarines and, perhaps the best example of all, sea mines, which even since 1945 have had a seriously damaging and delaying effect on the world's largest navy more than once.

I suppose the real difficulty for most of us is that we have spent much of our conscious lives in the shadow of the Cold War, the great superpower stand-off, and that biggest non-event of history, global nuclear war. If navies are to be sensibly structured for the decades ahead we will require a great deal of help from historians and others who understand how things were in the centuries which preceded this historically brief period. It really would be a terrible mistake to carry our Cold War experience and thinking directly forward to the twenty-first century. But there is a very real danger that we will do so – and of course not all the lessons and experiences of the last 50 years are irrelevant.

I believe that papers from the 1994 Exeter Conference which follow carry many of the essential verities of naval power in the twentieth century and, taken in context, should provide helpful pointers for the twenty-first.

Julian Oswald

Notes on the Contributors

George W. Baer is Chairman of the Department of Strategy and Policy, and Alfred Thayer Mahan Professor of Maritime Strategy, at the US Naval War College. His most recent book is *One Hundred Years of Sea Power: The U.S. Navy, 1890–1990*.

Correlli Barnett is Fellow and former Keeper of the Archives of Churchill College Cambridge. His many books include *The Collapse of British Power*, *The Audit of War* and *Engage the Enemy more Closely: The Royal Navy in the Second World War*.

Daniel A. Baugh is Professor of Modern British History at Cornell University, and author of *British Naval Administration in the Age of Walpole*, and *Naval Administration 1715–1750*. He has written on government and society in England, 1660–1830, especially on the relief of the poor. During the past decade his articles and essays have been chiefly concerned with the maritime, financial and imperial aspects of British defence policy from the sixteenth to twentieth century.

Hervé Coutau-Bégarie is director of studies at the École Pratique des Hautes Études and director of the 'cycle de stratégie' at the Collège Interarmes de Défense. He is a former President of the Commision Française d'Histoire Maritime, and the author of numerous works on naval strategy.

David Brown has been head of the Naval Historical Branch of the British Ministry of Defence for seventeen years.

W. A. B. (Alec) Douglas served in the Royal Canadian Navy from 1950 to 1973, then was head of the official histories programme of the Canadian Armed Services until 1994. He has published among other things *Out of the Shadows: Canada in the Second World War* (with B. Greenhous), and *The Creation of a National Airforce: The Official History of the RCAF* Vol. II.

Dr Michael Epkenhans is Research Fellow of the Reichspräsident-Friedrich-Ebert Memorial Foundation at Heidelberg, and honorary lecturer at Heidelberg University. He is the author of *Die wilhelminische Flottenrüstung 1908–1914* (soon to be published in English), and the forthcoming *Admiral Albert Hopman, 1865–1942. Tagebücher, Briefe, Aufzeichnungen*.

Commander James Goldrick, RAN, a former International Research Fellow at the US Naval War College, is at present Executive Officer of

HMAS *Perth*. He is the author of *The King's Ships were at Sea*, and the editor of *Reflections on the Royal Australian Navy* and (with John B. Hattendorf) *Mahan is not Enough*.

Eric Grove is a former lecturer in strategic studies at the Royal Naval College Dartmouth, Naval Research Director of the Foundation for International Security, and Research Fellow of the University of Southampton. His books include *Vanguard to Trident: British Naval Policy since 1945*, *The Future of Sea Power* and *Maritime Strategy and European Security*. He is now senior lecturer in Politics and Deputy Director of the Centre for Security Studies at the University of Hull.

Rear-Admiral Richard Hill retired from the Royal Navy in 1983. He has written six books, including *Maritime Strategy for Medium Powers*, and edited the *Oxford Illustrated History of the Royal Navy*. He is editor of *The Naval Review* and Chairman of the Society for Nautical Research.

Dr Andrew Lambert is a Senior Lecturer in the Department of War Studies at King's College, London. His books include *The Crimean War: British Grand Strategy against Russia 1853–1856*, and *The Last Sailing Battlefleet: Maintaining Naval Mastery 1815–1850*.

Dr Nicholas Lambert was until recently an Olin Fellow at Yale University, and now holds a Charter Fellowship at Wolfson College, Oxford.

Ian Nish is Professor Emeritus of International History in the London School of Economics and Political Science.

Admiral of the Fleet Sir Julian Oswald retired from the Royal Navy in 1993 after a career of 46 years, culminating in four years as First Sea Lord and Chief of the Naval Staff.

Captain Werner Rahn, Federal German Navy, is Commanding Officer of the Militärgeschichtliche Forschungsamt, Potsdam. He is the author of *Reichsmarine und Landesverteidigung, 1991–1928*, and joint editor of the *Kriegstagebuch der Seekriegsleitung 1939–1945*.

Dr N. A. M. Rodger is Anderson Fellow of the National Maritime Museum and Honorary Research Fellow of the Centre for Maritime Historical Studies of the University of Exeter. His published work includes *The Wooden World, An Anatomy of the Georgian Navy* and *The Insatiable Earl, A Life of John Montagu Fourth Earl of Sandwich*.

David Rosenberg is an Associate Professor of Modern Military and Diplomatic History at Temple University, and a Lieutenant-Commander USNR. He has published widely on post-Second World War military and naval history and on the history of nuclear strategy. He is at present editing a book on the Berlin Crisis of 1958–62, writing a biography of Admiral Arleigh Burke, and a history of concepts, plans and policies for a future world war from 1945 to 1990.

James J. Sadkovich is a graduate of the University of Wisconsin who has published a number of studies of modern Italy and Yugoslavia, including *The Italian Navy in World War II*.

Michael Simpson is a Senior Lecturer in History at the University of Wales, Swansea, and Hon. General Editor of the Navy Records Society. He has written extensively on British and American naval history in the twentieth century, and edited volumes on Anglo-American Naval Relations and the papers of Sir James Somerville.

G. Teitler is Professor of Military History and Strategic Studies at the Royal Naval College and Royal Military Academy of the Netherlands, and author of *Vlootvoogd in de knel: Vice-Admiraal A. S. Pinke tussen de marinestaf, Indië en de Indonesische revolutie*.

Geoffrey Till is Professor and head of the Department of History and International Affairs at the Royal Naval College, Greenwich, and Visiting Professor in Maritime Studies in the Department of War Studies, King's College London. He has written among other books, *Air Power and the Royal Navy, Maritime Strategy and the Nuclear Age, Modern Sea Power*, and (with Bryan Ranft) *The Sea in Soviet Strategy*.

Introduction
N. A. M. Rodger

A hundred years ago the influence of sea power on current affairs was an accepted fact. The sensational success of Alfred T. Mahan's book *The Influence of Sea Power upon History 1660–1783*[1] and its successors,[2] made naval power the most fashionable and potent of all weapons in the statesman's armoury. Mahan was not primarily a theorist, and his works have to be read with care to extract his ideas on when, where and how sea power could be used to effect, but it is the fate of fashionable books to be read hastily and carelessly more often than with attention, and cited more often than read.[3] His contemporaries like P. H. Colomb, Sir John Laughton, Sir Julian Corbett and Sir Herbert Richmond,[4] each of whom added dimensions to naval history which Mahan had not laid open, never equalled him in popular appeal. Corbett in particular, whose ideas of naval strategy remain valuable and influential today,[5] addressed them primarily to a naval and scholarly readership, and had much difficulty in carrying the naval men with him. His subtle and searching evocation of the ways and circumstances in which sea power had actually been used and useful in the past, carried much less weight with naval opinion than the simple idea which they found in Mahan that one great battle solved every problem. At the end of his life, and at the height of his powers and reputation as an historian and theorist, Corbett was publicly rebuked by the Board of Admiralty for suggesting that naval warfare could or should take any other direction than the decisive battle leading presently to command of the sea.[6]

The lesson the public derived from Mahan was that sea power consisted above all in a battle-fleet, whose function was to meet and defeat the fleet of the enemy in a decisive action. From victory would flow unnumbered, and often unspecified, blessings. The possession of a fleet, it was often assumed, was a talisman of great-power status; necessary, even perhaps sufficient, for the aspiring candidate to that eminence. It was no accident that this idea sprang from the popularity of Mahan's books, for one of his main underlying objects was undoubtedly to persuade his compatriots that they could never take their place in the front rank of nations until the United States Navy was equal to the greatest fleets of the world. This was not an easy argument to advance in strictly logical terms, for it was an inescapable fact that a small, weak and obsolete navy had not (since 1814) exposed the United States to any external danger, nor hampered its rapid economic rise. It therefore suited Mahan's purpose, as well as his genius, to present his case by implication rather than plain statement.

The Russo-Japanese War reinforced the more simplistic Mahanian views, but the First World War delivered a severe blow to them. Dominant sea power had failed to solve all the problems of Britain and her allies; the Grand Fleet had experienced great difficulty both in fighting and in winning the decisive battle for which it had been created. For all the claims advanced after the war for the effectiveness of naval blockade as the weapon which had really brought Germany to her knees, the stark fact remained that Britain had for the first time in her history been forced to raise a mass army and deploy it on the Continent. This had major political as well as strategic implications. The losses of the war – overwhelmingly military losses on the Western Front – bred a revulsion against war and armaments of all sorts which is with us yet. Moreover Kitchener's New Army shaped the political consciousness of its generation. From being a nation of civilians with some awareness of sea power, the British became a nation of infantrymen, and arguably remained so during and after the Second World War, with the experience of military service ('military' in both senses for the majority) prolonged into the 1960s. This war, too, though fortunate for sea power in general, gave much less comfort to the simple Mahanians. Decisive battles had been relatively few, and in several of the most decisive campaigns the main fleets had been notably absent. So far from being an autonomous and decisive weapon, the fleets seemed to have worked to best effect in conjunction with the other services, as enablers and guarantors of victory rather than the direct instruments of it.

By 1945 the only country in which simple Mahanism could still be said to maintain its intellectual credibility was the United States. This was natural enough, for the USN was not only the chief beneficiary of Mahan's ideas, but by then the dominant world sea power, and the only navy which had recently won anything like traditional fleet actions. Even so it was the admirals rather than educated public opinion which kept up the faith. For a sceptical outsider like Henry Stimson, the Navy Department 'frequently seemed to retire from the realm of logic into a dim religious world in which Neptune was God, Mahan his prophet, and the United States Navy the only true church'.[7] The USN was not alone in needing a new and more cogent intellectual justification for sea power. But no second Mahan arose in the 1950s. Sea power remained, as it had been between the wars, a matter of professional debate behind closed doors between naval staffs and politicians. It was no longer a question of vital public interest, and historians (seldom immune to the currents of fashion) generally ignored it.

Not until 1976, when Paul M. Kennedy published *The Rise and Fall of British Naval Mastery*,[8] did a serious scholar present a coherent study of the whole of British naval history which went far to replace Mahan's explanations, or implications. Kennedy emphasised the economic impact of sea power; always the most expensive and burdensome of all the state's activities, a navy could only justify itself when it 'paid its way' by assuring and protecting the sources of the nation's wealth. For Britain, sea power had made possible a rise to greatness which was founded on overseas trade and investment. By the end of the nineteenth century, however, Britain's economic lead was slipping towards countries (notably Germany and the United States) with better-endowed and more flexible economies, and the naval trident, he argued, was bound to follow. Kennedy also adopted arguments drawn from the Edwardian geographer Sir Halford Mackinder, suggesting that sea power in general (not just British power in particular) had derived its unique importance from economic circumstances which were passing away. So long as water transport preserved its economic advantages of cheapness, security and flexibility, littoral states were bound to dominate the fragmented and disunited economies of the interior with their high transport costs and numerous political and technical barriers to trade. The rise of the great land empires, however, and the spread of railways, would inevitably erode if not destroy the advantage of commercial shipping, and consequently of sea power.

Kennedy's interpretation was intellectually vastly more coherent than Mahan's, and its message that economics drives history, and that naval and imperial power belonged to the past, was readily acceptable, especially in Britain. It still has powerful advocates, even in this volume, but it is already beginning to show signs of strain. The collapse of Marxism has done nothing to strengthen the status of economic history as a teleology. The transport costs of railways remain stubbornly higher than those of ships, even when the ships have to cover much greater distances to reach their destinations. The inevitable triumph of the great land empires is looking a great deal less inevitable now that only the United States and (barely) China survive at all as unitary states. At the same time naval and military history have regained much of the public interest and intellectual respectability which they lacked for so many years, and new ideas and theories are coming forward. Colin S. Gray has published an impressive study arguing that in wars between a dominant land power and a dominant sea power, history shows the sea power consistently to have certain decisive advantages.[9] Rather than winning wars by winning battles, in the

Mahanian style, his sea power buys time for recovery. It preserves a defensive position and allows it to build up its strength while the land power exhausts and dissipates its own. In a global war of attrition, sea power is staying power.

This is a powerful argument, but it applies to a single, admittedly important, case. Like Mahan and Kennedy, it takes its text chiefly (though not only) from the experience of Britain as the leading case of a country whose rise to be a great power, and a great naval power, went hand in hand. It addresses itself to the distinctively British, and later American, problem of the dominant naval power facing a victorious land power. It does not claim to advance any universal theory of sea power.

Nor does this volume, but its focus is on sea power at large. The experience of a century of naval war has taught us many ways in which Mahan's ideas were inadequate and superficial, but it cannot be said that we have today any general explanation of how naval power works and why it is important which can credibly be applied to many different nations and navies (not just the British and the Americans) in the circumstances of the past and the present. The object of the conference (held at the University of Exeter in July 1994) whose proceedings are printed here was to look back over the century in search of some ideas out of which such a general theory of naval power might be constructed. The participants were selected and instructed to look at the experience of each of the major navies of this century, and some of the lesser ones, in order to examine what navies could and could not do; how, and why, and where sea power worked, or did not work. How far did naval power make nations great, and keep them great; to what extent was it an offensive weapon which won wars, or a defensive weapon which ensured national survival; what strategic objects in war and political objects in peace could be best, or only, met by a navy? Looking at the experience of different navies, we tried to work towards broad conclusions about which countries got value, or could have got value, from the money invested in their fleets, and which wasted it in pursuit of the irrelevant or the unobtainable. Would some countries have been better off to have saved the burden on their economies which building a fleet entailed? Did natural land powers waste their strength on chimerical naval ambitions, or natural sea powers drain their resources into futile continental campaigns? Can navies ever defeat armies, and should they try? These and the like questions were addressed to the experience of different countries; some of them over the whole century, some of them in the light of particular campaigns.

We cannot claim to have provided definitive answers to such large questions, but at least the volume clears much ground. Some conclusions are obvious. Wilhelmine Germany spent recklessly if not fatally in pursuit of a strategic chimaera, building a fleet which could not realistically have been expected to achieve what was hoped for, or anything else which would have justified a fraction of the money invested in it. The German Navy rose from its ashes in the 1930s having learnt nothing from its experience, and committed itself to exactly the same course. Here, clearly, was money ill-spent on an unnecessary and misguided fleet. The Japanese case, on the other hand, equally disastrous in the end, has more to do with political and diplomatic miscalculation, committing Japan to an unwinnable war. Though the Imperial fleet was thus destroyed, it had been an excellent investment for Japan, might still have been with less reckless handling, and is so again today. The Soviet Russian case seems to have many parallels with the German: a Continental military power, impressed by Mahanite doctrines, sought to buy her way out of the limitations of geography, and only bought her way into bankruptcy. The Italian Navy as it appears in this volume, though not always fortunate in battle, successfully applied in the Second World War the 'risk strategy' which was so fatal to Germany in the First. Never strong enough to fight its major enemy directly, the Italian Navy could and did cope with the local threat (France), and exploit geography to render the British position in the Mediterranean almost impossibly difficult when she faced so many other enemies at the same time. The United States presents yet another situation. Facing no external enemies capable of a credible threat to any part of the country (Hawaii perhaps excepted), the United States Navy always had to justify its existence either as a defence against unlikely enemies and improbable attacks; or as a means of offence, projecting power overseas in competition with other services which claimed to be able to do it better or faster. Hence the sense, so evident in most histories of the USN, that foreigners come and go, but the real enemies are always in Washington.[10]

In all these different histories, the influence of geography is paramount. The luxury of distance, of remoteness from threat, allowed the USN to develop in one way, and the Royal Canadian Navy in another, quite different fashion. Italy was able to exploit her position athwart the British imperial sea-route (and intelligently improve it with air power), while Wilhelm II tried to buy himself a place in the sun, and only got a place in the North Sea. France in the twentieth century found, as she had found before, that an impressive fleet was no defence against overland invasion of the homeland, or subversion of the colonial empire. Moreover the relationship of the French Navy and the state has more often than not been one of mistrust. The Dutch, with a much happier history of civil–naval relations, had no more success using ships against colonial rebels in the East

Indies than the French had in Vietnam. Britain, after two centuries of profiting from her insular position, kept safe from European rivals by the same navy which dominated their overseas trade, found the facts of geography turning against her in the twentieth century. Sir John Fisher attempted a radical technological solution to the new problem, but in essence it was insoluble. Only with allies was it possible to face primary threats in more than one part of the world at once.

This is as true in peace as in war. Navies, even more than most armed forces, are powerful instruments of diplomacy, deterrence and persuasion. For the major western navies, these have been central preoccupations for the past forty years, and much of the interest of the conference, which was enriched by the participation of officers with experience of naval planning and operations, lay in its treatment of war-planning, deterrence, peace-keeping and the whole range of activities short of major war in which navies may be engaged. The navies concerned are not only those of the major sea powers; time and space did not suffice to examine more than a few instances of second-rank naval powers, but it is clear that sea power may still be a good investment on quite a small scale, if intelligently matched to worthwhile objectives, attainable within the resources prudently available.

If there was one single theme which emerged from the conference, it is that there are not many simple, universal laws of sea power. Nothing in the experience of the past century or the situation of the present day suggests that naval power has lost any of its influence on history. On the contrary, the power to influence history by sea power is more widely spread than ever before, so that the freedom of action of individual navies is much restricted. The days are certainly gone when a single British squadron in the Western Approaches could effectively dominate the oceans of the world; and they are gone, not because British sea power has declined, but because other navies have arisen all over the world where once the threats came only from European powers conveniently close at hand. Now it is only broad alliances which can hope to face the number and diversity of naval powers, great and small, to be met with across the world. Within this context, the possibilities open to individual countries continue to be greatly influenced by geography. Open frontiers, especially with major military powers on the other side of them, are still a great obstacle to developing and exploiting sea power. Island states still have enormous advantages in using the sea for their own defence and profit. Distance remains a costly tyranny for the offensive as well as a precious security for the defensive. Most long-distance international trade still travels by sea, and no nation seriously

Introduction xxiii

involved in international trade can safely ignore it. Money matters, in this most expensive and complex of all state activities. Reckless investment in sea power is as likely to lead to bankruptcy as victory, even if the investment itself be well conceived. Arguably the surrogate war of a peacetime naval race has it in common with real war at sea that it is essentially a matter of attrition, in which the weaker ultimately goes to the wall. Logically it need not always be the strong military power which loses the naval war of attrition, but it is obvious enough why it has often been so. There is matter here to support those who see an integral link between successful sea power and democracy, even if the nature of the link might be argued. Perhaps there are few surprises here: the universal principles of naval power, if such they be, are simple enough, even banal. But the book is not altogether useless which calls the reader back to neglected truths, and lays foundations upon which the grander edifices of future thinkers may be built.

NOTES

1. Boston, 1890.
2. For which see *A Bibliography of the Works of Alfred Thayer Mahan*, ed. John B. Hattendorf & Lynn C. Hattendorf (Newport R.I., 1986).
3. On Mahan's influence see *The Influence of History on Mahan*, ed. John B. Hattendorf (Newport R.I., 1991).
4. *Mahan is not Enough: The Proceedings of a Conference on the Works of Sir Julian Corbett and Admiral Sir Herbert Richmond*, ed. James Goldrick & John B. Hattendorf (Newport R.I., 1993). D. M. Schurman, *The Education of a Navy: The Development of British Naval Strategic Thought, 1867–1914* (London, 1965); and *Julian S. Corbett, 1854–1922: Historian of British Maritime Policy from Drake to Jellicoe* (London, 1981). Colomb's major work *Naval Warfare: Its Ruling Principles and Practice Historically Treated* (originally London, 1891) is edited with an introduction by Barry M. Gough (Annapolis, Md., 1990, 2 vols).
5. *Some Principles of Maritime Strategy* (London, 1911).
6. In a note prefaced to Vol. III of his official history *Naval Operations*, published immediately after his death in 1922. See Schurman, *Corbett*, p. 193.
7. George W. Baer, *One Hundred Years of Sea Power: The U.S. Navy, 1890–1990* (Stanford, 1994), p. 114. Stimson's memoirs were published in 1948, but the remark is quoted in connection with the London naval conference of 1930.
8. London; 2nd edn 1983.
9. *The Leverage of Sea Power: The Strategic Advantage of Navies in War* (New York, 1992).

10. A foreigner cannot help remarking that the USN actually names some of its ships (*Forrestal, Carl Vinson, Henry M. Jackson, John C. Stennis*) after the allies and victors of the great battles of Capitol Hill and the Pentagon.

1 Parameters of Power: The US Navy in the Twentieth Century
George W. Baer

A parameter is defined as a characteristic element of a member of a system, an arbitrary constant whose value describes the member's behaviour or attributes. The characteristic of the US Navy in the twentieth century was a fleet strategy of offensive sea control. That was the way the service identified itself. Power was invested in an offensively oriented fleet.

The Navy said that offensive sea control was characteristic of its way of war, the prime element of its definition of purpose. This self-definition gave the Navy freedom for presumptive planning during the many periods when it received no political direction, when it had to make deductions from a vague national policy, or when it sought to influence the nature of an American war. Only in the 1990s did the Navy declare a new characteristic, when it exchanged the doctrine of combat on the sea for the doctrine of projection of force from the sea. That was a major parameter shift, closing the book on a century of Mahan.[1]

We all know that neither the role nor the force structure of any navy is self-evident, that navies are contingent creations. By defining its own central characteristic as offensive sea control, the US Navy was able to control the answer to the fundamental question: what's a navy for? Mahan and his sea-power supporters at the turn of the century put the Navy at the centre of national strategy and put an offensive battle fleet at the centre of the US Navy. America, the Navy averred, was a maritime state facing maritime challenges. In a competitive world it was accepted that great powers must command great fleets. The logic of operations meant that command of the sea came from offensive concentration of a battle fleet. Isolated coastal defence vessels, or independently sailing cruiser squadrons could not prevent Spain, Germany or Britain from establishing a threatening fleet in the Caribbean, or meeting the Japanese fleet in the Pacific. Bay-bound monitors and the Army's immobile coast artillery could not break an enemy blockade or prevent an insult to the American coast. Only a forward deployed offensive fleet of battleships could sink an approaching fleet.

Given what the Navy declared was so obvious a national need, with the Navy's strategic value so obvious, with the logic of naval warfare so clear, the Navy thought it could act almost autonomously. The Navy had declared itself as central to the national destiny, to national security, to national prosperity. The Navy had identified the threat in the fleets of rivals. It had a theory of victory based on sea control. It had a concept of operations based on fleet engagement. So comprehensive and coherent was the doctrine of sea power that the Navy in fact had empowered itself with strategic independence.

For fifty years after 1890 this characterisation held fast. For fifty years there really was a fleet threat at sea, or a challenge that could be plausibly imputed, or a political opportunity that a display of fleet power might serve. The battle of Santiago de Cuba and the acquisition of a maritime empire, the self-justifying acquisition of bases in the Pacific, the pressure against Germany at time of the Venezuelan blockade, the voyage of the Great White Fleet to Japan and around the world, the Black, Red, and Orange war plans, all pivoted on the concept of offensive sea control.

Experience in the First World War did not change the Navy's view. To be sure, no US battleship fired a shot at the opposing enemy fleets. No US battleship even saw the German High Seas Fleet. The Navy's most famous operation was to lay a minefield. Furthermore, the Navy gave up its autonomy and sailed in combined operations with the greatest navy in the world. The Navy in the war was mainly a transport service – the ferry to France. And, in the war, ships in convoy crossed the ocean before the Navy cleared the sea of predators. Effective sea control turned out to be local, not absolute.

But neither the operational or the political experience of the war caused the Navy's leaders to alter their fundamental position. The Secretary of the Navy might sigh that he wished he had built more destroyers. Critics might complain that the fleet was top-heavy. Others said that mining and convoying – to say nothing of the use of U-boats in a *guerre-de-course* – had changed the means of gaining sea control. But for the key US political and naval leaders the Mahanian analysis was still valid. The fleet challenge remained, part of a Darwinian maritime competition among great powers. Such zero-sum competition would continue in the postwar world. Great navies would still exist, whether Britain or Germany won. Against these, for hemispheric or imperial defence, or for the leverage to enforce a Wilsonian peace, the Navy sought a fleet second to none, battleships able to sail to the reaches of the oceans and engage thereupon. Strategic independence demanded parity with the world's largest navy, and more if one contemplated a two-ocean war.

The absence of a national enemy after the war, however, meant that strategic planning had to be presumptive. Congress refused to expand the battle fleet. Politicians tried to manage competition without force. Naval arms limitation depended on comparability, upon a symmetry of navies, upon the idea that decisive battle would be between mirror-imaged fleets. That was the core assumption of the naval arms limitation conferences of the 1920s and 1930s. Their purpose was not to reconfigure naval force structure, but to end warship building by establishing ratios of force with respect to geographic position. They were not intended to change naval strategy or the concept of fleet sea control. Although, quite rightly, the Navy bridled at the idea of a yardstick of combatant values, proportional settlement was possible because of comparability. Capital ships, fleet organisation and a Mahanian vision of naval power gave the three oceanic navies (the US, the British and the Japanese) their common denominator. The Navy's parameter of power was not denied at Washington, or at Geneva, or at London. It was confirmed and codified.

While US political leaders settled naval competition without an arms race and without sea battle, they also destroyed the practical ability of the US Navy to conduct its Pacific strategy. Forswearing fortified bases west of Hawaii meant that the US Navy could not send its battle line across the Pacific to deliver the decisive blow. Politics conceded sea control in the western Pacific to Japan. So naval strategy luffed. Without a declared enemy it was hard to make a case for an offensive. Without a fleet capable of sustaining a distant offensive, War Plan Orange was removed one step further from reality.

Naval force turned out not to be as enfeebled by the treaties as it at first seemed. In the 1920s and 1930s the service innovated with war games and the offensive use of carrier air power, and modernised its battleships. The beneficial results of this preparation were to be seen in the Pacific war. The Navy's weakness in the 1920s and 1930s, however, remained that politicians did not use its strategy of offensive sea control. Thus war games remained staff forecasts, and war plans remained hermetic exercises. In 1938 the Navy dropped its strategy for an offensive naval war in the Pacific. When in 1940 Franklin Roosevelt held the Pacific Fleet at Hawaii, he was hopeful the battleships might have some deterrent effect, but no one could say in support of what particular interest. All the Navy knew was that if its battle line was supposed to be preparing for war, it should be back on the west coast at its supply facilities. When its

Commander-in-Chief, Admiral Richardson, told that to Roosevelt he was sacked, but Richardson was right. To leave the ships in Pearl Harbor unprepared and undirected was contrary to offensive sea control.

In the Second World War, winning sea control, the Navy transported and supplied 7.6 million American servicemen across the seas. It thus met America's most essential strategic condition of keeping combat far from American shores.

Both the Americans and the Japanese began their war with a similar theory of naval warfare: offensive sea control hinged on decisive fleet engagement. Once war began, however, the contrast in strategic innovation could not be greater. The US Navy instantly moved to dispersal, attrition, and attack of the land. The Navy attacked cargo shipping without waiting to establish fleet command. It broke from concentration by turning fleet-support submarines loose on a *guerre-de-course*. Aircraft carriers became the centre of autonomous, ever-mobile strike forces, which were, like submarines, able to concentrate swiftly as needed. Amphibious warfare claimed land objectives, notably island airfields, that supported the maritime advance. All this was designed to apply unremitting pressure on an enemy dependent upon the sea.

US officers sought Mahan's benediction. An official historian of the submarine campaign wrote: 'though the introduction of the submarine changed the tactical picture, it did not change the rules of grand strategy outlined by Mahan'.[2] In the view of most naval officers, naval blockade, supplemented with Air Force bombing, would compel the Japanese to surrender. It would be enough to apply the 'remorseless, steady pressure' of which Mahan wrote, 'cutting the resources of the enemy'.[3] However, against the Navy's prescription for a protracted war of attrition stood the political need of a faster victory, created by the entry of the Soviet Union into the war against Japan and the eagerness of Americans to end the conflict. The Navy's way of war did not promise swift decision. Thus the Army's contention prevailed that only an invasion would force a fast surrender.

It was shipping that took US military power abroad, but not across open oceans as envisioned by Mahan's doctrine of command. Protection of that shipping showed another type of naval strategy, showed that fleet-determined, offensive sea control was not the only way to gain effective use of the sea. 'Put in a nutshell,' writes Marc Milner, 'the principal means of *defending* shipping in the Second World War was avoidance of the enemy.'[4] Shipping also reflected productivity, a key element of maritime success. The United States simply produced more cargo and transport ships than the Germans could sink, and more warships than could the Japanese.

The Second World War was the high point of American sea power. The Navy had integrated its ships, naval air, and Marines into a true maritime strategy, true to pragmatic and diverse naval traditions if not strictly to Mahan's prescriptions. Almost immediately after the war, however, the Air Force put the still-central doctrine of offensive sea control under a challenge that almost overwhelmed the Navy. First, the Air Force noted that there was no credible threat at sea. The enemy lay deep inland, at the centre of a continental empire, reachable only by air or land. Second, the Air Force claimed that strategic bombing was now the decisive mode of warfare. Command of the air replaced command of the sea. The Strategic Air Command, however, had no strategy below the level of all-out war, and few listened to Navy voices that said such a war would be politically meaningless. Third, the Air Force said that air-atomic bombing should be its mission, and the military services reorganised according to the weapons they used. That would mean the end of Navy air. Fourth, Congress weighed in with a call for a merger of the services into a single national defence establishment under unitary command. All this posed a mortal threat to the Navy's force structure, its sense of mission, its operational autonomy, and its diversity – the sources of the wondrous successes of the recent war.

Unprepared for peacetime politics and the pell-mell demobilisation, the Navy was not ready to face the threat that it might lose its air arm, that the Marines might be absorbed into the Army, and that its operations might be subordinated to a central command. The service had done no long-range planning. To avoid dissolution the Navy had to show that offensive sea control, its essential characteristic, was strategically useful against the Soviet Union, and to justify its diverse force.

It made its defence in terms of the policy of containment. Containment called for a defensive, peripheral, maritime strategy. Effectively an island power, the United States would support the sea-facing armies of continental allies in classic maritime form, to surround its continental enemy. It was no accident that the North Atlantic Treaty was named for an ocean.

Also, in the decisive years immediately after the war, Air Force bombers were not able to deliver the bomb to Soviet centres of gravity. That meant, and this was the Navy's argument, that a general war would not be a short atomic spasm but a protracted war of sequential campaigns in which sea control would be essential. That hypothesis fitted the Navy's paradigm. It justified the carrier fleet. The absolutely necessary sea lanes over which a maritime power supported a continental campaign would be secured by the destruction of Soviet submarines. This would be done not by hunting them down at sea but by bombing them at their source, in their pens. The

Navy's established skill at delivering *precision* air strikes would be directed against a continental foe *in the name of sea control*. Forward-deployed carriers would undertake immediate offensive operations against the land, in order to guarantee command of the sea.

Vice Admiral Sherman, as Deputy CNO for Operations, reconceptualised the Navy's strategy and justified its power just at the moment when the Navy most needed a contemporary restatement of its value. Sherman declared a sea-control need and a sea-control threat. His argument for naval force was as useful to the Navy as Mahan's had been fifty years before. As Norman Friedman wrote, the argument equated freedom of action at sea with freedom to strike at land.[5] Deep precision strikes by Navy air, *with or without* atomic bombs, were part of a sea-control strategy conducted by a forward-deployed fleet led by the contemporary capital ship, the aircraft carrier.[6]

The Navy thus described a naval air war against a continental power. It was a strategy that preserved the force structure that had won the Pacific war. Even the Air Force could not rebut the argument that such land strikes by Navy air served a sea control function. In 1947 the National Security Act told the Air Force it could not take control of naval aviation. The Navy's thinking, however, had limits. It did not take into account other possible maritime strategies, such as defensive sea control or limited war. And there remained the question of whether the country should adopt a wholly new air-atomic way of war, of intercontinental atomic bombing, as the Air Force wanted; and if so who was to deliver the new weapon, and in line with what national strategy?

Some Navy officers failed to heed Sherman's insistence on the centrality of sea control and joint operations, on function rather than on a weapon or a system. That drew the Navy into a confrontation with the Air Force, for they argued that the Navy's top priority was to deliver the atomic bomb. The National Security Act of 1947 had saved the carriers, and the Key West Agreement of 1948 gave the Navy access to the atomic bomb. The vision of an air-atomic war had whet Navy thirsts, and those had not been slaked. Admiral Nimitz had proposed that *land-based* Navy air be used for bombing targets beyond those related to naval sea control. Rear Admiral Gallery proposed that carrier air take over the strategic delivery of the atomic bomb into central Russia, leaving the Air Force the secondary follow-on missions. Vice Admiral Radford, the Vice CNO, proposed a 'full air program'. This shift to air power and strategic bombing accepted the Air Force contention that atomic bombs were the key to a general war, that an air-atomic war would be short, and that a short war made sea control unnecessary. That was a radical departure from Sherman's insistence on sea control as the rationale for Navy air. Naval aviators, grasping for ways to save the carriers, led the Navy up the Air Force's garden path. That was unwise because when the Navy gave up sea control as its reason for being, it gave up its best position from which to translate bureaucratic victories into an effective maritime strategy.

A few saw the danger and reasserted a Navy way of war. To less panicked Navy officers it was not the admirals who were in revolt but the Air Force, which was proposing an untenable form of warfare based upon an unsupportable theory of victory. In 1948, writing for the General Board, Captain Arleigh Burke called upon the Navy not to be misled by the notion of a wonder-weapon, and to return to 'established concepts and techniques of war'. While Burke did not reject tactical counterforce atomic bombing – because he taught the Navy's low-altitude pilots could land bombs on military targets whereas the less accurate high-altitude horizontal bombers of the Air Force could not – he argued that indiscriminate bombing of cities could not give a politically meaningful victory. A war with the Soviet Union, Burke said, would be drawn out. Prudence called for preparing a flexible strategy and a diversified war machine. What the Navy could do was keep the war overseas and mount a counter-offensive upon the continent. Accordingly, said Burke in 1948, the Navy's first job, and that of the fast-carrier task forces, was offensive sea control. That meant anti-submarine warfare.[7]

This position was lost in the two bruising debates of 1949, one over the fate of the Navy's new bombers and the supercarrier designed to carry them, and the other over service unification. Navy aviators thought the moment of truth was at hand. Unless they engrossed their air mission they would lose all strategic standing. And, if the Air Force's argument prevailed, that the services should reflect weapons systems, the Navy would lose its carriers as well, and its capacity to control amphibious operations.

The low point came when Secretary of Defense Johnson said to Admiral Conolly:

> Admiral, the Navy is on its way out. Now, take amphibious operations. There's no reason for having a Navy and a Marine Corps. General Bradley [Chairman of the Joint Chiefs] . . . tells me that amphibious operations are a thing of the past. We'll never have any more amphibious operations. That does away with the Marine Corps. And the Air Force can do anything that the Navy can do nowadays, so that does away with the Navy.[8]

That reopened the question: could the Navy put naval strategy together again?

Admiral Burke as CNO from 1955 to 1961 made a run up the centre of the air-atomic debate with the fleet ballistic missile and the doctrine of discretionary targeting called finite deterrence. Polaris was the Navy's answer to the Strategic Air Command; finite deterrence was the Navy's answer to the SIOP's (Single Integrated Operational Plan) inflexible bombing doctrine. Polaris put the Navy back in the forefront of national strategy. Burke made another run right around the air-atomic debate with the doctrine of flexible response, based on an expanded fleet for intervention in limited wars away from the central front. The crises of the late 1950s – Suez, Taiwan Strait, Quemoy and Matsu, and Lebanon – showed off the carriers and the maritime amphibious force. But Navy air was limited to these examples of flexible response in situations of regional, not general, conflict. In 1962 the Defense Department pulled the carriers out of the SIOP. Finite deterrence and flexible response had not added up to a maritime strategy, and indeed had forced sea control down the list of Navy priorities.

As offensive sea control was not at issue in Korea and Vietnam, the Navy made another strong assertion of power projection against the land, still, however, in the context of limited, regional war. Navy planes protected army troops around Pusan; Inchon vindicated the Fleet Marine Force and showed that amphibious operations had value in the atomic age. And while the Air Force never let the Navy forget that its pilots launched from carriers that were not facing a threat at sea, the Navy drew the lesson that power projection, that is, naval air and sea operations in support of land operations in a limited war, was now its most characteristic function. The Navy might have responded more aggressively to the Air Force that the absence of a challenge at sea was the result of its offensive sea control force, against which no naval force was willing to stand.

Expression of sea control doctrine receded further in the 1970s, and so did power projection except in the case of limited war, when the Soviet Navy adopted a defensive network comprised of land-based naval air, submarines, and shipborne missiles. The purpose of that was to stand off any approaching US carrier force. Such a defence made it much harder for the US Navy to envision an attack on Soviet targets on land, perhaps impossible to execute the 'attack at the source'. It made it much more difficult to operate near shore or in an enclosed space like the eastern Mediterranean where there was a strong Soviet presence. Thus it was more difficult for the Navy to claim an offensive or power projection role in a general war.

Open-ocean ASW remained a critical mission. But if Soviet attack submarines were *withdrawn* from the open ocean, then the importance of sea-control ASW was reduced. And shadowing Soviet SSBNs was really part of deterrence, part of the prevention of war, not part of a strategy of offensive sea control in time of war, except that Soviet SSBNs would be attacked should deterrence fail. In similar fashion, the American SSBN force was essentially removed from naval war-*waging* strategy. Then, in the 1970s, it appeared that even the Soviet SSBNs were being withdrawn back from the open ocean to the defensive bastions. Inside and outside the US Navy there was great confusion. While the Navy remained unchallenged at sea there was no doctrinal agreement on its purpose or on its main characteristics.

Admiral Zumwalt, CNO 1970–74, tried to get the service to look at procurement and strategy in terms of mission rather than in terms of exercising a delivery platform. He thought the headlock of the aviators had led the service to put undue emphasis on power projection by carrier air. He cancelled the offensive mission of 'attack at the source'. The big carriers were too vulnerable to deployed Soviet submarines and stand-off missiles. The Navy therefore wanted to keep its carriers out to sea as much as possible. What Zumwalt revived was the interest in localised sea control. He boosted low-value ships for broadly based sea-control campaigns. He proposed to disperse the carriers. A concentrated battle group around a heavy carrier was too tempting a target for Soviet land-based air, submarines, and missile-shooters. Admiral Kidd of the Sixth Fleet said, in 1970, that the missile age meant that no longer 'may naval task forces expect to group in classic manner, search out the enemy, and engage'.[9] Operation amidst the large Soviet presence in the eastern Mediterranean – the *locus classicus* of the resurgence twenty-five years earlier of the doctrine of forward deployment – led Zumwalt to declare in 1971 that if the fleets engaged in non-nuclear combat the US would probably lose.[10]

Zumwalt's critics said that his sea-control approach was only tactical, that it was not a naval or maritime strategy at all, still less a definition of sea power. They said that it was as inhibiting of strategic thinking as the operational perspective and parochial 'union' thinking that Zumwalt attacked. It is true that in reordering priorities Zumwalt did not integrate the elements of naval warfare into a long-range naval strategy. Elements of warfare remained unconnected to larger national political considerations. That disconnect, with the ensuing deductive nature of naval strategy, was the besetting conceptual weakness in Navy thinking throughout the 1970s.[11] And, finally, the damning argument against Zumwalt's low-end force was that it could not assure sea control on a global scale against a serious Soviet naval threat in a general war. Zumwalt's successor said dismissively of the low-end force: 'It's [for] a Third World strategy'.[12]

In 1975, the Navy's 200th anniversary, the active fleet had dropped below 500 ships, the smallest number since 1939. In 1976, Admiral Rickover, with reckless hyperbole, told Congress that in a submarine war he would prefer to be in command of the Soviet submarine force.[13] In 1977 the active fleet was down to 464 ships.

The confusion of the 1970s got worse as the decade came to an end. Strategic indecision was related to low budgets, a wish to deal with the Soviets through diplomacy, a hope for arms agreement, and a post-Vietnam aversion to limited war. Containment was to be pursued by a strong stand on the NATO central front. It was the late 1940s all over again. To the extent that military planners thought a central front invasion could be stopped in weeks, they paid less attention to naval force, to sea control, to forward presence, to power projection, and to those customary venues of the Navy, the Pacific and the Mediterranean. Sea control would not materially effect the course of a short war in Europe.

The Navy's offensive doctrine was thus rendered meaningless by the strategy it was supposed to support. Defense Secretary Brown said that the Navy was for ASW and convoy in the Atlantic, and for 'localised contingencies outside Europe and peacetime presence'. Navy Secretary Claytor charged that this denial of an offensive role in a 'Europe first' policy and the reduction of the Navy to gunboat diplomacy and patrol constituted 'one of the sternest assaults on the Navy's tradition roles and missions in decades'.[14] For a couple of years at the end of the 1970s, the navy lost its strategic focus. It was still pre-eminent, still maintaining its edge in technological innovation, still buying new equipment and serving practical needs, but it seemed to many irrelevant to a general war.

Mahan would have seen the problem in a moment. The Navy had thought its interests and value could be taken for granted. In fact those interests had to be established and defined, from inside as well as outside the service. The Navy had disassociated itself from broad national positions, and so disassociated itself from the source of its strength. Close adherence to heavy carrier doctrine, which re-emerged after Zumwalt's tenure, put the Navy in a double bind. It could not detach its central doctrine from a weapon that had lost its credibility. Everyone thought that it would be too risky to use the carriers close in, which thus negated 'attack at the source'. The divergence of dominant Navy thinking from national policy, and the debates that continued within the service, meant some years of discouraging confusion.[15]

That was the problem Navy leaders took in hand at the end of the 1970s. They rejoined service and political views in the form of an offensive 'Maritime Strategy', publicly declaring that the Navy's putative weakness was in fact the country's strength. The offensive 'Maritime Strategy' of the early 1980s revived a Mahanian answer to the question of why America needed a big, expensive, carrier-centred Navy. It combined sea control with power projection. It was a return to 'attack at the source' by carriers and now also by submarines, combined with a classical amphibious assault on the flanks of the central battlefront, as the Army and the Air Force now felt more confident about containing an invasion. The formulation of the 'Maritime Strategy' overcame the internal dispute on the use of naval force, and how the Navy should present itself to the nation. It tied together into a comprehensive, easily understandable synthesis the main elements of an offensive strategy. It was how the Navy presented itself to the nation.

The shrewdly promoted doctrine moved the argument about the Navy's mission away from reactive sea control and away also from limited, Third World interventionism. It moved the Navy to a world-wide offensive in a general war, using the strong force the Navy had at hand. It expanded the central front by attacks on the flanks and the rear. It characterised the Soviet naval and missile forces as strategically plausible targets whose defences could be overcome by the US Navy's high-end ships and airplanes. This confidence rested on new sources of intelligence and technological advances that, it was said, vastly reduced the risk factor. US warships and aircraft could now defend themselves. Thus they could execute sea, air, and land strikes *within* the Soviet bastion defence. High technology enabled US submariners to attack the Soviets' all-important SSBN reserve force, the Soviets' ultimate ability to control the outcome of a war. This would also reinforce sea control in terms of ASW, as Soviet attack submarines, withdrawn to defend the strategic reserve, would thus be removed from the open ocean where they would pose the major threat to the sea lanes. Likewise, a global US naval force would expose Soviet flanks to amphibious operations supported by carrier air in the north, south and west. More broadly, Navy planners hoped to move the national strategy away from a Soviet-initiated conflict on the central front towards a protracted, conventional, maritime war of attrition, one of global scope, the sort of war in which relative advantage would fall to the United States and its world-wide maritime allies. From its maritime position the US could regrasp the strategic initiative and control the shape of a general war, and thus define the terms of victory.

This line of thought was much criticised as unrealistic, self-serving, contradictory, and provocative. Unified commanders, directly responsible for developing specific naval strategy, realised the 'Maritime Strategy' was not a specific war plan but a broad public justification of how naval force could be used, a declarative strategy. At the same time, they were able to use it as a point of reference for operational exercises. In these many ways it helped the Navy to ride the crest of the rearmament of the 1980s and to save the high-performance, high-ticket attack carriers and submarines. Those, after all, were the Navy's main existing assets, and alone were available to execute an immediate offensive if war broke out.

The biggest drawback to the 'Maritime Strategy' was that it never redirected the national strategy. Few political leaders were willing to forsake the grotesque stability of Mutual Assured Destruction and envisioned war with the Soviet Union as an instrument of policy. We don't know the full impact of this Navy thinking on Soviet naval planning. We will never know if the war plan based on the 'Maritime Strategy' could have been employed successfully. The rationale for the large capital ship fleet and offensive sea control disappeared with the end of the Cold War. In 1990, a hundred years after Mahan, the United States found itself again without agreement on the use and composition of its Navy.

Everyone agreed that the US was a maritime state with innumerable global interests. Once again, however, there was no open-ocean threat, or one that the country could easily presume. So the Navy and Marine Corps found they had to restate what naval force meant to the United States. Such a position was published in 1992 in a Department of the Navy White Paper. It declared 'a fundamental shift away from open-ocean warfighting *on* the sea toward joint operations conducted *from* the sea'.[16] Instead of showing the value of offensive sea control in a general war, it turned attention back to limited fighting in regional war. Sea control was not thrown overboard – how could it be? What the Navy wisely noted was the plurality of uses that have characterised most navies for most of the time, and its own for most of American history, but something of a doctrinal revolution had taken place. In 1992, adopting ...*From the Sea*, the US Navy closed its book, at least for the time being, on the offensive sea control doctrine of Mahan.

NOTES

1. For critical readings and good ideas I am grateful to colleagues in the Strategy and Policy Department, US Naval War College, and to Frank Uhlig. My theme is developed in George W. Baer, *One Hundred Years of Sea Power: The U.S. Navy, 1890–1990* (Stanford, 1994). Special thanks to

Captain Paul Odell, USN, who delivered the paper to the Exeter Conference.
2. Philip M. Morse, 'The Antisubmarine Problem', in Office of Scientific Research and Development, *Summary Technical Report of Division 6, NDRC: Volume 1, A Survey of Subsurface Warfare in World War II* (Washington, D.C., 1946), p. 7.
3. Alfred T. Mahan, *The Influence of Sea Power Upon History, 1660–1783* (Boston, 1890), p. 209.
4. Marc Milner, 'The Battle of the Atlantic', in *Decisive Campaigns of the Second World War*, ed. John Gooch (London, 1990), p. 46.
5. Norman Friedman, *The Postwar Naval Revolution* (Annapolis, 1986), p. 22.
6. This appreciation of Sherman follows the pioneering study by Michael A. Palmer, *Origins of the Maritime Strategy: American Naval Strategy in the First Postwar Decade* (Washington, D.C., 1988).
7. David A. Rosenberg & Floyd D. Kennedy, *U. S. Aircraft Carriers in the Strategic Role*: Part I, *Naval Strategy in a Period of Change: Interservice Rivalry, Strategic Interaction, and the Development of Nuclear Attack Capabilities, 1945–1951* (Falls Church, 1975), pp. 46–54; David A. Rosenberg, 'American Postwar Air Doctrine and Organization: The Navy Experience', in *Air Power and Warfare*, eds A. F. Hurley & R. C. Ehrhart (Washington, D.C., 1979), pp. 256–7; and James L. Lacy, *Within Bounds: The Navy in Postwar American Security Policy* (Alexandria, 1983), pp. 86–7.
8. Quoted in Paolo E. Colletta, *The United States Navy and Defense Unification, 1947–1953* (Newark, 1981), p. 213.
9. Elmo R. Zumwalt, Jr., *On Watch: A Memoir* (New York, 1976), pp. 292–301, 444–5; Admiral Isaac C. Kidd, Jr., 'View from the Bridge of the Sixth Fleet Flagship', *United States Naval Institute Proceedings* (February 1972), pp. 19, 27.
10. Zumwalt, *On Watch*, pp. 295, 338.
11. See David A. Rosenberg, 'History of Navy Long-Range Planning: An Overview', in James L. George *et al.*, *Review of USN Long-Range Planning* (Alexandria, 1985).
12. Admiral Thomas B. Hayward, 'Remarks', *Wings of Gold* (Summer 1982), p. 59.
13. Cited by Lawrence J. Korb, 'The Erosion of American Naval Pre-eminence, 1962–1978', in *In Peace and War: Interpretations of American Naval History, 1775–1984*, 2nd edn., ed. Kenneth J. Hagan (Westport, 1984), p. 342.
14. James L. Lacy, *Within Bounds: The Navy in Postwar American Security Policy* (Alexandria, 1983), p. 452.
15. This discussion is informed by Thomas H. Etzold, 'The Navy and National Security Policy in the 1970s', in *Military Planning in the Twentieth Century*, ed. Harry R. Borowski (Washington, 1984).
16. Sean O'Keefe (Secretary of the Navy), Frank B. Kelso, II (Chief of Naval Operations), & Carl E. Mundy, Jr. (Commandant of the Marine Corps), *...From the Sea: Preparing the Naval Service for the 21st Century* (Washington, D.C., 1992).

2 Luxury Fleet? The Sea Power of (Soviet) Russia[1]
Geoffrey Till

In the view of Admiral S. Gorshkov, lately Commander-in-Chief of the Soviet Navy, 'The fleet wrote into the history of our homeland many remarkable heroic pages and played an important role in the history of the development of Russia',[2] hostile propaganda and endless difficulties notwithstanding. But to what extent can twentieth-century Russia in fact be counted as a maritime power? What form has Russian sea power taken and what influence did it have on Russian history? Was the Soviet Navy simply the latest iteration of a doomed and impossible dream for the landbound Russians?

The Soviet Navy should not be studied in a historic vacuum, for it inherited much, good and bad, from its Tsarist predecessor. Russia has the longest coastline in the world, one that is washed by two oceans and twelve seas. As Fred T. Jane reminded his readers at the beginning of the century, the Russians have a longer seafaring tradition than the British.[3] They were keen explorers, and often surprisingly innovative in developing naval technology.

But geography was a strategic and commercial hindrance too. It divided Russia's fleet between different areas in a way which made the concentration of force difficult. Access to the open ocean was climatically and strategically difficult, and the continuing threat of overland attack made the sea necessarily secondary in Russian defence. Indeed, success at sea was often dependent on the army's ability to win or retain territory, coastlines, and bases. The usual Mahanian model seemed to work in reverse as far as the Russians were concerned. Instead of power at sea leading to power on land, for them it seemed frequently the other way around – a relationship all too often demonstrated in the negative, failure on land producing failure at sea. Bases were more often treated as strategic commitments than as sources of oceanic strength. Accordingly, the sea was often seen not so much as a window out onto a wider world, more as an avenue by which the malignant sometimes came to spread dangerous ideas, or to threaten Russian interests.

Through much of the nineteenth century the deficiencies of Russia's industrial base forced its sailors to shop heavily in Western shipyards. Worse still, naval procurement was conducted in such a piecemeal fashion that it produced a heterogeneous fleet difficult to operate as a cohesive whole. In 1904–5 for example, the result was 'no fleet, but a chance concourse of vessels',[4] and this played an important part in Russia's defeat by the Japanese. Because the Russians were often fatally dependent on foreigners, in both the construction and the deployment of their fleets, the sea also was all too often seen as something not quite Russian.

It is not easy to summarise either the nature of Russian sea power in the Tsarist era, or its legacy for the succeeding regime. On the one hand, it could take orthodox Mahanian forms, against weaker powers like Sweden or Turkey, and sometimes even against the maritime British – as in the 1890s when the expansion of Russian naval power in the Far East '... was a more serious matter for British naval mastery than the much more famous 'race' with Tirpitz's fleet before 1914'.[5]

Tsarist sea power could equally well seem distinctly un-Mahanian, as in the Crimean War for example, or with the 'Fortress Fleet' and *guerre de course* conceptions of the 1860–80 period. In Richmond's terminology, Russia was not a natural sea power in which maritime consciousness welled up from the mercantile nature of the community as it had in England or the Netherlands; instead it was the product of an Imperial *ukase*, usually in response to some immediate military, dynastic, or political need. All too often, the Navy was seen as little more than an Imperial caprice. As one British ambassador put it in the 1830s:

> In this light is the Russian navy considered by almost every official person with whom I have conversed on the subject. They all declare it to be a 'toy', and a very expensive toy, with which the Emperor delights to occupy himself, but not one of them...anticipates the possibility of its ever being made use of as a means of attack or defence, and all openly deplore the expense which it occasions, as weakening their financial resources, and withdrawing large sums annually from the more useful national purposes.[6]

Indeed, the overwhelming response of the 'real' maritime powers to Russia's ill-advised ventures upon the sea led some to conclude that the whole enterprise was likely to be counter-productive. General Kuropatkin, for example, warned the Tsar just before the 1904–5 war that concentrating too many resources on the Navy and imperial adventures in the East could make Russia dangerously vulnerable in the West.[7] Navalism could reasonably be seen not just as strategically counter-productive but as a threat to the regime itself.

Some navalists like Admirals Nikolai Klado, or 70 years later, Sergei Gorshkov, disputed the relevance of the Tsarist legacy, good or bad. Russia, they said, had been allowed to degenerate into a non-maritime country through centuries of uneven development and often plain neglect, much of which could be ascribed to the deficiencies of the Tsarist system[8], rather than to the characteristics of the Russian nation. In the Soviet period, things would be different.

A number of what Stalin would have called 'permanently operating factors' were apparent in the Soviet Navy era. As in the Tsarist period, some were helpful to the development of power at sea, but some were not. Clearly the Navy, like the other services, reflected all the structural and economic weaknesses of the regime it served. Thus the Stalinist purges of the 1930s and the depressing effect of the *zampolits* (political officers) produced systemic constraints on military initiative. The tendency for Soviets to obey orders and 'go by the book' helps explain the mediocre performance, for example, of Soviet submarines in the Arctic theatre during the 'Great Patriotic War', or the Soviet failure to interfere with the German withdrawal from the eastern Baltic in 1945.

In some ways, such problems were likely to be exacerbated by the Navy's rather lowly status – which was usually fifth in the overall pecking order; behind, that is, the Strategic Rocket Forces, the Ground Forces, the Aerospace Defence Force and the Air Force. Typically, this was reflected in everything from spending priorities to the positions the senior commanders took on the reviewing podium for Red Square parades.

Geography also tended to limit the Navy more than it did the other services. The collapse of the Army in 1917 squeezed the Baltic fleet far up into the Gulf of Finland until the end of the Second World War, when the maritime border surged forwards to the edge of Denmark. Otherwise, in terms of coastal configuration and climate, conditions were just as bad for the Soviet Navy as they had been for its Tsarist predecessor.

Moreover, throughout its existence, the Soviet Navy faced a series of putative adversaries who had all demonstrated much more impressive levels of power at sea than it managed to achieve in the 'Great Patriotic War'. This was especially true in the Cold War era, when the anticipated foe was a great international alliance and inescapably maritime[9] with the naval forces, outlook and expertise to match.

But there were positive factors too. In 1904, for example, Mackinder had warned that 'the great industrial strength of Siberia and European Russia and a conquest of some of the marginal regions would give the basis for a fleet necessary to found the world empire'.[10] The Soviet Union finally became an industrial superpower, and the consequent level of industrial resource available to its Navy was very considerable, despite its relatively low status. The Soviet Ministry of Ship-building of the Cold War era provided about 50 significant shipyards, 30 of them very large indeed. Despite the climate, the construction yard at Severodvinsk on the White Sea, for example, produced more submarines than the rest of the world put together. The Soviet Union also took about 70% of the ship-building capacity of Eastern Europe and Finland. Nor was this merely a question of quantity. Where the Soviet leadership chose to concentrate its resources, its achievements were impressive. By the 1970s, the Soviet Union produced about 7000 naval architects a year; people from its prestigious Institute of Welding contributed to levels of expertise in certain aspects of construction (like welding titanium hulls for submarines) that were operationally highly advantageous and perhaps 10 years ahead of the Americans.[11]

Another strength was the Leninist stress, in the Soviet approach to war and strategy, upon the unity of forces. Gorshkov's successor, Admiral Chernavin put it like this:

> Today...there is no purely specific realm of warfare. Victory is achieved by the combined efforts of all [branches of the armed services] which brings about the need to integrate all knowledge of warfare within the framework of a united military science.[12]

The fact that its naval forces were consequently frequently put under the control of the generals during the 'Great Patriotic War' is portrayed by Western analysts and historians as a grave source of weakness, and so quite often it was. But it could be helpful too. Successful army operations could capture coastlines and ports for the Navy to use; air and missile forces could be projected deep into the ocean, providing, thereby, much power at sea.

But perhaps the biggest single maritime advantage that the Soviet Union could draw from its strategic circumstance was a corollary of a factor already mentioned, namely the fact that its principal adversary was maritime. While navalists like Mahan claimed that sea power was as a source of strength, it could sometimes be a source of weakness too. In the Cold War era, for example, NATO's maritime dependence on secure sea communications across the Atlantic and its vulnerability to attack from possibly quite small numbers of modern submarines provided a permanent leitmotif of strategic anxiety amongst analysts and practitioners alike. As Gorshkov noted, a glance at the disproportion between the Allies' efforts to defend their shipping in the Second World War and the Germans' efforts to attack it seemed to prove a point foreseen by Mackinder, amongst others. Western maritime vulnerabilities and, even more, sensitivities, could be regarded as a source of Soviet sea power.

A review of the development of the Soviet Navy, before and during the Cold War should help us analyse the varying impact of this cluster of negative and positive factors. As the strategy of Soviet Russia developed and changed, so did the tasks of the Soviet Navy, and the relative importance of the various factors influencing it.

When the cruiser *Aurora* opened fire on the Winter Palace in October 1917, she signalled the importance of the Navy in the forthcoming revolution and civil war. The Navy provided the Revolution's shock troops, thwarting the Kornilov conspiracy, seizing railway and power stations, capturing Army headquarters in Petrograd. But the Baltic Fleet acted more as an army than a navy, and its sailors were dispersed in order to stiffen Red infantry, defeat the counter-revolutionaries and suppress the Constitutional Assembly in January 1918. The fleet was the vanguard of the new Russia, probably more important to the outcome of events then than it was to be again for many years. The savage suppression of the Kronstadt mutiny in 1921 showed how swiftly it could fall from grace, however.

In the War of Intervention, its Black Sea, Northern and Pacific Fleets almost ceased to exist. Its riverine forces were topped up with men and materials from the Baltic and were effective against the Whites, but contributed only a little to the maritime defence of the country against external attack. Only in the Baltic could the fleet have any real impact on allied operations. The British were wary of the residual capacity of Soviet battleships like the *Petropavlovsk* and the *Andrei Pervozvanni* but were more worried, and with greater reason, about Soviet mines and submarines. Even so, the Allies' reluctance to attack Petrograd undoubtedly had more to do with a political reluctance to get too enmeshed in the Civil War, than with the operational effectiveness of this new 'Fortress Fleet'.

Nonetheless it was a significant campaign. Firstly, the fact that even the 'oceanic' British decided this was not an appropriate area in which to deploy battleships or fleet carriers sustains the impression that for reasons of geography, Soviet naval operations were bound to be different from those of the maritime West. Second, from the Soviet point of view, the fleet seemed to have achieved its purpose despite such disasters as the sinking of the cruiser *Oleg* and the British attack on Kronstadt in August 1919. In the North, the East and the South, where there were no effective naval forces, Soviet Russia's allies came ashore. But '... [i]n the Baltic where quite a strong fleet was maintained, the interventionists hesitated to make a landing.'[13]

The lesson seemed clear, and was enunciated by Frunze in February 1925: '... we cannot conceivably safeguard our maritime borders without a strong navy.'[14] But this was an ambitious aspiration. The bulk of the Navy's officers were ex-Tsarist and the Kronstadt Mutiny of 1921 had clearly demonstrated their political unreliability. The most recent and immediate threats were, as so often before, overland from Poland and Germany. Further, there were many who argued that in the new revolutionary circumstances the thinking of the 'Navy of Red Workers and Peasants' should be folded into an emerging 'Proletarian Military Doctrine'. Worst of all, Soviet shipbuilding capacity was in an appalling state. Given all this, the continued dominance of what became known as the Old School, where Professors Gervaise and Petrov at the Naval War College followed the example of Nikolai Klado in adapting Mahanian concepts of maritime strategy to Russian's semi-oceanic circumstances, seemed quite bizarre. They argued for a significant navy including battle ships and heavy cruisers intended for the forward defence of local waters by 'keeping command of the sea in dispute' just as the Baltic Fleet had tried, with some success, to do in 1919.

But as the practical difficulties of this policy became apparent, such slavish adherence to foreign concepts of maritime warfare was increasingly questioned:

> We often...identify with the classical sea powers and try to operate like they do. The battle of Jutland is our model which we study and attempt to imitate. Admirals Beatty and Spee – they are our role models. That which we learn from foreigners is good... . But to try to transplant all that directly into our conditions is not correct. We have other forces, other means, and we operate under different conditions. Consequently, it is necessary to work out the tactics for a small navy which acts together with the Army according to a single strategic plan.[15]

In some exasperation, Admiral Zof, the Navy's Chief, complained that the Old School seemed completely to ignore economic and technical reality, and the fact that '...perhaps tomorrow, or the day after, we will be called upon to fight. And with what shall we fight? We will fight with those ships and personnel that we have already'.[16]

Sensing the shift in mood, Petrov gradually retreated before the advance of the so-called New School, which argued for a much more localised defence of Soviet coasts against serious maritime attack using minefields, coastal artillery, submarines and motor torpedo-boats. Gervaise stuck to his battleships until forced to make a public and humiliating recantation in 1932. For the next few years the New School held the field.

But from 1936, the Soviet Navy slowly reverted to orthodoxy, under the tutelage, especially, of Professor Vladimir Belli, who argued that a more ambitious interpretation of 'homeland defence' justified a larger Navy. Stalin was now sympathetic to this, the caprice of the ruler once more working to the (at least short-term) benefit of the Navy. Molotov declared, grandly: 'Only the biggest High Seas Fleet will meet Soviet demands'. If the Soviet Union was to defend its national and revolutionary needs outside the confines of the Black Sea and the Baltic, the Northern and Pacific Fleets would need to be created (1933 and 1932 respectively) and a substantial new construction programme would be necessary, especially of battleships and heavy cruisers. Opponents were purged accordingly, and the right-thinking Kuznetsov took over as Commander-in-Chief. Shortly afterwards, the Soviet army moved into Finland, the Baltic Republics and Poland, hugely improving Russia's maritime geography. It seemed that the Soviet Union was once more on the road to becoming a great sea power in the orthodox mould.

Reality soon intruded and this turned out to be another false dawn. The rapid advance of the German army in 1941 cruelly reversed the geographic advances so recently made, and the Soviet Union lost the great majority of its naval bases and shipyards. Worse still, the overland threat to the survival of Russia was so severe that the air/land campaign naturally commanded the lion's share of the state's defence resources. More insidiously, the lesson that the younger generation of naval officers (who entered positions of command in the early 1940s) had learned in the late-1930s was that the reward for innovative thinking all too often was a bullet in the back of the head. All this contributed to a lacklustre performance in the 'Great Patriotic War'.

The Navy was probably at its best on Russia's rivers and lakes, but was reasonably active in the Black Sea, where it conducted numerous evacuation and landing operations, and both attacked and protected the sea transportation of supplies and military personnel. In the North, its success in the latter role was disappointing, but many small-scale landing operations were conducted. In the Baltic, constrained by the weather, by strategic geography and by thick German minefields, the fleet was barely able to act even as the 'fortress fleet' envisaged by the New School. Instead, the fleet went ashore, its components acting as infantry and artillery in the desperate defence of Leningrad. Later, when the strategic situation in the Baltic dramatically improved, the Baltic Fleet was largely unable to shake off the habits of maritime passivity.

But as Gorshkov, one of its most successful wartime commanders, remarked, the war was 'predominantly of a continental character', and therefore action at sea was bound to be important rather than decisive. Further, the Navy reflected the structural frailties of the regime. When the Germans launched their 'Sunday Blow', in 1941, the Navy was largely caught napping; operationally, even tactically, the Navy's ability to seize the fleeting opportunity was constrained by the need to do exactly what one was told and to refer everything new to higher authority.

In the Cold War era the Soviet Navy's mission structure was broadly as shown in Table 2.1.[17]

Its peacetime tasks included the general deterrence of potential adversaries, the use of naval forces as diplomatic instruments in situations short of conflict, and its possible participation in conflicts short of general war. In wartime success depended on the extent to which the Navy could control relevant sea areas. Strategic defence and strike involved the Navy's need to maintain its share of the country's nuclear deterrent force and to harass that of the opposition. The Navy had also to defend the territory of the state from all other forms of sea-based attack, protect or harass shipping, and project power ashore. Except for the two 'nuclear' roles, these missions also applied to the earlier period up to end of the end of the Second World War. The priority given these tasks shifted as Soviet strategy developed.

When victory came in 1945, Stalin seemed anxious to rid Russia of as many of its old maritime constraints as possible. Ambitious pre-war naval programmes were amended and restarted. The Army, by retaking all lost

Table 2.1 The Soviet Navy's mission structure during the Cold War

	Fleet	1.	Sea dominance
	v.	2.	Homeland defence
	Fleet	3.	Strategic defence
War			
Tasks	Fleet	4.	Strategic strike
	v.	5.	Operations v. shore
	Shore	6.	Maritime interdiction
Peace		7.	General deterrence
Tasks		8.	Naval diplomacy
		9.	Limited & local war

territory, by advancing almost to the Danish border, and by occupying Rumania and Bulgaria, Northern Korea, Sakhalin and all the Kurile islands, had already provided a maritime geography better for the Navy than it had ever been before.

Even so, Stalin sought to improve it. In 1944, Molotov told Trygve Lie, his Norwegian counterpart:

> The Dardanelles, here we are locked in...Øresund...here we are locked in. Only in the north is there an opening, but this war has shown that the supply line to northern Russia can be cut or interfered with. This shall not be repeated in the future.[18]

Pressure was put on the Norwegians over Bear Island and Spitzbergen, on the Danes over Bornholm, on the Turks over the Dardanelles and the Caucasus border; through links with Yugoslavia, and more reliably Albania, Russia became an Adriatic power for the first time since the eighteenth century; there was even talk (mainly in Moscow!) of Stalin's being rewarded with Libya for his contribution to the defeat of the Axis powers.

Although none of these ambitions in fact were realised, thanks in no small measure to the sea-based deterrence operated by the US Navy, they were a strong indication of Stalin's maritime ambitions. But the building of the *Sverdlov*-class cruisers, the slow priority given the development of organic aviation, and the multitude of short- and medium-range submarines, strongly suggests that what was envisaged at this stage was the maritime defence of the Soviet homeland against sea-based attack very much in the Klado/Belli style; this was neither the coastal/fortress fleet advocated by the New School, nor the forward offensive/defensive operations then envisaged by the US and British navies, but something in between.

Interestingly, Stalin's declaratory policy towards the arrival of atomic weapons was that they would not be decisive against the permanently operating factors of conventional warfare in which the Soviet Army more than held its own. In this context, at 1,800,000 tons, the Navy flourished; the Navy of 1957 was over three times bigger than it had been in 1917, and twenty times its 1923 size.[19]

When Khrushchev directed policy from 1956 to 1964, things changed. This was the era of the 'Revolution in Military Affairs' when Soviet leaders, like their British and the American counterparts, flirted with the notion that the imminent arrival of thermonuclear weapons would transform the processes of war, rendering obsolete great swathes of the existing conventional force structures of all three services. In the Soviet Union, this worked to the particular benefit of the submarine force which from the mid-1950s seemed likely to be charged with an important part of the strategic deterrent force, and which was also a means for keeping American nuclear carriers away from the Soviet coast. The intrusion of these new 'nuclear' elements into the Soviet Navy's mission structure transformed the rest. Only to the extent that the surface fleet could contribute to these two missions would it be spared from cuts. The air was thick with epithets to the effect that large surface ships were expensive 'metal-eaters' and 'floating coffins' in this new missile era, and new construction was badly hit.

Nonetheless, a strong and bureaucratically skilful defence was mounted by the new Commander-in-Chief, Admiral Gorshkov, who advanced the argument that such ships were an essential part of a balanced fleet, however dominated it might be by submarines and shore-based maritime aircraft. He was aided in this by Khrushchev's evident desire to cut a diplomatic figure on the global stage and to transform the potentially deadly East–West confrontation over Europe into a politico–military competition for the support of the emerging Third World. Only the Navy could provide Khrushchev with the geographic reach he needed. The humiliation of Cuba reinforced the point.

Upon Khrushchev's (connected) departure from office, there ensued a long confused and confusing period which, perhaps, culminated in Secretary Brezhnev's historic speech at Tula in 1970, when he declared that nuclear warfare of any sort would be an irrational act.[20] Through this period, in the view of the Soviet General Staff, both the relative likelihood, and the anticipated length, of the conventional non-nuclear phase of a systemic war with the West gradually increased. At the same time, the prospect of non-systemic conflict in defence of Soviet interests outside Europe was taken more seriously. All this was vastly encouraging to the Navy. Not surprisingly, its exercises grew steadily more ambitious, its ship-days-out-of-area totals mounted; the size and quality of the fleet expanded; battle-cruisers were built, fleet carriers were planned, amphibious forces expanded. Even Gorshkov's ambition of creating a properly 'balanced fleet', peaking at some $2\frac{1}{2}$ million tons by the early-1980s, was achieved. It was the Soviet Navy's golden age and the maritime West grew steadily more alarmed. Nor was this maritime expansion confined to the Navy. There were also huge and beneficial expansions in the merchant, fishing, and oceanographic fleets.

Unsurprisingly, this extraordinary phenomenon raised the question of what all this naval expansion was for, and what should be the West's reaction to it. Most Western analysts concluded that the Soviet Navy's top priority in this final stage of the Cold War was the custodianship of an increasing share of the country's nuclear deterrent. This mission attracted huge resources and resulted in a level of technological achievement comparable, and in some ways superior, to that of the West. The main task of the surface fleet was the defence of the submarines performing this duty. The Soviet Navy planned to harass Western nuclear missile-firing submarines, and pushed its defensive perimeter down to the Greenland–Iceland–UK gap and out into the North-west Pacific, a much broader concept of sea control than any Russian navy had had since the eighteenth century. The Soviet Navy's presence in more distant seas such as the Mediterranean, the Indian Ocean and, most provocatively of all, the Caribbean made it a global actor for the first time. Russia, it seemed, had finally arrived as a global sea power.

It is easy to see why there should nonetheless have been some doubt in the Soviet Union about the ultimate wisdom of this course of policy. The doubts were articulated as part, if a relatively small part, of the increasingly agonised general debate about defence that took place in the Soviet Union from about 1977 to 1985. The expansion of the Soviet Navy had certainly given the country's leaders far more political and operational possibilities than ever they had had before, but the price was heavy, and the demands on the economy severe. Worse still, the expansion of the Soviet Navy provoked a furious reaction from the United States. In the 1980s, the Reagan administration countered the Soviet challenge with a programme to produce a 600-ship navy, and a much more assertive national strategy, which became known as 'The Maritime Strategy'. Moreover, this new Western response was technically very sophisticated. Reflecting on the implications of the Strategic Defence Initiative, air- and sea-launched cruise missiles, microprocessors, electronic warfare, particle beam research and so on, Marshal Ogarkov warned grimly that future war would be waged on the basis of 'new physical principles' and that the Soviet Union was falling behind technologically. Only by spending even more on conventional defence could it hope to compete, at sea as elsewhere.[21]

Soviet leaders took this new maritime–technical threat very seriously indeed, and began to feel even more insecure than they had before. In that it seduced the Soviet Union into a naval arms race which it could not win, the expansion of the Soviet Navy could therefore be seen by sceptics as strategically counter-productive, just as perhaps it had been in the early part of the century. From 1985, the new leadership under Gorbachev concluded that the Soviet Union simply could not increase its defence expenditure still further. Only by present cut-backs in defence and, it was increasingly recognised, a remodelling of the structure of the state itself, could the Soviet Union hope to reform its economy and secure its future as a superpower. Thus did Gorbachev feel forced to initiate a policy that led inexorably to the end of the Cold War, the collapse of the Soviet Union and to his own downfall.

It is difficult to come to a final conclusion about whether the Soviet Navy represented roubles well spent. It certainly helped suck the creaking Soviet Union into an arms race it could not win. It seemed that Mahan had finally defeated Mackinder. But on the other hand, the naval expansion had helped turn the Soviet Union, for the first time, into a global superpower which could make its presence felt all round the world. Moreover, in many ways, the Soviet leadership really had no choice but to take to the sea in a significant way, when it was confronting a maritime adversary and a series of technological developments (such as sea-launched cruise and ballistic missiles and nuclear carriers) which it simply could not ignore. The Soviet leadership's real difficulty lay in the inefficiency of the structure of the state, not in the fact that it had, finally, gone seriously to sea.

In some ways, the final verdict on the role and utility of the Soviet Navy will be provided by what the new Russia does now and in the future. Will its new leaders deduce from past experience that Russia needs an open-ocean fleet, or will they conclude, as Kuropatkin did in the early-1900s and the New School did in the late-1920s, that it represented a dangerous distraction from Russia's real destiny? Or will Russia end up once more with a distinctive local-water fleet midway between a coastal defence force on the one hand and an oceanic western-style fleet on the other? As ever, the evidence is varied and contradictory, but at the moment it is far too soon to conclude that Russia's desire for oceanic or semi-oceanic power at sea is merely history.

NOTES

1. The opinions expressed in this article should not be taken necessarily to reflect official opinion.
2. S. Gorshkov, *The Sea Power of the State* (London, 1979), pp. 68–9, 70–71.
3. Fred T. Jane, *The Imperial Russian Navy: Past Present and Future* (London, 1904), p. 23.

4. V. Semenoff, *The Battle of Tsushima* (London, 1906), p. 10.
5. See C. J. Bartlett, *Great Britain and Seapower 1815–1853* (Oxford, 1963), p. 103; A. J. Marder, *Anatomy of British Sea Power* (New York, 1940), p. 13. Also Paul Kennedy, *Strategy and Diplomacy* (London, 1983), p. 168.
6. Bartlett, op. cit. p. 106.
7. William C Fuller, *Strategy and Power in Russia 1600–1914* (New York, 1992), p. 378.
8. Gorshkov, op. cit. p. 68.
9. A ringing declaration that this is so may be found of all places, in the German Defence White Paper for 1983, p. 40.
10. Halford Mackinder, 'The Geographic Pivot of History', *The Geographic Journal*, vol XXIII (1904).
11. Boris S. Butman, *Soviet Ship-building and Ship Repair: An Overview* (Arlington, Va, 1986). See also *Understanding Soviet Naval Developments* (Washington, D. C., 1985), p. 79.
12. Admiral V Chernavin, 'On Naval Theory', *Morskoi sbornik*, No. 1, January 1982.
13. Gorshkov, op. cit. p. 128.
14. Quoted in S. A. Tyushkevich, *The Soviet Armed Forces: A History of their Organisational Development* (Moscow, 1978). USAF English Language edition, p. 163.
15. Quoted, Robert Herrick, *Soviet Naval Theory and Policy* (Washington, 1988), p. 10.
16. Quoted in ibid., p. 7.
17. This matter is discussed much more extensively in B. Ranft & G. Till, *The Sea in Soviet Strategy* (London, 1989).
18. Quoted in C. Bertram & J. J. Holst (eds), *New Strategic Factors in the North Atlantic* (Oslo, 1977), p. 37.
19. Bradford Dismukes & James McConnell (eds), *Soviet Naval Diplomacy* (New York, 1979), pp. 15–16.
20. J. M. McConnel, 'The Soviet Shift Toward and Away From Nuclear War Waging', Arlington, Va, Center for Naval Analyses. Working Paper, 1984.
21. Christopher Donnelly, 'Planning Parameters for the Soviet General Staff' in J. Pay & G. Till, *East West Relations in the 1990s: The Naval Dimension* (London, 1990), p. 64.

3 Imperial Germany and the Importance of Sea Power
Michael Epkenhans

When writing his memoirs after the military and political collapse of the German Empire in November 1918, Grand Admiral Alfred von Tirpitz, who can rightly be called the builder of the Imperial German Navy, still remembered an encounter with an unknown English woman in Gibraltar some fifty years earlier. Boarding one of the very few German warships, which lay in the harbour of this outpost of the British Empire, and seeing a number of ratings, this woman exclaimed astonishedly: 'Don't they look just like sailors?' When Tirpitz, a young sub-lieutenant then, asked her what else they should look like, she replied bluntly: 'But you are not a seagoing nation'.[1]

Tirpitz, a representative of the most powerful nation on the continent, obviously regarded this answer as a humiliation, for his memoirs somehow still reflect his embitterment about this event. However, there can be no doubt that this woman, though perhaps in a slightly arrogant manner, had only stated a simple fact: while the German army was the strongest in Europe, marching from one victory to another, the Navy had contributed nothing to the wars of unification, and unlike the army, it was a negligible quantity internationally.[2] It is the aim of this paper to analyse the reasons for this insignificant role of the navy in mid-nineteenth century Germany, to describe the course of naval history in the years between the unification in 1870-71 and the final defeat of the Empire in 1918, as well as the changing importance of sea power for government policy, for naval strategy, and for the public, and, finally, to discuss the contribution of the attempt to become a sea power both to German greatness and fall.

As the incident described above illustrates, naval power did not seem very important in Germany for the greater part of the nineteenth century. In spite of its status among the European great powers, Prussia, as an embodiment of a military state, primarily relied on its strong army. Both a long-lasting tradition as a land power and the geographical situation in the centre of Europe as well as the lack of important overseas interests were responsible for the neglect of sea power.[3]

However, after the failure of the revolutionary movement to found a navy in 1848–49,[4] Prussia and, after the unification in 1870–71, Imperial Germany, slowly began to build up a fleet. With regard to later interpretations of sea power, it is, of course, necessary to keep in mind that this fleet, which, significantly enough, was commanded by army generals, Generals Stosch and Caprivi, until 1889, only aspired to second-class naval strength.[5] The small size of the navy and the operations plans, which were primarily aimed at defending the coast, at protecting commerce, and at supporting the army in case of war, as well as the poor state of the shipbuilding industry further underscore the fact that sea power was not yet an aim in itself.

There were, of course, already a few intellectuals and industrialists who advocated a strong navy. Heinrich von Treitschke, for example, told his students in 1864 that only 'sea powers, the rulers of overseas territories' could be called 'great powers'.[6] Similarly, Friedrich Harkort, one of the most important pioneers of German industrialisation, demanded a greater navy in order both to protect and to promote commercial interests overseas.[7]

However, under Bismarck's chancellorship, it was very unlikely that the Navy would play a more decisive role in political and military planning. In Bismarck's opinion, the precarious position of Germany in the centre of Europe required both a self-confident though cautious policy towards its neighbours, and a powerful army to support it if need be. The validity of the doctrine that Germany's fate was to be decided on land and not on the high seas can best be illustrated by Bismarck's famous answer to a German explorer of the dark continent who tried to convince the Chancellor of the advantages of larger possessions in Africa:

> 'Your map of Africa is very nice', he answered, 'but my map of Africa lies here in Europe. Here lies Russia, and – pointing to the left – here lies France, and we are right in the middle; this is my map of Africa.'[8]

Accordingly, the army was greatly increased twice within a few years, while the Navy still lived from hand-to-mouth. In this respect, it is also significant that General Caprivi, who had been Chief of the Admiralty until 1889, did not give naval development highest priority when he was appointed Chancellor after Bismarck's dismissal in 1890.[9]

The accession of the young Emperor Wilhelm II to the throne in 1888, however, definitely marked the end both of a long era of land power thinking, and of the relative decline of the navy.[10] To a certain degree, his sometimes childish naval passion, his manifold but often incompetent interference with naval affairs,[11] and his pride in wearing the uniforms of an Admiral of the High Seas Fleet as well as of the Royal Navy, illustrate that the Emperor regarded the navy as a kind of 'mechanical toy', as Tirpitz put it to a close confidant in early 1913.[12] However, there can be no doubt that Wilhelm II played a very important role in the promotion of sea power thinking in Germany in spite of his personal flaws. On the one hand, these flaws, which often enough caused those responsible for German politics in general and for naval affairs in particular to throw up their hands in despair, helped to make the navy popular. On the other hand, the Emperor's extraordinarily persistent attitude in his attempts to realise his naval plans, even if this meant a coup d'etat, finally paved the way for their approval by the government as well as by the Reichstag. Furthermore, he helped to end a decade of incompetent naval planning, of uncertainties about both naval construction and naval strategy, and, finally, of a lack of precise aims.

The Emperor's 'naval passion' and his direct or indirect pressure to enlarge the Navy, however, cannot sufficiently explain the shift in German politics as well as in military thinking in the 1890s.[13] It seems unlikely that Wilhelm II would have been successful if the importance of sea power had not been realised by a steadily increasing number of people, and, above all, if he had not had a man like Tirpitz at his disposal, who systematically dealt with the political, military, strategic, and economic aspects of becoming a sea power.[14]

What were the reasons for this change and what did sea power mean to the advocates of this new course, however? Firstly, many contemporaries were proud of their political, economic, and military achievements since the unification, and they felt that Imperial Germany was a vigorous young nation, bursting at the seams in many ways.[15] The ideas of imperialism, which had reached Germany in the 1880s, and the political and military events in East Asia as well as in other distant parts of the world in the mid-1890s further enhanced the conviction that Germany had to embark on 'world politics', and had to secure a 'place in the sun', in order to preserve its achievements, and, above all, its status in the Concert of the Great Powers.

Against this background, it was obviously a stroke of luck that just as the famous Prussian General Karl von Clausewitz had delivered a handbook for the role of the army in politics, Alfred Thayer Mahan's books on the 'Influence of Sea Power upon History' now provided both the much-desired 'recipe' to achieve these aims and, what is much more important, a comprehensive philosophy of sea power.[16] In an era in which the rise or fall of nations seemed to be particularly at stake, Mahan's claim that the 'key to much of history as well as of the policy of nations bordering upon the sea' would be found in the naval conflicts of the eighteenth century, deeply impressed his German contemporaries.[17]

Above all, Mahan's ensuing description of Britain's rise to world power was widely regarded as an example that simply had to be imitated. That is why it is not astonishing that the Emperor himself enthusiastically wrote to an American friend in May 1894: 'I am just now not reading but devouring Captain Mahan's book, and am trying to learn it by heart. It is a first-class work and classical in all points'.[18] Similarly, the German Secretary of State, Bernhard von Bülow, urged the industrialist Friedrich A. Krupp to accelerate the building of warships by referring to the writings of the American 'naval prophet'. As Mahan had proved, he wrote to Krupp in 1898, the 'flowering and prospering of great states is closely connected with the development of their naval forces'.[19] A modern propaganda campaign and more than 200 so-called 'fleet professors' further helped to make Mahan's ideas popular at least in bourgeois circles.[20] As a result, the 'real' meaning of sea power, its significance in former and present wars, the importance of the control of the seas, and the role of navies in cutting the supply lines and seizing the colonies of weaker sea powers quickly became the themes of a flood of pamphlets, as well as of many discussions in academic circles and among armchair strategists from almost all social classes. The German Navy League in particular, founded in 1898 and highly supported by the Imperial Naval Office, promoted the interest of the public in the Navy through organised visits to the High Seas Fleet and through regular lectures on naval affairs by leading members of the League or retired naval officers, and through other means of modern propaganda all over Germany.

Second, apart from the vague but psychologically important notion that sea power was a symbol as well as a precondition of national greatness, the rising emphasis on world politics and sea power since the mid-1890s also had important power-political implications. As Wilhelm II publicly declared at the launching of the pre-dreadnought *Wittelsbach* in July 1900, world politics and sea power meant that 'in distant areas [beyond the ocean], no important decision should be taken without Germany and the German Emperor'.[21] However, like other pithy speeches about the need to build a navy, this claim only vaguely described the political and naval concept underlying Germany's 'new course'.

In spite of the vagueness of the German demand for equal entitlement (*Gleichberechtigung*), and the corresponding lack of a catalogue of precise aims, it would, of course, be wrong to assume that the Imperial government did not know what it wanted. In a long conversation with the Emperor, Bülow, for instance, described the decaying Ottoman and

Chinese Empires as well as a number of islands in the Pacific as desirable objects of German expansion.[22] Tirpitz in turn always maintained that a powerful navy would greatly enhance Germany's alliance value (*Bündnisfähigkeit*),[23] and thus strengthen the nation's position in the emerging new world power system. The final aim of the Emperor's new men, Bülow and Tirpitz, however, was to replace the 'Pax Britannica' by a 'Pax Germanica' either through a cold or, if necessary, even a hot war against the supreme world and sea power.[25] After completion of the High Seas Fleet, Tirpitz assured the Emperor, Britain would lose 'every inclination to attack us, and as a result concede to Your Majesty such a measure of naval influence and enable Your Majesty to carry out a great overseas policy'.[25]

Third, sea power or, as Tirpitz more often put it, naval presence (*Seegeltung*) was allegedly also a prerequisite for the protection of the German colonies, as well as of economic wealth, industrial progress, and commerce. Without a strong navy, Tirpitz kept on arguing, with many people believing him, Germany, whose industrial production and commerce had risen immensely since the unification, would be unable to preserve its steadily rising 'sea-interests' and, subsequently, inevitably decline to the status of a pre-industrial, 'poor farming country'.[26]

Finally, sea power also had important domestic-political implications.[27] In contrast to the modernity of its industrial system, the German political and social order was pre-modern in many ways. The influence of parliament was restricted through the strong position of the Emperor and his government within the constitution. The military, the bureaucracy, and the diplomatic service were still parts of the traditional monarchical prerogative in which the Reichstag had almost no influence. Moreover, in spite of their decreasing economic importance in a quickly industrialising country, the old agrarian elites still exerted more political influence on the development of the state and society than seemed justified, with regard to their small number and their general decline, as well as, above all, to the democratic ideas of the nineteenth century.

After all other measures had failed in the past, the government hoped that the acquisition of sea power, and the envisaged great success of world politics through the plan carefully designed by Tirpitz, would safeguard the overall expansion of German industry, foreign trade, colonies and the Navy, and, what is most important, thus offer a permanent solution to the 'social problem' which threatened the existing political and social order.

There can be no doubt, however, that the 'Tirpitz-Plan' was at least in one respect also directed against parliament. With the difficulties of naval construction before his coming into office in mind, Tirpitz tried to make the Navy independent of the Reichstag, by stipulating in the first Navy Law that all ships, which were built at a rate of three capital ships a year, had to be replaced by newly built vessels after 20 years. Thus, the Emperor would have a powerful navy of 60 capital ships always at his disposal. With regard to the necessity of safe long-term planning, this provision indeed seemed to be justified. The history of the relationship between the army and parliament in the decades before, however, illustrates, that this aspect also had important political implications, namely the restriction of parliamentary influence on traditional royal prerogatives.

In order to achieve her ambitious aims, and to succeed Spain, Holland, and now Britain as the leading world and sea power, Germany began to build the High Seas Fleet in 1897–98. The main architect of this fleet was Admiral von Tirpitz, who was appointed Secretary of the Navy in 1897. In many respects, the concept he developed in the mid-1890s was congruent with Mahan's ideas, though, because of Tirpitz's own experience in high command, it is unlikely that he simply adopted them.[28] Like Mahan, Tirpitz was convinced that only a battle fleet could defeat the enemy's fleet in order to gain command of the sea, and thus attain sea supremacy.[29] As a result, he mercilessly fought all those who still adhered to the teachings of the French *jeune école*, instead of joining Tirpitz's and Mahan's battleship school. Germany's fate, Tirpitz alleged, was to be decided in the vital theatre of war, the North Sea, and there only ships-of-the-line could secure victory in a traditional and decisive naval battle.[30]

Accordingly, this fleet was supposed to consist of 41 battleships, 20 large cruisers, 40 small cruisers, 144 torpedo-boats, and 72 submarines in twenty years' time.[31] Of course, this remarkable force would still be inferior to the Royal Navy, but Tirpitz was convinced that Britain could not outbuild Germany because of financial restraints and lack of personnel, and that, therefore, the margin of inferiority between the Imperial Navy and its future enemy would not exceed one third. With high-quality ships, superior tactics, and better trained crews, Tirpitz regarded victory over the Royal Navy in the 'wet triangle around Heligoland' as possible. An integral part of this optimistic view, however, was the assumption that the latter would only be able to bring about half of its strength into action due to its overseas commitments.[32]

Though these were indeed bold assumptions, unless Tirpitz did not – and there are indications that this was his ultimate aim – want to build a fleet equal in size to the Royal Navy,[23] he himself, the public, and the Emperor took them for granted almost throughout the whole Wilhelmine era. As a result, the navy received priority over the army in the allocation of funds; the Reich's financial resources were almost ruthlessly exploited for the build-up of the fleet, and, what is more important, German foreign policy now also gravitated around the 'Tirpitz-Plan'.[34] Any criticism of this 'master-plan', whether it came from diplomats, who were increasingly concerned about the rising Anglo-German antagonism, or from naval heretics like Vice Admiral Galster, who in view of Britain's determination to accept the German challenge publicly advocated a *guerre-de-course* in 1907–08, was bluntly rejected.

However, Tirpitz's master-plan nevertheless slowly began to decay in the last years before the war: firstly, because of the unsocial distribution of the costs to build the fleet, the number of Social Democrats in the Reichstag increased and did not decrease. As a result the stability of the existing political system was again threatened by social discontent, but also, and more importantly, increasingly by the demands of a national opposition, which impatiently wanted to reap the fruit of world politics. Second, apart from a short boom at the turn of the century, the German shipbuilding industry as well as industry and commerce in general either did not benefit from Tirpitz's plan, or continued to prosper independently of it. Third, and most importantly, Britain took up the gauntlet and began to outbuild the High Seas Fleet, both in size and technically, in spite of the financial burden this entailed, while the state secretary himself had to admit that he 'simply could not build the ships assigned for lack of funds.'[35] Moreover, due to both the deteriorating position of the German Empire in Europe, and the visible failure of Tirpitz's plan, the importance of sea power, which seemed to have been recognised by almost everyone in Germany, was being questioned now: 'No success', the Prussian Minister of War convincingly argued in 1912, 'however striking it may be, can make up for a decisive defeat of the army. The fate of the Hohenzollern crown, the weal and woe of our fatherland, rest upon either victory or defeat of the German army'.[36] Accordingly, the army again received priority over the Navy in almost every respect in 1911–12, though Tirpitz still hoped that this decision would not fundamentally affect the realisation of his naval programme. On the eve of war, Tirpitz even seemed to be prepared to fight for his plan once again, and at least some members of his staff were confident that he would eventually succeed despite the growing difficulties then faced. As Captain Hopman, one of Tirpitz's close aides in the Navy Office, noted in his diary with regard to the disputed supplementary budget in June 1914: 'The nation and the Reichstag can't do anything else without damaging our national prestige severely'.[37] The war, which broke out only a few weeks later, was to prove both the correctness of this claim and, above all, the importance of sea power for Imperial Germany.

The war which broke out in August 1914 and for which Bethmann Hollweg's risk policy was highly responsible, soon proved to be a disaster for the Navy, both militarily and with regard to the concept of sea power in general. Firstly, contrary to Tirpitz's allegations or, at least, to his hopes, the Grand Fleet did not seek an open battle in the German Bight where conditions would have been favourable to the High Seas Fleet, but unfavourable for the Royal Navy.[38] Instead, the German squadrons were quickly bottled up in their home waters by a distant blockade, which became almost impregnable during the war. From a traditional naval point of view, this avoidance of a decisive battle in the German Bight may have been 'dishonest', but it proved 'wise' because it achieved its main aim, namely to preserve the Royal Navy's supremacy.

Moreover, the first skirmishes with British forces in August 1914 as well as the attempts to destroy isolated parts of the Royal Navy through raids on the British coast, sometimes ended with heavy losses. It is true, both at Coronel and in home waters, the Grand Fleet also suffered severe setbacks in the following years, but these neither affected its overwhelming superiority nor changed the strategic imbalance in the North Sea. Admiral Scheer, Commander-in-Chief of the High Seas Fleet since early 1916, painfully had to admit this after the famous Battle of Jutland.[39] Even though Scheer's ships may have been tactically successful at Jutland, this costly success was by no means comparable to Nelson's victory at Trafalgar as the Emperor proudly claimed when he welcomed the mauled vessels in their home ports.[40] Whether Tirpitz – then out of office already – and all the other adherents of the traditional concept of sea power liked it or not, the Imperial Navy was to remain a fleet-in-being, which, though this was important enough, only protected the German coasts and some U-boat exit routes, and which proved of some value in the eventual peace negotiations, but which could not gain command of the sea by successfully challenging British naval supremacy. From a naval point of view, only the submarine, which had been much neglected and despised by Tirpitz in pre-war years, proved successful, though it could neither break the blockade nor force Britain to enter into negotiations about a favourable peace for Germany.[41] The political consequences of the increasing reliance upon submarine warfare, though, were disastrous because they finally caused the USA to enter the war on the side of the allies. Only in the Baltic, the High Seas Fleet kept the upper hand, although the Russian navy was by no means as easy a match as had been expected. Strategically, however, the control of these waters was insignificant for the course of the war.

Second, the disappointment about the lack of success ranked second behind the widespread questioning of the whole concept of sea power.[42] Apart from finally falsifying Tirpitz's famous risk theory, in the eyes of many people the war only proved that the Navy was indeed a 'luxury' when compared with the task the army had to fulfil. Contrary to Tirpitz's allegations before the war, sea power did not seem to be decisive for Germany. Almost all colonies had been lost in the first months, the cruiser squadron stationed overseas had fought bravely and had been a nuisance for the Admiralty for some time, but it had achieved practically nothing apart from the destruction of a small number of enemy merchant vessels and a few outdated warships. And while the allies could still trade with the whole world, the German trade routes and supply lines had already been cut off by the Grand Fleet in August 1914.

Therefore, it was by no means astonishing that not 'sea power', as Mahan, Tirpitz, and their numerous disciples had argued, but, as the geographer Halford Mackinder had declared a decade before, 'land power' was now regarded as the real prerequisite of German greatness.[43] In an obituary on Mahan's death in December 1914, the liberal *Berliner Tageblatt* openly expressed this reversal of priorities. Though Mahan's ideas were appreciated in general terms, their validity for Germany was denied. 'It is true', the *Berliner Tageblatt* wrote, 'that we need an effective fleet, but the roots of our strength, which, in the heart of Europe, enable us to stand up against a superior force of enemies around, lie in the army'.[44] Accordingly, the attention of generals and even admirals as well as of the public soon focused upon annexations in eastern Europe, the 'heartland' of an almost unassailable superpower, instead of an unreachable 'place in the sun'.

This criticism, carefully registered by Tirpitz, is one of the reasons why he demanded a more offensive role of the High Seas Fleet in the North Sea. As he kept on writing almost in despair to his wife, and to close friends like Admiral Trotha, only success could secure the future of the Navy.[45] However, the Emperor, the Chancellor, and even his own admirals did not want to risk the fleet in what appeared to them a suicidal attempt to break the blockade, to defeat the Royal Navy in a decisive battle, and to establish control of the sea. In this context it is, however, necessary to remember that, contrary to his own assertions after the war, Tirpitz himself also hesitated to launch a full-scale attack upon the Grand Fleet, because he anticipated the probable outcome.

Although they did not question the principal importance of sea power, high-ranking naval officers also began to criticise the previous development of the Navy and Tirpitz's strategic premises in the first months of the war. In particular the battle fleet concept as well as the construction policy of the Navy Office were now openly disputed by many officers. Though no final decision about the future concept of naval power was reached during the war, the internal discussions made it clear that more weight should be laid upon the building of cruisers and submarines, and that Tirpitz's 'sacred cow', the Navy Law, had to be made more flexible, if not abandoned at all.[46] More important, especially in the long run, were the ideas developed by a younger staff officer, Lieutenant-Commander Wolfgang Wegener.[47] In several memoranda, he pointed out some of the mistakes made by Tirpitz and his followers in their attempt to follow Mahan's teachings. On the one hand, Wegener argued, Germany did not possess 'a fleet, of size and quality adequate to the proposed operations',[48] as Mahan had put it. On the other hand, in spite of Mahan's emphasis on this prerequisite of sea power, the importance of an advantageous geographical position had been completely neglected by Tirpitz. Similarly, Tirpitz had wrongly regarded a battle as an aim in itself, instead of developing a true maritime strategy. As long as both a favourable position, which allowed free access to the main sea routes, and a bigger, more powerful fleet were lacking, Wegener emphasised, the 'Tirpitz-Plan' was of no strategic value. In essence, Wegener thus rightly maintained that Tirpitz had never fully understood Mahan's ideas. By demanding the introduction of unrestricted submarine warfare and by recommending the seizure of Jutland and Funen, Tirpitz at least implicitly recognised the validity of Wegener's criticism.[49] During the First World War, these insights showed no results, of course, but a generation later, Grand Admiral Raeder obviously took them to heart by seizing the Norwegian and French Atlantic ports, though, ironically, with an even more inferior fleet.[50]

Did it pay for Imperial Germany to try to become a sea power? For historians, judging from hindsight, it is always easy to denounce an obvious historical mistake. However, in Imperial Germany, there were, as already indicated above, some, though unfortunately, not very many people who did not doubt the legitimacy, but the wisdom of Germany's naval aspirations, as well as the influence of sea power at all, and these critics were right for a number of reasons:

1. Germany had become a great power without being a sea power, and with regard to Germany's political, economic, and military strength, there was no reason to believe that the Empire would soon decline, unless it deliberately embarked upon an aggressive course which

entailed this risk.
2. Germany's geographic position was a decisive naval strategic disadvantage, which was very difficult to overcome.
3. Germany's position in the centre of Europe and its limited material and manpower resources, which simply did not allow it to grasp both the hegemony on the continent and the command of the sea, primarily required a powerful army, especially because it was highly unlikely that a future war would be an isolated war at sea.
4. It was more than a bold assumption that the relationships between the great powers would remain unchanged, and that the European alliance systems could be frozen for a generation in order to allow Germany to build up a powerful navy quietly and unmolested and, what is more important, without increasingly arousing the suspicion of the potential enemy.
5. In an era of rapid industrial and technological development, it was similarly bold to assume that warship construction and war technology would not change dramatically within short intervals, thus impairing the political, financial, and strategic premises of the existing concept.
6. The firm belief in a Mahanite blue-water battle fleet and the strategic premises this entailed neglected both important preconditions of this strategic school and the advantages offered by alternative naval strategies.
7. The flourishing of German industry and commerce did not depend upon sea power, at least not as long as a suicidal dagger-at-the-throat strategy against one of its most important customers was the precondition of achieving this aim.
8. With regard to the domestic – political aims, it was unlikely not least as a result of the unsocial distribution of the costs, that the 'wind of democratic change' would abate because of the vague promise of a great future.

Against the background of these grave errors, Tirpitz's ships, which lacked success at sea, which spent most of their time rusting in their home ports and which were finally shamefully surrendered to the enemy they had been supposed to defeat, demonstrated that, in contrast to the Emperor's claim, Germany's grasp for the 'trident', this ancient symbol of sea power, was not a precondition of Germany's greatness, but the main cause of its fall.

NOTES

1. Alfred von Tirpitz, *Erinnerungen* (Leipzig, 1919), p. 10. For a detailed survey of Tirpitz' ideas and plans cf. Volker R. Berghahn, *Der Tirpitz-Plan. Genesis und Verfall einer innenpolitischen Krisenstrategie unter Wilhelm II* (Düsseldorf, 1971), p. 58ff.
2. For a short description of German naval history in the 19th century cf. Wolfgang Petter, 'Deutsche Flottenrüstung von Wallenstein bis Tirpitz', in 'Deutsche Marinegeschichte der Neuzeit', in *Deutsche Militärgeschichte 1648–1939*, ed. by Militärgeschichtliches Forschungsamt, vol. 5 (Reprint) (Herrsching, 1983), p. 81ff.; Werner Rahn, 'Die Kaiserliche Marine', in *Grundzüge der deutschen Militärgeschichte*, ed. Karl-Volker Neugebauer, vol. 1, (Freiburg, 1993), p. 225ff., and Ivo N. Lambi, *The Navy and German Power Politics, 1862–1914* (Boston, 1984), p. 1ff.
3. Cf. Petter, 'Flottenrüstung', p. 41ff., 63ff.
4. Ibid., p. 50ff, and the omnibus volume ed. Walther Hubatsch: *Die erste deutsche Flotte 1848–1853* (Bonn, 1981).
5. Cf. Lambi, *Navy*, p. 3ff.
6. Quoted in: Peter Winzen, 'Zur Genesis von Weltmachtkonzept und Weltpolitik', in: *Der Ort Kaiser Wilhelms II in der deutshen Geschichte*, ed. John C.G. Röhl (Munich, 1991), p. 198.
7. Cf. Host Duppler, *Der Junior Partner. England und die Entwicklung der deutschen Marine 1848–1890* (Herford, 1985) p. 29f.
8. Bismarck in a conversation with Eugen Wolff, 5 December 1888, quoted in: *Bismarck Gespräche*, ed. Willy Andreas, vol. 2: *Von der Reichsgründung bis zur Entlassung* (Birsfelden-Basel, (no year) p. 525.
9. Cf. Lambi, *Navy*, p. 57ff.
10. On the role of the Emperor cf. Lambi, *Navy*, p. 31ff.; Winzen, 'Genesis', p. 190ff.
11. Cf. Tirpitz, *Erinnerungen*, p. 132ff.
12. Cf. the diary of Captain Hopman, 4 January 1913, BA-MA, Hopman-Papers, N 326/10.
13. Cf. Volker R. Berghahn, 'Des Kaisers Flotte und die Revolutionierung des Mächtesystems vor 1914', in *Der Ort Kaiser Wilhelms II in der deutschen Geschichte*, ed. John C. G. Röhl (Munich, 1991), p. 173ff.
14. On the 'Tirpitz-Plan' cf. the detailed analysis by Berghahn, *Tirpitz-Plan*, passim, and for the period 1908 until 1914 Michael Epkenhans, *Die wilhelminische Flottenrüstung 1908–1914. Weltmachtstreben, industrieller Fortschritt, soziale Integration* (Munich, 1991) Cf. also Werner Rahn's contribution to this book.
15. Cf. Thomas Nipperdey, *Deutsche Geschichte 1866–1918*, vol. 2: *Machtstaat vor der Demokratie* (Munich, 1992), p. 595ff., 629ff.
16. Cf. Michael Epkenhans, 'Seemacht = Weltmacht. Alfred T. Mahan und sein Einfluβ auf die Seestrategie des 19. und 20. Jahrhunderts', in *Kiel, die Deutschen und die See*, ed. Jürgen Elvert, Jürgen Jensen and Michael Salewski (Stuttgart 1992), p. 37ff., and the omnibus book: *The Influence of History on Mahan. The Proceedings of a Conference Marking the Centenary of Alfred Thayer Mahan's 'The Influence of Sea Power upon History, 1660–1783'*, ed. John B. Hattendorf (Newport, 1991).

17. Quoted in: Paul M. Kennedy, 'Mahan versus Mackinder. Two Interpretations of British Sea Power', in *Militärgeschichtliche Mitteilungen*, 16 (1974), p. 39.
18. Wilhelm II to Poultney Bigelow, May 1894, quoted in: Winzen, 'Genesis', p. 207, n. 82.
19. Bülow to F. A. Krupp, 22 May 1898, in: Krupp-Archives, FAH III B 145.
20. Cf. Berghahn, *Tirpitz-Plan*, p. 179f.; Wilhelm Deist, *Flottenpolitik und Flottenpropaganda. Das Nachrichtenbureau des Reichsmarineamtes 1897–1914* (Stuttgart, 1976), p. 88f., p. 147ff.
21. Cf. the speech of Wilhelm II in Wilhelmshaven, 3 July 1900, quoted in: *Reden des Kaisers. Ansprachen, Predigten und Trinksprüche Wilhelms II*, ed. Ernst Johann (Munich, 2nd edn, 1977), p. 81.
22. Cf. Bernhard Fürst von Bülow, *Denkwürdigkeiten*, vol. 1 (Berlin, 1930), p. 60.
23. Cf. Tirpitz, *Erinnerungen*, p. 51.
24. Cf. Berghahn, *Tirpitz-Plan*, p. 173ff.; for Bülow cf. Peter Winzen, *Bülows Weltmachtkonzept. Untersuchungen zur Frühphase seiner Außenpolitik 1897–1901* (Boppard, 1977), p. 61ff.
25. Cf. Tirpitz's report (Immediatvortrag) to the Emperor, 28 September 1899, quoted in: *Rüstung im Zeichen der wilhelminischen Weltpolitik. Grundlegende Dokumente 1890–1914*, ed. Volker R. Berghahn and Wilhelm Deist (Düsseldorf, 1988), p. 161.
26. Cf. Tirpitz, *Erinnerungen*, p. 167; Berghahn, *Tirpitz-Plan*, p. 129ff; Epkenhans, *Flottenrüstung*, p. 143ff.
27. Cf. Berghahn, *Tirpitz-Plan*, p. 145ff.; Epkenhans, *Flottenrüstung*, p. 15ff.
28. Cf. Tirpitz, *Erinnerungen*, p. 47.
29. Ibid., p. 49ff., 79ff.; Lambi, *Navy*, p. 62ff.
30. Ibid.
31. According to the last amendment in 1912 to the Navy Law of 1898, cf. Alfred von Tirpitz, *Politische Dokumente*, vol. 1: *Der Aufbau der deutschen Weltmacht* (Stuttgart, 1924), appendix.
32. Cf. Berghahn, *Tirpitz-Plan*, p. 184ff.; Paul M. Kennedy, 'Maritime Strategieprobleme der deutsch-englischen Flottenrivalität', in *Marine und Marinepolitik im kaiserlichen Deutschland 1871–1914*, ed. Herbert Schottelius and Wilhelm Deist (Düsseldorf, 2nd edn, 1981), p. 181ff.
33. Ibid., p. 208ff.
34. Berghahn, *Tirpitz-Plan*, p. 271ff.; Lambi, *Navy*, p. 174ff., 241ff., 269ff., 361ff.; Epkenhans, *Flottenrüstung*, p. 21ff., 931ff., 337ff.
35. Note by Tirpitz, 17 May 1914, cf. Epkenhans, *Flottenrüstung*, p. 391.
36. Heeringen to Bethmann Hollweg, 19 November 1911, quoted in: *Der Weltkrieg. Kriegsrüstung und Kriegswirtschaft*, ed. the Reichsarchiv, vol. 1 (Berlin, 1930), p. 125.
37. Diary of Captain Hopman, 15 June 1914, BA-MA, Hopman-Papers, N 326/10.
38. For an excellent summary of the strategic problems of German naval operations during the war cf. Werner Rahn, 'Strategische Probleme der deutschen Seekriegführung 1914–1918', in *Der Erste Weltkrieg. Wirkung, Wahrnehmung, Analyse*, ed. Wolfgang Michalka, (Munich, 1994), p. 341ff.
39. Ibid., p. 353f.

40. Cf. the speech of Wilhelm II in Wilhelmshaven, 5 June 1916, in: BA-MA RM 2/1970.
41. Cf. Rahn, 'Strategische Probleme', p. 354ff.
42. Cf. Epkenhans, 'Mahan', p. 40ff.
43. Ibid., p. 40, and by the same author, 'Die kaiserliche Marine im Ersten Weltkrieg: Weltmacht oder Untergang?', in *Der Erste Weltkrieg. Wirkung, Wahrnehmung, Analyse*, ed. Wolfgang Michalka, (Munich, 1994) p. 331f.; Kennedy, 'Mahan', p. 39ff.
44. *Berliner Tageblatt*, 3 December 1914.
45. Tirpitz to his wife, 3 September 1914, quoted in: Tirpitz, *Erinnerungen*, p. 397.
46. Cf. Epkenhans, 'Weltmacht', p. 332ff., and Friedrich Forstmeier, *Deutsche Großkampfschiffe 1915–1918. Die Entwicklung der Typenfrage im Ersten Weltkrieg* (Munich, 1970).
47. Cf. Edward Wegener, 'Die Tirpitzsche Seestrategie', in: *Marine und Marinepolitik im kaiserlichen Deutschland 1871–1914*, ed. Herbert Schottelius Wilhelm Deist, (Düsseldorf, 2nd edn., 1981), p. 236ff., and Wolfgang Wegener, *The Naval Strategy of the World War*, ed. Holger Herwig, (Annapolis, 1989).
48. Quoted in: Holger H. Herwig, 'The Failure of German Sea Power, 1914–1945: Mahan, Tirpitz, and Raeder Reconsidered', *International History Review*, 10 (1988), p. 75.
49. Cf. Holger Herwig, *'Luxury' Fleet. The Imperial German Navy 1888–1918* (London, 1980), p. 190ff., 224.
50. Cf. Herwig, 'Failure', p. 86ff.

4 The Opportunities of Technology: British and French Naval Strategies in the Pacific, 1905–1909

Nicholas A. Lambert

The formulation of British naval policy in the decade before 1914 is usually explained in terms of great power rivalry in Europe. The received opinion is that by 1902, the British Government had realised that the expansion of the High Seas Fleet was intended by German statesmen to gain diplomatic leverage over Great Britain by threatening British naval supremacy in home waters. Once recognised, the Admiralty initially responded by implementing a series of long overdue reforms to improve the Navy's fighting efficiency. As the competition intensified, however, Britain was obliged to concentrate a steadily larger proportion of her fleet in home waters in anticipation of imminent conflict; in a series of steps, beginning in December 1904, the Royal Navy gradually abandoned its world-wide sea control. And as the legions were recalled from the outer marches of empire, the security of imperial interests became steadily more dependent upon diplomacy. The idea that British defence policy was driven by a mainly anti-German imperative is simple, suits the standard political and diplomatic accounts of the period, and favours the predisposition of many, to view the decade before 1914 as a lead up to the outbreak of World War One.[1]

Recent work, however, has shown that there are substantial grounds for questioning the premises upon which this narrative has been based. New studies of pre-war British foreign policy indicate that for much of this period Germany was not in fact the uppermost concern in the minds of British leaders. At least until 1905, and probably beyond, many still regarded Russia as the British Empire's most persistent and dangerous foe. The formulation of British foreign policy during this period, moreover, was never determined exclusively by the continental balance of power. Distracting Russian eyes from central Asia, for instance, where British interests were most vulnerable, remained one of the principal goals of foreign policy before 1914.[2] Traditional accounts of naval policy have also been shown to require substantial revision. New scholarship using new methodological approaches has cast doubt on the reliability of existing core histories.[3] It has been proved that the motives and intentions for some key policy decisions by the Admiralty have been completely misread. For example, Sir John Fisher, who has always been regarded as the arch-instigator behind the so-called 'Dreadnought revolution' in capital ship design, was actually opposed to the continued construction of battleships, wanting instead to build new model armoured warships of his own conception later known as battle-cruisers.[4] Other new work has shown that contrary to popular belief, the Admiralty quickly recognised the potential of the submarine and from 1903 gave these craft a vital strategic role to play in the maritime defence of the empire.[5] Finally, new evidence indicates that the Admiralty did not become unduly concerned with the expansion of the German Navy until much later than previous historians have suggested. Unquestionably, the redistribution of the British fleet announced in December 1904, was not intended to affect a concentration of force in the North Sea against the German Empire.[6]

Taken together the revisionist scholarship presents a fundamentally different picture of imperial defence policy before 1914, and indicates particularly that the thinking of Britain's naval leadership has been badly misinterpreted. I do not intend to discuss why or how this happened. This story has been told elsewhere.[7] For this story, suffice it to say that when Admiral Sir John Fisher was appointed Senior Naval Lord in October 1904, he was very far from being an 'orthodox' naval strategist. He did not subscribe to the 'historical' principles of naval warfare nor did he believe that a navy centred around a battle fleet was the best force structure for protecting Britain's maritime interests. He had been convinced that the advent of the submarine heralded a revolution in methods of conducting naval warfare. After Fisher arrived at Whitehall he began to reconstitute British naval strategy and to create a new force structure: essentially, he believed that a force of dual purpose battle-cruisers and submarines could be built and maintained at significantly less cost than a mixed force of battleships and armoured cruisers. In addition, his strategic vision was not limited to the North Sea. Fisher's 'New Model Navy' was intended to protect imperial interests around the world and at an affordable price.[8]

The negotiation of a naval alliance with Japan in 1902 is generally held to mark the end of Britain's 'splendid isolation'.[9] Arguably, the permanence of this shift was confirmed in 1905 by the renegotiation of this treaty for another ten years.[10] That same year, the Admiralty recalled the China battle-squadron, allegedly to face the German fleet. Generally, the 'end of isolation' and the intensification of Anglo-German naval rivalry are regarded as an adequate explanation for imperial defence east of Suez after 1905. Effectively, the British Government jettisoned global commitments to ensure the safety of the United Kingdom.[11] Although it is true the Royal Navy may have deployed fewer warships and no battleships in the Pacific after 1905, this should not automatically be interpreted as signifying an abdication. Throughout Fisher's administration the Admiralty always claimed it had not 'given up' the Far East, and insisted the Navy could still protect imperial interests in those distant waters.[12] These claims, however, have been dismissed by historians out of hand.

A closer look at the preparations for the maritime defence in the Far East prior to 1904, reveals that for many years the Admiralty's plans had been in flux. Traditionally, the Pacific squadrons of all principal navies had consisted largely of gunboats and cruisers supported perhaps by an old battleship, and had been organised primarily to protect trade and police commercial interests. In 1897, however, the situation changed. Russia seized the ice-free anchorage at Port Arthur and immediately began to despatch first-class naval units.[13] By 1900, the Russian squadron had grown into a fleet of six modern battleships with more on the way.[14] Initially, the Admiralty responded in a conventional manner, by reinforcing the China squadron with armoured warships.[15] But as the Russian force continued to grow, the Admiralty found it could not maintain the pace. Subsequently, pressure grew for the Board to review the composition and distribution of all station fleets.[16] But the Senior Naval Lord, Walter Kerr, refused even to consider the idea for fear of undermining Imperial prestige.[17]

Contemplating how to bolster the China squadron, the Admiralty was faced with two main problems. Firstly, shortage of money to build more ships;[18] second, shortage of personnel.[19] Both these difficulties stemmed from the Admiralty's response to the more immediate threat to British naval supremacy posed by the development of the side-armoured cruiser. This was a new type of warship specially designed by the French Navy for commerce raiding; it could outpace and outdistance any British battleship or large cruiser then afloat and out-gun anything faster.[20] From 1897 the French Navy began investing heavily in these new warships and by 1900 armoured cruisers were absorbing two-thirds of its construction budget.[21] Despite some internal opposition, most French admirals were extremely proud of their new cruisers. When completed, they believed, they would provide the Marine Française with a force much better adapted to challenging the Royal Navy than the weak conventional battle-fleet available to them at the time of Fashoda.[22] Uninformed English-speaking publicists ridiculed this cruiser fleet. Citing Mahan they argued that commerce warfare was an ineffectual strategy and that historically war at sea was decided by battle-fleets.[23] The British Admiralty, by contrast, was secretly extremely concerned. Armoured cruisers, the First Lord of the Admiralty admitted, effectively rendered obsolete *all* its existing trade protection cruisers.[24] Accordingly, he argued, the Royal Navy had no alternative but to match the French initiative and build its own fast armoured cruisers.[25] The cost, however, was prodigious. The ships were as expensive to build as battleships and were more expensive to maintain.[26] Between 1897 and 1904 the Admiralty ordered a total of thirty-five armoured cruisers in addition to twenty-seven battleships.[27] But each year it encountered more difficulties in securing the funds to sustain this phenomenal pace of construction. Manning this armada presented an even greater problem. In 1900 not one armoured cruiser was in commission: by 1905 there were twenty-eight requiring almost 20,000 men.[28] According to the First Lord's seven-year programme, projected construction and recruitment up to 1907 would ensure the Royal Navy a superiority of force in European waters, but not for the Far East as well. Subsequently, the Admiralty agreed as an interim measure to the negotiation of a naval treaty with Japan.[29]

Over this same period, France was confronted with very similar problems in defending her Asian empire. Like Britain, she too could not afford simply to build new ships. In 1901, with an eye to alleviating her defence burden in Indo-China, France coaxed Russia into extending their alliance to be activated in the event of war against Britain.[30] Like their British counterparts, the French admirals regarded this treaty as a breathing space to allow the completion of modern warships in sufficient numbers to equip fleets at home and overseas.

During 1905, however, a combination of events dramatically changed the strategic environment in the Pacific.[31] The Anglo-French Entente (signed the previous autumn) was cemented during the Moroccan crisis; in May the remnants of the Russian Navy were annihilated at Tsushima; in June, Britain recalled her battle-squadron from the China station; shortly afterwards, the US recalled all its battleships from Manila. By the end of 1905, therefore, except for the Japanese Navy the Pacific was virtually deserted of armoured warships! And Japan's failure to win reparations at the peace talks, prevented her from waging another war in the immediate future. Confronted by this very different strategic climate, British and French admirals found it very difficult to calculate or justify to politicians an appropriate force level in these distant waters where threats to national interests no longer came in obvious form or direction. Having now to prepare against a range of possible threats and enemies, naval planners were confronted with the equally difficult problem of deciding upon an appropriate force structure. After the war, seeing no obvious threats, and experiencing continuing fiscal problems, the politicians in both Britain and France demanded what is known in modern parlance as a 'peace dividend'. In consequence, expenditures were cut and projected construction programmes slowed. Obviously, maintaining a strong force of armoured warships in the Pacific was no longer politically nor financially viable. Yet naval leaders in both countries regarded a return to station fleets of gunboats as impossible. Naval leaderships in Britain and France, therefore, had good incentives for considering new strategies for the defence of their maritime responsibilities in the Far East. Interestingly, both adopted radically new strategies which depended upon the successful exploitation of new technologies.

Since before the turn of the century, French imperial aspirations in south-east Asia had been declining steadily in favour of acquiring further territory in Africa bordering the Mediterranean. This trend accelerated after the appointment in 1898 of Théophile Delcassé as Minister for Foreign Affairs.[32] After the renegotiation of the Franco–Russian alliance in 1901, on the assumption that in time of crisis Russian naval support would be available, the strength of the French squadron in Indo-China was reduced and work suspended on the naval base at Port Courbet. In war against Britain, the French Navy planned eventually to base its armoured cruisers at Diego Suarez in Madagascar and Dakar in Senegal, and use them to wage a *guerre industrielle* against British trade.[33] Meanwhile, the Russian Pacific fleet would operate from the French naval base in Indo-China at Saigon.[34]

The poor performance of the Czar's Navy during the Russo-Japanese war, however, undermined French confidence in the alliance. Increasingly, opposition deputies expressed their concern at the virtually defenceless state of French Indo-China. This charge was difficult to refute. In 1904, the Marine Française based only one armoured, and one second-class cruiser plus three old torpedo-boats at Saigon. But demands for the Far East squadron to be reinforced could not be met without further weakening the Mediterranean fleet, a move which the government refused to consider. All the Navy could do was promise to send five new cruisers and some submarines as soon as they were completed. During the voyage of the ill-fated Russian Second Pacific Squadron, which left the Baltic in October 1904, France provided considerable assistance to the Russian

Navy far beyond the limits of benevolent neutrality. This, however, induced growing trepidation of a revenge attack by the Japanese against Tonkin: fears which were taken more seriously after the appalling condition of the Russian ships became known. More than a month before the Russian fleet had reached the Straits of Tsushima, the Minister of Marine – Gaston Thompson – instructed a committee of three senior admirals to propose an emergency plan for the defence of Indo-China.[35] On 21 April 1905, this committee submitted an interim report recommending the immediate dispatch to Indo-China of defensive submarines to prevent the two naval bases from being captured by *coup de main*.[36] This advice was accepted by Thompson and the Chief of Naval Staff, Vice Admiral Philippe Touchard.[37]

A week later the committee of admirals submitted their final report on the naval defence of Indo-China.[38] Until this time, French naval planners had always envisaged that conflict in the Pacific would be similar to the Spanish–American war of 1898 – more naval in character than maritime – limited to attacks on commerce and engagements between rival squadrons. The performance of the Japanese armed forces during 1904 shattered this notion. The admirals were disturbed at the audacity of Japan's use of amphibious attack to assault Port Arthur. If an attack could be mounted against Saigon before reinforcements could arrive, they reported, the colony and probably also the fleet would be lost. They were even more alarmed by the seemingly insuperable logistical difficulties in sending reinforcements from the metropolis to Indo-China. The committee subsequently concluded that the only practicable plan of defence would be to maintain a strong autonomous 'station' fleet at Saigon to deter attack.[39] But instead of advising the despatch of more armoured warships to Indo-China, the admirals suggested sending submersible torpedo-boats. With sufficient radius of action to patrol the entire littoral of Indo-China, they argued, a force of submersibles would pose a credible deterrent against hostile operations in the South China Sea. Moreover, as most of the major sea routes in the East passed within a radius of six hundred miles of Saigon, submersibles should be able to interdict enemy merchant traffic in the Gulf of Siam: conceivably they might even be capable of operating off an enemy's principal naval bases.[40] The only drawback to the scheme was that submersibles with anything like sufficient endurance for these missions did not yet exist.[41] However, one of the three admirals on the committee, Rear Admiral Philibert, was also chairman of the Navy's submarine committee. He would certainly have known that submarine designers were confident that suitable craft could be built.[42]

After a series of meetings of the Conseil Supérieur de la Marine held at the end of May 1905, the emergency plan for the defence of Indo-China was adopted.[43] The submersibles would be relatively cheap to build, thus ensuring that funding was politically feasible. Instructions were issued for naval engineers to prepare designs for a large 'offensive' submersible, with a surface range 'to cover the entire littoral of the Tonkin frontier in the Gulf of Siam' – approximately 2,500 miles.[44] The urgency which the Navy attached to the procurement of these submersibles may be inferred from the extraordinary rapidity with which they were ordered.[45] Within a month, sketch designs had been submitted for approval, and in July the Comité Technique had selected the plans of Engineer-Captain Maxime Laubeuf – the original pioneer of the submersible concept.[46] In August, twenty *Pluviôse*-class submersibles were ordered; four months later, twenty more; and in early 1907, another twelve. To avoid delay, because sufficiently powerful diesels had not yet been developed, the navy reverted to the use of cumbersome steam powerplants for surface propulsion for this class, a decision which made the vessels obsolete even before they entered service.[47] During 1905, expenditure on new submarines soared from eight to twenty percent of the Navy's construction budget, and remained at this level for three years. This shift in the Navy's pattern of expenditure is all the more significant because it occurred at a time when the budget for new construction was declining. Thus the money for the submersibles had to be found from actual reductions in spending on other types of warships.[48]

The scheme to defend Indo-China with submersibles was never implemented, even though the craft were eventually completed. Sometime during 1907 the plan was dropped.[49] In October, the military bureau of the Colonial Ministry and the Army General Staff advised the Navy that 'the autonomous defence of Indo-China was impossible owing to the shortage of personnel and money'.[50] The French Government, moreover, may have been encouraged to abandon the defence of Indo-China after the signing of a treaty with Japan promising to respect each other's spheres of interest in south-east Asia.[51] But there are other possible reasons. During the summer, the Navy was warned of further cuts in its construction budget. Contemporary French naval doctrine recommended the battle-fleet operate only in waters where it could be supported by submarines.[52] The Admirals may, in consequence, have decided to keep the submersibles in home waters to supplement the relatively weak French fleet. Alternatively, the scheme might have been abandoned because the Staff had finally decided to listen to Captain Lucien Mottez,[53] the Navy's leading expert on submarine warfare, who had repeatedly warned that figures for range and performance claimed by Laubeuf were wildly optimistic.[54] In any case, the *Pluviôse*-class submersibles (which were probably the least successful warships designed by the French Navy before the war) were never employed in the role for which they had been originally designed.

Fisher arrived at the Admiralty on 20 October 1904 charged with the task of finding significant economies in naval expenditure.[55] His basic reforms are well known; scrapping warships of little fighting value (which in wartime would have been decommissioned anyway); rationalising the global network of station fleets; poising a new fleet comprised of the newest battleships and cruisers at Gibraltar.[56] Contrary to popular belief, Fisher's redistribution of the fleet was not intended to affect a concentration of force against Germany. Actually, besides endeavouring to save money, he was trying to improve the Navy's strategic flexibility and to shift the emphasis of the Navy's operational capabilities away from fleet actions towards improving its capability to hunt down enemy armoured cruisers operating on the trade routes. If these changes do not seem obvious in retrospect, it is partially because his proposals for the reorganisation of the station fleets were never fully implemented.[57]

Critics, then and now, have portrayed the recall of the five British battleships as signifying the end of British naval dominance in the Far East.[58] In particular, the Australian government was furious at the recall of the China battle-squadron and refused to accept assurances from (unsympathetic) British diplomats that the Japanese naval treaty meant imperial interests in the Far East were safe.[59] Successive Australian Prime Ministers agitated loudly for a stronger Royal Navy presence in the Pacific, arguing that they believed Japan was actually the greatest threat to British interests in the Pacific. The best illustration of this Australian concern of the 'yellow peril' occurred in 1907 when, much to the embarrassment of the British government, the Australians issued an invitation for the US Navy's Great White Fleet to visit Australia during its world cruise.[60]

Assessments of British naval weakness in the Far East after 1905 give too much credence to the views of diplomats, and to public opinion as represented in newspapers. Historians have tended to overlook that the imperial interests that had to be protected were commercial rather than territorial. Another major oversight is the failure to appreciate the immense distances between points in the western Pacific and the magnitude of the logistical difficulties in operating a large fleet in the Far East.[61] The principal threat to British interests east of Suez was raids against seaborne trade. The deployment of battleships on the China station was 'misplaced power'.[62] Had a clash of imperial interests in China or the south-west Pacific occurred during this period, it is difficult to see how any power (except Britain) could have sustained a large maritime force in these waters, if only because of the difficulties in obtaining adequate supplies of steam coal. The best steam coal came from South Wales: the only coal mined in the Pacific region suitable for naval purposes came from Westport, New Zealand.[63] Quite simply, without plentiful supplies of coal offensive naval operations in the Far East would necessarily have been limited to sporadic raids by cruisers.

In 1898, the United States Navy was able to maintain only a very small squadron in Asiatic waters and even then relied upon access to British coaling facilities.[64] The lesson was relearned during the cruise of the Great White Fleet across the Pacific in 1907.[65] Subsequently, officers at the Naval War College proved that the General Board's vaunted *Plan Orange* was impossible to execute because 'the shipping under our own flag is inadequate to support the logistical requirements of our fleet, even for a campaign in the Caribbean'.[66] It has already been shown that the French Navy clearly understood the problems of fuel supply. Admittedly, Admiral Rozhdestvensky's Russian fleet did manage in 1904-1905 to limp halfway around the world, but only with considerable assistance from the French Navy and supported by a train of chartered British and German colliers.[67] During 1904-1905 the Japanese fleet had shown it possessed the tactical ability to operate effectively in home waters, but it could never venture more than five hundred miles from its bases because of inadequate logistical support.[68]

In contrast, the Royal Navy possessed an unrivalled fleet support infrastructure east of Suez. By July 1905, the Navy's own stockpile of Welsh steam coal in the Far East alone had grown to over 300,000 tons.[69] To put this in perspective, readers should note that the Japanese fleet burned a total of 375,000 tons of coal during the entire eighteen months of war with Russia.[70] Two years later, at the height of peace, British stocks in the region were still at 270,00 tons. The Royal Navy could also rely upon the largest merchant fleet in the world for logistical support – far more than it required.[71] In 1907, the Admiralty promised the Japanese that in the event of war within three weeks 140,000 tons of British shipping would arrive at Kobe.[72] Another 'hidden strength' was Britain's stranglehold on cable communications giving the Admiralty a monopoly on the control of information into or out of the Far East.[73] Furthermore, an expanded Naval Intelligence Department charged with the duty of monitoring movements of foreign steamers and warships, linked to a chain of wireless telegraphy stations intended eventually to encompass the globe, enabled the Admiralty to respond to enemy movement with economy of force and to vector cruisers towards enemy warships.[74]

After 1905 the Admiralty, very quietly, further improved upon the Navy's 'hidden' logistical strengths. Most tangibly, they continued to modernise overseas naval bases.[75] For instance, a victualling yard was built at Sydney, and the docks at Auckland, Bombay, Fremantle, Hong Kong, Simonstown, Singapore, and Sydney were all enlarged to take battle-cruisers.[76] The money spent before 1910 on new works at Simonstown alone contrasts sharply with the amounts set aside for Rosyth – which supposedly had been designated in 1902 as the Navy's main base of operations in the next war.[77] The funds committed by the Admiralty between 1905 and 1910 to improve 'imperial' naval bases in preference to developing those in the North Sea belies the notion that the imperial defence had been effectively abandoned.[78]

From 1905, the foundation of the Admiralty's plans for war in the Far East rested upon the fleet support infrastructure. The Royal Navy was the only maritime power which had the capability to dispatch large reinforcements to the South China Sea, and sustain a fleet of armoured warships. In 1909, the Director of Naval Intelligence, Rear Admiral Alexander Bethell, assured the Committee of Imperial Defence that in an emergency the entire Mediterranean fleet could proceed from Malta to Hong Kong within twenty-four days, and certainly inside a month.[79] In addition, within six weeks additional reinforcements detached from the Home Fleet could be sent east of Suez without any risk of compromising home defence. 'We could', he continued, 'even if we were engaged in war with Germany, send out twenty battleships to Hong Kong, with a proper proportion of armoured cruisers'.[80] These claims were perfectly realistic. After the elimination of the Russian Navy in 1905, the Royal Navy was left with a superiority in modern armoured warships equalling the combined strength of the next three naval powers. But even without this huge numerical preponderance, Fisher believed that sufficient battleships and battle-cruisers could be dispatched east of Suez when necessary, because torpedo craft and submarines would deter hostile navies from launching an invasion across the narrow seas around Britain.[81]

Even though Britain did not keep a large fleet in the Far East after 1905, clearly the Royal Navy retained a significant operational capability east of Suez. Fisher would have preferred to have seen more armoured cruisers based in China, but 'political' considerations prevented him from doing so.[82] In December 1905, a radical Liberal ministry came to power in Britain intent on reducing defence expenditure, and increasing spending on social welfare. The new Government insisted that the Navy was unnecessarily strong and could safely be cut without compromising national security. In July 1906 the Chancellor of the Exchequer, Herbert Asquith, ominously announced that he believed 'naval expenditure lends itself much more easily to retrenchment, because the amount of new construction to be put in hand is entirely within the discretion of the Government of the day'.[83] This was especially alarming to Fisher who needed new-model warships to accomplish his naval revolution. For political and financial reasons, therefore, the Admiralty was encouraged to conceal the true direction of naval strategic planning, understate its true strength and to exaggerate the threat from rival European powers in home waters. Fisher tried several ploys to protect the construction budget. One was to place a larger proportion of the fleet in reserve. Another was to blur the distinction between battleships (identified with home defence) and armoured cruisers (associated with imperial defence).[84] Similarly, the Admiralty could not keep an extravagantly large fleet on the China station: the consequences would have been obvious.[85]

In 1906, Australian frustration at Britain's refusal to strengthen the China squadron boiled over, and the Commonwealth began preparations to form its own Navy.[86] The threat caused great alarm in the Foreign Office and Colonial Office. Diplomats and civil servants were worried about complications this would cause to the conduct of foreign policy and terrified that brash 'colonial' gunboat diplomacy might drag Britain into war. Naval officials, by contrast, raised surprisingly few objections.[87] Indeed, at the 1907 Colonial Conference the Admiralty actively encouraged all the Dominions to provide flotilla craft 'and also to equip and maintain docks which could be used by the fleet'.[88] Surreptitiously, the Australians were steered away from their original plan to purchase 'useless' torpedo-boats, and persuaded to buy 'proper' ocean-going destroyers and also submarines – vessels which would be of assistance to a British fleet operating in the Pacific.[89] Meanwhile, behind the scenes, Fisher pressed even harder by lobbying Australian ministers to support his scheme for a new Imperial Eastern Fleet based at Hong Kong.[90] Sadly, the political differences between Britain, Canada, and Australia were too great to allow any coordinated scheme to be formally adopted at the 1907 conference. Not until the 1909 Imperial Conference was a practicable scheme of collective security in the Pacific finally agreed.[91]

Naval policies before the First World War have been very greatly misread largely because the historians who wrote the core histories of 'Edwardian' navies did so with preconceived notions of what naval strategy should have been. Like contemporary naval publicists, who too often thought of sea power in terms of battleships and Trafalgars, many scholars have tended to analyse naval policies in the light of Mahanian theories of naval warfare. This outlook has tended to restrict and distort the investigation of the evidence. How naval planners intended to apply sea power cannot be deduced simply by looking at the numbers, types and distribution of warships. The function of a warship, moreover, or the reason why it was originally built, is not implicit in its design. The size, structure, and distribution of fleets was largely determined by financial considerations, often set by politicians who were more concerned with national prestige than operational capability.[92] Students of naval policy, therefore, have to corroborate their basic interpretations with an analysis of more complex factors such as the tactical and operational capabilities each navy was trying to develop, or, say, the development of fleet support infrastructure. It is not sufficient to examine only 'naval' or 'strategical' factors. The conception of naval policy is not simply a matter of applying strategic principles. Naval policy is formulated by taking into consideration a wide variety of factors including finance, technological innovation, ship design, tactics, internal politics and imperial (foreign) relations, all of which are interlinked in manifold ways. No single element of the equation can properly be understood if studied in isolation: quite often the elements of 'policy' can conflict with one another and thus some will not give a true indication of policy direction. More fundamentally, however, naval policy cannot realistically be examined as an independent variable; the Admiralty (or Ministry of Marine) was a department of government in competition with other departments – most notably the Treasury (or Finance Ministry). Historians, therefore, need to look at naval policy from a much wider perspective, taking into account factors such as naval administration, industrial resources, economics, inter-service rivalry, national finance and politics, foreign policy and relations. Naval historians need more often to question old assumptions and also ask themselves the question 'so-what' more frequently.

NOTES

1. Arthur Marder, *From the Dreadnought to Scapa Flow* (London, 1961–70, 5 vols) I, 25–27, 36–43 & 105–50. Aaron Friedberg, *The Weary Titan: Britain and the Experience of Relative Decline, 1895–1905* (Princeton, N. J., 1988), pp. 189–208. Paul Kennedy, *Strategy and Diplomacy* (London,

1984), pp. 111–60; and *The Rise of Anglo-German Antagonism, 1860–1914* (London, 1980). George Monger, *The End of Isolation: British Foreign Policy 1900–1907* (London, 1963).
2. Keith Neilson, *Britain and the Last Tsar: British Policy and Russia, 1894–1917* (Oxford, 1995); and 'Greatly Exaggerated: The Myth of the Decline of Great Britain before 1914', *International History Review* XIII (1991) pp. 661–880.
3. Nicholas Lambert, 'British Naval Policy 1913/14: Financial Limitation and Strategic Revolution', *Journal of Modern History*, LXVII (1995). Jon Sumida, 'Sir John Fisher and the Dreadnought: The Sources of Naval Mythology', *Journal of Military History*, LIX (1995). Nicholas Lambert, 'Admiral Sir John Fisher and the Concept of Flotilla Defence, 1904–1909', *Journal of Military History*, LIX (1995).
4. Jon T. Sumida, *In Defence of Naval Supremacy: Finance, Technology and British Naval Policy, 1889–1914* (Boston, 1989).
5. Nicholas Lambert, *A Revolution in Naval Strategy: The Influence of the Submarine upon Maritime Strategic Thinking, 1898–1914* (forthcoming).
6. Ruddock F. Mackay, 'The Admiralty, the German Navy, and the Redistribution of the British Fleet, 1904–1905', *Mariner's Mirror*, LVI (1970) pp. 341–6; and *Fisher of Kilverstone* (Oxford, 1973) pp. 313–18. For new evidence to confirm Mackay's thesis see Lambert, *Revolution*.
7. Jon T. Sumida & David A. Rosenberg, 'Machines, Men, Manufacturing and Money: The Study of Navies as Complex Organizations and the Transformation of Twentieth Century History', in *Doing Naval History: Essays towards Improvement*, ed. John B. Hattendorf (forthcoming); also generally Sumida, 'Fisher and the Dreadnought', and Lambert, 'Flotilla Defence'.
8. Lambert, 'Flotilla Defence'.
9. For the origins of the naval alliance see Ian Nish, *The Anglo-Japanese Alliance* (London, 1966) pp. 174–238.
10. Nish, *Anglo-Japanese Alliance*; also Monger, *Isolation*, pp. 62 & 193–204.
11. Friedberg, *Weary Titan*, pp. 166–95. Paul M. Kennedy, 'The Relevance of the Prewar British and American Maritime Strategies to the First World War and its Aftermath, 1898–1920', in *The Maritime Strategy and the Balance of Power: Britain and America in the Twentieth Century*, ed. John B. Hattendorf & Robert S. Jordan (London, 1989) pp. 165–88, at p. 170.
12. PRO: CAB 2/1, 102nd meeting of the CID, 26 June 1909, remarks by Sir J. Fisher.
13. PRO: CAB 37/49/7, 'Navy Estimates 1899–1900', Goschen, 31 January 1899. Nish, *Anglo-Japanese Alliance*.
14. Gloucestershire Record Office: Hicks-Beach MSS D2455, PCC/83, Letters from Goschen (1st Lord of the Admiralty) to Hicks-Beach (Chancellor of the Exchequer) 17 December 1897, 6 June, 20 July, 21 July, 1898 (2 letters), 4 February 1899. See also *Brassey's Naval Annual* for 1898–1903.
15. *Navy List*, 1898–1904.
16. Bodleian Library, Oxford: MS Selborne 158 f. 156, Memorandum by Selborne, 4 April 1902. BL: Add. MSS 50280, f. 86–92, H. O. Arnold-Foster,

Naval Power in the Twentieth Century

'The Allocation of the Military Resources of the Empire as between the Army and Navy Respectively', 31 January 1902.

17. Bodley: MS Selborne 31 f. 62, Kerr to Selborne, 29 April 1902; f. 167, Kerr to Selborne, 15 October 1902. MS Selborne 41 f. 299, Kerr to Selborne 11 December 1904. MS Selborne 158 f. 156, minute added by Selborne, 21 October 1904, to his Memorandum of 4 April 1902.
18. Sumida, *In Defence* pp. 13–28. A. N. Porter, 'Lord Salisbury, Foreign Policy and Domestic Finance, 1860–1900', in *Salisbury: The Man and his Policies*, ed. Lord Blake & H. Cecil (London, 1987) pp. 148–84.
19. Lambert, *A. Revolution.*
20. Sumida, *In Defence*, pp. 19–21.
21. Figures extracted from *Brassey's Naval Annual.*
22. Theodore Ropp, *The Development of a Modern Navy: French Naval Policy 1871–1904*, ed. Stephen S. Roberts (Annapolis, Md., 1987). François Fournier, *La flotte nécessaire* (Paris, 1898). Edouard Lockroy, *La défense navale* (Paris, 1900) pp. 3–8, 77–81, 191–200, 233–9 & 364–97.
23. Arthur J. Marder, *British Naval Policy, 1880–1905: The Anatomy of British Sea Power* (London, 1940, repr. Hamden, 1964) pp. 275 n. 2, 276 & 283–7. *Brassey's Naval Annual* 1898 edn, p. 62.
24. PRO: CAB 37/56/8, 'Navy Estimates 1901–1902' (by Selborne), 17 January 1901, p. 10. CAB 37/73/159, Memorandum (by Selborne) on distribution of the fleet, 6 December 1904.
25. PRO: CAB 37/49/7, 'Navy Estimates 1899–1900' (by Goschen), 31 January 1899. CAB 37/59/118, 'The Navy Estimates and the Chancellor of the Exchequer's Memorandum on the Growth of Expenditure' (by Selborne), 16 November 1901 pp. 13–14. Hicks-Beach MSS D2455, PCC/83, Goschen to Hicks-Beach 23 July 1897, 20 & 21 (2 letters) July, 24 December 1898 & 4 February 1899.
26. Sumida, *In Defence*, pp. 18–28.
27. Fred T. Jane, ed., *Fighting Ships*, 1897–1904.
28. Lambert, *A Revolution.*
29. Nish, *Anglo-Japanese Alliance*, pp. 174–84. PRO: CAB 37/58/81, 'Balance of Power in the Far East', Selborne, 4 September 1901. Bodley: MS Selborne 26 f. 41, Kerr to Selborne 5 October 1901, cited in D. G. Boyce, ed., *The Crisis of British Seapower* (London, 1992) p. 128.
30. *Documents Diplomatiques Françaises 1871–1914*, 2nd. Ser. III, Annexe 3, pp. 605–607, 21 December 1901.
31. Robert de Caix, *Fachoda* (Paris, 1899), pp. 286–97.
32. Christopher Andrew, *Théophile Delcassé and the Making of the Entente Cordiale* (New York, 1968) pp. 87 & 225.
33. SHM: BB8 2424(5), CSM minutes, 11 November 1899; also Ropp, *Modern Navy*, pp. 352–5. Archibald Hurd, 'The New Flying Squadrons of France', *Fortnightly Review* XCII (1902) p. 351.
34. On the possibilities of neutral colliers supplying enemy cruisers see Keith Neilson, 'A Dangerous Game of American Poker: The Russo-Japanese War and British Policy', *Journal of Strategic Studies*, XII (1989), pp. 63–87; and 'The British Empire floats on the British Navy: British Naval Policy, Belligerent Rights and Disarmament, 1902–1909', in *Arms Limitation and*

Disarmament: Restraints on War 1899–1939, ed. B. J. C. McKercher (Westport, 1992), pp. 21–41. On the anticipated difficulty of intercepting neutral merchantmen and determining their true destinations and cargoes see J. Duroché, 'Le ravitaillement des croiseurs corsaires sur les théatres extérieures d'opération', *Revue Maritime* NS 166 (1933), pp. 481–511. See also Bodley: MS Selborne 41 f. 238, Kerr to Selborne 9 September 1904.

35. SHM: CSM index 1890–1925; Vice-Admiral de Maigret, Rear-Admirals R. d'Abnour & Philibert, secretary Lt. René Daveluy. This committee became the Permanent Section of the CSM in April 1905.
36. SHM: BB8 2424(6), dossier 2, paper 12, 1st report: 'Rapport présenté à la Section Permanente du Conseil Supérieure sur l'organisation de la défense d'Indo-Chine', n. d.; 2nd report, dossier 3, paper 16: 'Note sur les mésures transitoires et de circonstances, les plus efficaces pour couvrir dans le plus bref délai le littoral indo-chinois et donner au besoin un puissant appui dans les mers voisines à notre escadre d'Extrème Orient', 21 April 1905.
37. SHM: BB8 2424(6) dossier 3, paper 10, pp. 8–13.
38. SHM: BB8 2424(6) 2nd report, dossier 3, paper 16: 'Note sur les mésures transitoires'.
39. Ibid.
40. Ibid.
41. Henri Le Masson, *Du Nautilus au Redoutable: histoire critique des sous-marins de la Marine Française* (Paris, 1960) Ch. 7 & 8.
42. SHM: BB8 1815(d), Comité de Sous-marins, 1904–1905, Final Report 17 May 1905; for membership of the committee see *Liste Navale*, 1905.
43. J. Avice, *La défense des frontières maritimes* (SHM, Paris, 1922), pp. 180–85. SHM: BB8 2424(6) dossier 3, Fournier to Minister, 'Programme naval à adopter dans l'ordre d'urgence ...', 10 May 1905, & annexe 1, 'Note sur l'importance du rôle des flotiles sous-marines dans la guerre navale et sur les conséquences de ce rôle', 8 May 1905.
44. Ibid.; also BB8 2426(6), dossier 3, Fournier to Thompson 10 May 1905. Le Masson, *Du Nautilus au Redoutable*, pp. 183–4.
45. SHM: BB8 2424(8), CSM minutes 27 March 1906, remarks by Thompson, p. 13.
46. Le Masson, *Du Nautilus au Redoutable*, pp. 141–53. SHM: 6DD1 606-9499, folder G21-99, 'projet de submersible à 2 hélices, type 1905 à vapeur', July 1905.
47. SHM: 6DD1 626-8808, Comité Technique, minutes 7 August 1907, 'Rapport au installation de moteur à combustion intérieure sur les sous-marins Q.60 et similaires.'
48. Figures extrapolated from *Brassey's Naval Annual*, 1904–1909.
49. SHM: BB8 2424(9) dossier 2, 'Note au Ministère – défense de l'Indo-Chine', E. M. G. 2 + 3, 11 October 1907, p. 3 and Annexe A; also note letter cited from C-in-C Far East (de Marolles) to the Ministry, 14 March 1907.
50. Ibid.
51. Christopher Andrew & A. S. Kanya-Forstner, *The Climax of French Imperial Expansion* (Stanford, 1981), pp. 33–5.
52. SHM: BB8 2424(10) No. 27, précis of decisions, EMG 3, October 1907, pp. 25–7. BB8 2424(9) dossier 5, paper 8, 'Question: programme des

bâtiments à mis en chantier en 1909–10', EMG 3, October 1907. BB4 2437, dossier AT note 1, 'Note a pour but d'examiner les bases sur lesquelles pourraient être établies les nouvelles instructions des éscadres metropolitains pour le cas d'une guerre contre l'Allemagne'. EMG 3, 6 April 1907, pp. 2–12.
53. SHM: Service Records: Mottez, Lucien A. J., Capitaine de Vaisseau, né 29 August 1861.
54. SHM: 6DD1 606-8499, Minutes of Comité Technique, 30 January 1907, pp. 13–21, remarks by Mottez.
55. Bodley: MS Selborne 39 f. 137, Chamberlain to Selborne 10 May 1904. MS Selborne 42 f. 3, Selborne to Fisher, 17 October 1904. MS Selborne 39 f. 157, Selborne to Chamberlain 11 November 1904. Mackay, *Fisher*, pp. 306–308. Sumida, *In Defence*, pp. 18–28.
56. Mackay, *Fisher*, pp. 313–18.
57. Lambert, *A Revolution*. Peter Kemp, ed., *The Fisher Papers* (Navy Records Society Vols. 102 & 106, 1960–64) I, 129–31.
58. Friedberg, *Weary Titan*, p. 137.
59. PRO: CAB 18/11B f. 69, Deakin to Governor-General, 28 August 1905. ADM 116/1241B, Australian Naval Agreement, 1906, f. 6, Deakin to Governor-General, 26 April 1906. Neville Meaney, *A History of Australian Defence and Foreign Policy, 1901–1923* (Sydney, 1976) pp. 121–33.
60. Ibid., pp. 163–6.
61. PRO: ADM 1/8905, 'Australia', memorandum by Capt. Charles Ottley, April 1906.
62. Bodley: MS Selborne 44 f. 44, Battenberg to Selborne, 20 October 1904; for evidence that Battenberg was referring to the need for more cruisers see Lambert, *A Revolution*.
63. PRO: ADM 1/7934, 'The Fleet Coaling Service – Memorandum showing the general position on 1st February 1907', pp. 1–21. Note that warships required Welsh coal to obtain their maximum (listed) endurance and speed.
64. William Braisted, *The United States Navy in the Pacific, 1897–1909* (Austin, Texas, 1958), pp. 22–35.
65. J. H. Maurer, 'Fuel and the Battle-fleet: Coal, Oil and American Naval Strategy, 1898–1925', *Naval War College Review* (1981), pp. 60–77.
66. U.S. Naval War College (Newport, R. I.): RG8, XLOG, 'Logistics', 3 May 1915, by Paymaster-General T. J. Cowie (BuS&A), pp. 24–40 & statistical appendices. Assuming a fleet of approximately 20 battleships would need 300,000 tons of coal a month to operate in the Western Pacific, the USN required a minimum of 75 colliers of at least 6,000 tons capacity. In 1914 there were only 18 such vessels under the American flag in the Pacific, plus 22 smaller craft. For General Board assumptions see RG8, ULF, 2nd Committee of G. B., 'Coal Supply in the Event of War', 16 November 1912. For the RN's assessment of American logistical weaknesses see Bodley: MS Asquith 21 f. 245, Ottley to Nash, n. d. [early 1909]. Plan Orange was the code name given to war plans against Japan; see Edward Miller, *War Plan Orange* (Annapolis, Md., 1991). The discrepancy between the coal requirements of the US and Japanese fleets, even allowing for the fact that the Japanese were very close to their bases and the USN expected to be

5,000 miles from theirs, suggests that the Japanese must have been severely rationed (see n. 68).

67. PRO: ADM 231/48, NID Report 782, 'Coaling of Russian Fleet', 1906. Further details can be found in *British Documents on Foreign Affairs: Confidential Prints*, eds. D. C. Watt, K. Bourne & I. Nish, (University Publications of America, 1989) Pt. 1 Ser. E Vols. 11–12. Lamar Cecil, 'Coal for the Fleet that had to die', *American Historical Review* (1964), pp. 990–1005.

68. PRO: ADM 231/49, NID Report No. 835, 'The Russo-Japanese War – reports on technical subjects' (June 1908) p. 27. At the beginning of the war, the Japanese fleet was rationed to 50,000 tons of coal a month (although a stock was available for emergencies). Throughout the war, the Japanese fleet was usually supported by 24 colliers with a capacity of 67,750 tons.

69. PRO: ADM 231/42, NID Report No. 751, 'Annual Statement of Requirements, Resources and proposed Method of Supply of Coal, 1904–1905'; ADM 231/44, 1905–1906; ADM 231/46 No. 806, 1906–1907; ADM 231/48, No. 829, 1907–1908. More than half the stock was Starr Patent coal which could be kept for long periods without deterioration; see ADM 1/7934, 'The Fleet Coaling Service'. 1 February 1907.

70. PRO: ADM 231/49, NID Report No. 835, p. 27. Over 75,000 of the 375,000 tons of coal burned was inferior grade domestic coal.

71. In August 1914 (the only year for which accurate figures are available) the RN chartered colliers with a total capacity of well over one million tons.

72. PRO: ADM 1/8386/218, 'British Shipping available as Japanese Transports', 1907. According to the NID, on any day in 1907 there was over 500,000 tons of British shipping within three weeks' steaming of Kobe: PRO: FO 800/87 ff. 107 & 114, 'Memorandum by the Admiralty', July 1907, and minutes of meeting between British and Japanese representatives, 29 May 1907. Apparently, under the terms of the Anglo-Japanese Naval Treaty, the RN promised to supply the Japanese Navy with 20,000 tons of coal a month; ADM 231/42 p. 7.

73. Paul Kennedy, 'Imperial Cable Communications and Strategy, 1870–1914', in *The War Plans of the Great Powers, 1880–1914*, ed. Kennedy (London, 1985), pp. 75–98. See also Hicks-Beach, MSS D2455, PCC/83, Goschen to Hicks-Beach, 13 December 1898.

74. PRO: CAB 17/77 f. 11, 'Defence (Naval): Report of the Committee of Imperial Defence on the Question of a General Scheme of Defence for Australia', May 1906, pp. 1–7, is an excellent (and fairly truthful) explanation of the Admiralty's ideas on naval policy in the Pacific during this period.

75. Ministry of Defence Naval Library, London: Tweedmouth MSS, 1908/09 Estimates, 'Navy Estimates Committee' [January 1908], Expenditure under Navy Works Act, 1895–1905. PRO: CAB 37/90/101, 'Future Battleship Building', Tweedmouth, 21 November 1907, Appendix B, 'Statement showing total estimated cost as shown in The Navy Works Act 1905 and as subsequently revised, and the expenditure to October 31 1907', 19 November 1907. Parliamentary Papers 1902–14 *passim*, Navy Estimates Vote 10, sub-head B.

76. Total expenditure on works under the Navy Works Act, 1895–1905: Home bases, £16,597,830; Mediterranean bases £10,876,170; Overseas bases £4,416,480; other expenditure £2,366,000. For details of extensions to docks east of Suez see PRO: ADM 116/1265A, 'Trincomalee', minute by Bethell, 11 February 1910.
77. Total expenditure on new works 1906–10: Rosyth, £411,200 (of which £250,000 was under the 1910 estimates); Simonstown, £802,230; Hong Kong, £370,904.
78. Parliamentary Papers 1900–1914, Navy Estimates. Note the contrast between the proportion of expenditure on works spent overseas between 1906–1909 and 1910–14. Moreover during this period the Admiralty managed to hand over the burden of maintaining and developing many of its bases (including Sydney, Fremantle, Halifax, Simonstown, Bombay, Auckland and Colombo) to colonial governments, which invested considerable sums in modernising 'their' naval bases.
79. PRO: CAB 2/2, CID 102nd meeting, 29 June 1909, remarks by Bethell.
80. Ibid.
81. Lambert, 'Flotilla Defence'.
82. PRO: ADM 1/7946, 'C. O. 20 Nov 1907', Deakin to Fisher, 12 August 1907, also memorandum by Slade, 7 November 1907, and Fisher's minute thereon, 20 November. Kemp, *Fisher Papers* II, 129–133.
83. PRO: CAB 37/83/62, 'Naval Expenditure', Asquith 9 July 1906. Tweedmouth MSS, A62, Asquith to Tweedmouth, 23 & 24 May 1906. More generally, Neilson, 'The British Empire floats on the British Navy', pp. 21–41.
84. Lambert, *A Revolution*.
85. Nevertheless, between 1905 and 1913 the number of RN personnel manning ships on stations in the Far East remained constant at 10,500, and only dropped below that figure after the formation of the RAN in 1912.
86. PRO: CAB 17/77, Papers for the 1907 Colonial Conference, f. 11, 'Resolution of the Commonwealth of Australia that the provisions of the Naval Defence Agreement, 1902, be reconsidered.' Meaney, *Australian Defence*, pp. 133–41.
87. PRO: CAB 2/1, CID 88th meeting, May 1906, remarks by Tweedmouth. CAB 17/77 f. 65, Ottley to Colonial Office, 30 July 1906. I disagree with Meaney's interpretation of the RN's attitude towards the RAN.
88. PRO: CAB 18/11A, section on naval defence of speech by Tweedmouth, April 1907, p. 130.
89. Ibid. PRO: CAB 17/77, 'Defence (Naval)', f. 21, 'IV–Local Naval Defence', pp. 11–12.
90. PRO: ADM 1/7949, 'C. O. 20 Nov 1907' Deakin to Fisher 12 August 1907.
91. Nicholas Lambert, 'Economy or Empire: The Fleet Unit Concept and the Quest for Collective Security in the Pacific, 1909–1914', in *Far Flung Lines: Studies in Imperial Defence*, eds Keith Neilson & Greg Kennedy (London, 1995).
92. Ibid.

5 French Naval Strategy: A Naval Power in a Continental Environment
Hervé Coutau-Bégarie

En général, nous avons déployé dans notre marine notre véritable caractère: nous y paraissons comme guerriers et comme artistes. Aussitôt que nous aurons des vaisseaux, nous reprendrons notre droit d'aînesse sur l'Océan comme sur la terre. Nous pourrons faire aussi des observations astronomiques et des voyages autour du monde, mais, pour devenir jamais un peuple de marchands, je crois que nous pouvons y renoncer d'avance.[1]

This sentence by Chateaubriand, a penetrating observer as well as a celebrated author, places us immediately in the very heart of the ambiguous atmosphere which has always been characteristic of the relationship of France with the sea; or perhaps more exactly, of French awareness of this relationship. It is worth remembering that in the thirteenth century King Philip Augustus became so disenchanted that he claimed that, 'Les Français ne connaissent point la voie de mer'.[2] In the later eighteenth century his remote descendant Louis XV echoed the sentiment: 'Il ne peut y avoir en France de marine que celle de M. Vernet'.[3]

This kind of remark has given credit to the idea that France and the sea were unfamiliar with each other, and incidentally encouraged the exaggerated notion that Louis XV was resolutely opposed to the Navy. The abandonment by Louis XIV of his grand naval policy after the defeat of La Hogue in 1692, the scanty results of the Napoleonic navy, the excesses of the *jeune école* debate at the end of the nineteenth century, are all presented as further proof. English-speaking historians have continued to advance such arguments: Mahan depicts a French Navy incapable of sustained achievement; Ronald Chalmers Hood[4] draws an exaggerated portrait of a certain number of French naval officers as devotees of the past, if not definitely reactionaries; and E. H. Jenkins, at the end of a detailed and sound history of the French Navy, comes to the stark conclusion that 'France has had little just cause to be ashamed of her navy; the navy may have had some just cause to be ashamed of France'.[5]

This picture has been presented without qualification, and French sailors are for the most part convinced of it. Many have developed a siege mentality, acknowledging the ignorance and ingratitude of their country towards its navy with sardonic pleasure or resigned scepticism according to their temperaments. In France there is no marked interest in the Navy, and the disasters of the Second World War have created a climate of distrust on both sides which has not yet disappeared. When the Naval Staff presented President Pompidou with its 'Plan Bleu' in 1973, he commented that, 'il n'y aura jamais de grande marine en France'. When they asked him why, he referred to the scuttling of the fleet at Toulon in 1942.[6]

It seems difficult if not impossible to contradict all this evidence, but we may at least correct the balance somewhat. Let us simply recall that France has a long and rich naval history. Certain Gaulish tribes, notably the Venetae, had strong maritime traditions; the Franks were using the North Sea in the sixth century; and throughout the expansion of the monarchy the sea was seldom absent for long. Undoubtedly French naval history is uneven, but the periods of naval decline are linked to national crises like the Wars of Religion which shattered the first efforts of the Valois, the rebellion of the Fronde which ruined Richelieu's work, and the French Revolution which disorganised the Navy for a generation. Government neglect, however, was exceptional. Louis XIV did not abandon his fleet after the defeat of La Hogue in 1692, but from absolute necessity in the face of invasion in 1704–1705.[7] Under Louis XV, Choiseul developed an active policy of reconstruction, and Napoleon devoted very large resources to his fleet, though the strategic context was unfortunate. The efforts of the July Monarchy and the Second Empire to rebuild the Navy are well known. People are less aware that between 1870 and 1914 France spent as much as Germany on her Navy. No doubt the results were less decisive, but French naval setbacks did not flow from neglectful governments refusing financial support.

Overall, French naval history was uneven, with resounding victories (Agosta, Palermo, Beachy Head,the Chesapeake), contrasting with many periods of relative or absolute decline. Historians today are more inclined to blame geopolitical factors than governments. The French coasts are divided between the Atlantic and the Mediterranean, with difficult and dangerous links between the two. A further problem was the lack of good naval ports, Toulon excepted, and especially the lack of one on the Channel coast until Vauban's dream of Cherbourg was finally achieved in the 1860s. Brest is well situated but the prevailing westerlies made it difficult to get out of. These factors tend to be overlooked by modern studies, which emphasise instead a different handicap, the permanent shortage of seamen. The population of fishermen was always too small to man the fleets, and the longer the war lasted, the more the problem was felt.

Nevertheless we must not forget that France achieved respectable results even against Britain, the leading naval power. Though France could never be a naval power like Britain, if only because she was not an island, her achievement is not to be despised. One is reminded of the jest of Jules Siegfried, the great French authority on political science; meeting a Polish politician who declared his intention of imitating British policy in every respect, Siegfried asked him if he proposed to make Poland an island.[8] France has often been threatened with invasion, and not only on the north-eastern frontier. She has equally often been tempted by continental expansion, as in the Italian Wars. There were logical and unavoidable considerations drawing her that way, which cannot be ignored. The supremacy of the army corresponds to an historical reality, which we do not need to be determinists to recognise.

The main task of French strategists has always been to fit the Navy into a continental environment. Hence the remarkable flowering of naval thinkers, unparalleled in any other country including Britain. In the seventeenth and eighteenth centuries the great naval authors were French: Hoste, Bigot de Morogues, Bourdé de la Villehuet, Grenier, all of whom were translated into English and Dutch. As late as 1830, Hoste was translated into Greek. In the nineteenth century there was intense debate between such writers as Paixhans, Bouet-Willaumez and Grivel, forgotten today, but influential in their day. At the end of the century the *jeune école* was an intelligent attempt to apply technical advances to overturn British industrial supremacy by exploiting her dependence on imported food, though in the end it lapsed into absurd extremes in its advocacy of the small torpedo-boat against the battleship. Admiral Aube was a naval thinker of real breadth before he became a less successful Minister of Marine. Though the *jeune école* was doomed to failure, the triumph of orthodox Mahanism as preached by Darrieus and Daveluy depended on France's new diplomatic position. As part of the Triple Alliance against the Triple Entente, France's naval enemy became Italy, against which a conventional fleet victory was perfectly feasible. By the early years of the twentieth century France had abandoned her longstanding pretensions to rank as the second naval power after the Dutch, later the British, and was content to be the leading continental naval power, facing Italy before 1914, Italy and Germany after 1918. All this was achieved in a difficult financial and diplomatic context, for old reflexes die hard, and Britain strove to limit France's ambitions in international disarmament conferences.[9]

We may conclude that France is not and never could be a 'thalassocracy', but until the twentieth century she was always a great European, later world power. Contrary to what has often been said, she was seldom unaware of the maritime dimension of her power, and with a few exceptions, her ministers have not been fools, though they had to take account of France's situation and the unavoidable needs of defence by land. They have frequently been disappointed by the poor returns yielded by heavy investment in those defences. France has had great sailors, exceptional privateers, talented squadron commanders, but few great admirals. Even the great Tourville lacked boldness: 'courageux de coeur, poltron d'esprit', Louis XIV called him.[10] Suffren was always an exception. The Navy has been accepted as a necessity, but seldom with enthusiasm. On the Arc de Triomphe there is only one naval battle, Grand Port in 1810 (four frigates against five); it was hardly in the same league as Austerlitz. Admiral Auphan noted, perhaps without realising the full significance of the fact, that the only French naval victory of the twentieth century was the defeat of the Siamese at Koh Chang in January 1941 – not the most decisive battle of the Second World War. How could Grand Port and Koh Chang outweigh in the public mind Trafalgar or the scuttling of the fleet at Toulon?

This unhappy inheritance bears on the development of a new strategy nowadays. Under the Fourth Republic, the Navy was viewed with suspicion, and its links with Vichy were not forgotten. No naval review was held until 1958, and no officers were promoted full admirals. The material reconstruction of the fleet was successful, in part thanks to American assistance, but for want of political support the sailors were unable to gain the NATO positions the Naval Staff had hoped for. They had to be contented with command of the Western Mediterranean (MEDOC) and a limited area in the Bay of Biscay (BISCAYLANT).

Under the Fifth Republic the Navy was rehabilitated. General de Gaulle did not care for it, but his policy of national independence served its interests. The Americans were ready to make concessions to keep France in the integrated military organisation of NATO, and in 1963 the Navy was on the verge of achieving its ambitions to control the IBERLANT command, creating an extended zone of command embracing the Eastern Atlantic and the Western Mediterranean, and allowing France to take a high line with the British. But General de Gaulle had other ideas, and the Navy was forced to submit to his determination to leave NATO. It had to be content with secret, non-binding agreements prescribing rules of co-operation with the NATO allies; the Barthélémy–Smith agreement for the Atlantic in 1964, and Barthélémy–Woods for the Channel in 1965. For reasons which have never been officially clarified, the equivalent agreement for the Mediterranean (Tardi–Turner) was not signed until 1977.

For diplomatic reasons, the Navy attempted to define unilaterally some Zones of National Interest, later the 'National Security Zone' in the Atlantic and the 'Maritime Interest Zone' in the Mediterranean. These zones were too large; they did not correspond to national capabilities nor enhance the status of the French Navy. More realistic zones were called for; a 'Zone of Regular Action' in the Atlantic, and a 'Zone of Naval Action' in the Mediterranean within which, in turn, was a smaller 'Zone of Priority Action'. All were vague paper concepts; they had no official existence and their operational status seems to have been slight or non-existent.

The real rehabilitation of the French Navy occurred elsewhere, with the creation in the 1960s and the 1970s of the 'Oceanic Strategic Force', the practical expression of the statement (so often quoted by French naval officers) made by General de Gaulle at the École Navale in 1965: 'Pour la première fois dans l'histoire, la Marine est en première ligne de défense de la France et cela sera dorénavant de plus en plus vrai.'[11] It was a development all the more remarkable in that the Navy did not initially want nuclear ballistic-missile submarines.

But this rehabilitation came at a heavy cost in funds diverted from other forces. In 1958 the third carrier, the *Verdun*, was cancelled; while the *Suffren*-class guided-missile frigates, of which there were to have been eight, were reduced first to four and then two. Between 1962 and 1967 only one major surface warship was built, the *Aconit*. Initially the decline was not obvious. The Fifth Republic was fortunate to inherit from the Fourth two new carriers, an impressive fleet of escorts, and the submarines of the *Aréthuse*- and *Daphné*-classes. The problems began to emerge in the 1970s. In 1973 the Naval Staff proposed a very ambitious scheme, the 'Plan Bleu', based on two aircraft carriers, two helicopter carriers and more than 300,000 tons of other warships. It was approved but never carried out, and there followed an inexorable decline. Of more than 200 ships in the 1960s, about 120 remained at the end of the 1980s, and there will be fewer than 110 at the end of the century. France still has 300,000 tons of ships and ranks fourth among the naval powers, but she keeps that rank only thanks to the ballistic-missile submarines and the carriers. In 'classical' forces the French Navy is markedly outclassed by the Japanese. More worrying, in surface ships both the Italian and Indian navies are stronger. The most acute problems at present are the nuclear-powered attack submarines, (the building of the seventh has been suspended and no more are planned, though there is a new class projected for 2007); and the anti-aircraft destroyers (only four remain, of which the two *Suffren*-Class will come to the end of their lives about 2004).

During the 1980s a gap between objectives and means has become ever more evident. From the mid-1970s France has been involved in many local or regional crises calling for naval involvement for humanitarian purposes (evacuation of French and other foreign residents from Lebanon, Somalia, and Aden); to support a client state or friend (Tunisia against Libya in 1976 and 1980); to sustain Djibouti in the face of Ethiopian or Somali threats; to deter or intimidate a potential adversary (deployments off Libya during the Chad crisis of 1984); and to protect trade in the Arabian Gulf during the final phase of the Iran–Iraq War. Formerly undertaken in a strictly national basis, such actions now tend to occur in a multilateral context following UN, NATO or WEU decisions – as in the Gulf War – the Adriatic blockade of former Yugoslavia, and the Haiti embargo.

All these tasks make it ever more important to have the means to project power; the Navy has never been more in demand, but never more burdened. Operations in tropical waters lead to increased wear and tear, while money for maintenance is reduced as budgets are more and more restricted. Outside the Navy the problem is little understood, and there is no appetite in political circles for any fundamental debate on national defence. There was no White Paper between 1972 and 1994, and the one just published is remarkably discreet about the choice of ships and weapons. Consensus on the doctrine developed in the 1960s has ossified into a refusal to face awkward questions. Too often, hackneyed phrases about the search for a European defence identity serve to deflect hard questions about its compatibility with a reformed NATO or a reinforced WEU. Experience with Yugoslavia suggests that European agreements lead to paralysis. In Rwanda, France reluctantly agreed to act alone, and she would have to do so again if there were another crisis in Lebanon. For some time yet, French naval strategy may have to be defined in a national context. There is no lack of tasks, but the means have to be provided to carry them out.

NOTES

1. Chateaubriand, *Réflexions et aphorismes*, ed. J. P. Clément (Paris, 1993), p. 28.
2. Michel Mollat, 'Philippe Auguste et la mer', in *Philippe Auguste, Colloque international* (Paris, 1982).
3. Quoted in François Caron, *La guerre incomprise ou les raisons d'un échec. Capitulation de Louisbourg, 1758* (Vincennes, 1983) p. xxi. Joseph Vernet was a celebrated painter of ports and harbours.
4. *Royal Republicans: The French Naval Dynasties between the World Wars* (Baton Rouge, 1985).
5. *A History of the French Navy* (London, 1973), p. 344.
6. Information from a staff officer of the period.
7. Jean Meyer, 'Louis XIV et les puissances maritimes', *XVIIe siècle*, No. 123 (1979).
8. Quoted in Jean-Louis Seurin, *Analyse des systèmes politiques* (University of Bordeaux political science course, 1978).
9. Cf. generally *L'évolution de la pensée navale*, ed. Hervé Coutau-Bégarie (Paris, 1991–95, 5 vols).
10. Philippe Masson, *Histoire de la Marine* (Paris, vol. I, 1982).
11. For many years quoted as an epigraph to successive editions of the *Flottes de Combat*.

6 The Indispensable Navy: Italy as a Great Power, 1911–43
James J. Sadkovich

Although it is uneven in quality and coverage, there is an extensive literature on the Italian navy, including an impressive list of publications by the navy's historical office, and numerous scholarly and popular works by individual historians, from patriotic works on the First World War to critical accounts of the Second and studies dealing with everything from naval policy to strategy and tactics.[1] Italian writers have generally conceded that the Italian state needed a large navy, although they have differed in their assessments of how well their navy was constructed and managed. Yet if a large navy was a burden on the Italian budget and could not alone determine Italy's destiny, it was nonetheless essential to the Italian state in an era of naval power.

In their study of Italian naval policy, Gabriele and Friz concluded that a navy was 'indispensable' to Italy, thereby echoing Aldo Valori's popular work of the 1930s, which argued that a navy was 'absolutely necessary' for Italy and had to occupy a 'conspicuous and irreplaceable position' among its armed forces.[2] Today, this seems an odd assertion, because the outcome of the Second World War has strongly coloured our assessment of the value of its navy to Italy. But navies performed tasks other than combat. Possession of a navy enhanced a state's status and prestige in the early twentieth century, and our impressions would have been different in 1912, 1918, or 1936.

There is no question that to be counted as a great power Italy needed a powerful fleet. Just as strategic nuclear weapons and regional alliance systems have determined a state's status and its relationship to other powers since 1945, so a powerful navy and colonies established a state's ranking prior to 1940. As one writer observed in the late 1930s, great powers had 'always been maritime powers', and 'naval effectiveness' was still 'the yardstick by which the stature of the Powers' was determined.[3] Indeed, governments expended so much money and effort to stay ahead of their naval rivals that a later critic wondered whether the 'progress of civilization' had 'reached the stage at which the nation taking the highest place does so by virtue of its war fleets, the calibre of its guns, and the weight of deadly projectiles it can handle'.[4]

Certainly, many Italians saw themselves as a maritime people whose well-being depended on their navy. Balliano and Soavi believed that Italy's future lay on the seas, and Pietro Silva considered it natural that Italy secure the Adriatic before expanding in the Mediterranean.[5] A large navy seemed indispensable both to defend Italy's extensive and vulnerable coastline and to enable it to compete in the scramble for colonies. By the turn of the century Italy had a powerful fleet; and if it had fallen to seventh place in tonnage by 1914, it still held the naval balance in the Mediterranean, its mere existence paralyzed the Austrian Navy, and Rome's conclusion of naval accords with Vienna in 1913 raised the spectre of an Austro-Italian force powerful enough to check the French fleet and close the Mediterranean to the British.[6]

The navy also provided a link with a glorious past eclipsed by decades of foreign domination, and the 'shame' of the fleet's loss to Austria at Lissa in 1866 became a prod to reclaim Italy's honour. Young naval officers like Alberto Da Zara were therefore anxious to bring the Austrian fleet to battle and 'avenge' Lissa in the spring of 1915. If Italy's fleet stayed in port during the war and its allies were generous with their criticism, the Italian Navy had checked the Austrian simply by remaining neutral in 1914; and a year later it assured the Entente control of the seas by entering the conflict on their side. Geography and Austrian strategy, more than an inefficient fleet or a poorly conceived naval policy, precluded the decisive naval battle that might have redeemed Lissa, and led to heavy Italian naval and merchant losses as the conflict in the Adriatic settled into a war of attrition fought with mines, submarines, torpedo-boats, aircraft and MAS (motor torpedo-boats).[7]

Unable to engage the Austrian fleet, the Italians waged a 'guerrilla' war, parrying raids by surface ships, interdicting submarines, and supporting land operations in the Balkans. Armoured trains and MAS were more conspicuous than battleships, and the largest operations were the evacuation of the Serbian army in 1916 and the laying of the Otranto barrage in 1918.[8] If Ettore Bravetta exaggerated when he claimed that by defeating Turkey and Austria the Italians had shown themselves 'worthy' descendants of Roman and Venetian mariners, the navy had performed its tasks tolerably well, and the commanders and sailors of its smaller vessels had shown both dash and daring. Criticism was therefore all the more galling, and the Italian Naval League prefaced its volume on the war by noting that its intent was to combat foreign accounts that ignored or misrepresented the Italian Navy's actions during the war, while Bravetta accused the French of lying and treating Italy as badly as her elder sisters had Cinderella.[9]

Yet if Italy's fleet had earned little respect during the war, it had emerged victorious, leading one writer to herald Italy as 'a new maritime nation of great potentialities' and 'rich' traditions, and enabling Carlo Schanzer to confirm Italy's credentials as a great power at the Washington Naval Conference by obtaining parity with France in capital ships.[10] With its Austrian rival removed, the Italian Navy could become an essential element in an assertive foreign policy calculated to transform Italy from a regional power into a world or, in naval terms, an oceanic power – a logical development for a state whose survival depended on seaborne commerce, which provided Italy with its raw materials and the markets for its finished goods.[11]

If possessing a navy established Italy as a major power, Rome asserted its status and prerogatives by exercising naval power, and both liberal and fascist regimes used the navy to intimidate smaller states and to assert their presence during diplomatic disputes.[12] How useful the navy could be was demonstrated in 1923 when its occupation of Corfu enabled Rome to assert its dominance in the lower Adriatic, to contest Greek and Yugoslav influence in Albania, and to force Belgrade to accept Italy's annexation of Fiume and tacitly acknowledge Italian hegemony in the upper Adriatic.[13] Such successes were clearly addictive, and by the 1930s Fioravanzo had concluded that an even larger navy was needed to realise Italy's political and strategic objectives.[14]

Yet strategic improvements could create precarious diplomatic situations. In 1911–12 Rome used the Navy to gain a foothold in the Aegean Sea by seizing the Dodecanese Islands, but doing so alarmed the British. Mussolini's subsequent annexation of the islands was strategically logical, but discomfited London and annoyed Athens and Ankara.[15] Having more enemies might have conferred more honour, as the fascist leader argued, but an aggressive navy clearly conjured up competitors, including Italy's erstwhile Austrian ally in 1913 and its former British patron in 1935, and led to such contradictory actions as simultaneously planning to fight the Austrian fleet and signing naval accords with Vienna.[16]

As an expanding imperial power, Italy needed a navy to appropriate and secure its 'living space' abroad. However, because only states with a large industrial plant and abundant resources could build a navy powerful enough to guarantee access to the resources Rome needed to develop a powerful industrial base, the logic of imperialism seemed inverted in

Italy's case. Yet it was precisely Italy's lack of agricultural and mineral resources that led the Italian Naval League and the Nationalist Party to advocate a strong navy as necessary to obtain colonies and new markets overseas.[17] Naval officers were crucial to initial penetration of East Africa, and some, like Enrico Millo, who forced the Dardanelles in 1911, became heroes during Italy's defeat of Turkey, which one British contemporary felt had justified the 'care and forethought' spent on the Navy before 1911.[18]

Prestige, heroes, and colonies, the stuff of navalism, were also fascist propaganda themes, and by the late 1930s, colonies appeared fundamental to prestige and power, the 'basis of economic vigour', and an arena for Italian development. To lose them was to be seriously damaged as a nation and as a state, especially after the First World War had shown them to be sources of cheap raw materials, labourers, and troops.[19]

Whether Mussolini had transformed liberal Italy's 'expansionist colonial policy' into 'a military quest' for bases on which to build his empire, his consolidation of East Africa gave Italy outposts near the Indian Ocean. But the Italian Navy lacked the first-rate bases it needed at Massawa and Assab to make it a serious threat to British communications, and many observers discounted the Italian Navy because they considered its equipment poor, its training faulty, and its officer corps second-rate.[20]

Still, just as Italy needed colonies, however poor, to be a great power, so it needed a large fleet, however incomplete, to show the flag abroad, because MAS were too small to do so. Even in the late 1930s, well after navies had air arms and aircraft carriers, capital ships were considered the 'backbone' of a navy and the naval equivalent of 'gold reserves', because their possession served as a deterrent and provided the fleet with its 'strategic and moral power'. Fioravanzo thus argued that a country fell in rank and could not claim an 'imperial' role without big-gun ships, which Edwards saw as still 'the ultimate arbiter of sea power'.[21]

Criticism of the Italians for building such vessels rather than aircraft carriers ignores both contemporary opinion and the Mediterranean realities which made carrier-based aircraft seem less useful than those flying from fields on land.[22] To get territories abroad, therefore, both increased Italy's prestige and improved its strategic position by obtaining the air and naval bases needed to protect and expand its empire.

Denied Dalmatia at the peace table in 1919, Italy had nonetheless obtained harbours along the eastern coast of the Adriatic, part of the Austrian fleet, torpedo works at Fiume, and shipyards at Monfalcone and Trieste. Rome thus controlled the Adriatic Sea and was in a position to continue prewar efforts to create an integrated heavy industry able to supply the navy with ships and equipment.²³ By 1914 the Terni steelworks had joined shipyard owners in large conglomerates, and governmental subsidies enabled firms like Armstrong of Pozzuoli to increase output and improve the quality of their products. A decreasing dependence on foreign suppliers, while masking a continuing reliance on foreign licenses, led to a better use of resources and prompted boasts that the Navy's ships and their equipment were produced in Italy, a point of honour as well as a practical advantage during a conflict.²⁴

During the interwar period, Italy's Navy assured its invitations to international conferences, which Rome used to urge global disarmament and to argue for parity with France. Mussolini also used Italy's growing naval and air power to press London and Paris to concede him a larger role in the Mediterranean and Red Sea.²⁵ With an industrial plant able to supply most of its needs by the mid-1930s, and with bases in Libya, the Dodecanese Islands, Eritrea and Somalia, the Italian Navy had evolved into a dangerous enemy whose light vessels were a serious threat in the Mediterranean's restricted waters.²⁶ Indeed, not only did the Italian Navy play a crucial role in the conquest of Ethiopia, it appeared to have faced down the British Navy.²⁷

Although Italy would have lost a war with Britain in 1935, London's effort to use its fleet to deter Rome failed badly, leading one Briton to complain that the British empire was 'a stranded whale from which any bold hand may cut blubber with impunity'.²⁸ Perhaps Mussolini was bluffing when he warned that while London could order its fleet into the Mediterranean, the Italians would decide whether it could leave. But it was an effective bluff, and the Italian fleet emerged from the crisis with its reputation enhanced, even if Italian troops in Libya and Italian aircraft on Sicily had been as important as the Italian Navy in London's calculations.²⁹

By 1937, thanks in large part to its navy, Italy was positioned to extend its political influence in the Middle East, to contest control of the Red Sea, and to threaten Britain's communications with India. But if all this led Vansittart to view Italy as a first-class power, it also earned Rome a place on Britain's list of potential enemies, and Mussolini's use of submarines to blockade the Spanish Republic alarmed both Paris and London.³⁰ However, by the time that Britain and France reacted, the Italian boats had disrupted Soviet shipments to the Spanish Republic. The Italians then joined in anti-submarine patrols, transforming themselves from 'suspected pirates' into 'policemen', as Italian aircraft sporting Nationalist insignia underscored the isolation of the Soviets and the Spanish Republic by continuing to sink merchantmen bound for Republican ports.³¹

Rome was even able to conclude an important agreement with London in early 1938, and thanks to the efficiency of Italian submarines and merchantmen, Mussolini could consider suspending operations in Spain.[32] In short, Italy's use of its navy and air force had unnerved Britain, paralysed France, guaranteed a Nationalist victory, and stymied the Soviet Union. That such successes created dangerous illusions and weakened the Italian Navy by spending funds needed to rearm on operations in Ethiopia and Spain was not yet obvious.[33]

In 1939 it seemed as if naval expenditures had been justified. The navy had confirmed Italy's status as a great power, secured the Adriatic, enhanced the fascist regime's foreign and domestic image, faced down the British fleet in 1935, and checked the Soviets in 1937. Italy's merchant fleet had weathered the Depression, and naval building had stimulated Italian industry, which by the late 1930s was providing the navy with armour-plate, guns, and electro-mechanical devices that, if not always of top quality, were significant steps toward autarky.[34]

Italy's strategic position had improved appreciably with the suppression of the Senussi revolt in Libya and the development of air and naval bases in East Africa and the Dodecanese, while Franco's victory in Spain gave Rome a nominal ally in the western Mediterranean. If it was unlikely that the colonies would repay their cost anytime soon, they still bolstered the regime's image at home and abroad, and by 1939, only French control of Tunisia and British possession of Malta kept the Italian fleet from dominating the central Mediterranean.[35]

Although the Navy's performance between 1940 and 1943 was disappointing, it was far from dismal, despite its lack of radar and its inability to use French bases in Tunisia. For almost three years, it sustained a convoy effort to North Africa, effectively closed the Mediterranean to regular shipping, and harried the British in port and at sea.[36] The Navy suffered embarrassing defeats, but these were often due to British advantages in radar and intelligence, and must be set against Italian successes, including the performance of its light craft and special units.[37] For example, in March 1941, while the Italians lost three cruisers and two destroyers, they sank two British cruisers in turn. In December 1941 Italian frogmen crippled the last two British battleships in the Mediterranean, and in the summer of 1942 Italian units were crucial to Axis air–naval victories that cost the British 100,000 tons of merchant shipping and several major naval units.[38] But Rome could not afford to trade naval pieces with London, and a crushing Anglo-American material superiority made even such victories meaningless. In other words, if the British never dominated the Italian Navy, they wore it down, and all that the Italians could do after 1940 was to perform well, which they did despite enormous handicaps.[39]

Because possessing a navy was seen as essential to national security and prestige, an analysis based on the outcome of a single war is misleading and criticism of autarkic and protectionist policies designed to subsidise naval industries are misplaced. Few states have been indifferent to questions of national prestige, and even Adam Smith argued that the invisible hand is irrelevant in matters of national security.[40] Modern states have subsidised their military and naval industries, because that has been the only way to guarantee the forces needed to assure themselves a niche within a highly competitive and constantly shifting international hierarchy.

Its Navy cannot therefore be judged a luxury simply because Italy lost a war and a fleet in 1943. The destruction of the Italian fleet was as much a tribute to its importance as the dismantling of the German and Austrian Navies in 1918 was an admission that they had seriously threatened British, French, and Italian control of the seas. Italy's fleet had enabled it to be taken seriously as a great power, and if its rank in the hierarchy of states was relatively modest, in 1914 its fleet held the balance of naval power in the Mediterranean. After 1940 it took the combined forces of Britain and the United States to defeat it. This was no mean achievement for a navy that was stitched together in 1866, hampered by an embryonic industrial base and tight finances, and humbled by its loss to the Austrians at Lissa. Whether being a good second-class navy justified its cost is largely moot, because after 1918 Italy's fleet was matched against first-class navies, and at that point one could argue that even a draw was a moral victory.[41]

NOTES

1. For a discussion of the literature, see the essays by Brian Sullivan and James Sadkovich in *Ubi Sumus? The State of Naval and Maritime History*, ed. John B. Hattendorf (Newport, RI, 1994). Also Giuseppe Fioravanzo, *A History of Naval Tactical Thought* (Annapolis, MD, 1979); and Giorgio Giorgerini, *Da Matapan al Golfo Persico. La marina militare italiana dal fascismo alla repubblica* (Milan, 1989).
2. Mariano Gabriele and Giuliano Friz, *La flotta come strumento di politica nei primi decenni dello stato unitario italiano*(Rome, Ufficio Storico della Marina Militare, 1973), p. 304; Aldo Valori, *Esercito-Marina-Aeronautica* (Milan 1938), p. 88; also Ezio Ferrante, *Il Mediterraneo nella coscienza nazionale* (Rome, 1987).

3. Gary E. Weir, *Building the Kaiser's Navy. The Imperial Navy Office and German Industry in the von Tirpitz Era* (Annapolis, 1992), p. 1, notes that 'At the turn of the twentieth century, possessing a navy was a sign of national greatness and power, and a strong naval force was virtually required for a nation to compete for economic and political influence around the world'. Paul G. Halpern, *The Mediterranean Naval Situation, 1908–1914* (Cambridge, MA, 1971), p. 203, and Kenneth Edwards, *Uneasy Oceans* (London, 1939), pp. 16, 77.
4. Arthur Guy Enock, *This War Business. A Book for Every Citizen of Every Country* (London, 1951), p. 84.
5. Adolfo Balliano and Giuseppe Soavi, *L'Italia sul mare nella grande guerra* (Turin, 1934), pp. 9, 14; and Pietro Silva, *Il Mediterraneo dall'unità di Roma all'impero italiano* (Milan, 1942), esp. pp. 454–5.
6. Mariano Gabriele and Giuliano Friz, *La politica navale italiana dal 1885 al 1915* (Rome, Ufficio Storico della Marina Militare, 1982), pp. 23–6. Halpern, *1908–1914*, p. 358–64, thought Italy held the balance in the Mediterranean because it could jeopardise or assure Franco-British naval supremacy there. Richard Hough, *The Great War at Sea, 1914–1918* (New York, 1983–84), pp. 41–3, 70, considered Italy's navy a solid second-class force.
7. Alberto Da Zara, *Pelle d'ammiraglio* (Milan, 1949), pp. 60, 119–20; Balliano and Soavi, *L'Italia sul mare*, pp. 15–16; and Halpern, *1908–1914*, pp. 362–7, and *The Naval War in the Mediterranean, 1914–1918* (Annapolis, 1987), pp. 84, 264, 276–7, 451–2, 579–80; also Camillo Manfroni, *Storia della marina italiana durante la guerra mondiale, 1914–1918* (Bologna, 1923), *passim*, and Lawrence Sondhaus, *The Naval Policy of Austria-Hungary, 1867–1918. Navalism, Industrial Development, and the Politics of Dualism* (West Lafayette, IN, 1994), *passim*.
8. Arturo Riccardi, 'La guerra sui mari d'Italia', in Luigi Segato, *L'Italia nella guerra mondiale. II. Dalla resistenza sul Piave-Grappa a Vittorio Veneto* (Milan, 1927), pp. 967–1002; Balliano and Soavi, *L'Italia*, p. 55; Royal Italian Navy, Historical Section, *The Italian Navy in the World War, 1915–1918* (Rome: 1927), pp. 33–5; and Lega Navale Italiana, *La marina italiana nella guerra mondiale, 1915–1918* (Rome, 1920), pp. 62–3; also Angelo Gatti's polemical *La parte dell'Italia. Rivendicazioni* (Milan, 1926), esp. pp. 126–61, for the evacuation of the Serbians.
9. Ettore Bravetta, *La grande guerra sul mare. Fatti, insegnamenti, previsioni* (Milan, 1925), pp. 196, 240–41, 246–8; Lega Navale Italiana, *La marina italiana*, prefatory note and pp. 62–4, 68, saw securing communications overseas as the navy's 'first and natural task.' It also stressed the difficulties facing the Italian navy at the outset of the war, focused on the exploits of individuals like Luigi Rizzo and Costanzo Ciano, and underscored the role played by the navy in saving the Serbian army in 1916, supporting land operations on the Isonzo front, and securing communications overseas.
10. Archibald Hurd, *Italian Sea-Power and the Great War* (London, 1918), pp. 24, 122–4; Lega Navale Italiana, *La Marina*, pp. 174–80. Thomas G. Frothingham, *The Naval History of the World War. The United States in the War, 1917–1918* (New York, 1971/1924–26), p. 257, saw the Italian navy as having dominated the Austrian, and the sinking of the *Viribus Unitis* as 'one of the most daring feats of the war.'

11. Ferrante, *Coscienza*, pp. 44, 68–9, 89–93. For Italy's dependence on the sea, see E. Manzini and M. Monterisi, *Economia pubblica e nazione armata* (Milan, 1939), *passim*, who calculated that up to 85% of Italy's raw materials arrived by sea; Giuseppe Fioravanzo, *Basi navali nel mondo* (Milan, 1936), pp. 113–14, who believed the navy could only assure supplies to Italy and communications with the empire by establishing its control of the sea; and James J. Sadkovich, 'Minerali, armamenti e tipo di guerra: la conflitta italiana nella seconda guerra mondiale', *Storia contemporanea* (1987), for the importance of seaborne sources of raw materials to Italy's war effort from 1940 to 1943.

12. Matteo Pizzigallo, 'L'Italia alla conferenza di Washington (1921–1922)', p. 587, and 'Il ruolo della Regia Marina nella politica estera. La missione dell'*Audace* a Tangeri nel 1923', both in *Rivista marittima* (1975); and Silva, *Il Mediterraneo*, pp. 448–50, for the dispatch of a naval division to Tangiers in 1927.

13. James Barros, *The Corfu Incident of 1923* (Princeton, NJ, 1965), esp. pp. 101–102; Matteo Pizzigallo, 'L'incidente di Corfu e la politica italiana nel Levante', *Storia e politica* (1974). Silva, *Il Mediterraneo*, p. 455, saw the shelling as 'eloquent proof of the new energy that animated Italian policy.' Since the Entente threatened to shell Athens in 1916, such demonstrations were not uniquely fascist. See Halpern, *1914–1918*, pp. 292–300.

14. Gabriele and Friz, *Flotta*, pp. 304–305; and Fioravanzo, *Basi*, pp. 46–7.

15. Ferrante, *Coscienza*, pp. 48–50; Fioravanzo, *Basi*, pp. 135–6, and *Documenti Diplomatici Italiani*, Series 7, vols. 1, 2, and 3, *passim*, esp. vol. 3, docs. 228 and 789, for the potential of the Dodecanese islands to serve as major air and naval bases.

16. Gabriele and Friz, *1885–1913*, pp. 231–49.

17. Jacopo Mazzei, 'Il problema degli "spazi vitali"', in *Rivista di studi politici internazionali* (1941); Valori, *Esercito–Marina–Aeronautica*, p. 104, saw the fleet as 'the indispensable instrument of the Duce's imperial policy.' For the Lega Navale, which was chartered in 1899, Gabriele and Friz, *1885–1915*, pp. 40–45; for the ANI, Franco Gaeta, *Nazionalismo italiano* (Naples, 1965), pp. 80–85, and Enrico Corradini, *Discorsi*, esp. pp. 112–18, 141, 462, 472–3.

18. Hurd, *Italian Sea-Power*, pp. 33–9; Halpern, *1908–1914*, pp. 194–5; and Giuseppe Fioravanzo and Guido Viti, *L'Italia in Africa. Serie Storico-militare. Vol. II. L'opera della marina (1868–1943)* (Rome, 1959), for colonial expansion, and Paolo Alatri, *Nitti, D'Annunzio e la questione adriatica (1919–1920)* (Milan, 1959), *passim*, for Millo.

19. Rafaele Ciasca, *Storia coloniale dell'Italia contemporanea. Da Assab all'Impero* (Milan, 1938), pp. 1–8; and Jacopo Mazzei, 'L'utilità della colonie', *Rivista di studi politici internazionali* (1947), pp. 335–56. Also Giorgio Rochat, *Il colonialismo italiano* (Turin, 1974); Luigi Goglia, 'Sulla politica coloniale fascista', *Storia contemporanea* (1988); and Carlo Zaghi, *L'Africa nella coscienza europea e l'imperialismo italiano* (Naples, 1973), esp. 393–8, 404–405.

20. Fioravanzo, *Basi*, pp. 84, 205, 213–14; and Brian Sullivan, 'A Thirst for Glory: Mussolini, the Italian Military, and the Fascist Regime, 1922–1936', (Columbia University PhD, 1984), pp. 212–29, and his 'A Fleet in

Being: The Rise and Fall of Italian Sea Power, 1861–1943', *International History Review* (1988). For Libya, see Claudio Segrè, *Fourth Shore: The Italian Colonization of Libya* (Chicago, 1974), *passim*.

21. Fioravanzo, Basi, p. 123; Valori, *Esercito–Marina–Aeronautica*, pp. 93–4; Edwards, *Uneasy Oceans*, pp. 68, 78–9; Halpern, *1914–1918*, p. 561.
22. James J. Sadkovich, 'Aircraft Carriers and the Mediterranean, 1940–1943: Rethinking the Obvious', *Aerospace Historian* (1987).
23. For early problems, Lega Navale Italiana, *La Marina*, pp. 18–20. Valori, *Esercito–Marina–Aeronautica*, pp. 89–90, listed its tasks as securing communications with Asia Minor, the Dodecanese, the Black Sea, and Libya; threatening enemy communications; protecting convoys; and preparing to operate on the oceans.
24. Paolo Ferrari, 'La produzione di armamenti nell'età giolittiana', *Italia contemporanea* (1986), esp. 114–15, 14–7, Table 2; and James J. Sadkovich, 'Reevaluating Who Won the Italo-British Naval Conflict, 1940–42', *European History Quarterly* (1988), pp. 457–60, and *The Italian Navy in World War II* (Westport, CT, 1994), Chapter I.
25. Luca Pietromarchi, 'La questione del disarmo', *Rivista di studi politici internazionali* (1934), pp. 79–92. For naval disarmament, see Giovanni Bernardi, *Il disarmo navale tra le due guerre mondiali, 1919–39* (Rome: Ufficio Storico della Marina Militare, 1975); and Dino Grandi, *Italia fascista nella politica internazionale* (Rome, 1930).
26. Edwards, *Uneasy Oceans*, pp. 54–6, 112, 156–8, thought that even without aircraft carriers, the Italian navy was 'an exceedingly strong force' owing to its submarines, minelaying capabilities, and 'great strength in fast vessels peculiarly suited to the narrow waters of the Mediterranean'.
27. See Pietro Varillon, *L'aspetto navale del conflitto anglo-italiano in Mediterraneo* (Rome, 1936), *passim*; Luigi Barzini, *La guerra all'Inghilterra. Commenti e spiegazioni* (Verona, 1941), p. 148; and Daniele Varè, 'British Foreign Policy through Italian Eyes', *International Affairs* (1936), *passim*.
28. Gaines Post, Jr., *Dilemmas of Appeasement. British Deterrence and Defense, 1934–1937* (Ithaca, N.Y., 1993), pp. 91,125, sees the British as trying to avoid war with Italy.
29. Romeo Bernotti, 'Il Mediterraneo nel prologo del secondo conflitto mondiale', *Nuova antologia* (1956), pp. 263–7, thought the conflict had convinced Mussolini that the Italian armed forces could neutralise the British navy. Also George W. Baer, *The Coming of the Italian-Ethiopian War* (Cambridge, MA, 1967), pp. 463–70; Esmonde M. Robertson, *Mussolini as Empire-Builder. Europe and Africa, 1932–1936* (London, 1977), pp. 176–9; Massimo Mazzetti, *La politica militare italiana tra le due guerre mondiali (1918–1940)* (Salerno, 1974), pp. 165–8.
30. Ciasca, *Storia coloniale*, pp. 501–506; Rosaria Quartararo, *Roma tra Londra e Berlino. La politica estera fascista dal 1930 al 1940* (Rome, 1980), esp. 169–74; 312–36; and Lawrence R. Pratt, *East of Malta, West of Suez. Britain's Mediterranean Crisis, 1936–39* (London, 1975), pp. 75–87.
31. No Soviet supplies reached Spain via the Mediterranean from August 1937 to early 1938. John F. Coverdale, *Italian Intervention in the Spanish Civil War* (Princeton, 1975), pp. 300–16; Renzo De Felice, *Mussolini il Duce. II. Lo stato totalitario, 1936–1940* (Turin, 1981), II, pp. 411–12,

427–41; Willard C. Frank, Jr., 'Naval Operations in the Spanish Civil War, 1936–1939', *Naval War College Review* (1984), p. 37–48; James W. Cortada, 'Ships, Diplomacy and the Spanish Civil War: Nyon Conference, September 1937', *Il politico* (1972), pp. 683–4.

32. Dino Grandi, *Il mio paese: ricordi autobiografici* (Bologna, 1985), p. 430; Coverdale, *Italian Intervention*, pp. 317–32; and Hugh Thomas, *The Spanish Civil War* (New York, 1963), pp. 394–5, 437.

33. Lucio Ceva, *Storia della forze armati italiane* (Turin, 1981), pp. 274–5; Bernotti, 'Prologo', p. 261.

34. Manzini and Monterisi, *Economia*, pp. 153–74, saw Italy's successful conclusion of the war in East Africa in 1935–36 as proof that autarky was a valid principle. Also Erminio Bagnasco, *Le armi delle navi italiane nella seconda guerra mondiale* (Parma, 1978), for weaponry. Italy also continued to build ships for export. See Giorgio Arrighi, 'Un secolo di costruzioni in Italia per l'estero', *Rivista marittima* (1976).

35. Edwards, *Uneasy Oceans*, pp. 162, 242–3, for worries over Tunisia.

36. Giorgio Giorgerini, *La battaglia dei convogli in Mediterraneo* (Milan, 1977), and 'The Role of Malta in Italian Naval Operations, 1940–43', *New Aspects of Naval History* (Baltimore, 1985), *passim*; and James J. Sadkovich, *The Italian Navy in World War II, passim*.

37. For intelligence, Alberto Santoni, *Il vero traditore. Il ruolo determinante di Ultra nella guerra del Mediterraneo* (Milan, 1981); For the X MAS, which specialised in 'guerrilla' tactics, see Virgilio Spigai, 'Italian Naval Assault Craft in Two World Wars', and with L. Durand de la Penne, 'The Italian Attack on the Alexandria Naval Base', *United States Naval Institute Proceedings* (1965, 1956); Junio Valerio Borghese, *Sea Devils* (Chicago, 1954).

38. Sadkovich, *Italian Navy*, pp. 138, 256–65, 285–301; Francesco Mattesini, *La battaglia aeronavale di mezzo agosto* (Rome, 1986), and *Il giallo di Matapan. Revisione di giudizi* (Rome, 1985), *passim*.

39. For the Second World War, see Romeo Bernotti, *Storia della guerra in Mediterraneo* (Rome, 1960); Marc' Antonio Bragadin, *Il dramma della Marina italiana, 1940–1945* (Milan, 1982), and with Giuseppe Fioravanzo, *The Italian Navy in World War II* (Annapolis, MD, 1957, 1980); and Aldo Fraccaroli, *Italian Warships of World War II* (London, 1968); Alberto Santoni and F. Mattesini, *La partecipazione tedesca alla guerra aeronavale nel Mediterraneo (1940–1945)* (Rome, 1980).

40. For Smith, see Edward Mead Earle's 'Adam Smith, Alexander Hamilton, Friedrich List: The Economic Foundations of Military Power', in Peter Paret, *et al.*, *Makers of Modern Strategy from Machiavelli to the Nuclear Age* (Princeton NJ, 1986).

41. As Vittorio Di Sambuy does in *Match Pari tra due grande flotte. Mediterraneo, 1940–1942* (Milan, 1976).

7 Japan and Sea Power
Ian Nish

One of the leading naval studies in Japanese uses as its translation of sea power the word '*Shi-paa-waa*'. That is, because there is no appropriate word, it chooses to use the English word in an obscure Japanese version. I believe that this is of more than passing interest. One may speculate either that sea power is deemed to be a concept alien to the Japanese (which is self-evidently untrue) or that it is genuinely difficult to translate the concept into Japanese. I have some sympathy with this difficulty. I can understand the concept of naval power but find it harder to make sense of sea power.[1]

Japan is an island kingdom and was from her earliest beginnings conscious of sea power. Most prominent in her history were the seaward invasions of Korea by Hideyoshi at the end of the sixteenth century when the Japanese fleet may have come off second best in the encounters. But, apart from national fleets, there were bold maritime adventurers sailing on their predatory raids to Korea, China and south-east Asia. Japan had her Drakes and Frobishers and also her Spanish Main. But from about 1630 the so-called seclusion policy was imposed on the seafaring Japanese under the Tokugawa shogunate and endured for two centuries. It would now appear from a number of historical studies that this seclusion applied largely to contacts with European countries and their trading and missionary emissaries. It was not rigorously applied to the junk traffic to Korea and China and perhaps further afield. So seamanship continued to be in the blood of many Japanese, even if overseas contacts were discouraged by the regime in power.[2]

The wisdom of neglecting sea power came to be challenged. The appearance of Commodore Perry's black ships in Tokyo Bay in 1853 was both menacing and daunting. Because of the prevailing isolationist policy, Japan did not have a single warship capable of opposing them. The shogunate central government in Tokyo and the individual daimyo, particularly those of Satsuma and Tosa, set about purchasing warships from abroad. By the time of the Meiji Restoration in 1868 Japan nominally possessed some ten warships, though many of these were destroyed in the sea battles of the ensuing civil war.

In the years that followed the Restoration, Japan, whose defence depended on sea rather than on land, created the nucleus of a fleet, but it is in some ways surprising that she did not do more to increase her navy in order to deter possible 'foreign barbarians'. One explanation lies in the nature of the clan rivalry which developed under the new government. Satsuma, the naval clan, rebelled in 1877–78 and was suppressed by the newly formed Japanese army. The Navy, therefore, came to be regarded as a secondary arm in the scheme of national defence. As a symbol of this, when an Imperial Headquarters was set up for the duration of the war with China (1894–95), both services came under the Chief of the General Staff, a general in the army.

It stands to reason therefore that the naval authorities had a fight on their hands in order to get access to funds for the creation of what was inevitably an expensive service. At the end of the nineteenth century Japan wished to acquire naval power. Professor Aoki in his discussion of Japan's thoughts about sea power writes:

> In the view of naval officers at the time, the object of holding sea power was not for the sake of protecting lines of communication for the sake of commerce, as Mahan considered, but was for the sake of destroying enemy fleets which came to attack Japan, and protecting Japan's coasts.[3]

In Aoki's view the Japanese who comes closest to the great naval figures like Mahan, Holland, Fisher, Makarov, Perry and Tirpitz, is Admiral Yamamoto Gonnohyoe (generally shortened to Gombei). Yamamoto, 1852–1933, is generally regarded as the father of the Japanese Navy. He was born into the Satsuma clan and entered the naval college as a clan cadet in 1870. He gained his practical experience on board a German warship. After various commands at sea, he became secretary to the Navy Minister in 1891, eventually becoming Navy Minister in 1898. He was the key figure in determining the systems, personnel, and plans for battleship construction. During the period of his dominance Japan won wars against China (1894–95) and Russia (1904–1905), in whose victories Yamamoto played a conspicuous (though land-based) part.

The breakthrough came with the peace treaty which ended the war with China, the treaty of Shimonoseki. This laid down that an indemnity would be payable by China and it worked out that a sum of over eight million pounds sterling was payable to Japan through the City of London. The importance of Japan's naval victories in the war and the continuing menace of the European powers, conspicuously Russia, convinced her that now was the time to consider her naval power. If she was to benefit from the new technology, she had to build abroad and it was natural that she should try to build in British yards where she already had long-standing links.[4] The Navy Ministry at this time was able to complete the programme of building a '6–6' fleet, based on six battleships and six armoured cruisers. It was relatively successful in steering the concept of defence and security from army-first navy-second to one of army-navy equality.

In the Russo-Japanese War the newly created fleet exceeded even its highest expectations. The round-the-world voyage of the Russian Baltic fleet was every bit as daunting as the coming of Commodore Perry half-a-century earlier. The battle of the Japan Sea (or Tsushima) was a test for the Japanese fleet which had up to that time largely been involved in blockade and mining operations. As a symbol of the new state of dependence on sea power, the heads of the two services were for the first time given equal status in the Imperial Headquarters which was set up during the war with Russia. But this did not last. In the domestic storms between the army and navy which followed the war with Russia, Yamamoto was politically adept enough to secure the Navy's objectives.[5] He obtained a promise that the Navy should be expanded to two squadrons, each of which was to consist of eight super-battleships (Dreadnoughts) and six cruisers. But he was immediately confronted by the financial demands of an increase in the army in Korea and the expanded navy had to be deferred by the Saionji cabinet (1912–1913) until finance was available. Yamamoto himself formed a Satsuma-based cabinet in 1913 and immediately tried to push the Navy's plans. There was determined opposition in the Diet to its budget which called for increased naval estimates. Coincidentally his cabinet became implicated in the Siemens bribery scandal which led to court cases and the resignation of the ministry in March 1914. The scandal certainly damaged the reputation of the Navy in the eyes of the media and the people. Yamamoto himself was placed on the reserve list of officers along with other officers allegedly involved, notably Admirals Saito and Takarabe. For Yamamoto this was an unprecedented disgrace since his political rivals argued that 'the father of the Japanese Navy' had 'damaged the honour of Japan abroad'.[6] The Navy as a whole felt itself to be under a cloud, though Yamamoto himself was later recalled to head a short-lived cabinet in the 1920s.

The opportunity to change from being a west-Pacific to a world naval power occurred in 1914. The fact that Germany had a leased territory in China within 600 miles of Nagasaki and possessed a number of strategically placed Pacific islands meant that, when the war between Germany and the western allies broke out, it would have a Pacific dimension.

Moreover Britain had issued an ambiguous and reserved invitation for Japan to become a belligerent. But the opportunity was not automatically grasped by Japan's naval leadership. In an outstanding study by the naval historian, Professor Hirama, he differentiates between groups, the positive and negative schools. The positivists held that, if Japan became a belligerent, it would redound to her credit but, if she did not enter the war early on, the German territories in the east would be gobbled up by Britain and France; it would be futile for Japan to look on enviously, 'putting her fingers in her mouth' and abstaining from the meal. The more cautious line was that it would be to Japan's advantage to preserve peace in the east, to plan the development of the Navy and expand Japanese trade; but this would mean either refusing Japan's help to Britain or at least postponing entry into the war.[7]

Somewhat surprisingly the Navy's overall approach towards entering the war was one of reluctance. Uncertain about the movements of the German squadron, it advised delay. But the heavyweights in the cabinet favoured early entry and the Navy went along with the decision once it had been taken. But there was always at the back of the naval mind the urgent business of achieving the plan for the '8–8' fleet, modified to eight battleships and eight cruisers as a result of wartime thinking. Clearly the navy was more likely to win support for this if it could, through its wartime activities, win back the good reputation which it had lost in the 1913 scandal. But there was always the uncertainty about how the Togo fleet would perform.

During the First World War the Navy recovered its reputation and paved the way for a new role in the world. By its help to Britain over convoys (1914), over the Singapore mutiny (1915) and in the Mediterranean in 1918, it won the goodwill of its ally. As a result of these activities it could take part deservedly in the victory parade in London in 1919. It had demonstrated its capacity for carrying on world-wide operations. On a broader plane, most Japanese recognised that Japan had lost its reputation internationally by her Twenty-one Demands on China. There is a sense in which the actions of the Navy did something to atone for this in the minds of the allies.

At the same time the First World War taught the Japanese some of the realities of life. On the one hand, it was a boom period economically, but their prosperity ended abruptly in 1919. Moreover, the material on which her shipbuilding programmes depended, steel, was not made available by the United States in 1917 when she asked for it. Her own steelworks at Yawata had disastrous strikes in 1920. The fact that the world's navies moved over to oil as a source of power left Japan all too well aware of her lack of raw materials. Finally the peace settlement at Paris, while it gave Japan Class C mandates on many Pacific island groups to the north of the equator, did not give her Yap. She did not obtain many of the strategic points which some of the naval positivists had hoped for in 1914. Some of those officers who went as observers to Jutland and European waters began to harbour doubts about whether one could measure naval strength any longer by the number of vessels alone. It was equally important to develop economic self-sufficiency on the industrial front and keep on good terms with sources of supply.

On 29 June 1920 the 43rd Diet assembled to consider the 8–8 budget which had been drawn up as the result of a long political struggle for support from the political parties, which were anxious to economise, and the army, which had its own claims. In spite of rumours of corruption involving cabinet ministers, it passed the budget a month later. On the whole, the party politicians did not confront the government over defence issues.

But the 8–8 programme now had to face international pressure for arms limitation. There were discussions in preparation for the League of Nations' meeting on disarmament in December. Japan agreed that it would be best to instruct its delegate, Ambassador Ishii, to leave arms limitation initiatives to those in Washington. No sooner was this completed than a new crisis loomed with the receipt of President Harding's invitation to Washington for a conference on naval issues on 21 July 1921.[8] The admirals had to confront the issue of whether the 8–8 fleet should be abandoned in the light of possible international agreement on arms control. The internal investigation within the Navy concluded that Japan might abandon her existing fleet expansion plans on the basis of inferiority to the American and British fleets provided fortifications in their colonial territories in the west Pacific were limited or destroyed. The Japanese cabinet wanted to improve Japan's militarist image abroad, and also to encourage the Americans to drop their 1916 building programme. The American Secretary of State carried through the 10–10–6 ratio for battleships, but accepted a formula for non-fortification, only excluding Hawaii from it. The Japanese delegate, Admiral Kato Tomosaburo, one of the architects of the 8–8 programme, telegraphed Tokyo from Washington that limitation was a prize which the US and Britain were determined to win and Tokyo must not lose the opportunity to cooperate. Kato offered to scrap the *Settsu* in order to keep *Mutsu*.

As a result of the Washington naval treaty, the 8–8 programme was reshaped. Only the *Mutsu* and *Nagato* were retained of the capital ships laid down; the battle-cruisers *Akagi* and *Amagi* were converted into aeroplane tenders. The programme which was first scheduled for completion by 1927 was ultimately accomplished in March 1929: cruisers 25; destroyers 81; submarines 67. The treaty did not cover cruisers. Japan decided to build light cruisers of 7,000 tons (instead of 5,500 tons) and four 10,000 ton high-speed cruisers equipped with 8-inch guns, following the worldwide preference for larger vessels.

The Washington naval treaty was due to last for 15 years. The naval limitation formula which it enshrined continued to fuel an argument within the Japanese naval establishment throughout that period. It is conventional to divide naval leaders into the treaty faction, those prepared to comply with the Washington treaty, and the fleet faction, those who were determined to secure a Big Navy.[9] But this classification is not wholly satisfactory. The Japanese Navy (like other navies) bred individualists and there are countless shades of opinion on the issue. After Washington the treaty faction was in the ascendant. How else can one interpret the appointment of Admiral Kato Tomosaburo as Prime Minister on his return from the States? In June 1922 he was chosen as Prime Minister, acting simultaneously as Navy Minister. But his tenure was short-lived for he died in August of the following year. It was he who led Japan to act on realistic calculations and to seek accommodation with new thinking about navies. In his view a nation could not be satisfied merely with the bigness of its fleet; it had to have money and resources behind it; and Japan was deficient in both. This view was not universally accepted and the staff of the naval delegation in Washington had been fundamentally divided. Kato's opponents thought that naval strength was one of the factors which had led to Japan becoming a world power and that she needed a big fleet to defend her shores and patrol her main trade routes, allowing for the poor resource base which she possessed.

During Kato's tenure the National Defence Plan was revised in 1923. Russia which had been the main enemy contemplated in previous defence plans, had become less of a menace since the revolution. It was agreed therefore that the United States – the enemy contemplated by the navy – should become the main enemy, followed by the Soviet Union and China. The United States would become the fleet against which Japan's strength should be measured.[10]

During the next decade the party opposed to naval limitation for Japan was gaining ground. But there were still senior voices which expressed sober international sentiments. Thus Admiral Saito who represented Japan at the abortive Geneva Naval Conference in 1927 urged moderation on his colleagues: 'The only way to attain both security and expansion is to stick to our present position'.[11] Meanwhile Japan had been building up her strength in the category of cruisers which had not been covered in the Washington naval treaty.

The culmination of this confrontation – it might be called the confrontation over sea power – took place against the background of the London Naval Conference of 1930. Eventually a compromise was worked out in London which imposed a naval ratio of 10–10–7 for heavy cruisers and a reduction of total submarine tonnage from 78,000 to 52,000. Ignoring the international arguments and concentrating on the internal debate, we may say that the naval moderates and the government party approved acceptance because of the state of the economy after the depression and the need for keeping on good terms with the US and Britain. Admiral Okada who had to act as mediator during the long-drawn-out discussions in Japan (over six months) before the treaty was ratified, tried to convince the hardliners of the futility of unlimited rearmament:

> No matter how many arms are piled up, there never comes a point for saying 'That's enough; with that much we are secure'. It would be fine if we were well enough prepared to engage in a contest; but no matter how dogged our efforts, that sort of thing is impossible for a country like Japan whose national resources are inferior to those of the major powers.[12]

But the opposition felt they had many grounds for dissatisfaction: the corrupting influence of party politics; a constitutional disagreement over the roles of the Naval General Staff and the Navy Ministry; and the government's failure to comply with the General Staff's wishes over the naval balance.

These opponents, though they were defeated in 1930, came into the ascendant after the Manchurian crisis of 1931–33. They maneuvered the leaders of the treaty faction into early retirement and reorganised the Navy to reflect more the wishes of the General Staff.[13] While there were those who stayed on and formed a moderate brake on policy, the majority now favoured uncoupling from international commitments to restrict building. If they won within the naval hierarchy, they still had difficulty in getting their way over shipbuilding targets because they were in competition with the army over the annual budget. They argued that increased tension with the United States made necessary the building of new ships; and it was no surprise when they gave notice at the end of 1934 that they wanted complete parity with major naval powers or would pull out of the naval limitation treaties.

After New Year 1936 the situation deteriorated. Japan left the second London Naval Disarmament conference, thus indicating her intention to embark on a new phase of naval building. The mutiny of the Guards regiments in February gave the navy a new popularity over the army. The mutiny included the assassination of Finance Minister Takahashi who had for a few years been a brake on demands for naval spending. There were no international restraints from 1937 so the main limitation on naval ambitions came from the army. The necessity to seek common ground with the army led on 7 August 1936 to the revision of the National Defence Policy. This was based on the assumption that Japan had a stabilising position in the west Pacific. While taking account of the 'contemplated enemies' of previous Defence Policies, the United States and the Soviet Union, the nation would prepare itself also against China and Britain (the first time that Britain had featured as an enemy): 'While avoiding provoking other countries as much as possible, we will undertake our economic advance in the South Seas, particularly the Outer South Seas regions, over the next five years'.[14] This seemed to reflect naval rather than army aspirations, the latter being still worried about the Soviet threat in north-east Asia, while the former was stressing priorities in the south. Whether the southward expansion was perceived as a matter of national security for Japan or merely as a pretext for a further shipbuilding programme is an open question for the historian.

From 1937 Japan became engaged in war with China; and tension increased. Accordingly the Navy became preoccupied with its third and fourth Replenishment Programmes which largely came to fruition in 1940–41. These included a number of aircraft carriers and two *Yamato* class battleships, among the most powerful craft ever constructed. The naval air force was expanded to the 1941 strength of 1,750 Zero fighters, torpedo-bombers and bombers and some 530 flying boats for reconnaissance purposes. From these exertions the admirals concluded that Japan had not the means to embark on a further building plan in the short term. It was therefore the ships of the third and fourth plans with which she took her critical decision for war in 1941. This was probably what bred the mentality that Japan must strike without delay while she still had prospects of victory. Behind the Armada strength, however, there were vulnerable points: the lack of submarines; the inadequacy of the merchant marine; and the shortage of naval pilots for the demands of the wide-ranging war that would have to be fought.

As the crisis developed, the Japanese Navy leaders were inclined to go beyond arms to explore other means of achieving their national goals. There was of course diplomacy. But Japan's approaches to China (1938–45) failed as did her overtures to the United States in 1941. Only her Tripartite Alliance with Germany and Italy and the so-called Great

East Asia Co-Prosperity Sphere boosted her morale, though whether they made a great contribution to the ongoing war is doubtful. Japan's missions to the Netherlands East Indies in search of regular oil supplies, so vital for the navy, also failed. To compensate for weaknesses in other directions, the Japanese leaders relied on the human factor, believing that the Japanese people, taken individually, were solidly behind the government and would make very great sacrifices for their emperor and state. Thus Count Okabe, discussing the wartime role of civilians in developing new technologies, wrote in 1943:

> Our enemy, America, has adopted the same measures [national mobilisation of science] according to information which we have received. But we are quite aware of the difference between our scientists and hers, in that, while American scientists base their efforts on material gains, ours are burning with patriotic spirit. We can fully expect differences in the results also.[15]

This was an example of the wartime optimism about the natural patriotism of the people which would overcome Japan's technological shortcomings and her lack of resources. This willingness to make sacrifices for the state found its clearest manifestation in the exploits of the kamikaze pilots.

Given that Japan in the first half of the twentieth century had continental ambitions, her armed forces had to be both land-based and sea-based. Without a formidable navy, she could not have made such spectacular land conquests as she did. Down to the purge of 1933 there were many voices which drew attention to the folly of engaging in a spiral of naval building in which Japan was likely to come off worse because of her poor resource base. But those who were in charge of her navy in the 1930s were, on the whole, Big Navy men. They were striving to enlarge the scale of her armaments against the United States as the country entered the entanglement with China in July 1937. Even then there was a strong rearguard action between 1938 and 1940 on the part of the minority (still identified with the treaty faction); but it was less over the size of the fleet than over Japan aligning herself politically with Germany and Italy and assuming excessive world commitments. Eventually, however, their resistance was worn down after the apparent successes of the Germans in the European war, and Japan entered the Tripartite Pact in September 1940. As a recent study by the naval historian, Professor Asada, has shown, an atmosphere was developing before the war where the top naval leadership was avoiding responsibility and pure opportunism was prevailing.[16]

It is easy to argue retrospectively that money could have been better spent than on building up a 'Dreadnought fleet'. After all, other nations were doing the same so far as their economic resources permitted and the Japanese resented any suggestion that they occupied a position of inferiority. The Japanese people tightened their belts for decades and missed out on improvements in their standard of living because of the very large share of the national budget which went to the armed services. But they had little choice in the matter as their political representatives were generally willing to take the line of least resistance over military budgets. This was one of the factors which caused Japan to keep down her post-1952 armaments expenditures until recent decades.

NOTES

1. Aoki Eiichi, *Shi-paa-waa no sekaishi* (Tokyo, 1983, 2 vols).
2. Oba Osamu, *Edo jidai no Nitchu hiwa* (Tokyo, 1980); Marius Jansen, *China in the Tokugawa World* (Cambridge, Mass., 1992); and Ronald Toby, *State and Diplomacy in early modern Japan* (Princeton, 1984).
3. Aoki, op. cit., p. 355.
4. Marie Conte-Helm, *Japan and the North-east of England* (London, 1990), pp. 38–44; Fred T. Jane, *The Imperial Japanese Navy* (London, 1904), ch. 8.
5. Ikeda Kiyoshi, *Nihon no kaigun*, 2 vols, (Tokyo, 1987), vol. 2, pp. 20–26. This appears to have continued with the setting up of Seikosho at Muroran, about which the British ambassador reported that this Vickers-Armstrong enterprise 'has received a considerable amount of patronage from the Navy [due] partly to the chairmanship of the Company being occupied by Admiral Yamanouchi'. (PRO: FO 371/1140 [49453], Col. Somerville to MacDonald, 26 October 1911).
6. *British Documents on Foreign Affairs*, series E, part I, vol. 10 (Bethesda, MD, 1989,) doc. 135, Greene to Grey, 13 May 1914.
7. Hirama Yoichi, 'Dai 1-ji sekai taisen e no sanka to kaigun', in *Gunji Shigaku*, 22 (1986), pp. 30–31.
8. Asada Sadao, 'Japan's special interests and the Washington Conference' in *American Historical Journal*, 1961, pp. 62–70; Roger Dingman, *Power in the Pacific: The Origins of Naval Arms Limitation, 1914–22* (Chicago, 1976), p. 186ff.
9. Ikeda Kiyoshi, 'Togo Heihachiro', in *Britain and Japan: Biographical Portraits*, ed. Ian Nish (Folkestone, 1994), pp. 119–20.
10. Ikeda, *Nihon no kaigun*, II, pp. 86–8; *Senshi Sosho, Dai-hon'ei: Kaigunbu-rengo kantai*, vol. I (Tokyo, 1975), pp. 197–9.
11. Admiral Saito as quoted by Kobayashi Tatsuo, 'London Naval Treaty' in *Japan Erupts*, ed. J. W. Morley (New York, 1984), p. 14
12. Admiral Okada as quoted by Kobayashi in Morley, op. cit., p. 36.
13. *Kaigunbu-rengo kantai*, vol. 1, p. 246.

14. *Kaigunbu-rengo kantai*, vol. 1, pp. 315–18; Stephen E. Pelz, *Race to Pearl Harbor* (Cambridge, Mass, 1974), pp. 174–7.
15. Count Okabe Nagakage in *Nippon Times Weekly*, 16 September 1943, p. 3.
16. Asada Sadao, *Ryo-daisenkan no Nichi-Bei kankei: Kaigun to seisaku kettei katei* (Tokyo, 1993), contains a large section dealing with the influence of Admiral Mahan's thinking on the Japanese naval establishment.

8 German Naval Power in First and Second World Wars
Werner Rahn

During the nineteenth century Great Britain, the dominant sea power, had an influence on the naval policy of all other Great Powers having any kind of navy.[1] Based on the theories of Alfred Th. Mahan[2], at the end of the nineteenth century, navies, in the form of a battle fleet, were increasingly regarded as an essential instrument for a great power wishing to represent and enforce world-wide interests. Owing to the German Reich's position in Central Europe, with potential enemies in both East and West, the build-up of the Navy was for a long time overshadowed by the army. Until 1897, its strategic horizons were limited to forward coastal defence. It was not until the time of Alfred Tirpitz[3] that the systematic building of a battle fleet got under way.

Tirpitz regarded Great Britain as the most dangerous potential enemy at sea against whom Germany must have a certain degree of naval strength.[4] Cruiser warfare was out of the question due to a lack of bases; the German fleet would therefore have to deploy its war effort between Heligoland and the Thames.

In his concept for the building of the fleet, Tirpitz assumed that the Royal Navy would always act offensively in a war against Germany, establishing a blockade close in to the German coast. Such a blockade by the British fleet would then create favourable conditions for Germany to enter into a battle. There was, however, a great deal of confusion regarding the true purpose of a battle.[5] Notwithstanding the fact that the German Naval Command had willingly adopted Mahan's theory of sea power, they had paid only lip-service to a central element of that theory: namely the importance of geographical position and the resultant strategic options.

This led to a wrong assessment of British strategy. Despite the tradition of offensive action in the Royal Navy, Britain never had a definite war plan which included a close blockade of Germany. It was considered that the development of such modern means of naval warfare as mining and the submarine made such an operation too risky.[6]

When Great Britain joined the war on the side of France and Russia in August 1914, the few German cruisers stationed overseas were soon neutralised by the Royal Navy, though they achieved a few notable successes. However, one small but powerful German task group was to influence the balance of forces and the overall course of the First World War. It was the Mediterranean Division comprising one battle-cruiser and one light cruiser. The breakthrough of the two units to Constantinople, and their formal handover to Turkey in August 1914, so enhanced German influence on that country that it joined the war on the side of the Central Powers in October 1914. Thus the Turkish Straits became impassable to the Allies. The second most important sea route to Russia after the Baltic remained closed and this contributed to that country being lost as an ally to the Entente in 1917.[7]

The operations of the High Seas Fleet in the North Sea and the Baltic, culminating in the Battle of Jutland in May 1916, cannot detract from the fact that the Fleet primarily performed the function of a 'Fleet in Being'; protecting the coast of Germany, blocking the Baltic approaches and keeping submarine exit routes clear.[8]

During the first months of the war the submarine had proved to be an efficient naval weapon, although its early successes also gave the leadership in the Reich an exaggerated idea of its capabilities. The problem of how to use the submarine in the most effective military way against Great Britain, whilst still being able to justify attacks on merchant shipping politically to the neutral powers, led to repeated arguments between the political and military leadership which lasted until the end of 1916.

Notwithstanding the successes achieved against merchant shipping whilst following the Prize Regulations, the Naval Command called again and again for 'unrestricted submarine warfare'. At the end of 1916, the leadership of the Reich saw unrestricted submarine warfare as the only remaining means of bringing about a victory.[9]

The breaking of relations with the United States was taken consciously into account and was indeed followed by the American declaration of war in April 1917. However, with the introduction of the convoy system the submarine war was practically in ruins.

In the fall of 1918, the German Navy stood before the bitter realisation that despite individual successes, its concepts of a decisive battle and of submarine warfare had failed. The whole point of having a fleet seemed to be placed in question. It was from this assessment that the idea arose to send the fleet out for one final battle so that it could at least justify its existence. The ships' companies of the High Seas Fleet saw that the Naval Command was acting arbitrarily in the operation and refused to obey. Within a few days it developed into a revolt which led to the collapse and end of the Imperial Navy and accelerated the general uprising in the Reich.[10]

Under these circumstances the question was bound to arise as to whether and how the continued existence of a navy could be justified. The answer was provided by the allied powers, who laid down important military stipulations in the Versailles Peace Treaty of 1919. However, the peace treaty drastically limited the strength of the Navy.[11]

A few weeks after the 'seizure of power' by the National Socialists in January 1933, the new Reich Chancellor, Adolf Hitler, made it clear to the military commanders that he intended to develop the armed forces into an instrument of his power politics.[12] However, Hitler and his naval commanders were operating with different assumptions, as far as their strategic thinking was concerned. For Hitler, strategy and ideology were 'inextricably and dialectically linked with each other' and geared to the forthcoming struggle for hegemony in Europe, whereas the Navy believed that Hitler would take into consideration the necessary industrial constraints and time required to construct a new fleet.[13]

Following the conclusion of the Anglo-German Naval Agreement on 18 June 1935[14], the Navy's planning was thus based wholly on the structure of the other naval powers. Its motto was: 'What the other navies, with their rich traditions, consider proper, and what Germany is now permitted within the 35 per cent ceiling, is what Germany will now build'.

From 1928 onwards, the Navy's thinking was marked by the experiences of the man who was to command the Navy until early 1943. In his study of the cruiser campaign in the First World War, Admiral Erich Raeder had come to the conclusion that there had been a strategic correlation between the operations of the cruiser squadron in the Pacific and South Atlantic and in the North Sea campaign during the autumn of 1914.[15] Following the ideas of René Daveluy, Raeder developed a concept of naval strategy which he designed to enable the weaker of two naval forces to perform both its protective tasks and attacks on its enemy's sea lines of communication. He based this concept on the realisation that all naval theatres of war form a homogeneous whole and that consequently any operation had to be viewed in its correlation with other sea areas.[16]

Raeder formulated his strategic thinking most clearly in a briefing he gave on 3 February 1937 to Hitler.[17] Analysing war experiences, Raeder pointed out the correlation between strategy and a country's military–

geographical situation. However, Raeder was aware of the totality of a future war, which would be a struggle not just between forces, but of 'nation versus nation'. In this struggle, 'final success would go to the nation which [had at its disposal] the greater number of people and, more importantly, unlimited material and food supplies'. He emphasised the negative consequences for Germany 'if she is unable continually to procure the raw materials she lacks'.[18] Thus, Raeder had pointed out the glaring weaknesses in the Reich's war potential, without being able to influence Hitler's policies which were aimed at confrontation.

A fundamental change in the Navy's strategic planning commenced in 1938. As it became apparent that the western powers opposed German expansion, Hitler issued the directive that all German war preparations should consider not only France and Russia, but also Great Britain, as potential enemies. Raeder followed Hitler's hazardous course of confrontation without protest, erroneously assuming that the Navy would still have several years of peace to continue its buildup.[19]

In the summer of 1938, the Naval Staff's strategic study concluded that, given a geographical starting position similar to that of 1914, only oceanic cruiser warfare, with improved pocket battleships and U-boats could hold out any prospect of success.[20] Despite this realisation, a naval planning committee busied itself with the question as to what task battleships would perform in a cruiser campaign.

To the traditionalists, who considered capital ships as the most important arm of a naval power, this meant that the concept of sea denial was pushed into the background by the concept of sea control. Unlike Tirpitz, the Naval Staff had repeatedly proposed a sea denial strategy in the 1930s. The new suggestion to develop a strategy of sea control was, in the words of the then Commander-in-Chief of the Fleet, Admiral Carls, nothing less than 'according to the will of the Führer ... to achieve a secure world-power position' for Germany.[21] Nevertheless, Raeder was more inclined towards a sea denial strategy in an oceanic cruiser campaign with pocket battleships and intended to give this strategy his priority in the future armament programme. In November 1938, however, he was unable to gain Hitler's support for his programme. The dictator demanded that the Navy step up the pace of its battleship construction so that he would have at his disposal an instrument of power which could be employed throughout the world as soon as possible.

Disillusionment came on 3 September 1939. Totally unexpectedly, Hitler ordered the Navy to launch a naval war against Great Britain. The Navy was in no way prepared. Raeder's initial estimate of the situation was very pessimistic, and he resigned himself to the realisation that neither the few U-boats nor the surface forces would have any decisive effect on the outcome of the war. All they could do, he said, was to 'show that they know how to die gallantly and thus are willing to create the foundations for later reconstruction'.[22] Like the end of the war in 1918, the Navy once again faced a hopeless situation. It seemed to believe that the only purpose of its actions was to go down fighting, thereby proving its *raison d'être*. The progress of the war soon demanded a new estimate of the situation.

The Naval Staff concentrated on an offensive concept of naval warfare aimed solely at destroying the maritime transport capacity of the English-speaking powers. With this strategic aim, the Naval Staff hoped to weaken their enemy's potential for waging war to such an extent that it would bring about a decision in the struggle against Great Britain.[23] The surface force was insufficient for such warfare. To supplement it, the Navy concentrated on constructing and employing a means of naval warfare that had proven its worth during the First World War: the U-boat.

The Naval Staff knew from the experience it had gained during the First World War, that employment of the 'U-boat' against the enemy's merchant marine could only be successful if as many U-boats as possible were continuously deployed along the enemy's sea lanes. The Navy calculated that the number of U-boats permanently at sea should range from 100 to 150 boats. Taking into consideration the time it took to carry out maintenance and supply, this meant that the Navy needed approximately 300 operational boats at its disposal. To achieve this, time was an important factor:[24]

1. In an economic war waged against a country that depended on supplies by sea, a success could only be achieved in the long run. It was therefore a question of continuously weakening the enemy's maritime transport capacity to a degree which exceeded the rate at which she was able to construct new merchantmen.
2. From the summer of 1940 onwards, it became apparent that the British war effort was being increasingly supported by the resources of the United States. Therefore, the Naval Staff was intent on 'putting Britain out of action soon, before the effects of even greater American aid make themselves felt'.[25]
3. Since it took around two years to construct U-boats and to make them operational in the quantities envisaged by the Navy, plans had to be made at a very early stage in order to have the necessary concentration of forces.
4. While a numerically increasing U-boat fleet held out the prospect of success, the Naval Staff had to take into account that the enemy

would do everything to strengthen his anti-submarine warfare effort, in view of the threat that was looming.

In October 1939, the Naval Command presented a plan for the building of U-boats at a monthly rate of 29 boats. Though Hitler approved the plan, he refused to sanction priority, since he was at that time more concerned with the demands of the imminent land campaign against France.[26]

One year later, in November 1940, the Navy had to realise that the U-boat building was held up by shortages and that the building rate of 1940 would barely cover the losses. The Naval Staff foresaw that there were limits to the Reich's own production capacities and its material resources. In December 1940, it viewed America's growing support of Britain as a dangerous development 'towards a marked prolongation of the war'. This, the Naval Staff considered, would have a 'very negative effect on the overall German war strategy'.[27] This statement obviously expressed the simple fact that Germany would not be able to win a prolonged war of attrition against the two Atlantic naval powers.

For this reason, in December 1940, Admiral Raeder requested Hitler 'to recognise that the greatest task of the hour is concentration of all our power against Britain'. To Raeder, this meant the concentration of air and naval forces against the British supplies. The Admiral was firmly convinced that U-boats were the decisive weapons against Britain. Although Hitler did not reject Raeder's view, he did refer to the allegedly new political situation, requiring 'to eliminate at all cost the last enemy remaining [i. e. Soviet Russia] on the continent, before he can collaborate with Britain.... After that everything can be concentrated on the needs of the Air Force and the Navy'.[28]

In Hitler's eyes, Great Britain was not the enemy on which all weapons had to be concentrated in order to defeat him, but a potential partner, who had to be made to 'see reason' by applying an appropriate amount of military pressure. Hitler also knew that a forced economic war could not lead to any marked success in one year. Furthermore, an effort of this kind would imply the danger of the United States entering the war, which he was seeking to avoid at this point.[29]

In July 1941, after the first successes in the war against Russia, the Naval Staff tried to convince both the Wehrmacht Command and Hitler of the immediate strategic necessity of concentrating German warfare on fighting the Allied naval powers. Matter-of-factly analysing the threat to which the Reich was exposed, the Naval Staff pictured the dilemma of a European continental power lacking the vital elements of a naval power which was forced to fight against the greatest naval powers:

While in World War I we had the second strongest battle fleet in the world but no appropriate operational base, we now dispose of a strategically favourable operational base, however, we do not have the required battle fleet to operate in the Atlantic.[30]

The Naval Staff predicted that the two allied naval powers would continue to fight even if the Soviet Union collapsed, in order to reach their 'final goal' of destroying Germany on the continent. The Naval Staff came to the conclusion that 'the enemies' prospect for the battle in the Atlantic ... for the year 1942 must be assessed as favourable'.[31] For this reason, the Naval Staff advocated that Germany take advantage of the political assets of cooperation with France and Japan in order to bring about a decision in the Atlantic through concentrated employment of all available forces, and in particular with the help of U-boats and the air forces.

At the same time, Raeder tried to influence Hitler into making a clear decision on the matter. Some of the dictator's statements had made Raeder doubtful as to whether Hitler still ranked the naval war in the Atlantic highly. Raeder tried to convince Hitler to authorise more freedom of action for the navy. Hitler was not prepared to do this in view of the still undecided situation in Russia. However, when Raeder hinted at the hazards arising from a possible occupation of North-west Africa by British and American forces, he revealed the great strategic weakness of the axis powers in Europe. So Raeder demanded 'a clearing up of the relations between Germany and France' as a basis for political and military cooperation. Moreover, he advocated an extension of the naval war against American merchant ships by stopping and sinking them in accordance with prize regulations. This would be a further step in cutting the increasing American support to the British.

In saying that this political decision probably could not be taken unless the military campaign in the East was brought to an end, Raeder expressed the entire dilemma which lay at the heart of the German prosecution of the war in the summer of 1941. Hitler immediately took the cue and assured the C-in-C of the navy that he still had the same concept of the effects of obstructing British supply lines. Hitler continued to say that he was only trying 'to avoid having the USA declare war while the Eastern campaign is still in progress', and that afterwards he would reserve 'the right to take severe action against the USA as well'.[32] The German strategy thus did not and could not change. The Naval Staff's large-scale plans could not be realised, not only because of the lack of forces to carry them out, but because there was no 'afterwards' to the military campaign in the East.

On 27 October 1941, Hitler informed Vice Admiral Kurt Fricke, the Chief-of-Staff of the Naval Staff[33], that 'to win the military campaign in the East' was a necessary 'precondition for a successful fight against Great Britain'. To *'secure the continental zone'*, he said, was now the *'prime necessity of the hour'*. This, he added, also meant the securing of the Mediterranean position, since morale in Italy was going from bad to worse. This critical development made Hitler determined to reinforce German air and naval forces in the Mediterranean. Fricke, however, was in line with the Naval Staff's point of view, saying that it was necessary to concentrate all forces available for the disruption of British supply lines in the Atlantic. Hitler was not prepared to change his attitude and said that there had to be 'an immediate concentration of forces' in the Mediterranean, since 'a German/Italian loss of position in this area represented an intolerable hazard for the European continent'.

When Fricke expressed his opinion that 'the total defeat of England was necessary to guarantee a new order in Europe', Hitler frankly let him know that he and Naval Staff saw the enemy with quite different eyes. Even then Hitler was still prepared to conclude peace with England, since the geographic area in Europe, which Germany had been able to occupy so far, was sufficient to secure the future of the German people. Hitler's directives were unmistakable, and so the Navy had to send the requested number of U-boats into the Mediterranean. The transfer of 23 U-boats into the Mediterranean until December 1941 and the concentration of additional boats off Gibraltar seriously weakened the concept of sea denial in the Atlantic. It soon became clear at this point that the Axis Powers had overreached their potential and that they were only able to maintain their respective positions by alternating their concentration of forces. Meanwhile, the number of boats in the Atlantic had diminished to an extent that Admiral Karl Dönitz, Flag Officer U-boat Command, was speaking of a 'U-boat vacuum', which the enemy could not but welcome.[34] The inferior status of the Atlantic within the framework of German strategy became very clear when Germany declared war against the United States on 11 December 1941: of 91 operational U-boats, only six were immediately assigned for the American East coast.

At the end of 1941, Hitler was rather inclined to neglect the possible long-term results of effective warfare in the Atlantic. Now he was more concerned about 'sinking 4 ships in Arctic Waters delivering tanks to the Russian front line than to sink 100,000 GRT in the South Atlantic'.[35] This statement brought up again the fundamental question as to what was the strategic goal of naval warfare in the Atlantic. Would the fight be decided by a 'race' between the number of ships sunk and ships constructed? Or should the Atlantic be the front court of the 'Fortress Europe' that had to be defended against an enemy, who was definitely superior in all terms? So far, the U-boats had turned out to be very effective. However, this led to the fact that Hitler and others were inclined to overestimate this naval weapon.

In view of the fact that his weapon potential was tied up in the Mediterranean and the Norwegian Sea, Dönitz at the beginning of January 1942 was seriously worried 'that we will finally arrive too late for the Battle of the Atlantic'. He therefore called for a radical concentration of U-boats in order to cope with this task and once again lashed out most severely at the policy of dissipating the limited naval forces:

> We are in a tight spot, but that again makes it perfectly clear that every resource, simply everything should be channelled into the U-boat, and that the notion that we are still a naval power with surface forces collapses as soon as we are confronted in any area with any requirement of war at sea.[36]

Faced with the heavy fighting and the high monthly losses of U-boats in the spring of 1943, the new Commander-in-Chief of the German Navy, Grand Admiral Dönitz, told Hitler as early as April 1943 that he had serious doubts whether the U-boat war in the Atlantic would be successful in the long run. His hopes and demands concentrated on increasing the monthly output of the U-boat construction programme to 30 boats, 'in order to prevent the ratio of losses to newly built boats from becoming too unfavourable'.[37]

However, the offensive and defensive anti-submarine warfare of the Allies soon showed that the previous concept of submarine operations – submersibles which operated on the surface whilst remaining mainly stationary below – was doomed to failure. In May 1943, the U-Boat losses reached a height of 41 submarines. These losses were out of all proportion to the successes. Now, Dönitz was forced to discontinue the convoy attacks in the North Atlantic, to clear out towards other areas of operations where there was less air reconnaissance.

This decision meant the ruin of an offensive naval strategy which, in giving up on the struggle for sea control, sought to win victory solely by denying the sea to the superior Allied sea powers in the attrition and elimination of their transport capacity. It was a concept based solely on the performance of a one-weapon system which had in the meantime lost its ability to avoid enemy surveillance and defences. All later attempts to take up the war against the convoys yet again, but with better equipped submarines, brought only minor successes and a high loss rate. The defeat of the U-Boats in the Battle of the Atlantic had become inevitable.

CONCLUSIONS

1. For the German Reich, any power policy which included a claim to rule the seas interfered with Great Britain, and was bound to encounter mistrust of this sea power. The German Navy overestimated the possibilities of a naval war against Great Britain. Due to the geographical conditions, the British were capable of achieving their strategic aims without entering into a decisive battle.
2. The outbreak and the course of the First World War showed that the German Naval Command's political and strategic concept did not work. During the July crisis of 1914 the High Seas Fleet was no deterrent. The employment of the fleet had no effect on the conduct of the war as a whole. Germany's one-sided and inadequate concept of submarine warfare was a large factor in the USA's entry into the war. In November 1918, the Navy became the starting-point for political turmoil within the Reich.
3. After 1933, the Navy eventually became subject to Hitler's long-term ambitions for dominating the world and the seas in particular. But the Second World War broke out before the plans for a gigantic build-up could take effect. When the war came, the Navy was totally unprepared for it. To compensate, Germany attempted to force a strategic decision by destroying the Allies' shipping capacity (sea denial) rather than fighting them for mastery of the Atlantic (sea control).
4. From 1940 onwards, Germany possessed a good geographical basis for naval warfare in the Atlantic, but this basis could not be fully exploited due to insufficient weaponry. The U-boat did supply an effective weapon in the fight against enemy shipping up to 1942, but, as a result of the general war situation, and the critical situations in the Mediterranean and the Eastern front, the Naval Command was forced to employ its last remaining offensive capability as a 'strategic fire brigade'. The concept of U-boat war failed in 1943 because the submarine had lost its capability of escaping from enemy surveillance and defence as the allies developed their anti-submarine weapons.
5. In the course of this century, Germany has twice tried to force a strategic decision in confrontation with Britain and the USA by cutting the Atlantic shipping routes. Both attempts ended in failure. The second defeat brought with it the end of the German Reich and the dissolution of

all German armed forces. The Western orientation of the Federal Republic of Germany led to the close binding of the new German armed forces into the Atlantic Alliance. This meant, for the Navy, the smallest of the armed services within the Bundeswehr (Federal Armed Forces), that for the first time in her history she was obliged merely to perform that function 'which a German Navy can actually perform' in close cooperation with the great maritime powers.

NOTES

1. Cf. in this context my articles: 'La réflexion stratégique dans la marine allemande de 1914 à 1945', in *L'évolution de la pensée naval II*, éd. Hervé Couteau-Bégarie (Paris, 1992), pp. 135–62. And 'Strategische Probleme der deutschen Seekriegführung 1914–1918', in *Der Erste Weltkrieg, Wirkung, Wahrnehmung, Analyse*, ed. Wolfgang Michalka (Munich, 1994), pp. 341–65.
2. Cf. now *Mahan on Sea Power. Selections from the Writings of Rear Admiral Alfred Thayer Mahan*, ed. John B. Hattendorf (Annapolis, 1991).
3. Cf. Volker R. Berghahn, *Der Tirpitz-Plan. Genesis und Verfall einer innenpolitischen Krisenstrategie unter Wilhelm II* (Düsseldorf, 1971) and Ivo N. Lambi, *The Navy and German Power Politics, 1862–1914* (Boston, 1984).
4. Cf. Jonathan Steinberg, *Yesterday's deterrent: Tirpitz and the Birth of the German Battle Fleet* (London, 1965), pp. 208–210.
5. Cf. Paul M. Kennedy, 'Maritime Strategieprobleme der deutsch-englischen Flottenrivalität', in *Marine und Marinepolitik im kaiserlichen Deutschland 1817–1914*, ed. H. Schottelius & W. Deist (Düsseldorf, 2nd edn, 1981), pp. 178–210, see also Edward Wegener, 'Die Tirpitzsche Seestrategie', ibid., pp. 236–62.
6. Kennedy, 'Maritime Strategieprobleme', pp. 197–8.
7. Richard Hough, *The Great War at Sea 1914–1918* (Oxford, 1983), pp. 81–2, and Ulrich Trumpener, *Germany and the Ottoman Empire 1914–1918* (Princeton, 1968), pp. 25–7.
8. Rahn, 'Strategische Probleme', pp. 351–4.
9. Ibid., pp. 354–9.
10. For details see Werner Rahn, 'Führungsprobleme und Zusammenbruch der Kaiserlichen Marine 1917/18' *Die deutsche Marine. Historisches Selbstverständnis und Standortbestimmung*, ed. Deutsches Marine-Institut (Herford, 1983), pp. 171–89.
11. For details see my publication *Reichsmarine und Landesverteidigung 1919–1928. Konzeption und Führung der Marine in der Weimarer Republik* (Munich, 1976).
12. Jost Dülffer, *Weimar, Hitler und die Marine. Reichspolitik und Flottenbau 1920–1939* (Düsseldorf, 1973), pp. 237–9.

13. Michael Salewski, 'Das maritime Dritte Reich – Ideologie und Wirklichkeit 1933–1945', *Die deutsche Flotte im Spannungsfeld der Politik 1848–1985*, ed. Deutsches Marine-Institut (Herford, 1985), pp. 113–139, quotation on p. 117.
14. Cf. Wilhelm Deist, 'The Rearmament of the Wehrmacht', *Germany and the Second World War*, vol. I: *The Build-up of German Aggression* (Oxford, 1990), pp. 462–472.
15. Erich Raeder, *Der Kreuzerkrieg in ausländischen Gewässern*, vol. 1: *Das Kreuzergeschwader*, 2nd edn (Berlin, 1927), pp. 253, 265, 339 and 341. Compare Klaus Schröder, 'Zur Entstehung der strategischen Konzeption Grossadmiral Raeders', *MOV-Nachrichten*, vol. 46 (1971), pp. 14–18, 45–8.
16. Schröder, 'Entstehung', p. 48 and Michael Salewski, *Die deutsche Seekriegsleitung 1935–1945*, vol. 1 (Frankfurt, 1970), pp. 32–3.
17. Lecture of the C-in-C Navy, 3 February 1937: 'Grundsätzliche Gedanken der Seekriegführung', BA-MA RM 6/53. Compare in this context Salewski, *Seekriegsleitung*, vol. 1, pp. 32–3; Dülffer, *Weimar*, pp. 435–6, and C. A. Gemzell, *Raeder, Hitler und Skandinavien* (Lund, 1965), pp. 49–51.
18. Lecture of the C-in-C Navy, 3 February 1937, pp. 64–5.
19. Deist, 'The Rearmament of the Wehrmacht', p. 472–80.
20. Memorandum of Commander Hellmuth Heye: 'Seekriegführung gegen England und die sich daraus ergebenden Forderungen für die strategische Zielsetzung und den Aufbau der Kriegsmarine' [Conducting a naval war against Britain and the resulting requirements for strategic objectives and the build-up of the navy]. Cf. Salewski, *Seekriegsleitung*, vol. 1, pp. 43–6; Dülffer, *Weimar*, pp. 471–3; and Deist, 'The rearmament of the Wehrmacht', pp. 473–5. The final version of the memorandum is printed in Michael Salewski, *Die deutsche Seekriegsleitung 1935–1945*, vol III, (Frankfurt, 1973), pp. 28–60.
21. Comment of the C-in-C of the Fleet, Admiral Carls, on Heye's memorandum of September 1938, quoted in Dülffer, *Weimar*, p. 486–7; and Deist, 'The rearmament of the Wehrmacht', p. 475.
22. 'Gedanken des Oberbefehlshabers der Kriegsmarine zum Kriegsausbruch' [Reflections of the C-in-C, Navy, on the outbreak of war], 3 September 1939, *Lagevorträge des Oberbefehlshabers der Kriegsmarine vor Hitler 1939–1945*, ed. Gerhard Wagner (Munich, 1972), pp. 19–20., pp. 29–496], for the translation see *Fuehrer Conferences on Naval Affairs, 1939–1945*, (Annapolis, 1990), pp. 37–8. [i. e. reprint of *Brassey's Naval Annual 1948*].
23. The following basic sources and literature are necessary for any research in German naval strategy in the Second World War: Salewski, *Seekriegsleitung*, 3 vols, *Fuehrer Conferences*, *Lagevorträge*, Günther Hessler, *The U-Boat War in the Atlantic, 1939–1945*, ed. Andrew J. Withers (1 vol. in 3 parts (London, 1989). Commander Hessler, who was Dönitz's son-in-law, wrote the original report for the Admiralty in 1946–47. Karl Dönitz, *Memoirs, Ten Years and Twenty Days*, with an Introduction and Afterword by Jürgen Rohwer, (Annapolis, Md, 1990); and *Kriegstagebuch der Seekriegsleitung 1939–1945, Teil A*, vol. 1 (August/September 1939) – vol. 56 (April 1944), ed. Werner Rahn & Gerhard Schreiber with the assistance of Hansjoseph Maierhöfer, (Bonn, Herford, 1988–95), [to be continued].

24. See Vice Admiral Kurt Assmann, 'Why U-boat warfare failed', *Foreign Affairs*, XXVIII (1950), pp. 659–70, esp. pp. 665–6.
25. Naval Staff, War diary, Part A, 20 December 1940, p. 238 (published *Kriegstagebuch der Seekriegsleitung 1939–1945, Teil A*, Vol. 16, December 1940, Herford, 1990).
26. Hitler's long-term war policy and strategy is thoroughly examined by Andreas Hillgruber, *Hitlers Strategie: Politik und Kriegführung 1940–1941* (Munich, 2nd edn 1982).
27. *Kriegstagebuch der Seekriegsleitung 1939–1945, Teil A*, vol. 16, December 1940, pp. 233 and 238 (20 December 1940).
28. *Lagevorträge*, pp. 171–3 (27 December 1940), cf. also *Fuehrer Conferences*, pp. 160–3. See also Hillgruber, *Hitlers Strategie*, pp. 352–77 and Bernd Wegner, 'The Road to Defeat: The German Campaigns in Russia 1941–43', in *Decisive Campaigns of the Second World War*, ed. John Gooch (London, 1990), pp. 105–27, esp. pp. 106–107.
29. See Hillgruber, *Hitlers Strategie*, pp. 144–78, and Michael Salewski, 'The Submarine War: A Historical Essay', in Lothar-Günther Buchheim, *The U-boat War* (New York, 1978) [unnumbered].
30. 'Denkschrift zum gegenwärtigen Stand der Seekriegführung gegen England Juli 1941' (21 July 1941), published by Michael Salewski, *Die deutsche Seekriegsleitung 1935–1945*, vol. 3 (Frankfurt/M., 1973), pp. 189–210, citation on pp. 195–6.
31. Ibid., p. 196.
32. Conference Raeder with Hitler, 25 July 1941, *Lagevorträge*, pp. 271–3. Compare *Fuehrer Conferences*, pp. 222–3 and Salewski, *Seekriegsleitung*, vol. 1, pp. 407–12.
33. Best summary of the Conference Vice Admiral K. Fricke with Hitler in *Kriegstagebuch der Seekriegsleitung, Teil A*, vol. 26 [October 1941], (Herford, 1991), pp. 474–8. Quotations ibid.
34. Memo of B. d. U., 3 November 1941, BA-MA: RM 7/845, pp. 220–21. See also *Kriegstagebuch der Seekriegsleitung 1939–1945*, part A, vol. 27 (November 1941), pp. 43–4.
35. Memo Capt. v. Puttkamer of a conference Raeder with Hitler, 29 December 1941, BA-MA: RM 7/133, fol. 331–35.
36. Conversation by teletype between Dönitz and German U-Boat Command in Italy, 4 January 1942, BA-MA: RM 7/2868.
37. *Lagevorträge*, pp. 475–7. [Conference of 11 April 1943] and *Fuehrer Conferences*, pp. 316–18. Detailed research of the U-Boat-Crisis in Spring 1943, based on files of the German Naval Staff: Salewski, *Seekriegsleitung*, vol 2 (Munich, 1975), pp. 293–312.

9 Confusions and Constraints: The Navy and British Defence Planning, 1919–39
Daniel A. Baugh

In the long history of British defence policy nothing has attracted more interest and controversy than the interwar period of the twentieth century. The controversy has been dominated by two themes. One theme emphasises the inadequacy of Britain's industrial and financial resources in the newly emerging circumstances of world power; the predicament of national and imperial defence between the wars is thus seen in a large context of 'British decline', and the implication is that the situation was rather hopeless.[1] The other concerns the politics of delayed rearmament and appeasement. It is generally treated as a history of errors and illusions, but a discussion of these ought to be carefully situated in the context of the defence problem that Britain faced.

This chapter rests on a premise that the object of British defence planning in the interwar period was military preparedness, that is, the capacity to choose and carry on warfare if it should become necessary. Given the British nation's intense (and rational) desire to avoid war, this premise may seem unrealistic, but my purpose is to shift the focus from the politics of defence planning and war-avoidance – which are familiar subjects – to the configuration of Britain's defence problem.[2]

The history of British defence planning in the interwar period should be divided into two principal periods. The first period, from 1918 to 1934, was one in which the task of diagnosing Britain's defence needs was extremely confusing. As will be seen, the level of confusion did not simply or even mainly arise from economic constraints. To be sure, Britain now lacked the enormous industrial and financial *advantages* that it had possessed in earlier epochs, but was still better-off industrially and financially than most of its rivals. Yet its position as a great power was understood to rest on the overseas empire. An extended burden of naval responsibility was thus incurred, and imperial defence was an important source of complication and confusion. The second period, from 1934 to

1939, was one in which confusion gave way to crisis. By 1936 no one in government doubted that something drastic had to be done. Yet by this time there was no practicable solution to Britain's problem of national defence that either the Cabinet (or posterity) could consider adequate.

Attention will be chiefly directed to the first period. We shall examine the measures and omissions that left the defence planners with so little room for manoeuvre in the crisis period: as has been observed, 'politics is always confronted with the necessity of dealing with the consequences of previous policies'.[3] The inquiry is limited to selected topics and will give a measure of emphasis to naval matters.

It is part of my purpose to raise the issue of why Britain's uncomplicated problem of defence planning in the eighteenth century becomes so complicated in the twentieth. For this reason, items from Britain's eighteenth-century catalogue of experience will be brought to bear at certain junctures. This practice will also furnish a sense of proportion as well as serve to indicate the uncanny influence and endurance of traditional British attitudes toward national security.[4]

Perhaps the greatest source of confusion lay in the perplexities of British foreign relations after 1918. It was remarkably difficult for British statesmen to identify friends and enemies. This important subject, which of course forms an essential background of defence planning, cannot be dealt with properly here, but it is necessary to set forth some basic propositions even though they cannot be historically demonstrated in the space available.

In the eighteenth century the task of defining Britain's national security objectives was comparatively simple. The object was to prevent the expansion of French power, especially French maritime power and French means of invading 'the island realm', while enhancing British maritime power, looking to European coalition partners whenever feasible. In the 1920s, by contrast, it was by no means easy for statesmen to identify Britain's primary enemy. Political instability ruled the Continent, and no one knew what the Soviet Union would do. There was no balance of power in Europe – hardly even a possibility of imagining one.[5] With benefit of hindsight it has been easy to mark out Germany as the prime threat throughout the period, to speak metaphorically of a twentieth-century 'Thirty Years War'. Certainly the French always saw it this way, and no one today doubts that the British should have kept Germany's underlying war-making potential and possible disposition toward expansionism in view.

Turning from the question of European enemies to that of friends, there can be no dispute that Britain's most valuable ally on the Continent between the wars was France. It was a virtual certainty that France and Britain would not make war on each other; France, fearing Germany, dared not alienate Britain, and Britain had no desire to provoke France. Because Britain did not wish to maintain in peacetime an army suitable for Continental warfare, a defensive military alliance with France was all the more compelling, and coordination of the two countries' forces with plans for various forms of British assistance in case of war should never have been allowed to lapse. There was even more at stake. If France collapsed Britain's position would be dire, if for no other reason than geography. For in such a case German bombers would be flying from nearby air bases; the task of defending the far-flung empire would become much more difficult; and, not least, it would be much harder to fend off a German invasion of Great Britain. There was also the danger that French warships might be transferred to German use. When France suddenly fell in 1940, the resulting situation was reminiscent of that which obtained in 1804 – in many ways worse.

All of the considerations above, and the obvious policy conclusions therefrom, would have been consonant with eighteenth-century precedents *if* Germany had been clearly marked out as the primary enemy to be guarded against. The fundamental question of the 1920s was whether Germany should be so regarded. In the eighteenth century a powerful France was Britain's 'natural enemy' because of its extensive coastline and maritime interests; if France overran the Low Countries, the British problem of invasion defence was made doubly difficult and expensive. By comparison, even a consolidated Germany was geographically less of an *immediate* strategic threat than France. As just noted, the German danger lay in the *possibility* of German conquest of France (and the Low Countries).

The undeniable problem with Germany, of course, lay in its potential military strength. In the 1920s men from all points of the political compass wished to encourage the stabilisation of a tamed Germany, under the sort of non-militaristic, republican regime that it had been a British war aim in 1914–18 to install. As such, Weimar Germany was useful to Britain for commercial, financial, and balance-of-power reasons against possible Russian expansionism, and its existence was deemed to be the best hope of insuring a peaceful Europe. Even after 1934, when Germany's clear intention to rearm should have ended British confusion as to which European power constituted the main threat, it was difficult for British statesmen to abandon the hope of a tamed Germany and commit the country to a formal military alliance with France. Moreover, such an alliance, they reasoned, would make a general European war more likely.

Thus, France's alliances with Eastern European countries were regarded not as assets but as vehicles for exacerbating that danger of war which it was a British statesman's first priority to prevent.

It is well known that British statesmen allowed their desire for war-avoidance to take charge of their alliance policy, far too earnestly and too long, although it ought to be remembered – it seldom is – that none of the experts in any country foresaw the sudden, catastrophic defeat of France that occurred in June 1940. When one also remembers, however, that British statesmen even failed to make provision for the defence of the Low Countries, it raises the question of whether British policy was too strongly inclined towards not sending military forces to the Continent.

Eighteenth-century experience helps to put the issue in perspective. British statesmen in that century were aware that major wars followed a more or less standard form. There was an *initial* phase, lasting about three years, and an *endurance* phase, lasting four years or more. The main concern in the initial phase was simply to survive in order to bring about the endurance phase in which Britain had the advantage. The pattern was partly shaped by geography and naval power, but also dictated by British political culture and material interests. In other writings I have called the amalgam of defence preparedness, foreign policy, and grand strategy that produced this pattern, 'blue-water policy'.[6] It applies to all major European wars fought by Great Britain after 1689, except the First World War. It does not apply, in any century, to Britain's smaller scale and often pre-emptive overseas wars. This policy did not shun European alliances and coalitions, nor did it rule out the use of British troops on the Continent, but it was defensive, and this agreed well with the British public's strong desire to avoid engagement in Continental wars. Pre-emptive forms of strategic planning and preparation – measures that might appear manifestly provocative, or likely to entail unnecessary commitments to allies whose objects might be only remotely related to 'British objects' – were thus to be avoided. (For this reason, the League of Nations scheme of collective security, even if its implementation had been practical, did not accord well with traditional British defence policy.)

Whether this policy remained viable in the circumstances of the twentieth century may be disputed, but there are indications – most of which for reasons of space must be left to the reader's inference here – that its main elements were still ingrained (though their mode of interaction was not always clearly grasped) in the minds of responsible authorities and the public. But the question of whether the British government actually adhered to such a policy during the interwar period turns out to be interesting.

There can be no dispute that in choosing friends the government consistently kept the endurance phase in mind. Great Britain's most important 'ally' between the wars was the Empire–Commonwealth. Most people regarded it as politically inseparable, but defence planners rightly regarded it as an allied resource. In fact, the various territories, dependencies, and tied economies produced the whole range of strategic raw materials in impressive quantities, and the Dominions and India contributed fighting men.[7] The soldiers and sailors of this 'ally' were especially valuable because they could be asked to fight according to a harmonised strategy if war came. The empire provided a world-wide network of bases. Its role in British commerce and finance was prodigious: it was the main foundation of the 'sterling area', which developed in the 1930s and quickly became indispensable.[8] In sum, the British Empire really mattered; aside from traditional ties and emotional influences, it could help mightily in coping with the economic and financial problems of a war of endurance. Until the final year of the interwar period, and even then though to a lesser extent, 'imperial defence' was, in fact, the touchstone of all British discussion of defence policy.

There were four drawbacks, however. One was that the empire provided very little to enable Great Britain to absorb the initial shock of war in Europe and the resulting threat to the homeland, while its defence requirements, military and naval, dispersed scarce military resources. In other words, it was of little value for the initial phase. A second was that without security for its long-distance sea linkages it was useless, and therefore a large naval investment in ships for trade protection was needed. The third drawback was that the Far Eastern outposts and dominions were fearful of Japanese aggression, and the Japanese were eager to build up their battle fleet. Finally, the empire provoked the jealousy, and the sterling area the animosity, of the United States' government, and the United States had to be considered Britain's most important friend next to the empire. However thin and remote, and in many respects unappetising, the prospects of alliance with America might appear, its assistance was indispensable in any war of endurance.[9]

In terms of defence planning, the second, third, and fourth of these were all entwined and conspired to produce a huge naval problem. The United States's opposition to Japanese expansion meant that the British government could not choose, after the Washington Naval Treaty of 1922, to deal with its Far Eastern naval problem by allying with Japan, as it had done in the immediate past. But neither could it count on the readiness of the Americans to use their navy to deter Japanese aggression, even though there was a strong probability that the contentions of Japan and the United

States would at some point place Britain in a posture of hostility toward Japan. There was really no way out of this dilemma – only the hope that Japan's leaders would carefully consider the hazard of provoking such a war. Yet the existence of this dilemma, and the naval obligations and expense that it entailed, should not authorise a leap to the conclusion that Great Britain was unwise in considering the Empire–Commonwealth to be of the first importance to her national security.[10]

Among the greatest distractions to well-conceived defence planning in this period was interservice contention. It operated at an extreme level of intensity between the wars. Nothing like it had existed in eighteenth-century Britain because no one then questioned that national security depended vitally upon the navy's capacity to rebuff invasion and protect trade. Thus, naval planning and defence planning in time of peace were practically synonymous.

The situation changed suddenly and profoundly in the opening decade of the twentieth century. It was then that the army made a bid for a primary role in national defence. The bid failed, but during the 1914–18 war the army ascended to the primary position in British warfare; it did not maintain that position after the war. Also during the First World War, in 1918, the Royal Air Force was born. Thus, when peace came there were suddenly three players: the proud senior service, the newly risen but somewhat eclipsed army, and the newborn air force.

At the end of the war, the Admiralty and War Office sought to recover control of tactical air warfare, and the RAF's dynamic chief, Sir Hugh Trenchard, fought this off with paranoid intensity, under the belief that the other services aimed at no less than the RAF's elimination. That may well have been an accurate assessment in 1921, but the RAF was soon thereafter authorised to build up a sizable peacetime bomber force, and after that it chose not only to tie its fortunes chiefly to strategic bombing but also to propose schemes of 'force substitution', that is to say, substitution of air power for land and sea power wherever that seemed plausible. The insertion of this new, ambitious, and anxious player in the contest for prestige and budgets did not augur well for the future of defence planning.

Interservice contention in the interwar period had a peculiarly distorting effect on policy because of the British government's system for assessing defence needs. As we have seen, during the 1920s it was hard to identify any compelling, near-term external threats. The system, however, invited departments to parade their assessments of various threats before the Cabinet in justification of appropriations, and the armed forces eagerly complied. Initially, the Admiralty sought to match the announced naval building programme of the United States. This was mainly, as everyone admitted, a prestige question. After 1922 the Admiralty focused attention on Japan's threat to British interests and territories in the Far East. Japan was the only potential enemy (the United States being ruled out) that was actually building up a battle-fleet, and the Admiralty, which remained devoted until the later-1930s to the concept that naval power rested upon battle-fleets, used Japan as a rationale for budgeting a fleet of capital ships.[11] In a similar manner the Royal Air Force, under Trenchard's guidance, used the irritation felt by the British government at France's high-handed conduct in 1923 and the size of the French air force (the largest in existence at the time) to postulate France as a serious threat to Great Britain. This enabled him to obtain a countering force of bombers called the Home Defence Air Force. This was granted on the ground that the very threat of France's being able to bomb London might give her undue diplomatic influence, despite the fact that everyone in the British government recognised that France, fearing Germany, would never dream of alienating Great Britain by such an action.[12] For its part, the army played the old Northwest-frontier-of-India card, but made nothing out of it. All this promoted an atmosphere of unreality in the deliberations over defence planning.

The Cabinet's mode of protection against distorted claims was the 'Ten-Year Rule'. This was first enunciated in 1919. The service departments were asked to revise their estimates on the 'assumption that the British Empire would not be engaged in any great war during the next ten years'. This rule was made automatically perpetuating in 1929 and not countermanded until the end of 1932. The most pernicious effect of the Ten-Year Rule, however, was not that it delayed a vigorous rearmament – for no rule, of itself, could have such an influence – but rather that it was a simple rule of thumb which inhibited a true conception of long-term defence planning.[13]

The extreme paranoia that marked interservice contention in the 1920s moderated in the early-1930s, but sources of serious confusion and distraction had been sown by those contentions. The most important of these was an idea that had been readily seized upon by the public and which the RAF was of no disposition to discourage. This was the fearful prospect of devastating aerial bombing attack, to which the only answer, it was firmly held by the masters of the RAF, was a threatening counterforce of bombers. The leaders of the RAF cannot be said to have deliberately set out to promote public fear of this – they hardly needed to – but it was, after all, a precondition of a budget for building the countering force of bombers and it deeply influenced public perceptions about national defence. Moreover, although the Air Staff bore responsibility for probing and understanding the true efficacy of their instruments, no serious attempt was made to do so. Thus the limitations and difficulties of carrying out an effective bombing attack remained hidden from everyone – government, public, and air force authorities themselves, until about eighteen months before the war when the Air Staff realised that they might actually be called upon to deliver bombs on Germany. It will be seen presently that public fears of air attack and overinflated claims for the efficacy of strategic bombing had an extremely distorting impact on defence planning in the mid-1930s.

It has been noted that the government's methods of determining defence needs in the 1920s were not conducive to a broad appraisal of the main problems; year-to-year foreign policy concerns and interservice budgetary contentions played too prominent a role. Nevertheless, the armed services, especially the Navy, were aware of longer-term issues and did manage to develop fairly sensible procurement programmes. Beginning in the later-1920s, however, successive British governments – Conservative, Labour, and National Coalition – seriously undermined these programmes. The Navy was particularly hard hit. Yet in the interwar years more than ever, Great Britain needed a strong degree of steadiness in defence procurement.

A comparison with the eighteenth-century situation reveals how crucial this factor of steadiness had become. To be sure, defence analysis was a simple matter then; as noted above, for Britain, defence preparedness and naval preparedness were practically synonymous. Still, if we focus on the naval aspect of the 1919–39 period – in which, interestingly, about 60 per cent of the total defence budget went to the navy, a percentage that almost exactly replicated the eighteenth-century peacetime figure – it is possible to detect two vital needs that did not change across the centuries: the maintenance of a body of manpower with superior skills (in respect to such tasks as gunfounding, shipbuilding, and repair as well as combat), and a constancy in maintaining the fleet, especially the larger ships. When the latter was neglected, as occurred in 1775–77, the operational results were dire, and only the nation's superior finances and maritime resources enabled it to pursue a massive building programme and eventually recover sea supremacy in the war of 1778–83 against the Bourbon powers.[14]

Britain's capacity for a war of endurance depended, in both centuries, upon wartime continuance of production for export and maritime trade. In the First World War, however, the situation was massively transformed. Industry became heavily devoted to war production not only for the navy but also the army. The cost of expanded wartime imports vastly exceeded earnings from exports. By 1916 debts incurred for purchases from the

United States were growing ominously. Admittedly, a massive increase of the national debt in wartime was a standard British phenomenon in the eighteenth century, but it now involved a substantial portion that was owed to a major foreign power. Britain's traditional war-of-endurance strategy now depended upon the actions of the United States.

The change was permanent. A new future for British war-making was thus marked out. Furthermore, other powers with greater industrial capacity than Britain's had now emerged, powers that could probably – in the case of the United States, certainly – build up armaments on a faster timetable.[15] To minimise the degree of dependency British defence policy between the wars needed to take these new constraints into account. It would have been necessary even if the pace of change in weapons technology and tactical needs – a minor consideration in the eighteenth century – had not complicated the problem.

A suitable plan for the 1918–39 period might therefore have included the following measures:

1. purchase and retain on active service sufficient numbers and varieties of ships and equipment to train numerous fighting men;
2. steadily procure enough new guns, ships, planes, and tanks to keep vital manufacturing skills and facilities in being, and to upgrade them in accordance with technological change;
3. maintain steady construction of heavy units, such as heavy ordnance, capital ships, and large cruisers;
4. avoid scrapping older ships except those of little combat value or those not worth upgrading;
5. maintain large numbers of destroyers and other escort vessels, but expect to build lots more at the start of a war.

No special insight into the strategic future was needed for any of these measures. In fact, almost all of them had their counterparts in the practices of British naval administration in the eighteenth century. Only the problems posed by technological obsolescence were new.

What in fact occurred? For its part, the Admiralty in the 1920s and 1930s was consistent in calling attention to the need to keep up Britain's industrial capacity for building and equipping the heavier classes of warships. Until the mid-1920s this was substantially achieved.[16] There then began a serious erosion of the naval budget. In the later-1920s the main motive behind defence cuts – urged by the Chancellor of the Exchequer, Winston Churchill – was budgetary saving to make funds available for social programmes.[17] The Navy's proposals at the time were 'excessive and its priorities were often misguided', but the six-year programme of 1925 for building '31 cruisers, 2 carriers, 44 submarines, 92 destroyers, and 42 auxiliary vessels' reflected a generally sound assessment of future naval needs.[18]

The Conservative government's approval of the naval cuts was made possible by the atmosphere of the Locarno agreement. When a Labour Government under the prime-ministership of Ramsay MacDonald took office in 1929, the pressure for naval arms reduction intensified. For one thing, MacDonald was devoted to the idea of improving relations with the United States, and the Americans had been pressing to extend the 1922 Washington Naval Treaty's principle of ratios for capital ships to lesser classes. The result was the London Naval Treaty of 1930, which the Labour government signed over strenuous Admiralty objections; it violated the hitherto firmly held principle that Britain's cruiser needs, because of her world-wide task of 'imperial trade' protection, could not be subjected to parity.[19] The Navy's allowance of cruisers was reduced from 70 to 50, while the Japanese demanded and were given an increased quota: 70 per cent of the British level. A scholar who has closely studied these matters concludes:

> MacDonald's second government made Britain's single gravest error of the interwar years. At the London naval conference of 1930, for no compelling reason, it destroyed the navy's ability to match the IJN [Imperial Japanese Navy] and any European power. It forced the navy to scrap many warships, its actions precluded any major naval armament until 1937.[20]

In fact, nearly all the anticipated benefits soon vanished. The improvement of relations with the United States did not extend to non-naval issues, the French and Italians could not be induced to sign anything, and before long the Japanese withdrew. In effect, Britain unilaterally reduced its great Navy without receiving anything significant in return.

None of this would have been persisted in if MacDonald and his Labour colleagues had not been fixated on disarmament.[21] In the later-1920s and early-1930s disarmament had the power of an ideology. It captivated public opinion in nearly all countries, but especially in Great Britain. It was seen as reducing diplomatic tensions and tending toward the elimination of a supposed cause of war. (In fact, a case can be made that the principle of ratios and the publicity surrounding them actually had the perverse effect of heightening patriotic jealousies.) Disarmament was also seen as easing the task of implementing League of Nations sanctions. However true this may have been in general, the British naval reductions served to diminish the relative power of the only League navy that could reasonably be expected to enforce sanctions. If there had been any second thoughts about these issues, they were submerged by the great financial crisis that hit the British government in 1931, in consequence of which naval reductions were regarded as unavoidable anyway.

To summarise, in 1929, notwithstanding the naval cuts begun in 1926, Britain possessed 'the strongest navy on earth and a reasonably large and modern army and RAF'.[22] Thereafter the three armed services experienced famine, which did not end for the RAF until 1935, the Navy until 1937, and the army until 1939. The Navy was permitted to build new cruisers in this period, but its overall strength declined, intrinsically as well as relatively. Many older ships that could have been usefully upgraded if war came were scrapped. Among these was a serviceable class of destroyers, which would have been of much use as convoy escorts a decade later.[23] But most important, the Admiralty's long-term programme of steady accumulation and replacement (only a portion of which deserved oblivion) was derailed, and the regeneration of industrial skills in the armaments industry was stifled. In the event, when massively accelerated naval rearmament became absolutely unavoidable in 1937, it was not the creation of manufacturing facilities but the sudden need for skilled craftsmen that posed the most intractable problem.[24]

On 28 February 1934 the Defence Requirements Committee, appointed the preceding October after Germany walked out of both the Disarmament Conference and the League of Nations, made its first report. This is rightly regarded as opening a new era in British defence policy, but that must be qualified. The report assessed probable needs in a balanced manner, even calling for a 'Field Force' to help to defend the Low Countries. The Cabinet's response to the report gave the RAF clear priority, brushed away the army's Field Force, and put off much of what was listed for the Navy. The reluctance to authorise the Field Force, though unwise, was understandable given the abhorrence of Continental warfare ('Never again'). However, the refusal to attend to the naval requirements was both historically unprecedented and politically unnecessary, for there is no reason to suppose that the British government could not have succeeded in persuading the public, by 1934, to accept the expense and opprobrium in the arena of 'world opinion' which naval rebuilding entailed. But Ramsay MacDonald and Neville Chamberlain, each for his own reasons, adhered to the old course.[25]

By 1936 the government suddenly realised that it was in the grip of a defence crisis. The suddenness and severity of the crisis stemmed from the pace of German rearmament, the mounting aggressiveness of Italy and Japan, and a growing sense that England was threatened with German aerial bombardment. The prevailing view of strengthening an alliance with France (that it was likely to bring on the thing most feared, a European war), and the ominously unhelpful posture of the United States, were major constraints on the scope of remedies.[26]

The threat of air attack had a tremendous influence. In every country during the 1930s the power of the bomber was greatly overrated; public fear and fascination was heightened by allegedly expert publicists and the press. Perhaps, however, the people of the island realm, for whom this was something doubly new – they had been peculiarly immune to external assault for two centuries – had a special claim to be forgiven their fears.[27] One may even excuse Winston Churchill for aggravating these fears in 1935, since his larger purpose was to arouse the nation to rearm and this was an issue on which the public was willing to listen to him – there weren't many. But here was an extraordinary source of distraction and confusion. The game of numbers called 'air parity' that commenced in 1935 was underpinned by public pressure. In respect to policy, the British government conceived of air parity, that is to say, matching the German bomber force's projected growth, as both the correct means of air defence and a deterrent to German aggression. But the task of quantifying the German side of the equation – in early 1935 the German air force consisted of little more than planning-paper listings – was fraught with projections that were really predictions, and worst-case analyses distorted by the Air Staff's assumption that the enemy's strategic priorities were the same as theirs. The RAF was firmly convinced that the first order of business was to defend Britain from an early 'knock-out blow' from the air.[28] On the other hand, the RAF's well-publicised doctrine held that there was no real defence against bombing, except to launch a countering action of the same kind, and the Air Staff had never critically examined the probable efficacy of this method. Of all the sources of confusion in the interwar period, this was the most egregious.

Its result in terms of defence preparedness was that during a crucial period from 1934 to 1937 programmes for rebuilding naval and ground forces were given lower priority. New ship construction and the upgrading of the older capital ships, already postponed in the early-1930s, were now further delayed, thus postponing claims on specialised industrial facilities and skills to a time when they were badly needed for other heavy equipment, such as anti-aircraft and field guns. In sum, the policy of suddenly increasing the numbers of British bombers to keep pace with Germany's alleged striking power caused a major distortion in the allocation of resources at a critical moment. And, sadly and ironically, it was the worst possible moment in the history of aviation technology to emphasise production over development.[29] In the eighteenth century there had been no real distinction for Britain between instruments ordered for effective fighting and instruments of deterrence. Now there was.

Moreover, the British bomber force was bound to fail as a deterrent to German aggression. For one thing, Hitler's first move was exceedingly unlikely to be made against England and he had no reason to fear a pre-emptive move from England; for another, Germany had placed emphasis on its industrial infrastructure and could readily overmatch Britain in aircraft production. Britain's goal of air parity with Germany did in fact prove impossible to attain. It has been remarked that on this count 'Britain was outdeterred by Germany' during the Czechoslovakian crisis of 1938.[30]

Not only that, the RAF's strategic force of long-range bombers proved to be almost useless for the initial phase of the war. Despite the priority it had enjoyed when financial and industrial resources were most precious, Bomber Command had nothing to bring to the table when war broke out in 1939, and even in 1940. It could not recommend a plan for early strategic bombing: Britain was more vulnerable than Germany; compact, urban, southern England had always been more vulnerable to bombardment from the air than Germany.[31] Whatever value the development of British long-range strategic bombing capability had, it proved to be suited only for helping to win a war of endurance, and then only with more advanced aircraft.

The month of December 1937 was a decisive moment of change. The Minister for Co-ordination of Defence (a recently created office to supervise appropriations under the circumstances of escalating defence expenditures and strategic urgency) was Sir Thomas Inskip. His reports to the Cabinet – inspired, it appears, by his expert adviser, Sir Maurice Hankey – altered the perspective and the priorities. It is fairly well known that the Air Staff was forced at this time to reduce allocations for bombers and increase allocations for fighters.

Of greater interest for our purposes is the fact that this change had the result of bringing the methods of deterrence more in line with the necessities of war-preparedness. Inskip's December memorandum outlined a general plan of grand strategy for the war that might come. It postulated an initial phase of survival, followed by an endurance phase in which financial capacity and global access to resources would provide the keys to victory.[32]

By the time this change of orientation occurred, however, it was too late to prepare all three armed forces adequately while still maintaining a capacity for financial endurance. The army's Field Force was given the lowest budgetary priority, the Air Force continued to receive large appropriations, and the Navy's appropriations were sharply increased. On the whole, the Navy wound up in the best shape of the three when Britain went to war in 1939.

Procurement of ships, planes, vehicles, and weapons does not produce war-readiness. Histories of defence policy generally focus on material factors and seldom devote much space to the hidden dimension, human skills and teamwork. Yet when one considers the question of Britain's readiness to fight in 1939–40, this dimension is of immense importance – much greater than space allows us to explore. But it is the appropriate subject for a brief conclusion.

Human skills accounted for most of the Royal Navy's advantage in the eighteenth century. The old navy did not outbuild its opponents, it kept the sea and outfought them; it captured their ships and added the best of those ships to the British fleet.[33] This advantage was almost impossible for opponents to overcome. It all but disappeared when the age of sail came to an end. Yet it is arguable that skills became even more important to British warfare in the machine age. We have seen that skilled workers for war production were both vital and scarce. But there were also the vital combat skills, most notably: habituation to new weapons and coordination of disconnected fighting units.

In the eighteenth century an admiral or general could rely substantially on past experience, often personal, for tactical guidance. As is well known, rapid technological change requires that military planners and leaders must try to integrate their experience and critical understanding of combat history to imagine an arena of battle not yet experienced. This point was well understood in the interwar period.

Yet there were egregious failures in the 1930s, for which the professionals of Britain's fighting services were often responsible. The RAF, as we have seen, was negligent in its failure to assess the difficulties of strategic bombing critically through candid evaluations of demanding operational exercises.[34] The Navy's inferiority in the sphere of aviation was not only an inferiority of machines but also of tactics and war-fighting imagination. All in all, it appears that the deficiencies of naval aviation were not so much owing to the dominance of the 'big-gun' surface-warfare school as to the insidious effects of the RAF's retention of the Fleet Air Arm, a situation which the Admiralty tried very hard and persistently to rectify throughout the interwar period, with the sole effect, until the FAA was finally released from the RAF in 1937, of annoying important leaders of government.[35]

On the plus side, the most striking and important initial-phase combat success of the war belonged to the RAF, namely the success of Fighter

Command in 1940. The path to success was launched by civilian pressure in the Cabinet; nevertheless it stemmed from developed skills, integrated new technology (especially radar), and well-conceived coordination – all planned by RAF professionals in peacetime. Among the peacetime developments for which the navy deserved credit was proficiency in surface-ship night fighting; this paid off spectacularly in the battle off Cape Matapan (March 1941).[36]

The other variety of skill, the coordinating of the three fighting forces, had very seriously deteriorated in the interwar period. The service insularity of former eras posed mild problems when compared with the problems that came to the fore in the 1920s and 1930s, chiefly as a result of the air force's indifference to, sometimes even wariness of, combined-arms operations.

It is a large subject and cannot be entered upon here, but the basic cause may be traced to the doctrines adopted by the leaders of the RAF in the 1920s to insure the independence of their service. These doctrines pointed diametrically away from cooperation with, or attention to, matters of vital importance to the army and Navy, yet the leaders of the RAF clung tenaciously to the coordinate tactical responsibilities which they had been given at the time the separate service was founded in 1917. They held firm to the doctrine of the 'Unity of the Air', a doctrine that ran so clearly counter to basic realities of land and sea warfare as to provoke our retrospective amazement that it was not squelched.[37] Thus, the Royal Air Force retained responsibility for developments in military and naval arenas that it had too many incentives for neglecting. Its conduct led to serious deficiencies that, though they do not mainly account for, certainly contributed greatly to, the three most prominent military catastrophes of the war's initial phase: the sudden collapse of the defences of Norway, France, and Singapore.

NOTES

1. The most influential exponent of this approach has been Paul M. Kennedy, in many writings but see particularly his mature assessment in *The Rise and Fall of the Great Powers* (New York, 1987), ch. 6.
2. Even today, it remains possible, though this is admittedly a bit extraordinary, for a textbook to be issued in which the account of the prewar crisis is rendered entirely in terms of politics and foreign policy with no mention whatsoever of the question of armament; see Keith Robbins, *The*

Eclipse of a Great Power: Modern Britain, 1870–1992 (London, 2nd edn, 1994), pp. 172–6.

3. Gustav Schmidt, *The Politics and Economics of Appeasement: British Foreign Policy in the 1930s* (London, 1986), p. 11; also relevant are pp. 13 and 21. It seems to me that, though he focuses more on individual actors rather than a governing group, D. C. Watt is suggesting a similar point in his introduction to *Succeeding John Bull: America in Britain's Place, 1900–1975* (Cambridge, 1984), pp. 3–5.

4. Unlike the nineteenth century, the eighteenth provides a fairly stable frame of reference. More importantly, it provides 'real prices', by which I mean that peacetime ideas and arrangements were actually tested and adjusted by the experience of successive wars. That is no doubt why the eighteenth century has provided the paradigm for 'the British way in warfare'.

5. For a richly documented account of how difficult the task was in the early 1920s see Lorna S. Jaffe, *The Decision to Disarm Germany: British Policy towards Postwar German Disarmament, 1914–1919* (London, 1985), ch. 3.

6. See Daniel A. Baugh, 'Great Britain's "Blue-Water" Policy, 1689–1815', *International History Review*, 10 (1988), 33–58.

7. For a statistical account of the size and scope of production of strategic raw materials in the Empire–Commonwealth as a whole, when compared with the quantities produced by the United States, Soviet Union, and Germany in 1938, see Williamson Murray, *The Change in the European Balance of Power, 1938–1939* (Princeton, 1984), pp. 5–6.

8. For a succinct assessment of the importance of the sterling area, see P. J. Cain & A. G. Hopkins, *British Imperialism: Crisis and Deconstruction, 1914–1990* (London, 1993), ch. 5.

9. For a concise catalogue of the United States government's exasperating misunderstandings and conflicting goals at this time see Watt, *Succeeding John Bull*, pp. 66–7, 80–89. Neville Chamberlain, the one major British statesman who was inclined to forget the importance of the USA, was regularly reined in by his Cabinet on this matter.

10. Some influential historians have argued that the empire had become an anachronism in terms of power and therefore an expensive distraction from the real problem of national defence. See Michael Howard, *The Continental Commitment: The Dilemma of British Defence Policy in the Era of the Two World Wars* (London, 1972, repr. 1989), esp. pp. 100–103; Correlli Barnett, *The Collapse of British Power* (1972, repr. 1987), ch. 4. There has been a response to this argument which has emphasised the tremendous value of the empire in a long war and also suggested that imperial defence was not in fact a large drain on the United Kingdom's peacetime military budget. See G. C. Peden, 'The Burden of Imperial Defence and the Continental Commitment Reconsidered', *The Historical Journal*, 27 (1984), 405–23.

11. See especially John Robert Ferris, *The Evolution of British Strategic Policy, 1919–26* (Basingstoke, 1989), p. 139; the book was also published under the title *Men, Money, and Diplomacy* (Ithaca, NY, 1989).

12. See John Ferris, 'The Theory of a "French Air Menace", Anglo-French Relations and the British Home Defence Air Force Programmes of 1921–25', *Journal of Strategic Studies*, 10 (1987), 62–83.

13. Cf. Barnett, *Collapse*, p. 278: 'It took all sense of urgency and reality of purpose from strategic planning and defence policy'.
14. See Daniel A. Baugh, 'Why Did Britain Lose Command of the Sea during the War for America?' in *The British Navy and the Use of Naval Power in the Eighteenth Century*, ed. Jeremy Black & Philip Woodfine (Leicester, 1988), pp. 148–69.
15. At the time of the Washington Naval Conference in 1921-22 Arthur Balfour, the chief negotiator (who was accompanied by Beatty), pointed out in a telegram to London that the treaty's provisions did not prevent 'richer countries like America or some other Power under militaristic control' from keeping building facilities in existence; obviously, a long cessation of capital-ship building could mean 'violent spells of armament activity' later, a situation, he remarked, that would not be to Britain's advantage. See B. McL. Ranft, ed., *The Beatty Papers: II, 1916–1927*, Navy Records Society (London, 1993), p. 194.
16. For Beatty's consistent concern for the reservoir of industrial skills and facilities, see Ranft, ed., *Beatty Papers, II*, pp. 78, 92, 104–109, 146, 194, 351. See also Hugh Lyon, 'The Relations between the Admiralty and Private Industry in the Development of Warships' in *Technical Change and British Naval Policy*, ed. Bryan Ranft (Sevenoaks, Kent, 1977), pp. 62–4.
17. Stephen Roskill, *Naval Policy Between the Wars. I: The Period of Anglo-American Antagonism 1919–1929* (London, 1968), pp. 498–516, 544–56. William Manchester, *The Last Lion: Winston Spencer Churchill: Visions of Glory, 1874–1932* (New York, 1984), pp. 788–91.
18. Ferris, *Evolution*, pp. 163, 187.
19. A detailed political history is provided in David Carlton, *MacDonald versus Henderson: The Foreign Policy of the Second Labour Government* (London, 1970), ch. 4–6.
20. Ferris, *Evolution*, p. 181.
21. See Barnett, *Collapse*, pp. 285–98 for a brief and penetrating discussion. For a glimpse of its ideological hold on the non-trade union element of the Labour Party see John F. Naylor, *Labour's International Policy: The Labour Party in the 1930s* (London, 1969), esp. the account of the Brighton Conference in 1935, pp. 102–11.
22. Ferris, *Evolution*, p. 181.
23. Information given to author by Professor Jon Tetsuro Sumida. I am greatly indebted to Professor Sumida for assistance in other ways, and particularly for sending me his unpublished paper on Churchill and the issues of naval procurement.
24. See mainly G. A. H. Gordon, *British Seapower and Procurement between the Wars: A Reappraisal of Rearmament* (Basingstoke, 1988), esp. pp. 162–7, 286–9. Also G. C. Peden, 'A Matter of Timing: The Economic Background to British Foreign Policy, 1937–1939', *History*, vol. 69 (1984), esp. p. 23; and Norman Gibbs, *Grand Strategy, Vol. I: Rearmament Policy* (London, 1976), pp. 310–11.
25. Howard, *Continental Commitment*, pp. 103–10; Barnett, *Collapse*, pp. 412–16. Barnett rightly gives credit to MacDonald for preventing naval reductions beyond a certain point (pp. 295–6), but it appears that MacDonald's pacifistic instincts delayed naval recovery. See the diary entry

for 18 May 1936 of the army's member of the D. R. C. See also his comment on Chamberlain, 30 July 1933: 'And they (the Board of Admiralty) are right to fight, for the Chancellor's thesis does involve giving up the one power standard and the ability of the Fleet to protect our interests whenever threatened or attacked', Brian Bond, ed., *Chief of Staff: The Diaries of Lieutenant-General Sir Henry Pownall* (London, 1973), pp. 50, 130. For a comprehensive yet penetrating account of the whole history see Gibbs, *Grand Strategy, I.*

26. The concept of such a crisis is central to the interpretation of Gustav Schmidt; see *Politics and Economics of Appeasement*, esp. p. 21.
27. For a monograph on the subject see Uri Bialer, *The Shadow of the Bomber: The Fear of Air Attack and British Politics 1932–1939* (London, 1980). I am inclined to place much greater emphasis than Schmidt does on the influence of this threat, although objectively it was grossly exaggerated.
28. Historiographically this is still a developing story, but there have been some remarkable contributions in the past few years. Evidently, the British government's inclination (though not the Air Staff's in the beginning) was to overestimate the current numbers and capabilities of Germany's bomber force and to underestimate the German economy's underlying capacity for aircraft production. See R. J. Overy, 'German Air Strength 1933 to 1939: A Note', *The Historical Journal*, 27 (1984), pp. 465–71; R. J. Overy, *War and Economy in the Third Reich* (Oxford, 1994), ch. 6; Wesley K. Wark, *The Ultimate Enemy: British Intelligence and Nazi Germany, 1933–1939* (Ithaca, NY, 1985), ch. 2–3. One fact brings the level of misapprehension into sharp focus: in September 1939 Germany did not have a bomber in service that could bomb England from German airfields.
29. The later-1930s witnessed a quantum leap in airframe design and aviation engines.
30. Wark, *Ultimate Enemy*, p. 69.
31. Two recent books are important. Malcolm Smith, *British Air Strategy between the Wars* (Oxford, 1984), maintains a balanced tone, but the impression of a national-defence fiasco cannot be dispelled. Harvey B. Tress, *British Strategic Bombing Policy through 1940* (Lewiston, NY, 1988) is a closely researched scholarly monograph that developed along the lines of investigative reporting; see esp. pp. 88–95, 136. D. C. Watt, 'The Air Force View of History', *The Quarterly Review* (Oct. 1962), pp. 428–37, though dated in terms of now-available archival information, still provides the most succinct and forceful critique.
32. See G. C. Peden, *British Rearmament and the Treasury: 1932–1939* (Edinburgh, 1979), pp. 130–31; and Smith, *British Air Strategy*, pp. 183–6. Deterrence, such as it was, was now based on the idea that Hitler would think twice before commencing a long war of endurance.
33. See Jan Glete, *Navies and Nations: Warships, Navies and State Building in Europe and America, 1500–1860*, 2 vols. (Stockholm, 1993), I, 264–6, 271–6, 284–8; II, 383–4. Working from Glete's figures, I have provided a brief overview in chapter 5 of J. R. Hill, ed., *Oxford Illustrated History of the Royal Navy* (forthcoming, 1995).
34. Tress, *British Strategic Bombing Policy*, p. 88. Smith, *British Air Policy*, p. 270. Howard, *Continental Commitment*, pp. 111–12.

35. Geoffrey Till, *Air Power and the Royal Navy 1914–1945* (London, 1979), esp. pp. 188–9.
36. For prewar development and practice of night-fighting tactics see Jon Tetsuro Sumida, '"The Best Laid Plans": The Development of British Battle-Fleet Tactics, 1919–1942', *International History Review*, vol. 14 (1992), pp. 688–9; this was spearheaded by Rear Admiral Reginald Drax.
37. The 'Unity of the Air' doctrine led to further Air Ministry enunciations which Geoffrey Till has termed 'strategic gibberish' – a reasonable characterisation. These enunciations produced insidious effects on defence preparation generally, as high-ranking officers in the army and navy were well aware; see Till, *Air Power and the Royal Navy*, esp. pp. 192–3.

10 The Influence of History upon Sea Power: The Royal Navy in the Second World War
Correlli Barnett

It is the purpose of this paper to capsize Admiral A. T. Mahan. He published his thesis, *The Influence of Sea Power upon History 1660–1783*, at what appeared at the time to be the very apogee of British world power in the last decade of the nineteenth century, when the bounds of the British Empire had reached their widest ever (with the exception of the post-1919 mandates, not properly part of the Empire, and the former German East Africa, also a post-1918 acquisition); when Britain was the world's greatest creditor nation, indeed the financial centre of a world-trading economy in which she enjoyed by far the biggest share; when British industrial production remained second only to that of the United States as a percentage of the world total; and when the Royal Navy by its size and prestige rendered Britain overwhelmingly the world's greatest sea power.

It was from this vantage point of 1890 that Mahan looked back at his chosen period of 1660–1783 and sought to demonstrate that sea power had served as the midwife at the birth of this British world predominance, or, as he put it, that England's 'war fleets' grew along with 'her colonial system' and her merchant shipping, and her wealth 'grew yet faster'. However, Mahan also offered some passing comments on what he saw as the sinews of British predominance in its full maturity at his own time of writing. In his words, the broad basis of British sea power 'still remains in a great trade, large mechanical industries, and an extensive colonial system...'[1] Distant naval stations were essential, he remarked, whether they depended for protection on direct military force, like Gibraltar or Malta, or on a friendly surrounding population as in Australia, and

> when combined with decided preponderance at sea, make a scattered and extensive empire like that of England, secure; for while it is true

that an unexpected attack may cause disaster in some quarters, the actual superiority of naval power prevents such disaster from being general or irremediable. History has sufficiently proved this. England's bases have been in all parts of the world; and her fleets have at once protected them, kept open the communications between them, and relied upon them for shelter.

Colonies attached to the mother-country afford therefore the surest means of supporting abroad the sea-power of a country. In peace, the influence of the government should be felt in promoting by all means the warmth of attachment and a unity of interest which will make the welfare of one the welfare of all, and the quarrel of one the quarrel of all; and in war, or rather for war, by inducing such measures of organisation and defence as shall be felt by all to be a fair distribution of a burden of which each reaps the benefit.[2]

Thus Mahan was highly impressed with the swathes of imperial red across the map of the world, as with the sheer size of the Royal Navy of his day. But, his book being weakest in the realm of technology, he failed to perceive the dry rot – in the form of Britain's growing industrial backwardness, as revealed by various reports by Royal Commissions and House of Commons Committees from the 1860s through the 1880s – which was already weakening the very keel of British power. He failed therefore to imagine a future time when British wealth, instead of 'growing yet faster' than 'her extensive colonial system' and that system's need for adequate 'war fleets', would actually grow more slowly than them; too slowly, indeed even shrink. In other words, it did not occur to Mahan that the British Empire might in due time become a strategic burden to Britain rather than an asset, and hence a grievous source of overstretch. Nor did it occur to him that the United Kingdom's dependence on a huge seaborne trade, especially in the form of imports of food and raw materials, might likewise constitute a source of strategic vulnerability and thus of further overstretch, especially naval.

Nonetheless, it is interesting that Mahan, seeing more clearly astern than ahead (like most of us), could well perceive and comprehend this problem of overstretch – i.e. the disparity between imperial obligations bequeathed by history and the current strength of the mother country – in the case of eighteenth-century Spain. Whereas in that epoch, he writes, 'the might of England was sufficient to keep alive the heart and the members (of Empire) ... the equally extensive colonial Empire of Spain, through her maritime weakness, but offered so many points for insult and injury.'[3]

Change the context to the 1930s and 1940s, and the name of the colonial power from Spain to Britain, and Mahan's observation will serve well enough as the moral for this paper. For the influence of history on sea-power in the case of Britain in the Second World War lies largely, but not solely, in the predicament presented by the existence of the British Empire. It was therefore the Royal Navy even more than the other British armed forces which had to pick up the bill, and especially in the first half of the war.

To summarise the predicament as it had come to exist by the mid-1930s, the British Empire was not a buttress of British strength, as Mahan had believed and public opinion still believed (particularly when the Empire was on show at Jubilees or Coronations), but a drain on it. Global in its sprawl, its constituent parts – the dominions, especially Australia and New Zealand; India, Burma and Malaya – were quite incapable of their own defence. The whole ramshackle historic structure depended on British – i.e. United Kingdom – sea-power paid for by the British taxpayer. The British Empire was in fact, as I wrote in 1972 in my book *The Collapse of British Power*, one of the most outstanding examples of strategic overextension in history. By 1937 there had arisen a triple threat to this Empire right across its global sprawl – Nazi Germany, Fascist Italy, and militaristic Japan – very largely because of the misjudgements of Conservative, Labour, and 'National' governments since the early 1920s.[4]

A triple threat to the Empire, then, with the Royal Navy having the main task of parrying it. But at the same time the Navy had been drastically cut back from its 1918 strength in the name of disarmament and the League of Nations, to say nothing of saving money. Re-armament only began in 1936, with the new ships and their weaponry not expected into service until 1940 and after. Even then the Navy was only going to be modernised – *not* expanded into a force capable of fighting Germany, Italy, and Japan simultaneously. Such a navy simply could not be afforded by an economy with visible exports hit by increasing industrial uncompetitiveness and 'invisibles' hit by diminishing dividends on overseas investments. In any event, thanks partly to technological backwardness and partly to desuetude owing to the stop on capital-ship construction under the Washington Treaty, Britain in 1936 simply lacked the shipyards, armourers, and precision-engineering industries to build such a navy. As is well known, when the Royal Navy finally went to war in 1939 its inventory still contained unmodernised capital ships like the First World War 'R' class and the battle-cruiser *Hood*.

To sum up the dilemma bequeathed to Britain by history at the outbreak of the Second World War, on the one hand was the global imperial burden – what Admiral of the Fleet Lord Chatfield called in 1939 'this heavy commitment', with special reference to our obligation to send the battle-fleet to Singapore when needed to defend Australia and New Zealand from Japanese attack – and on the other a Navy far too small to carry the burden.

The pay-off is quickly narrated. In June 1940 Italy entered the war and France, our only ally, left it. The Royal Navy now had to fight two wars – one against Germany, the other in the Mediterranean against Italy. By the autumn of 1941, when it became plainer and plainer that Japan was likely to move in the Far East, the Royal Navy had lost so many ships, especially in the Mediterranean, and had such large commitments in northern and Atlantic waters, that the Admiralty could only send the *Prince of Wales*, an unworked-up new battleship, and the *Repulse*, an unmodernised battle-cruiser, to Singapore, with results all too notorious.[5]

However, the fall of Singapore and the virtual extinction of British sea power east of India led to one enormous uncovenanted benefit, in that the 'heavy commitment' of defending Australia and New Zealand mercifully passed for ever from Britain to the United States. Nevertheless, in a further example of the influence of history on sea power, Britain still remained stuck with the obligation to fight a major war against Japan in defence of India – a possession which in the nineteenth century had provided a major source of British wealth thanks to its opium exports to China, but was now a poverty-stricken, sometimes famine-stricken, burden on scarce wartime shipping resources.

The existence of the British Empire also led to catastrophic *indirect* strategic consequences for Britain during the Second World War. Throughout the interwar period, but especially from 1934 onwards, British governments had pursued a policy of strategic isolation from Europe, refusing to commit Britain diplomatically, let alone militarily, to an alliance with France to resist Nazi-German expansion. Apart from the liberal delusion common to most British politicians of the time that a settlement could be negotiated with Hitler if only Germany's 'legitimate' grievances were appeased, the principal reason for this military isolationism from Europe lay in the competing demands of the Empire for protection in the face of the threats from Italy to the imperial lifeline through the Mediterranean and Middle East, and from Japan in the Far East (not forgetting the imagined overland threat to India from the Soviet Union).

It was this combination of naval and military weakness across the global spread of the Empire, coupled with direct pressure from the dominions to avoid war, that reinforced Chamberlain in his decision to sacrifice Czechoslovakia as a military power at Munich in 1938, thus transforming the strategic balance of Europe in Hitler's favour. Only in the spring of 1939, after Hitler's occupation of Prague, did Chamberlain accept the historically obvious – that the security of the United Kingdom was inescapably bound up with the security of Western Europe, indeed even more so in the age of air power. But Chamberlain's conversion came far too late to enable Britain to re-create a mass British army on the Western front before the enemy struck. When the panzer divisions began to roll towards the Meuse crossings on 10 May 1940, Britain had only 10 divisions in the field, none armoured, whereas France had 94 divisions. It is thus possible to argue that, largely thanks to the historical legacy of the British Empire, Britain betrayed France both diplomatically and militarily from 1930 to 1940.

After France capitulated in June 1940, closing down the Western Front, Britain began to pay an enormous strategic price for that betrayal – and once again, it was the Royal Navy which picked up the bill. In the first place, with the French Navy out of the war, the Royal Navy had to contend alone against the triple threat until the US Navy began to take up some of the burden during 1941. Secondly, the switch of imports from Europe over short sea routes to the long haul from North America sharpened the already grievous problem of protecting Atlantic convoys from the U-boat and the surface raider. But above all, the fall of France meant that Britain no longer had a nearby land front on which eventually to deploy a great army, as in 1914–18, and which could be supplied at minimum cost in shipping and naval protection. Instead Britain was forced to resort to what Basil Liddell-Hart lovingly called 'the British way of Warfare' and what General J. F. C. ('Boney') Fuller more accurately described as 'the strategy of evasion': in other words, expeditionary forces deployed and maintained in far-off peripheral theatres thanks to British sea power.

In the case of the Second World War, this meant the Mediterranean and Middle East, where the historic growth of the Empire and the consequent need to protect the route to India and beyond had resulted in a British presence extending from Malta and Cyprus to Egypt, the Sudan, Aden, British Somaliland and the Persian Gulf. In the summer of 1940 the First Sea Lord, Admiral of the Fleet Sir Dudley Pound, urged that the Mediterranean be evacuated in order to concentrate the inadequate resources of the Navy on the war with Germany and still have a margin against the Japanese. He was overruled by Churchill and the War Cabinet Defence Committee, who saw Britain's only current chance of early military successes as lying in North Africa and the Mediterranean theatre.

In other words, unable to kick Hitler, Britain was reduced to kicking his dog, Mussolini.

To telegraph what followed from this decision, this initial British commitment to 'blue-water strategy' in the Mediterranean grew ever greater in scale from 1940 to 1942, not least because of repeated setbacks in the land campaigns. From 1942 onwards the Americans became drawn in as well. It was a classic case of, to paraphrase Lord Kitchener, making war as we must rather than as we ought – a step by step entanglement that led from Egypt in 1940 to the cul-de-sac of the valley of the Po in 1945.

Not only at the time but also in retrospect Churchill and Lord Alanbrooke presented this 'blue water' commitment in the Mediterranean as brilliant strategy rather than as a series of expedients. In *Engage the Enemy More Closely* I argue that this strategy was cost-ineffective in the highest degree. To build up the main base for a great army in Egypt, a backward country with poor ports and no industrial resources, to bring in that army and all its stores and equipment, and to keep it and its weaponry and supplies up to strength over a sea route 13,000 miles long took a gigantic investment in shipping tonnage and covering naval forces. To run vital convoys directly through the Mediterranean to Egypt – or to Malta, the Verdun of maritime war, a heroic symbol rather than a profitable asset – demanded major operations by the Mediterranean Fleet and Force H, and incurred very heavy losses.

To this general picture must be added Churchillian follies like the Greek adventure in 1941, undertaken in pursuit of the fantasy of a Balkan front that would hold against the Luftwaffe and the panzer divisions, which calamitously resulted in the gutting of the Mediterranean Fleet to little purpose, with the consequent inability to send a fleet to Singapore. A few figures prove the point. The Mediterranean campaign from 1940 up to the point when the Anglo–American conquest of Sicily in July 1943 at last opened the sea to merchant traffic again, cost the Royal Navy a battleship, two carriers, 14 cruisers, two anti-aircraft ships, 2 fast minelayers, 44 destroyers, 41 submarines and over a hundred other ships of all kinds.[6] And for what profit? The Eighth Army itself never fought more than 3½ German divisions, at a time when the Red Army was engaging about 200. Certainly the North African campaign led on to the invasion of Italy in 1943 – but that mountainous and stoutly defended peninsula proved very far from a soft underbelly. And maintaining the allied armies in Italy demanded a huge shipping lift because of the distances back to UK or US ports. A few further figures demonstrate the cost-ineffectiveness of Anglo–American Mediterranean 'blue-water strategy'. The total allied manpower in the theatre in 1944 amounted to nearly 1,700,000 – as against the German forces actually engaged in Italy of just over 400,000.[7] More striking still, whereas an average total of one million deadweight tons of shipping supported the 90 Allied divisions on the Western Front in 1944-45, nearly seven million allotted to the Mediterranean theatre supported only 27 divisions on the Italian front.[8]

To sum up Mediterranean 'blue-water strategy', this legacy of Britain's historic imperial involvement in the region, it was not only cost-ineffective throughout but also plunged the Royal Navy into its most desperate battles of the Second World War and caused its most grievous losses: the worst of them in the evacuations of British expeditionary forces from Greece and Crete at the end of Churchill's foredoomed Balkan adventure in 1941.

This brings me to a further factor which pervasively affected the Royal Navy's war until 1944, indeed here a case of sea power being influenced by history in the human flesh. I refer of course to the Prime Minister, Winston Churchill, that child of Victorian and Edwardian Empire, student of Marlborough's and other eighteenth-century wars, and architect of the First World War 'blue-water' catastrophe of the Dardanelles expedition in 1915-16. As First Lord of the Admiralty in the Great War Churchill had controlled the largest navy and most powerful battle-fleet in the world, a privilege all too conducive to large gestures over the map, at Borkum here and Gallipoli there. But when as Prime Minister during the Second World War he again succumbed to grand waves of the cigar over the map, including his old fantasy of defeating Germany in the eastern Mediterranean and the Balkans, he no longer controlled the greatest navy in the world but one shrunken and desperately over-stretched in trying to protect an Empire which from the United Kingdom to Hong Kong was – to cite Mahan's words about the Spanish Empire – vulnerable to 'insult and injury'.

In these circumstances Churchill's romantic sense of history, his faulty strategic judgements and his itchy-fingered interference with actual operations at sea, as documented by Cabinet and Cabinet Defence Committee papers, proved even more dangerous than in the Great War. There is only space here to cite briefly some notable examples:

1. Operation 'Catherine' late in 1939. Four 'R' class battleships were to be turned into armoured 'turtles' (invulnerable to air attack). With armoured tankers, this force was to proceed through the Skaggerak and Kattegat into the Baltic, where it would then cut off Swedish iron-ore supplies to Germany and, Churchill hoped, probably bring Sweden into the war on the allied side, so winning the war. This was

at a time when Britain was desperately short of heavy ships for the open seas, and her steel industry could not produce enough armour-plate for the Navy's ships and the Army's tanks.
2. The Norway campaign in 1940, where Churchill's fist can be seen in all the shifts of allied strategy, the constantly changing operational priorities, and the overall inability to measure grand schemes against available fighting strength by land, sea and air.
3. The fatuous expedition to Dakar in summer 1940 – pushed through by Churchill against all military and naval advice.
4. The 1940–41 proposal to capture the tiny Italian island base of Pantellaria, demanding scarce naval and military forces – luckily scotched after months of wasted staff work.
5. The Greek adventure in 1941. The story is well known of how it was decided to stop O'Connor's desert offensive against the Italians in Libya in its tracks and send an army to Greece instead. What is not so generally known is that the decision was taken despite the prior knowledge that Britain lacked the shipping and the munitions to keep a Greek front going even if the initial German onslaught were repelled.
6. Churchill's proposal that Admiral Cunningham should sink the battleship *Barham* as a blockship in Tripoli harbour in Libya in order to hinder Rommel's supplies – again at a time of desperate shortage of heavy ships.
7. The despatch of the *Prince of Wales* and *Repulse* to Singapore. The documentary records demonstrate beyond doubt that this was done at Churchill's insistence, in the pursuit of yet another fantasy – that these ships would be a deterrent to Japan, on the analogy of the anxiety caused to the Admiralty by the *Bismarck* and then the *Tirpitz*.
8. The attempt to seize the Dodecanese Islands in Autumn 1943 – a complete reversion to the *ad hoc* opportunism of the Dardanelles and likewise a disaster.

But perhaps potentially the most dangerous episode of Churchill's conduct of the naval war lay in his failure fully to back the Navy's and RAF Coastal Command's demand for a diversion of long-range aircraft from the Bomber Offensive to the Battle of the Atlantic in 1942. Thanks to the pigheadedness of Portal and the Air Staff, to say nothing of that man of tunnel vision, Sir Arthur Harris, Britain very nearly lost the Battle of the Atlantic in late 1942 and early 1943 for want of a handful of very long-range 10 cm radar-equipped aircraft. I have dealt with this 1942 'Battle of the Air', as Dudley Pound called it, in detail elsewhere, because,

At issue, then, in the 'Battle of the Air' had been nothing less than Britain's very survival. This renders it the most important single British strategic debate of the war. It is, moreover, the one case where Britain's survival was imperilled not so much by enemy action in itself as by blind folly within Britain's own leadership.[9]

The Admiralty and Western Approaches Command perfectly understood that to beat the U-boat demanded aircraft and surface escorts working together, and that escorts alone were not enough. And as Dudley Pound also said in 1942: 'If we lose the war at sea, we lose the war... .'[10] To be beaten by the U-boat would mean not only British industry at a standstill, the nation starving and Bomber Command grounded for want of fuel, but also no possibility of a later Anglo–American liberation of Western Europe. Here was the absolute crux of Britain's war against Germany – that being the one war that really mattered. There is a fascinating parallel between U-boat Command's attempt to defeat Britain by wrecking her economy and national life; and Bomber Command's attempt to defeat Germany likewise. The question in 1942 was: who was winning the race? And the answer according to the then available evidence was clearly the U-boat, although the bomber barons refused to accept this.

Just as in the First World War the U-boat was exploiting the long-term consequences of Britain's adoption of Free Trade in the nineteenth century, of the Victorian development of Britain as the centre of a world economy, more geared into overseas trade than any other industrial country, and contrariwise the least self-sufficient. Thus Britain's absolute minimum requirements of imported food, raw materials and fuel in 1943 were estimated at 27 million tons.[11] This dependence on seaborne imports, this vulnerability to national strangulation, constitutes an example of the influence of history on British sea power in the Second World war hardly less important than that of the imperial legacy.

Had the Royal Navy entered the war with a numerous flotilla of well-equipped escort vessels, backed by a Coastal Command with enough of the right kind of aircraft equipped with effective find-and-destroy systems, this historic vulnerability would not have posed such a mortal threat. But the Battle of the Atlantic in the years 1941–42 found both the Royal Navy and RAF Coastal Command wanting in numbers as well as combat effectiveness – again the result of the belatedness of pre-war rearmament coupled with the limited resources of the British economy and industrial base.

Woven into this major theme of the influence of economic history on British sea power in the Atlantic is a minor theme – that of the long-term pernicious results of the creation of the Royal Air Force in 1918 as an 'independent' air force at the expense of the Royal Naval Air Service. For from its inception the Royal Air Force had been shaped by its leadership's belief, quite unjustified by technological and operational realities, that the bomber could win wars on its own, and that all other use of air power was diversion. We must recall Sir Arthur Harris's thoughtful remark in 1942 that Coastal Command was 'merely an obstacle to victory'.[12]

Even after the Fleet Air Arm was handed back to the Royal Navy in 1937, British naval aviation remained backward tactically and technologically compared with the United States and Japanese navies. This was partly because its hiving off from the Navy between 1918 and 1937 had consolidated the dominance of the traditional 'Big-gun' battleship admirals in the Royal Navy, who simply refused to comprehend the potential of air power over the sea – even as late as 1941 when Admiral Sir Tom Phillips sailed from Singapore to his doom off Malaya. But British backwardness in naval aviation also owed itself to the peculiar incompetence of the aircraft firms allotted to building for the Navy and Coastal Command. Again to telegraph a complicated story, the Fleet Air Arm all too often received aircraft already obsolete at the time of new delivery. As late as the British Pacific Fleet's operations in 1945, the Royal Navy's carriers had an assorted ragbag of types which could not compare with the aircraft in American carriers. More Seafires (an adapted Spitfire) were destroyed or damaged in landing accidents in the Pacific than in combat.[13] Coastal Command likewise suffered from poor British aircraft, but in its case largely at the beginning of the war; it came later to rely on American types – the Hudson, the Catalina, and the Liberator, although it must be said that the Vickers Wellington did good service.

This brief discussion of the quality of maritime aircraft produced by British industry raises another key aspect of the influence of history on sea power – in the shape of the prolonged relative decline of British industrial and technological capability from the 1850s to the 1940s. In particular the inefficiency, human and technical, of the British shipbuilding industry meant that to embark on a major wartime programme to expand the numbers of battleships and fleet carriers, as the Admiralty would have wished, was out of the question. Instead, all possible resources had to be concentrated on building or repairing escorts. Even so, by 1943 Britain had been compelled to turn to North America for the bulk of her supplies of escort vessels and the invaluable escort carrier.[14] In a sentence, the British industrial base could no longer sustain a large 'battle-fleet' navy such as the Americans created between 1941 and 1945. Partly because of this, partly because of operational necessity, the balance of the Royal

Navy shifted during the war towards being an anti-submarine force instead. This marked the final eclipse of Britannia's rule of the waves after two centuries: the pay-off for the failure of Britain's 'mechanical industries' (in Mahan's phrase) and her wealth to keep pace with her need for 'war fleets' large enough to protect 'her extensive colonial system' and 'great trade'.

Britain's technological shortcomings are particularly evident in the case of anti-submarine warfare, even though the Royal Navy and Coastal Command by 1943 had become not only masters of the necessary tactical techniques, the training methods and command and control organisation, but had also deployed a marvellous armoury of kit to detect, locate, and destroy U-boats: 10 cm radar, HF/DF, the Hedgehog, lethal depth-charges, the escort support group. But it had taken a very long time to develop all this shore, sea-going and airborne apparatus which (along with Ultra) enabled the British and Canadian navies and air forces finally to defeat the U-boat in 1943. To summarise a necessarily complex story, the heavy delays are to be explained by a combination of bureaucratic rivalry and obstruction within the Admiralty – and the Air Ministry too – and the sheer dearth of radio and precision-engineering firms capable of fabricating the brilliant inventions of world-class British scientists. The problem of this dearth was sharpened because Bomber Command was competing hard with Coastal Command for broadly the same kind of electronic kit, such as H2S and 10 cm ASV radar. The lack of high-quality precision-engineering firms also explains why the Admiralty before the war had settled for a system of anti-aircraft fire-control much inferior to American and German – British industry simply could not fabricate anything as finely precise as tachometric fire-control.[15]

From history's bequest to Britain of a global empire, utter dependence on seaborne imports, and an inadequate industrial base there emerges a poignant paradox which supplies the underlying theme of *Engage the Enemy More Closely*. Whereas the Royal Navy itself had never in its history shown greater seamanship and fighting spirit, the economic buoyancy which had once sustained the Navy, the technological dynamism which had once driven the expansion of British sea power, had disappeared. These were now factors sustaining the United States Navy, the new mistress of the world's seas.

It was of course the ships' companies who bore the brunt of the disparity between the Royal Navy's resources and the demands loaded on to it in the Second World War by British history. The leitmotif of the Royal Navy's war thus lies in operations – the unceasing and ubiquitous demands of the sea service from the first day to the last of a six-and-a-half-year conflict. There is here a striking contrast with the Royal Air Force's dominant theme of the gradual development of the bomber offensive against German cities, or its secondary theme of the equally gradual development of effective tactical support of the Army and Navy. There is a no less interesting contrast with the British Army's wartime theme of expansion, after early disasters and unpreparedness, into a mass citizen army.

These contrasts between the three services go further. It was only in 1943, with the introduction of Oboe and H2S that Bomber Command entered into its period of severest fighting and heaviest casualties; only in that year too that the British Army re-entered the Continent in Italy; and only in 1944 that the Army for the first time in the war fought a mass battle against a main body of the German army; that is, in Normandy. But by 1943 the Royal Navy had already fought its most desperate battles and suffered the majority of its wartime losses: all five of those capital ships that were sunk; all five of the fleet carriers that were sunk. In fact, the worst of the Navy's losses in ships larger than a corvette had been sustained by April 1942. All five of the lost heavy ships; four out of five lost fleet carriers; sixteen out of a total loss of 28 cruisers; 78 out of a total loss of 133 destroyers; 44 out of a total loss of 74 submarines.[16]

These stark figures demonstrate a truth easily forgotten – that, with one outstanding exception in the Battle of the Atlantic, the worst of the Royal Navy's war was over well before the British Army or the Royal Air Force had got their acts together and begun to wage war on a mass scale. Why? Because the Royal Navy even more than the Army's unlucky expeditionary forces bore the brunt of the early war years of defeat, disappointment and struggle, and, it might be added, of Winston Churchill's ill-considered opportunist strokes of strategy; in short, the brunt of British overstretch at its most desperate.

Only with massive American help did the diminished Britain of the 1940s escape the plight into which she had been plunged by the legacy of her past history as the world's greatest and richest power. With the passing of the Lend–Lease Act in April 1941 the United States began to tow Britain home economically and technologically, British sea power being henceforward kept afloat by American economic buoyancy. A year later, as has already been noted in this paper, the United States took Australia and New Zealand under her protection. Moreover, the deployment of a great American army and air force in the United Kingdom in 1943–44 thanks to the British and Canadian victory in the Battle of the Atlantic alone made it possible realistically to contemplate re-creating the Western Front. And, as not only the First World War but also the Napoleonic Wars, the Seven Years' War, and the war against Philip II of Spain demonstrate, the only effective application of sea power against a great Continental enemy such as Germany lies in opening and sustaining a land front where his armies may be ground down in battle by an allied army.

It could be argued that Operation Neptune, the climax of the Royal Navy's endeavours in the Second World War, was itself a product of the influence of history on sea power, in that it was rendered necessary by the collapse of the Western Front in 1940, that collapse being in turn the product of the history of the previous twenty years. Yet Neptune/Overlord has no precedent in the annals of British naval or military operations, for it was unique in its scale and complexity – and unique also in the thoroughness and professionalism with which it was planned by the Allied Naval Commander Expeditionary Force, Admiral Sir Bertram Ramsay, and his staff.

It was thanks to Neptune, and most of all the Royal Navy, that the Western Front was successfully reopened four years to the month after it had been closed down by the French collapse, and that at long last allied armies engaged a main body of the German army. The Battle of Normandy, in which the enemy lost 5 panzer and 20 infantry divisions, constituted a complete victory; victory on a scale that dwarfed the peripheral Anglo–American successes in the Mediterranean; victory on the shortest route to the enemy heartland; the first victory won by Western democracies over a great German army since 1918; victory which abundantly fulfilled the object of Operation Neptune as defined back in April by Admiral Ramsay on page one of his Operation Neptune Naval Orders: '. . . to carry out an operation from the United Kingdom to secure a lodgement on the Continent from which further offensive operations can be developed... .'

From the break-out from Normandy to the final German surrender in May 1945 the advancing allied armies depended on sea power – above all, British sea power – for all their supplies and reinforcements. Here then lay the decisive offensive role of the Royal Navy in the one struggle that mattered – the struggle against Germany for Britain's own survival. Here at last was a case of making war as we ought rather than as we must.

The successful execution of Neptune on 6 June 1944 therefore marks the moment when British sea power once again influenced history rather than the other way round.

NOTES

1. A. T. Mahan, *The Influence of Sea Power upon History 1660–1783* (London, 1965), p. 67. This is a facsimile of the original edition (Boston and London, 1890).
2. Ibid., pp. 82–3.
3. Ibid., p. 30.
4. See Barnett, *The Collapse of British Power* (London, 1972), Parts III and IV, for an analysis of imperial weaknesses and mistaken British 'total strategy' (a term first coined in this book to describe the interrelated elements of foreign policy, grand strategy, defence policy, economic policy, technological resources and even education and national motivation which make up a nation's total capability in rivalry with other nations). This was the first study to argue (on the basis of Cabinet, Cabinet Committee and Committee of Imperial Defence files) that the British Empire was a burden rather than an asset, distracting Britain from her own direct security interests in Europe. It was also the first work to relate Britain's growing financial, economic and technological weakness in the 1920s and 1930s to the strategic demands of her imperial commitments. Since 1972 numerous works have examined in detail various aspects of this 'total-strategic' dilemma, though without overturning the original thesis in *The Collapse*. As it might be said, after the Pathfinders come the lumbering academic heavy-bomber stream.
5. See Barnett, *Engage the Enemy More Closely: the Royal Navy in the Second World War* (London, 1991, 2nd edn. 1992), *passim*, but especially Chapters 12 and 13.
6. *Engage the Enemy More Closely*, p. 670.
7. Dominick Graham & Shelford Bidwell, *Tug of War: The Battle for Italy, 1943–1945* (London, 1986), p. 401.
8. Barnett, *Engage the Enemy More Closely*, p. 852.
9. Op. cit., p. 476. See Chapter 15, 'The Battle of the Air', *passim*.
10. Ibid., p. 440.
11. C. B. A. Behrens, *Merchant Shipping and the Demands of War* (London, HMSO 1955), p. 363.
12. Quoted in John Terraine, *The Right of the Line; The Royal Air Force in the European War 1939–1945* (London, 1985), p. 426.
13. *Engage the Enemy More Closely*, pp. 885–6, p. 892.
14. Ibid., p. 585.
15. See ibid., pp. 46–8 and 886–8.
16. Ibid., p. 429.

11 Wings over the Sea: The Interaction of Air and Sea Power in the Mediterranean, 1940–42
Michael Simpson

On the eve of Italy's entry into the war, Sir Dudley Pound told Cunningham, the C-in-C, Mediterranean, 'The one lesson we have learned here is that it is essential to have fighter protection over the Fleet'.[1] Norway and Dunkirk demonstrated the devastating effect of bombing on ships and sailors' morale and the ineffectiveness of AA fire. Cunningham and Somerville (Force H) were determined to exercise sea power in the historic manner. 'Our position in the Middle East', declared Cunningham, 'depends almost entirely on the fleet and I want to keep it active and able to go anywhere with moderate security'.[2] However, the Regia Aeronautica was numerous and highly trained and Cunningham complained that 'the Italians ... send planes over Alexandria every day and no force in the last three weeks has been at sea without being discovered and bombed'.[3] The enemy quickly learned to keep below a radar beam and thus 'enjoy a fair degree of immunity from fighter interception'.[4] Waves of up to 40 bombers attacked the fleet, dropping 400 bombs in 4 days. Though 'more alarming than dangerous', Cunningham observed 'the sailors, especially those in the destroyers, look a bit askance at going to sea knowing they will be bombed for two or three days running'.[5] Low-level torpedo-bombers, attacking in the moonlight were 'rather a menace – very difficult to meet'.[6] Force H was also beset by shadowers and bombers on its frequent 'club runs' to Malta. Carriers were especially vulnerable when conducting flying operations:

> You have to keep an eye cocked all the time for fear that the enemy may come and attack when you are stuck to one course, i.e. straight in the wind's eye and therefore have no freedom of manoeuvring.[8]

Thus Cunningham remarked that 'We are well able to look after the Italian Fleet, but I doubt if we can tackle their Air Force as well'.

However, Italian bombing 'had produced throughout the Fleet a determination to overcome the air menace' and Cunningham observed that 'The pre-requisite of successful operations ... is constant and complete air reconnaissance' and 'We should be able to quarter this end of the Mediterranean and not a thing should move without our knowing it'.[10]

Adequate base defence was vital. In June 1940, neither Gibraltar nor Malta had fighters, while at Alexandria, 'the fleet base and repair facilities are exposed to enemy air attack with very limited fighter protection' and Cunningham was compelled to dock major vessels only during moonless periods. Radar was primitive (and the Rock distorted signals at Gibraltar); AA and searchlight defences were deficient everywhere. After one raid on Gibraltar, Somerville complained 'the AA fire on this occasion [reached] a new low level of efficiency ... a deplorable exhibition'. Moreover, 'When this harbour is packed with ships, there's not enough water to catch the bricks'; when heavy raids were expected, Force H put to sea. Characteristically, Somerville shook up the radar and AA organisations.[11] Malta, which the Navy 'had always regarded ... as the keystone of victory in the Mediterranean and considered should be held at all costs', was dismissed by the Army and RAF as indefensible. 'Was there ever such a folly as to allow our Mediterranean fortress to fall into such a state?' Cunningham fumed, arguing that 'Malta is of immense value to us' as a base for central Mediterranean and Aegean operations, particularly the interdiction of Italian traffic with Libya. Pound agreed that 'we must get the fleet back to Malta; unless we do this the situation will be an impossible one when the Italians have six battleships', as the enemy would control the central Mediterranean if Cunningham was confined in Alexandria. At the height of the Battle of Britain, the Government was persuaded to despatch fighters to Malta and later reconnaissance, bomber, torpedo, long-range and night-fighter units, and 112 AA guns.[12]

The air threat compelled units to leave harbour at night, adopt evasive routeing and develop fleet AA techniques. At first, 'AA fire was bum', reported Somerville, 'all short again'. Radar and 'firing up ladders for range' helped but the best interim answer was barrage fire, highly effective against torpedo-bombers.[13] As Somerville recommended,

> ... keeping well locked up is the answer should the bombers be able to press home their attacks, since this ensures that every gun in the force is

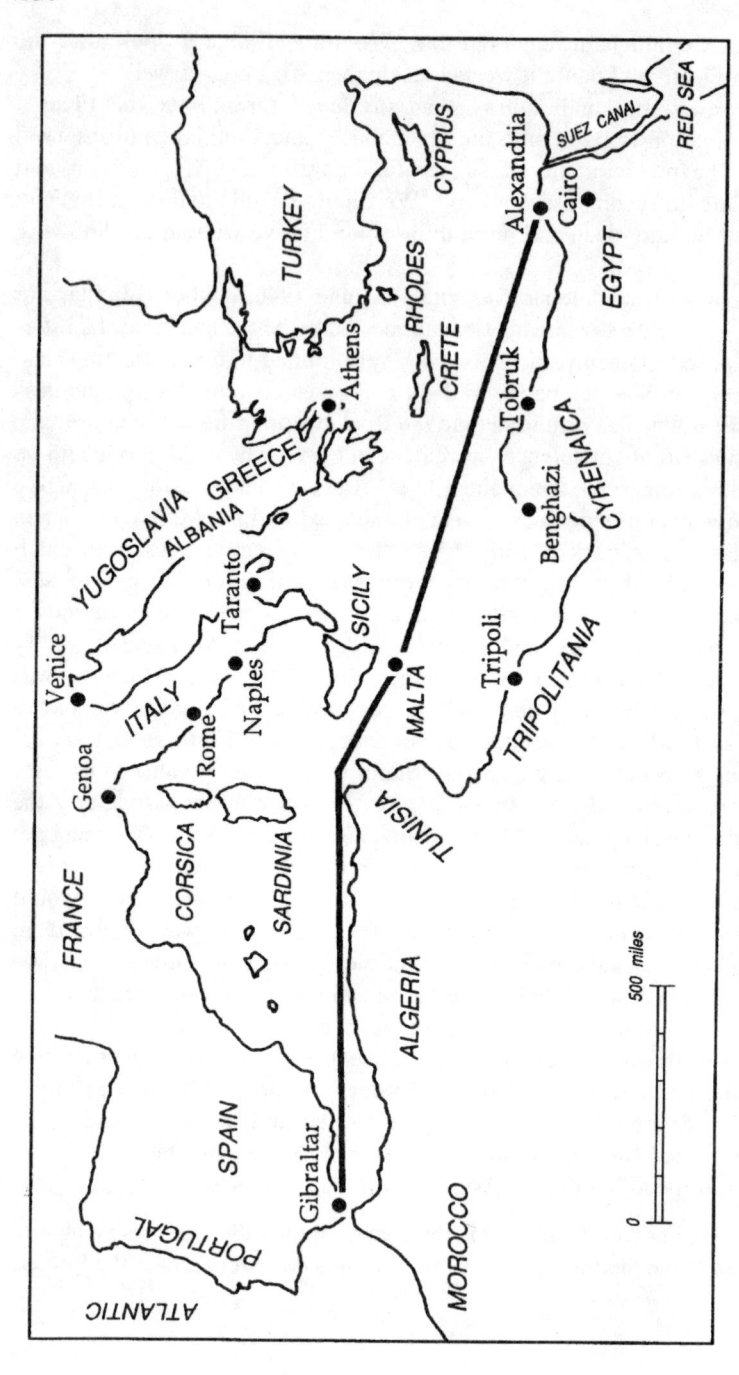

Map 11.1 The Mediterranean, 1939–42. Principal British Convoy Route indicated by solid black line.

in action before the bombers can reach the point of bomb release .... By staggering the line and stationing cruisers and AA ships on the bows and quarters, you get a compact formation which can be 'blued' in any direction to keep the 'A' arcs open.[14]

Much the best solution was carrier-borne fighter cover. Though inferior to shore-based fighters, Skuas and Fulmars performed miracles. During the 'Tiger' convoy of May 1941, Somerville exulted.

> ... our Fulmars ... mixed it up magnificently. I can't say too much in praise of the wonderful show they put up, ... [as] it was always a case of two or three of ours against six or nine of them.[15]

At one point 6 Fulmars drove off 30 German planes. Following the arrival of *Illustrious* (September 1940), Cunningham reported that 'whenever an armoured carrier was in company, we had command of the air over the fleet'. Carrier fighters disposed of the persistent shadowers, forcing bombers to 'unload on the horizon', thus heartening the sailors. Radar tracked approaching enemies and fighters were vectored onto them; Somerville also sought the advice of an RAF fighter direction expert.[16] So confident did he become that he welcomed encounters:

> Heavy air attack had been anticipated and hoped for, since with the heavy AA concentration and number of fighters available, I felt it should be possible to deliver a blow to the Italian Air Force which might have a telling and lasting effect.[17]

The handful of fleet fighters was the vital factor in the remarkably successful operations of 1940–41. Churchill wrongly complained that 'an exaggerated fear of Italian aircraft has been allowed to hamper operations', for by the end of 1940, Cunningham recalled, 'We had the measure of the Regia Aeronautica'.[18]

Carriers, of which both admirals made optimum use, facilitated reconnaissance, anti-submarine patrols, aerial mining, gunnery spotting, conventional and dive-bombing, and torpedo strikes. Somerville, the Royal Navy's first true 'air admiral', introduced new technology and techniques, and gave his carrier captain operational freedom 'in accordance with the general situation and what he knows to be the Admiral's views'. Exercising his planes constantly, he flew on 'torpedo runner exercises, dive-bombing practices, and fighter interception and encounters', arguing 'that it is most desirable that Senior Officers should take part in such practices that they may acquire a full appreciation of the problems which face the FAA pilots and observers'.[19] His nephew, a Fulmar observer aboard *Ark Royal*, expressed the aircrews' appreciation:

The general view ... is that the ship is now operating under a Flag Officer who not only understands the general aspect of naval aviation but who has also taken the trouble to investigate the practical and personal side of it.[20]

At sea, six of *Ark Royal's* Swordfish fanned out on long-range reconnaissance, another pair performed anti-submarine patrols, a strike force was at readiness, a section of fighters patrolled for shadowers, and further sections were ranged against bombing raids. *Ark Royal* (54 aircraft) was the core of Force H; when she was detached for the Dakar operation in September 1940, Somerville lamented 'I ... am very lost ... without her ... without air [cover] we are singularly ineffective in the big wide open spaces.'[21]

Ark Royal's Swordfish attacked Italian shore targets successfully and at small cost but, given their low numbers and limited bomb loads, these could only be pinpricks. Moreover, 'The very low performance of the Swordfish makes her such easy meat for shore-based fighters that unless the attack was carried out in the dark we should get none of them back'.[22] At sea, however, torpedo attacks

> on high speed targets during the present war have fallen far short of the estimates based on peacetime practices adjusted for 'opposition'. ... this is attributable entirely to lack of initial training and subsequent runner practice.[23]

After one unsuccessful dive-bomber sortie, Somerville exchanged his Skuas for Fulmars, observing that there were 'few opportunities of using Skuas for offensive operations in the Western basin'. Given the general success of dive-bombers at sea, the FAA might have persisted longer with the Skua.[24]

Cunningham's carrier, the obsolescent *Eagle* (17 Swordfish, 3 Sea Gladiators), scored numerous successes against Italian shipping and military targets, though after Calabria (July 1940), Cunningham lamented 'Had the FAA been able to hit ships steaming at about 25 knots, we would have had him [Riccardi] in his own snare'.[25] The arrival of *Illustrious* (36 aircraft) made possible the Taranto attack (November 1940). For the loss of two planes, three battleships were disabled for several months, the remainder retiring from the central Mediterranean. Taranto further dented fragile Italian morale and allowed the release of two British battleships. Praising the 'admirably planned' and 'determined and gallant' attack, Cunningham believed 'It will be some time before [the Italians] face the FAA'. Arguably the FAA's finest hour, 'As an example of "economy of force" it is probably unsurpassed' (even by Pearl Harbor). 'Most significantly', he concluded, 'this successful attack has greatly increased our freedom of movement in the Mediterranean.'[26]

The FAA also brought about the victory at Matapan (March 1941). *Formidable* (replacing the damaged *Illustrious*) flew several strikes against the Italian fleet. Though only two hits were registered, the first attack saved the British cruisers from a certain mauling and a later one damaged the *Vittorio Veneto*. A further strike crippled the *Pola*; with two of her sisters and two destroyers, sent to rescue her, she was sunk by Cunningham, ironically forced into a night action because the enemy 'would be well under cover of the Ju.87 dive-bombers at daylight'. Matapan discouraged Italian surface intervention during the Greek and Cretan campaigns in the spring.[27] Thus the FAA, 'in spite of the rotten aircraft they find themselves with', had crippled and inhibited the enemy battle fleet.[28]

However, on 10 January 1941, 43 Stukas, achieving surprise, hit *Illustrious* with 6 bombs, putting her out of action for a year. Fliegerkorps X, a specialist anti-ship group, had arrived in Sicily; the Axis now had 500 maritime aircraft. Cunningham understood at once the strategic significance of the Luftwaffe's arrival:

> ... it is a potent new factor in the Mediterranean war and will undoubtedly deny us that free access to the waters immediately surrounding Malta and Sicily which we have previously enjoyed, until our own air forces have been built up to a scale adequate to meet it.[29]

Before the Luftwaffe came, 'our control of the Mediterranean was close on being re-established ... [and] such movements would have been increasingly practicable.' Against dive-bombers, 'the only real answer is fighters' but without its carrier the fleet would have to rely on alterations of course at night, umbrella barrages and the feverish installation of radar – or avoid waters within dive-bombing range. Ironically, this was now impossible, for Malta was under more intensive air attack, thus requiring more sustenance, and the Government decided to support Greece, hold Crete, subdue the Vichy Levant, and supply beleaguered Tobruk.[30]

Cunningham doubted 'if our resources, particularly naval and air, are equal to the strain' of supporting Greece. Vulnerable to attack from Rhodes and the Dodecanese, convoys suffered 'increasing losses which must be attributed ... to inadequate air support'. Following Germany's intervention in April 1941, the Luftwaffe destroyed Piraeus and 22 merchant ships in 2 days. The British evacuation took place 'under direful conditions. About 400 bombers attacking troops and ships all day and not a plane of our own to defend them'.[31] Nevertheless, the Navy performed with determination and success, but Greece was only a prologue to the tragedy of Crete (May 1941), 'a trial of strength between the Mediterranean Fleet and the German Air Force'.[32]

Crete was vital, for 'If in enemy hands the supply of Malta would be most difficult, thereby affecting the Navy's ability to interrupt enemy sea traffic to Libya.' However, the Army was unable to supply an adequate AA defence and the RAF stated that 'it would be impossible for some time to provide sufficient fighter protection for Crete'. In any case, 'it would be difficult to operate aircraft from Crete if Greece were overrun' and therefore 'unlikely that we could use it as a naval or air base without strong fighter protection'.[33] Lacking RAF support and *Formidable*, reduced to four fighters, Cunningham's strategy was to operate north of Crete by night but withdraw southwards before dawn. 'The Navy succeeded in its object' of defeating a seaborne invasion 'but paid a heavy price for this achievement'. Suda Bay was 'subjected to frequent air attack which caused heavy casualties among the ships unloading' and 'Without air support of any sort, the fleet had to be exposed to a scale of air attack which is believed to have exceeded anything of the kind yet experienced afloat.'[34] The destroyer *Kipling* dodged 83 bombs in under 5 hours. Ships were often overwhelmed by the sheer mass of attackers and it required only one or two bombs to sink a destroyer and two or three for a cruiser. Vessels sank 'like a stone' – the *Kashmir* in only two minutes – and all ran short of AA ammunition.[35] Losses occurred generally when ships were caught alone or in small groups, Cunningham observing ruefully that 'past experience had gone to show that when under heavy scale of air attack it is essential to keep ships together for mutual support' and 'Together, the fleet's volume of AA fire might have prevented some of our casualties.'[36] However, it was undoubtedly true that 'gunfire from the best of ships cannot deal with aircraft which one there likened to a swarm of bees'.[37]

Despite Cunningham's order to 'Stick it out. The Navy must not let the Army down. No enemy forces must reach Crete by sea', Churchill accused him of faintheartedness and the Chiefs of Staff supported the Prime Minister's insistence that if necessary half the fleet must be sacrificed in defence of the island. Cunningham pointed out 'the need to avoid losses which without commensurate advantages to ourselves will cripple the fleet'.[38] However, after a week's fighting the Army had to be evacuated, at night, from beaches. As both ships and men were 'nearing exhaustion' and 'in some ships the sailors began to crack a bit', Cunningham confessed that 'I have been rather anxious about the state of mind of the sailors after seven days' constant bombing attacks.' He was driven to offer to relinquish command and even told Mountbatten (a dive-bombing victim) that he felt like going out on a destroyer into the thick of the bombing and getting killed.[39] Somerville commented,

> I'm not surprised that the sailors were shaken. I watched carefully what happened at Dunkirk and saw the results of continuous bombing at sea. On land you don't feel that *you* are the target. At sea it is just too bloody obvious and has its effect accordingly.[40]

In two weeks, the Luftwaffe sank 3 cruisers, 6 destroyers and 22 merchantmen. Two battleships, a carrier, 5 cruisers and 8 destroyers were damaged, many seriously, and several hundred troops and 2,000 sailors had become casualties. Only 2 battleships, 1 cruiser, 2 AA cruisers, a fast minelayer and 9 destroyers remained fit for operations.[41]

Cunningham acknowledged 'There is no question that [the Luftwaffe] have had the best of it and I suppose if one operates 30–40 miles off the enemy aerodromes it is to be expected.'[42] Enemy planes from Crete now posed a greater threat to Egypt. Most seriously, *Formidable* had been severely damaged by two bombs late in the Cretan saga, necessitating eight months' repairs.[43] Thus,

> the fleet will have to face serious loss by day whenever at sea outside the range of effective fighter protection. We are thus for the moment driven back on a defensive role and our liberty of action is greatly restricted.[44]

Crete reinforced the lesson that 'you can't conduct military operations in modern war without air forces which allow you at least to establish temporary air supremacy'. The situation for British sea power was now dire, for 'We are on the verge of disaster here for we stand to lose the fleet and thus Malta, Cyprus and Egypt unless we act at once (Repeat) once.'[45] Cunningham pleaded for another carrier but Pound believed it would be 'a sheer waste' since a new vessel was 'bound to be knocked out within a very short time'. Cunningham accepted that 'with the arrival of the Luftwaffe ... our carrier could no longer expect the immunity she had enjoyed' but, pointing out that many other ships would be lost for lack of air cover, argued that 'one good carrier filled with fighters should be able to look after herself'.[46] However, deteriorating relations with Japan meant the assignment of the new *Indomitable* and the repaired *Illustrious* and *Formidable* to the Far East. Throughout the remainder of Cunningham's stay, the fleet was 'restricted in its activities by the lack of an aircraft carrier'.[47]

Cunningham thus advocated a revised strategy. 'Until we get Cyrenaica', he declared, 'our movements will be very limited.' Cyrenaican airfields would enable bombers to attack enemy islands and northern shores of the Mediterranean; torpedo-bombers could cover most of the Italian convoy routes; Tripoli could be bombed relentlessly; and fighters could more easily defend convoys, Alexandria and the Canal. If Axis forces reached Mersa Matruh, 'it will be questionable whether Alexandria will be usable for the Fleet against fighter escorted aircraft.'[48] Furthermore, Tobruk was enduring an 8-month siege but the destroyers and small craft carrying troops and supplies 'get bombed going there and coming back all night when there is sufficient light'. Tobruk was 'mercilessly bombed' and thus 'The running in of supplies became a fine art.' The AOC-in-C regarded the defence of these ships as a 'costly commitment' diverting strength from the desert war but, as Cunningham pointed out, 'Without fighter protection the small ships now being used had little chance of accomplishing their journey in safety.' By the end of 1941, 27 naval vessels and 4 merchantmen had been lost and 27 warships and 6 merchant vessels damaged on this run. Lacking radar and suitable AA weapons, their crews 'felt pretty naked' and exhibited 'a gloomy cynicism'.[49]

Even more serious was the plight of Malta. Though Cunningham always maintained that 'Malta was really the linchpin of the campaign in the Mediterranean', in 1941–42 it was more of a millstone.[50] Following the arrival of the Luftwaffe in January 1941, the island was reduced to 'a very bad state', morale was low, the dockyard severely damaged and fighter strength down to eight. 'Seriously alarmed', Cunningham told Pound in May that 'They are having a very bad time; never a let off from continual bombing' and 'The enemy air forces are operating just as they please.'[51] At that point, Fliegerkorps X moved east. Malta's air component and AA batteries reached full strength and enabled the Navy to station Force K there. Aided by good reconnaissance and in conjunction with submarines and anti-shipping squadrons, it did good execution on the Tripoli convoys, while the air group afforded long-range convoy protection and bombed ports and bases in Italy and North Africa.[52]

However, the Luftwaffe returned in strength in December 1941, inaugurating Malta's worst ordeal. In October 1941, there had been 50 air raids; by January 1942, these had risen to 275, up to 200 heavily escorted bombers raiding day and night, dropping monthly up to 2,000 tons of bombs. Cunningham feared that invasion was imminent 'particularly observing the increased scale [of] air attack to which they are now being exposed and appear unable to defeat'.[53] Admiral Ford at Malta explained that AA defence was poor, pilots were inexperienced, night fighters were scarce, many aircraft were destroyed on the ground and the Hurricanes were outclassed. As for reconnaissance planes, 'God knows we've screamed hard enough for them' and he appealed for '100–200 fast fighters'.[54] His successor, Admiral Leatham, reported in February 'our troubles here ... are from the weakness of our fighter strength. Reconnaissance is dreadfully weak too and our striking power is none too grand either.'[55] Warships and merchantmen were sunk or damaged in harbour, unloading was virtually impossible and submarines had to lie on the bottom during the day. All warships save minesweepers and submarines were withdrawn. Though 1,000 anti-shipping sorties were flown in the first three months of 1942, poor reconnaissance and lack of training led to many missed opportunities. When Cunningham left the Mediterranean in March, 'The dockyard was a shambles of rubble and twisted girders'; Malta was being 'neutralised' and 'to a great extent the enemy had achieved his purpose'.[56]

Convoys from Alexandria lost most of their ships and Cunningham concluded that it was 'useless to pass in a convoy until the air situation in Malta and the military situation in Cyrenaica has been restored'. He thought 'if we hold the line at Derna it would just be possible to run Malta convoys with a reasonable degree of safety' but 'It was the German Air Force in Crete on the flank of our convoy route to Malta that made the maintenance of that island from the east so costly and hazardous.'[57] Most convoys therefore sailed from Gibraltar but still ran a gauntlet of air, surface and submarine attacks. The Chiefs of Staff were determined that Malta should hold out and in March 1942 the American carrier *Wasp* twice flew in Spitfires, fighters at last equal to enemy planes. Nevertheless, Malta's survival 'was a very close thing'.[58]

Given the increasing weight of Axis air power (by the end of 1941 they disposed of 600 bombers), Cunningham and Somerville sought closer cooperation with the RAF. Cunningham recognised that 'The key ... which will decide the issue of our success or otherwise in holding the Mediterranean lies in air power.'[59] Egypt could not be saved without substantial air support nor could the Tripoli convoys be halted without it for 'the Libyan communications battle is between the Navy and the enemy Air Forces and that battle can only be won in close partnership with an adequate Air Force'. All bases needed more fighters while as to long-range fighters, 'Lack of them is one of our greatest wants in all theatres.'[60] The Canal and Red Sea were under attack by bombers from Greece and Crete, the Canal often being closed for weeks; FAA fighters and AA cruisers had to defend it as the Army and RAF could not do so. There was need, too, for 'Adequate reconnaissance aircraft. Of these we are desperately short.' Here, the gaps were alarming; during the evacuation of Greece, 'Only one flying boat at a time from Malta could be kept on patrol in the Ionian Sea' and the two admirals often had no knowledge of Italian fleet dispositions for weeks. Cunningham underlined the grim prospect: 'if our Air Forces cannot be increased ... to reach some measure of parity with those of the enemy we may have to face some very unpleasant alternatives'.[61]

There were many successful joint operations – for example, the photo-reconnaissance of Taranto, reconnaissance at Matapan, and long-range fighter cover for the 'Halberd' convoy, during which 'the bombing and machine gunning of enemy aerodromes in Sicily and Sardinia undoubtedly reduced to a considerable extent the scale of air attack which the enemy intended to launch'.[62] Nevertheless, both admirals identified weaknesses in RAF operations over the sea, such as inaccurate reconnaissance, erratic navigation, the lack of anti-ship strike training, unwillingness to attack enemy warships by day, and inability to hit them when under way. 'Quite untrained for sea work', it was little surprise that bombing was 'inaccurate and ineffective'.[63] Cunningham expostulated that 'Yet again we are learning the lesson of the lack of shore-based long-range torpedo-bomber aircraft and of their enormous value to the enemy' and he was 'continually pressing' for aerial mining beyond naval air range. He noted that 'the German reconnaissance and bombing performances are infinitely better than ours, neither does our record approach the Italians in efficiency'. In exasperation, he wrote 'I can't get the RAF to see that it is all wrong for our ships to be bombed all day and that the enemy ships go unattacked for the three days they were in the Central Mediterranean.'[64]

The solution was

> ... more aircraft diverted to fleet cooperation and personnel that is trained in work over the sea and we shan't get these without ... a special organisation running them in close touch with us.[65]

Somerville and Cunningham had 'pressed for the allotment of air forces specifically for naval cooperation' on several occasions but the RAF 'was unable to agree ... that air forces should be locked up for this purpose'. To do so would be uneconomical since naval forces were not always at sea; it was prepared only to support specific operations.[66] The Navy demanded Mediterranean versions of Coastal Command, which was under Admiralty operational control. Somerville obtained No. 200 Naval Cooperation Group at Gibraltar but Cunningham, 'in no mood for a compromise', had to fight a 'pitched battle' with Tedder. The issue was resolved in London and No. 201 Naval Cooperation Group was set up in October 1941. By February 1942, it had become a balanced force of 16 squadrons.[67]

The RAF's reluctance was the result not only of a critical shortage of aircraft but also of different strategic concepts, the desire of the junior service to preserve its independence, and a clash of personalities. Cunningham enjoyed excellent relations with Longmore, AOC-in-C, Middle East, until May 1941, but disliked and distrusted his successor, Tedder.[68] Cunningham's exasperation reached a peak during the Greek and Cretan debacles: 'Why the authorities at home could not see the danger of our situation in the Mediterranean without air support passed my comprehension.' Thus, the abiding memory of 1941 for the British seaman was: 'There on watch like birds of ill omen silhouetted against the early dawn, hung four Ju88s.'[69]

By 1942, British sea power in the Mediterranean had been reduced to its lowest ebb for two hundred years. Force H, which had lost *Ark Royal* in November 1941, was a pale shadow of its former self, while the Mediterranean Fleet was reduced to a handful of light cruisers and destroyers. Thus the Admiralty considered withdrawing all major units from the Mediterranean, replacing them by shore-based aircraft. Momentarily, in December 1941, Cunningham ' rather grudgingly admitted that it might be possible to control the Central Mediterranean waters with air forces instead of surface forces'. However, the next two Italian convoys reached Tripoli undetected and Cunningham 'learnt the utter futility of our air forces over the sea'. He was convinced that 'Battleships can only be replaced by air forces trained in sea operations consisting of adequate reconnaissance and striking forces operating under my close control.'[70] Somerville had left in January 1942 and by March, Cunningham, reflecting 'there is now no fleet to go to sea in', was about to do so, remarking ruefully that 'our lack of air power, and the huge superiority of the Luftwaffe, had dominated the whole situation in the Mediterranean'.[71] By June 1942, the entire British position in the Mediterranean and Middle East was at risk. Cunningham, now in Washington, declared that

> ... control [of the Mediterranean] has lapsed to an alarming extent owing to our weakened sea power which is due in part to war losses and weakness in the air and in part to the enemy success on land in capturing the important air and sea bases which we need. ... Our reverses ... are due to our inability to provide sufficient strength at sea to enable our forces and their supplies to pass unhindered whilst denying the vital routes to the enemy. In modern war sea power is compounded of surface force and its essential component in the form of air support.[72]

Air power nevertheless conferred many benefits on the Royal Navy. Carriers became indispensable, versatile capital ships projecting sea power up to 200 miles. Both Somerville and Cunningham maximised the multi-role capabilities of their carriers. Aware that they were priceless and vulnerable, they resisted their employment on minor operations. The Fleet Air Arm struck terror into the Italian fleet. At Taranto, 21 lumbering Swordfish dispatched in a few minutes 3 battleships which the British battle-squadron could not reach. At Matapan, 6 of *Formidable's* Albacores saved Pridham-Wippell's cruisers from the superior and faster Italian fleet when the British battleships were still well out of range; otherwise, it might have been the Italians who went home with the scalps of 3 cruisers. Moreover, a handful of obsolescent fleet fighters enabled the Navy to defy the formidable Regia Aeronautica, establishing control of the Central Mediterranean and making possible the speedy reinforcement of Malta and the Middle East at vital moments. There were, however, too few carriers and their capacity was too small, their aircraft (hampered by multiple roles) too limited, their technique too primitive, for them to have the impact of their counterparts in the Pacific war. Incapable of overwhelming battleships under way, they were intended only to slow the enemy, delivering him to the battle fleet.

Though carriers greatly enhanced British sea power, Axis air power imposed severe limitations. Enemy bombing ensured that Malta was not a 'cost effective' military investment during 1940–42. Comprehensive Axis reconnaissance generally denied Somerville and Cunningham the element of surprise; Taranto, Matapan, several undetected Malta convoys, and the unmolested bombardments of Tripoli and Genoa testified to what could be achieved when bad weather, engagements elsewhere, or breakdowns in communications deprived the enemy of vital knowledge. Ceaseless bombing undermined morale; AA gunfire was not generally effective in any navy until the days of proximity fuses, sensitive radar and massed barrages in 1944–45. The agonies endured by seamen off Crete even permeated to the stalwart Cunningham. Enemy air power also underlined the imperative necessity of integrating the land, sea, and air campaigns; the Navy required the Army to hold Cyrenaica so that the RAF could fly from its airfields in defence of bases, the Suez Canal, convoys and other naval operations and thus enable the fleet to reinforce the Middle East and offer inshore support to the desert army. The RAF lacked not only the aircraft numbers and types required but also adequate maritime training and organisation and a sufficiently flexible strategic vision. At sea, more elaborate ruses and defensive precautions were necessary, radar was vital and sustained reconnaissance in depth was at a premium.

The Luftwaffe made naval operations costly as the deadly skills of massed dive-bombers were brought to bear on ships generally unprotected by fighters; it displayed 'economy of force', reaping rich rewards for minimal losses. Between April and December 1941, British Mediterranean naval strength sank to a parlous state, its losses attributable largely to aircraft, supported by U-boats, mines, and human torpedoes. Confined to the margins, total naval withdrawal was seriously considered, proof of air power's ability to nullify and destroy sea power inadequately defended by its own air forces.[73]

Somerville and Cunningham, though wary of untested enemy air power, were determined to command the sea in Nelsonian fashion. That they were able to do so was testimony to the courage of their men, their exploitation of naval aviation, the intermittently effective support of the RAF, and their determination to carry out their duties in the face of overwhelming enemy air power and grievous, indeed crippling, losses. They came to appreciate the interdependence of air and sea power in the realisation of the Navy's objectives in the modern age.

NOTES

Sources: The papers of Admiral of the Fleet Viscount Cunningham of Hyndhope, Manuscripts Division, British Library (BL Add Mss); the papers of Admiral of the Fleet Sir James Somerville, Churchill Archives Centre, Churchill College, Cambridge (SMVL); Cabinet (CAB) and Admiralty (ADM) records, Public Record Office. I am indebted to John Somerville, son of the late Admiral, for his comments on the paper.

1. Pound to Cunningham, 20 May 1940, BL Add Mss 52560.
2. Cunningham to Pound, 13 July 1940, BL Add Mss 52560.
3. Cunningham to Pound, 3 August 1940, BL Add Mss 52561.
4. Somerville, *Report of Proceedings, 26 Aug–14 Sept 1941*, SMVL 7/13 (hereafter *R of P*).
5. Cunningham to Pound, 3 August 1940, BL Add Mss 52561.
6. Cunningham to Pound, 16 October 1940, BL Add Mss 52561.
7. Somerville to Cunningham, 11 June 1941, BL Add Mss 52563.
8. Somerville to his wife, 10 November 1940, SMVL 3/22.
9. Cunningham to Pound, 13 July 1940, BL Add Mss 52560.
10. Cunningham, *Report of an Action with the Italian Fleet, 9 July 1940*, CAB 106/338; Cunningham to Pound, 10 September 1940, BL Add Mss 52561; to V-Adm Blake, 29 August 1940, BL Add Mss 52568.
11. Cunningham to Pound, 7 June 1940, BL Add Mss 52566; 3 August 1940, BL Add Mss 52561; Somerville, *R of P, 10–25 Aug 1940*, ADM 199/391; to

Blake, 17 October 1940, SMVL 7/28; *R of P, 1–8 March 1941*, SMVL 7/7; 1–9 Nov 1941, SMVL 7/16; Cunningham, *A Sailor's Odyssey* (London, 1951), pp. 280, 288.

12. Cunningham to Pound, 1 August 1939, 29 May 1940, 27 June 1940; Pound to Cunningham, 18 August 1939, 6 June 1940, 24 July 1940, BL Add Mss 52560; to Blake, 29 August 1940, BL Add Mss 52568; Cs-in-C, Middle East, Cttee., 11 September 1940, CAB 106/722; *A Sailor's Odyssey*, p. 257. I. S. O. Playfair, *The Mediterranean and Middle East*, vol. 2 (London, HMSO, 1959), pp. 43–4.

13. Somerville to his wife, 28 November 1940, SMVL 3/22; *R of P, 7–11 Jan 1941*, SMVL 7/6; *Report on Operation HALBERD, 24–30 Sept 1941*, SMVL 7/15.

14. Somerville to Blake, 4 September 1940, SMVL 7/28. 'Blued' meant a turn together.

15. Somerville to Adm North, 14 May 1941, NORTH 2/8 (Churchill Archives); *R of P, 28 April–12 May 1941*, SMVL 7/12.

16. *A Sailor's Odyssey*, p. 273; Somerville, *R of P, 30 Aug–3 Sept 1940*, SMVL 7/4; to Blake, 4 September 1940, SMVL 7/28; *R of P, 7–11 Nov 1940*, SMVL 7/5; *R of P, 12–20 Jan 1941*, SMVL 7/6; *Report on Operation HALBERD, 24–30 Sept 1941*, SMVL 7/15; Cunningham to R-Adm England, 23 November 1940, CUNN 5/3 (Churchill Archives).

17. Somerville, *R of P, 30 Aug–3 Sept 1940*, SMVL 7/4.

18. M. Gilbert, *Winston S. Churchill*, vol. 6, *Finest Hour, 1939–41* (London, 1983), pp. 771–2; *A Sailor's Odyssey*, p. 298; Cunningham to Pound, 13 July 1940, Pound to Cunningham, 24 July 1940, BL Add MSS 52560.

19. Somerville, *R of P, 7–11 Nov, 29 Nov–14 Dec 1940*, SMVL 7/5; *Observations on the Action off Cape Spartivento*, 18 December 1940, SMVL 7/21; *R of P, 26 Aug–14 Sept 1941*, SMVL 7/13; *A Sailor's Odyssey*, p. 263.

20. Lieut. Mark Somerville to Somerville, 12 December 1940 (in John Somerville's possession).

21. Somerville, *R of P, 30 July–9 Aug 1940*, ADM 199/391; to his wife, 4 October 1940, SMVL 3/22; to Blake, 17 Oct 1940, SMVL 7/28.

22. Somerville to Blake, 7 July 1940, SMVL 7/28; to his wife, 2 August 1940, SMVL 3/22; and e.g., *R of P, 30 Aug–3 Sept 1940*, SMVL7/4; to North, 26 August 1941, NORTH 2/8.

23. Somerville, *Observations on the Action off Cape Spartivento*, 18 December 1940, SMVL 7/21.

24. Somerville, *R of P, 19–29 Nov 1940*, SMVL 7/5; 12–20 Jan 1941, SMVL 7/6.

25. Cunningham to Pound, 15 June, 13 July 1940, BL Add Mss 52560.

26. Cunningham, *Fleet Air Arm Operations against Taranto on 11 Nov 1940*, CAB106/616; Cunningham to England, 23 November 1940, CUNN 5/3.

27. Cunningham, *Despatch on the Battle of Matapan*, 11 November 1941, CAB 106/628.

28. V-Adm Royle to Somerville, 28 December 1940, SMVL 7/21.

29. Cunningham, *Report on Operation EXCESS*, 19 March 1941, CAB 106/346.

30. Cunningham, *Report on Operation COLLAR*, 20 July 1941, ADM 199/797; *A Sailor's Odyssey*, pp. 302–304; Pound to Cunningham, 27 January, 8 February 1941, BL Add Mss 52561.
31. Cunningham to Pound, 11 March 1941, BL Add Mss 52561; to Pound, 22 April 1941, BL Add Mss 52567; to England, 1 May 1941, CUNN 5/3; Cunningham, *Despatch on Evacuation of the Army from Greece*, 1 July 1941, CAB 106/639.
32. Cunningham to Pound, 23 May 1941. BL Add Mss 52567.
33. Cs-in-C, Middle East, Cttee., 9 & 28 April 1941, CAB 106/722.
34. Cunningham, *Report on the Battle of Crete*, 4 August 1941, CAB 106/640.
35. *A Sailor's Odyssey*, p. 373; *Report on the Battle of Crete*, CAB 106/640.
36. *Report on the Battle of Crete*, CAB 106/640; *A Sailor's Odyssey*, pp. 370–86.
37. *A Sailor's Odyssey*, p. 374.
38. O. Warner, *Cunningham of Hyndhope: Admiral of the Fleet* (London, 1967), p. 150; Gilbert, *Churchill*, vol. 6, p. 1095; Chiefs of Staff to Cs-in-C, Middle East, 25 May 1941, Cunningham to Admiralty, 26 May 1941, BL Add Mss 52567.
39. Cunningham, *Report on the Battle of Crete*, CAB 106/640; to Pound, 30 May 1941, BL Add Mss 52561; to Admiralty, 26 May 1941, BL Add Mss 52567; to Rear Admiral H. M. Burrough, 30 June 1941, CUNN 5/2; O. Warner, *Admiral of the Fleet: The Life of Sir Charles Lambe* (London, 1969), p. 101.
40. Somerville to Cunningham, 12 June 1941, SMVL.
41. Cunningham, *Report on the Battle of Crete*, CAB 106/640; to Admiralty, 26 May 1941, to Pound, 31 May 1941, BL Add Mss 52567.
42. Cunningham to Pound, 30 May 1941, BL Add Mss 52561.
43. Cunningham to Pound, 28 May 1941, BL Add Mss 52567.
44. Cunningham to Pound, 28 May 1941, BL Add Mss 52567.
45. Cunningham to Pound, 28 May 1941, BL Add Mss 52567.
46. Pound to Cunningham, 19 June 1941, BL Add Mss 52561; Cunningham to Pound, 2 November 1941, BL Add Mss 52567.
47. *A Sailor's Odyssey*, p. 309.
48. Cunningham to Pound, 30 May 1941, BL Add Mss 52561; to Pound, 10 April 1941, BL Add Mss 52567.
49. Cunningham to Pound, 15 August, 28 December 1941, BL Add Mss 52561; Cs-in-C, Middle East, Cttee., 4 June 1941, CAB 106/722; John Somerville (a destroyer officer on the Tobruk run, 1940–41) to the author, 8 June 1994; Playfair, *The Mediterranean and Middle East*, vol. 3, pp. 24–6.
50. *A Sailor's Odyssey*, p. 421; Cunningham to Pound, 18 January 1941, BL Add Mss 52561.
51. Cunningham to Pound, 17 March 1941, BL Add Mss 52567; to Pound, 3 May 1941, BL Add Mss 52561.
52. Churchill to Cs-in-C, Middle East, 16 April 1941, and subsequent correspondence with Cunningham, BL Add Mss 52567; Pound to Cunningham, 3 September 1941, BL Add Mss 52561.
53. Cunningham to Admiralty, 10 January 1942, BL Add Mss 52567; *A Sailor's Odyssey*, p. 421.

54. V-Adm Ford to Cunningham, 26 October 1941, BL Add Mss 52569; 3 and 19 January 1942, BL Add Mss 52570
55. V-Adm Leatham to Cunningham, 12 February 1942, BL Add Mss 52570.
56. Leatham to Cunningham, 24 January, 12 and 25 March 1942, BL Add Mss 52570; Cunningham to V-Adm Moore, 9 January 1942, BL Add Mss 52561; *A Sailor's Odyssey*, pp. 457–8; Playfair, vol. 3, p. 173.
57. Cunningham to Pound, 6 and 14 February 1942, BL Add Mss 52567; *A Sailor's Odyssey*, p. 391.
58. Leatham to Cunningham, 12 March 1942, BL Add Mss 52570; *A Sailor's Odyssey*, pp. 457–8.
59. Cunningham to Admiralty, 25 April 1941, BL Add Mss 52567.
60. Churchill to Cunningham, 26 April and 1 May 1941; Cunningham to Churchill, 29 April and 2 May 1941, BL Add Mss 52567.
61. Cunningham to Churchill, 29 April and 2 May 1941, BL Add Mss 52567; Somerville to Cunningham, 11 June 1941, BL Add Mss 52563.
62. Cunningham, reports of operations on 9 July 1940, CAB 106/338; 17 August 1940 and 9–15 October 1940, ADM 199/466; 8–14 November 1940, CAB 106/616; Somerville, *R of P, 14–24 Sept 1941*, SMVL 7/14; *Report on HALBERD Convoy, 24–30 Sept 1941*, SMVL 7/15.
63. Somerville, *R of P, 29 Nov–14 Dec 1940*, SMVL 7/5; Pound to Cunningham, 24 October 1939, Cunningham to Pound, 18 December 1939, BL Add Mss 52560; to Pound, 22 April 1941, BL Add Mss 52567; to Pound, 25 July, 15 August, 28 December 1941, BL Add Mss 52561; S. W. Roskill, *Churchill and the Admirals* (London, 1977) p. 186.
64. Cunningham to Pound, 18 September, 14 October 1941, 28 December 1941, BL Add Mss 52561; to Pound, 26 November 1941, BL Add Mss 52566.
65. Cunningham to Pound, 25 July 1941, BL Add Mss 52561.
66. Cs-in-C, Middle East, Cttee., 4 June 1941, CAB 106/722.
67. Cunningham to R-Adm Willis, 12 June, 20 Nov 1941, CUNN 5/9.
68. Somerville to Cunningham, 12 June 1941, BL Add Mss 52563; Cunningham to Willis, 6 July 1941, CUNN 5/9.
69. *A Sailor's Odyssey*, p. 351; ADM 234/320, quoted in C. Barnett, *Engage the Enemy More Closely: The Royal Navy in the Second World War* (London, 1991), p. 361.
70. Cunningham to Moore, 9 Jan 1942, BL Add Mss 52561.
71. Cunningham to Pound, 15 March 1942, BL Add Mss 52561; *A Sailor's Odyssey*, p. 437.
72. Cunningham, *Memorandum on Command in the Middle East*, 10 June 1942, BL Add Mss 52561.
73. Pound to Cunningham and reply, 10 December 1941, Cunningham to Admiralty, 26 December 1941, BL Add Mss 52567; Cunningham to Moore, 9 January 1942, BL Add Mss 52561.

12 Seizing the Initiative: The Arctic Convoys 1944–45
Andrew D. Lambert

Victory in the Second World War was secured by the sound application of overwhelming resources. In the context of 1939–45, a total war, victory required the allies to reduce the axis to a position where they *could not* fight on. In a limited war the enemy has only to be reduced to the position where he *will not* fight on. The former is not achieved by defensive success, or superior tactical skill; it requires one side to apply superior resources to seize and maintain the strategic initiative, impose battle on the enemy and grind down his forces in campaigns of attrition.

Second World War maritime strategies reflected the nature of the conflict. Britain and her allies wanted to use the sea to move men, munitions and raw materials around the world. Germany tried to deny them this capability. After a period in which lack of resources forced the allies onto the defensive, mid-1940 to early 1943, they shifted to an offensive strategy, once they had the resources to pursue U-boats to destruction, without compromising the security of convoys. Within two months U-Boat Command ended pack operations in the Atlantic. However, as the U-boats remained a threat to Operation Overlord, they had to be engaged. The Arctic convoys, with other operations in the Northern Seas, provided the best opportunity.

The Arctic convoys of the period 1944–45 carried over one million tons of supplies to Russia, much of which remained unused at the end of the war, and helped to sustain the Grand Alliance. However, their most important role after 1943 was to bring the German forces based in Norway to battle. As the strategic situation improved, after U-boat Command lost its French bases, Britain adopted an offensive strategy focused on Norway. The Arctic convoys were integral to this strategy, for they alone could draw the enemy into attacking, the time when he proved most vulnerable. They were not run to provide this opportunity, but they were exploited for this purpose.

This strategy was only possible because the strategic and tactical balance had shifted firmly in favour of Britain. When Dönitz abandoned

Atlantic pack operations he was relying on the new Type XXI submarine to restart the campaign. In the interval older boats, particularly those without *Schnorchel*, were vulnerable. These boats could have been withdrawn and their crews transferred to the Type XXI, to rebuild morale and enhance effectiveness. Well aware of the advanced U-boats, the British exploited the fact that the Arctic was a defensive commitment for the Germans. Simply pushing the convoys through forced the U-boats to engage, something that no amount of 'offensive' activity could achieve. The object was to sink U-boats. Linked assaults on coastal shipping, and the *Tirpitz*, exploited German fears that Norway would be invaded.

The Arctic convoys allowed the Royal Navy to maintain the initiative so hard won in the Atlantic. By portraying the anti-submarine campaigns of 1939–45 as 'defensive' victories, existing accounts mislead. Although tactically defensive, the Arctic operations of 1944–45 had an offensive strategic purpose. Only by seizing and maintaining the initiative could the enemy be defeated, and this was the aim of Western Approaches Command under Admiral Sir Max Horton. Horton wanted to sustain the allied successes of mid-1943 in an attempt to break U-boat morale.

In 1944–45 there were eleven round-trip convoys to Northern Russia. While they sustained light losses, their escorts destroyed a significant number of U-boats. In 1943 convoy escorts did not sink a single U-boat, in 1944–45 they accounted for 21, shore-based aircraft added 4, making 25 from a wartime total of 32. By contrast U-boats had only sunk 1 escort before 1944, thereafter they accounted for 7, 4 of them in 1945. In 1943, there were no mercantile casualties, in 1944–45, 11. In the first half of 1944 the Germans were defeated. Hitherto success had been measured by the 'safe and timely arrival' of convoys, but by the time the British suspended the convoys to release resources for 'Overlord', the criteria had become U-boat kills. The most recent history of the Royal Navy in World War Two assumes that the object of the convoys was restricted to 'safe and timely arrival' throughout the war.[1] This approach links the convoys with the Home Fleet, concentrates on early difficulties, the dispersal of PQ17, and the destruction of two German capital ships, which is a major distortion. The Arctic was a sub-theatre of the Battle of the Atlantic.[2]

Down to the end of 1943 convoys to Northern Russia had been menaced by German capital ships, submarines and approximately 100 combat aircraft.[3] The surface threat, allied to the shift of resources from the Home Fleet to Western Approaches and the Mediterranean, forced the suspension of convoys in March 1943, but they were resumed in November, following the midget submarine attack on *Tirpitz*. The destruction of *Scharnhorst* removed the surface threat, until *Tirpitz* could be repaired.

Concurrently allied success in the Atlantic released experienced ASW forces from Western Approaches Command. The combination of a reduction in the dimensions of threat, with a marked increase in escort strength prompted a new approach to convoy operations. The Germans responded with new U-boat tactics. In turn these shifted the emphasis of British operations. As Bletchley Park was normally reading U-Boat and Air Force signals on a real-time basis it is a measure of the difficulty of convoy operations in Arctic waters that there were still casualties.

Defeat in the Atlantic forced Dönitz to shift resources to other theatres, in search of weak defences and a diversionary effect, until the Type XXI entered service. Serious reverses on the Russian front emphasised the need to stop the Murmansk convoys. Consequently the Arctic was the only area where pack attacks continued. In December 1943 and January 1944 Dönitz responded to the new convoys by moving 20 Atlantic U-boats to Norway, raising the number on station to 33. He considered the Arctic suitable for pack operations with old boats, largely because air reconnaissance was available to locate convoys in the North Channel in time to form patrol lines.[4] The Norway flotilla was not accorded priority for new equipment, notably the *Schnorchel*. The first boat equipped at Bergen only reached the Arctic in mid-September 1944.[5] Furthermore while Horton recognised the shift into distant theatres as a diversion, the Arctic, as a sub-theatre of the Atlantic, was reinforced by Western Approaches.

The first convoy of 1944, JW56A, left Loch Ewe on 12 January 1944. It comprised 20 ships escorted by 9 destroyers and 2 corvettes. Despite Ultra intelligence 3 ships were sunk by a group of 10 U-boats in the Bear Island passage, losses attributed to the limited experience of some Home Fleet escorts. The U-boats then moved west to intercept the second convoy, JW56B. When Vice Admiral Sir Bruce Fraser, C-in-C Home Fleet, received Ultra intelligence of this concentration, he cancelled the return convoy RA56A and recalled the escorts to reinforce JW56B. Just as the U-boats, now 15 strong, encountered JW56B the escort doubled, with those from JW56A acting as a Support Group; in consequence the U-boats never came close to the convoy. The destroyer *Hardy* was lost following a hit by a Gnat homing torpedo, but U.314 was sunk by the escort.[6] The 37-ship convoy RA56, covered by 23 escorts was only located by the Luftwaffe north of Bear Island, and then they reported it to be proceeding east.[7]

The JW-RA56 convoys demonstrated that escort strength would have to be increased, as there was simply too little room around Bear Island for effective evasive routing. A larger convoy with an adequate escort would, as Horton recognised, translate successful defence into attack.[8] In June 1943 Horton recognised that he had secured the initiative, and he determined to maintain it, shifting experienced Escort and Support Groups to the Arctic. His aim was to crack the will of the enemy by inflicting crippling losses.[9]

After RA56, the largest convoy to date, Fraser decided to sail future convoys in a single, large, formation. This reflected the reduced surface threat and new tactics. Additional escorts could establish a double screen, with an escort carrier from Western Approaches, to deal with air shadowers and surfaced U-boats. JW57 sailed from Loch Ewe on 20 February with 42 ships, 1 tanker, the escort carrier *Chaser*, the light cruiser *Black Prince*, Vice Admiral Glennie (1st Cruiser Squadron), and 17 destroyers. Fraser could now supply the escort commander with Ultra, which immediately revealed a fourteen-boat patrol line. Air contact was made on the 23rd, and the U-boats engaged the escort the following day, but could not reach the convoy. U.713 was sunk by *Keppel*, and U.601 by a Coastal Command Catalina working at extreme range, a major benefit of real-time Ultra; *Matabele* was sunk by Gnat the following night. On the 28th the U-boats were called off.

The 31-ship return convoy RA57 left the Kola Inlet on 2nd March. Warned by Ultra that U-boats were grouping north-west of the inlet, Fraser arranged for increased Russian air patrols and ordered a wide eastward detour. This gave the convoy a two-day start, which was fortunate as the weather was too severe for carrier operations. The U-boats located the convoy on the 4th, just as the weather improved, only to lose U.472, U.336, and U.973 to air attack on consecutive days; two more were badly damaged. One ship was lost.

In his report on the JW-RA57 convoys, Fraser, who appreciated the '*offensive* value of convoy' for Western Approaches, paid particular attention to the success of Western Approaches Support Group B1, keeping the U-boats outside the convoy screen, and the value of the aircraft.[10] Aircraft added a crucial element to convoy defence. They could follow DF fixes and force submarines down more quickly and economically than destroyers, with no risk from Gnat and without compromising the outer screen that kept the enemy away from the merchant ships.

Dönitz accepted that carrier aircraft denied the U-boats any opportunity to close the convoy and requested aircraft to deal with the carriers. Without air cover, tactics had to change; on March 20 boats were ordered to stay submerged all day, attack on the first night and then withdraw quickly. These were the tactics of the last Atlantic operations; it is indicative of British success that they were adopted within range of German air cover. As the period of near permanent daylight was approaching Dönitz recognised that success would be limited.[11]

For the British the safe arrival of these convoys, with the destruction of five U-boats was a major success. At the Admiralty the 'offensive capacity of air and surface escorts' was discussed. Two escort carriers accompanied the next convoy, with two Western Approaches Support Groups. The carriers helped to compensate for the poor sonar conditions found in Arctic waters, and could deal with shadowing aircraft.

The 49-ship JW58 sailed on 27 March covered by 20 destroyers, 5 sloops, 4 corvettes, the cruiser *Diadem*, Rear Admiral Dalrymple-Hamilton (10th Cruiser Squadron) and the 2 carriers. German aircraft located it on the 30th; 6 were shot down. That evening the U-boats concentrated in the Bear Island passage. By nightfall on the 31st 16 were in position. U.961 had been sunk on the 29th while on passage to the Atlantic; 3 more (U.355, U.360, U.288) were destroyed on the 31st and 2 April by the carrier aircraft and surface escorts. The convoy arrived safely. RA58 was unmolested. Dalrymple-Hamilton recognised that while the primary role of the Home Fleet was 'safe and timely arrival' the Western Approaches Escort Groups had been deployed to sink submarines.[12]

Commenting on JW-RA58 Horton agreed that at least two carriers should accompany each convoy. His thinking reflected both a shortage of targets in the Atlantic and the offensive emphasis of Western Approaches ASW policy. He observed the Arctic:

> represents the only prolific area remaining where heavy losses can still be inflicted on both enemy U-boats and long-range aircraft, and this consideration should in no way become secondary in importance to securing the safe and timely arrival of the convoy.

Fraser did not agree, 'I still consider that the safe arrival of the convoy is the primary object of these operations'.[13]

This distinction would become more significant in the last twelve months of the war. However, the failure of evasive routing, even with real-time high-grade intelligence, demonstrated that the convoys would have to be fought through, and if they were U-boats would be sunk. Concurrently with JW58 the Home Fleet staged a carrier strike on *Tirpitz*, leaving her disabled for three months.

After RA58 the convoy cycle was suspended, to release escorts for 'Overlord'. In April Rear Admiral McGrigor led a strong escort comprising 2 carriers, a cruiser, 16 destroyers and 4 frigates to recover ships from Russia. As RA59, 45 ships left for home on 28 April. Twelve U-boats concentrated in the Bear Island channel, sinking one merchant ship on the 30th, but three U-boats, (U.277, U.959, and U.674), were sunk by

Fencer's experienced aircrew. Roskill attributes the success of this period to the carriers; Dönitz agreed, arguing that if only the submarines could get close to the convoy they would still sink ships; he urged Goering to redeploy strike aircraft from the Mediterranean.[14]

While the convoys were suspended, the Home Fleet staged carrier attacks on the German inshore traffic to reinforce German fears that Norway would be invaded, as part of Operation 'Fortitude (North)'. This kept 22 U-boats in harbour.[15]

On D-Day+1 Churchill realised that destroyer casualties off Normandy were far lower than anticipated, and decided to resume the convoys, if the United States could provide cargoes.[16] The new C-in-C Home Fleet, Admiral Sir Henry Moore, would have to contend with an enemy increasingly fitted with *Schnorchel*, and a renewed surface threat. Ultra warnings of a new patrol line led Coastal Command 18 Group to conduct a series of offensive patrols between 17 and 24 July, sinking three boats, (U.361, U.742, and U.992), all non-*Schnorchel* units. Once *Schnorchel* had been fitted shore-based air patrols could only keep the U-boats submerged, crippling their mobility.

JW59 sailed from Loch Ewe on 15 August with 33 freighters, a rescue ship and 11 Soviet submarine-chasers, escorted by the carriers *Vindex*, for the first time as the flagship of Rear Admiral Dalrymple-Hamilton, and *Striker*, a cruiser, 7 destroyers and 11 escorts. Shifting the Admiral's flag into a carrier reflected the importance of air operations to the escort, and the advantages of combining the command and control facilities of the air and sea units in one ship. Concurrently Admiral Moore conducted an unsuccessful attack on *Tirpitz*.[17] The nine-boat patrol line in the Barents Sea could not reach the merchant ships, and although the U.344 sank the sloop *Kite* with a Gnat on the 21st, she was destroyed by a Swordfish the following day. JW59 demonstrated that U-boats could still score the occasional success, but these were normally against the escort, and prohibitively expensive.

RA59A, only nine strong, left Kola on the 28th, sinking U.394 the same day. The remainder of the passage was uneventful. Home Fleet carrier operations against coastal shipping had been so effective that the U-boats had been diverted to Scapa Flow. JW60 left Loch Ewe on 15 September, 30 ships, with 2 carriers, a cruiser and 12 escorts. There was no contact and the convoy reached Kola on the 23rd. RA60, also 30 strong, sailed on the 28th. Twelve U-boats were waiting in two groups. The following day the convoy ran right over U.310, which torpedoed two ships; later a Swordfish sank U.921.

The RAF crippled *Tirpitz* on 15 September, and sank her on 12 November. At the same time U-Boat Command had to change tactics.

Mobile operations by conventional boats were impossible when they were forced to remain submerged all day by aircraft. *Schnorchel* boats would abandon the Bear Island passage and Barents Sea and lie in wait off the Kola Inlet, hoping to ambush the convoy as the escort was constricted, or on the return, before it had formed.[18] Ultra ensured that Admiral Moore was aware of the problem, and he responded by sending two Support Groups to attack the concentration.

JW61 comprising 29 ships, 3 carriers, 1 cruiser, and 24 escorts left Britain on 20 October. Off Kola 18 U-boats formed. When the convoy reached Bear Island unmolested the 21st and 24th Escort Groups were sent ahead. Despite bad weather and poor sonar conditions they suppressed the U-boats. RA61, with 33 ships, left on 2 November. Again two escort groups went ahead, the frigate *Mounsey* being damaged by a Gnat. There were no further casualties.

At this time approximately 70 torpedo-bombers moved from the Mediterranean to Norway; largely in response to Home Fleet carrier attacks, Dönitz had already been obliged to make the carriers his priority.[19] The 28-ship JW62 left Loch Ewe on 29 November. RA62 left Kola on the 10th of December, the escort having sunk U.387 the previous day in clearing the passage. A Swordfish accounted for U.365 on the 13th.

In the second half of 1944 159 ships left for Russia, all arrived safely; 100 set out for home, only 2 were lost, along with 1 sloop. In return 9 U-boats were destroyed. This was the most successful period of the Arctic convoys. Thereafter the old tactics, based on radar, HF/DF, aircraft and Ultra proved less successful as U-boats stayed submerged, ceased talking and, belatedly, improved the security of Enigma. The link with Western Approaches and the Atlantic theatre was reinforced when the Germans abandoned the Biscay ports in the autumn. Submarines heading for the Atlantic now crossed the Arctic convoy route, and at least one was sunk by Arctic escorts. Furthermore the choke points around the North of Scotland and the related minefields were patrolled. This marked a return to the strategy of 1939–40, under more favourable circumstances.[20]

By early 1945 the Home Fleet, much reduced by the demands of the Pacific, comprised only seven cruisers, four destroyer flotillas and eight escort carriers, relying on Western Approaches for Escort and Support Groups. The Russians could not help, even in the Kola Inlet where the U-boats congregated. This concentration to attack the convoy at its destination rendered Atlantic ideas on 'safe and timely arrival' irrelevant. The shipping would have to be fought through. However, the Germans still required some warning; changing the cycle, and the weakness of German intelligence and reconnaissance, gave JW-RA63 a free trip.

Convoy JW64 left Greenock on 3 February with 26 ships, 2 carriers, 1 cruiser and 17 escorts. This time the Germans established and held air contact almost continuously. Eight U-boats were deployed, and on the 7th 48 torpedo-bombers were sent, but missed the convoy. Contact was re-established at night on the 8th and 9th as the carriers had no night fighters. On the 10th 30 aircraft attacked, but were beaten off with heavy losses. Although up to 11 U-boats were active the only contact resulted in the loss of a corvette in the Kola Inlet.

RA64 met with sterner opposition, largely from the weather. Forewarned of trouble off Kola by Russian losses Admiral McGrigor sent his escorts to clear the passage late on the 16th. *Lark* and *Alnwick Castle* sank U.425 that evening. RA64, with 34 ships, left on 17 February, running into trouble almost immediately. Six submarines were off the Inlet, U.968 crippled *Lark* and sank a merchant ship, another boat destroyed the corvette *Bluebell*. The following day the weather deteriorated, ending flying and dispersing the convoy. German air activity increased, but an attack on the 20th demonstrated the futility of torpedo-bombing against fighters and radar-controlled guns, although they sank a straggler on the 23rd. Admiral McGrigor was forced to detach several escorts which ran low on fuel, but shore-based air cover and fresh destroyers ensured that there were no losses to U-boats. The severe weather resulted in twelve of the sixteen destroyers that escorted RA64 being docked for hull repairs.

McGrigor reported the need for night fighters, and long endurance escorts to operate in the Kola Inlet while the main escort force turned round. The persistence of the U-boats, and their continuing ability to sink ships was worrying, particularly in view of the long-anticipated arrival of advanced boats. Equally worrying was the fact that U-boat command had finally tightened up signals procedure, providing each boat with an individual code. These came into effect between November 1944 and February 1945. Sinkings rose everywhere, including the Arctic.[21] Bletchley Park claimed they could have cracked the system, had the war continued, but the concurrent loss of Ultra and the arrival of Type XXI boats would have strained British resources. Consequently Britain was anxious to terminate the JW series by the middle of 1945.

In January, Churchill requested the Admiralty to consider sending all Russian cargoes via the Black Sea.[22] The request was not unwelcome at the Admiralty. The First Sea Lord, Admiral Cunningham, saw the Arctic as 'one of our major and most difficult commitments', and shared the view of many that the Royal Navy received neither help nor hospitality from their allies.[23] Cunningham, who lacked Western Approaches experience, and did not have a close relationship with Horton, undervalued Arctic operations.[24] The Admiralty observed that the Arctic convoys were a full-time task for two Escort Groups, 16 ships, and a major task, although not the only one, for 2 escort carriers, 1 cruiser and 10 fleet destroyers. In February 200,000 tons of stores were still lying on the quays at Murmansk. Short of rail capacity, the Russians had moved the ammunition, machinery, and vehicles, but left food, machine tools, and raw materials lying in the open. In April, the War Cabinet asked the Americans to support a joint approach to advise the Russians that the Arctic convoys would be ended in favour of the Black Sea route.[25]

JW65 left Greenock on 11 March. Six days earlier the Germans sent six *Schnorchel* boats to patrol west of Bear Island, others congregated off Kola. Despite excellent weather the Luftwaffe failed to locate the convoy, forcing the Germans to rely on traffic analysis. As JW65 approached Kola on 20 March the weather broke, six U-boats closed in, sinking the sloop *Lapwing* and two ships. Forewarned of the U-boat ambush in the Kola Inlet RA65 used a new channel through the German minefield north of Murmansk, which allowed a more direct exit on the 23rd, while four escorts staged a demonstration in the old channel. There was no further contact, reflecting good radio discipline and poor Luftwaffe reconnaissance.

In late April, before the next convoy, the Russians belatedly allowed the Royal Navy to lay a deep minefield where the U-boats assembled, with immediate effect. The last convoy of the war, JW66, led by Rear Admiral Cunninghame-Graham, included 2 carriers, 1 cruiser, and 18 escorts. In addition, for the first time an Escort Group went ahead to clear the U-boat concentration. There were 21 boats at sea, 11 off Kola, with others en route. There were no losses on either side. Even the best escort could only hope to suppress *Schnorchel* boats in the heavily layered temperature bands found in the Arctic. The convoy was then escorted in by aircraft dropping sonobuoys. RA66 sailed on the 29th. Ten U-boats were still lying off Kola, but the preliminary sweep accounted for U.307, a textbook Squid kill, and U.286. That evening the frigate *Goodall* was sunk. This was the last contact of the war.[26] Concurrently a carrier strike on Narvik sank a U-boat and a depot ship. After VE-Day JW-RA67 was escorted, without incident.

The Arctic had provided the most severe test of the war; convoys were fought through in waters where air reconnaissance made evasion rare. The escort forces were large; by 1945 there were as many escorts as merchant ships, and most of the escorts were large, modern units. By 1945 the U-boat barrier was composed of *Schnorchel*-equipped boats with secure Enigma, and Gnat. Consequently the worst case scenario that post-war planners could conceive for the 1950s was a barrier of Soviet Type XXI derivatives blocking a critical route, with air and possible surface support.

The Arctic convoys have been widely studied, yet few have considered them as part of the Atlantic campaign that dominated the U-boat war. Roskill considered that the turning point in the Arctic came with PQ18 in September 1942, basing his argument on the low level of mercantile casualties sustained thereafter, and placed much of the credit for this with the escort carriers.[27] This analysis, based on 'safe and timely arrival' as the critical indicator, is not relevant to the Arctic convoys. Unlike the Atlantic convoys they were sustained by political objects, and were never critical to the British war effort, narrowly defined. They were suspended in periods of great danger, or great need elsewhere, notably for the Atlantic crisis of mid-1943 and 'Overlord'.

The Arctic was a sub-theatre of the Atlantic. The bulk of all Arctic shipping came from the United States, via the Atlantic. If losses in the Atlantic became insupportable there would be no Arctic convoys. Indeed the turning point in the Atlantic came at a time when the Arctic route had been suspended, releasing escorts for Support Groups. Until the Atlantic battle had been won the Arctic was a luxury. When the Arctic convoys resumed in late-1943 Horton had secured the initiative and was determined to break the will of the U-boat arm, by sinking U-boats. The U-boats had become combat shy, they had to be tempted to attack heavily escorted convoys, and would only do so in the Arctic. From February 1944 the critical factor in the Arctic was the ability of convoy escorts to inflict casualties on the enemy.

In 1943 the contending forces in the Arctic had been in balance, the tide turned in 1944, and although the German forces were increased and modernised, they continued to sustain heavy losses. By taking on the Norway flotilla the Royal Navy kept a large number of U-boats engaged in a secondary theatre during 'Overlord', and sustained the success of the last Atlantic battles, with serious impact on U-boat morale. The U-boat arm was not beaten by the ability of the allies to evade and beat off attacks; it was beaten because it suffered insupportable losses whenever it attacked. By 1945 carrier strikes were hitting U-boat bases and supply ships in Norway; Support Groups were detailed to attack known concentrations, ahead of convoys, and cruised in transit points. The U-boat was being hunted, with success. As this approach was an anathema to the early post-war analysts, who believed that such tactics had been responsible for the problems of 1939–41, it was ignored.

The Arctic was an effective battleground because the Germans considered the convoys were critical to the Eastern Front. German attacks persisted down to the end of the war, because it was the only way in which U-boats could support land operations. As a result the Arctic convoy became, as Peter Gretton observed, 'essentially offensive for it forced the enemy to give battle if he was to achieve his object'.[28] Superior resources and sound strategy allowed the Royal Navy to create a battle of attrition in the Arctic that the Germans could not win. The Naval Staff were convinced that had the positions been reversed the Royal Navy would have destroyed every convoy.[29]

The Arctic campaign demonstrated the ultimate futility of a submarine-based *guerre-de-course*. The only convoys to be threatened with complete destruction were those attacked by surface ships. The submarine, in 1939–45 form, was simply too vulnerable and slow to operate against adequate surface and air escorts. Dönitz's successes were produced by allied weakness, not by any inherent merit of his method. Only a balanced force could deal with convoys, escorts and single ships, by taking effective control of the sea, even if only locally and temporarily. By relying on one arm the Kriegsmarine was vulnerable to allied countermeasures. The U-boat was a weapon of denial; unaided it was incapable of obtaining or exercising control.

The Germans effectively stopped the Arctic convoys in 1943, but they were simply unable to match the sheer weight of allied resources deployed in 1944–45. Consequently their efforts led to a further erosion of the strength and morale of the U-boat arm. This was not an end in itself, merely part of the process of destroying Nazi Germany.

NOTES

For details of all Arctic convoys see B. Ruegg & A. Hague, *Convoys to Russia 1941–1945* (Kendal, 1992).

1. C. Barnett, *Engage the Enemy more Closely* (London, 1990), p. 744.
2. Ibid., pp. 695 and 730. PRO: ADM 234/369, Admiralty Staff History (1954).
3. Air Ministry, *The Rise and Fall of the German Air Force* (London, 1948), p. 357. German aircraft in Norway 13 April 1945; PRO: ADM 223/50.
4. Günther Hessler, *The U-Boat War in the Atlantic 1939–1945* (London, 1989), Pt. 3, p. 55. J. Mallman-Showell, ed., *The Führer Naval Conferences* (London, 1991), [*FNC*] pp. 311, 331, 369, 374, 377, 379.

5. Hessler, *U-Boat War*, p. 69. P. Padfield, *Dönitz* (London, 1986), p. 393.
6. F. H. Hinsley et al., *British Intelligence in the Second World War* (London, HMSO, 1979–90, 5 vols in 6) III, i, 269. 'Gnat' was the British name for the German T5 Zaunkönig acoustic homing torpedo; N. Campbell, *Naval Weapons of World War Two* (London, 1985), p. 264.
7. PRO: ADM 199/2027, Staff Analysis.
8. PRO: ADM 116/5456, Horton, 20 March 1943.
9. W. S. Chalmers, *Sir Max Horton and the Western Approaches* (London, 1954), pp. 192, 202 and 222.
10. R. Humble, *Fraser of North Cape* (London, 1983), p. 229. PRO: ADM 199/327 p. 239, Fraser to Admiralty 17 April 1944.
11. *FNC* 12–13 April 1944, p. 377.
12. S. W. Roskill, *The War at Sea, 1939–1945* (London, HMSO, 1954–61, 3 vols in 4) III, i, 272. Information provided by Commander M. Chichester, former flag-lieutenant to Vice-Admiral Dalrymple-Hamilton, at Exeter on 5 July 1994.
13. PRO: ADM 199/327, pp. 382–3, Horton to Fraser, 31 May 1944, Fraser to Admiralty, 9 June 1944.
14. Roskill, *War at Sea*, III, i, 280–1. *FNC*, 4–6 May 1944, p. 391.
15. Hinsley, *British Intelligence* V, 111–112 (this vol., by Sir Michael Howard, is also published separately)
16. F. L. Loewenheim, H. D. Langley & M. Jonas, eds, *Roosevelt and Churchill: Their Secret Wartime Correspondence* (London, 1975) pp. 460, 521, Churchill to Roosevelt 4 March and 7 June 1944.
17. David MacIntyre, *U-Boat Killer* (London, 1956) pp. 164–71.
18. *FNC*, 17 February 1945, p. 447.
19. *FNC*, 30 November and 3 December 1944, pp. 418–19.
20. A. D. Lambert, 'Seapower 1939–1940: Churchill and the Strategic Origins of the Battle of the Atlantic', *Journal of Strategic Studies* XVII, No. 1 (1994), pp. 86–108.
21. David Kahn, *Seizing the Enigma* (London, 1991), p. 262.
22. PRO: CAB 87/7, War Cabinet, 26 January 1945.
23. A. Cunningham, *A Sailor's Odyssey* (London, 1951), espec. p. 617.
24. F. Ruge, *The Soviets as Naval Opponents* (Annapolis, Md., 1979), pp. 176–8.
25. PRO: ADM 116/5402 on re-routing the convoys to Russia, 1945.
26. David Syrett, 'The last Murmansk Convoys 11 March–30 May 1945, *The Northern Mariner*, IV (1994), pp. 55–63.
27. Roskill, *War at Sea*, III, i, 261–2.
28. P. W. Gretton, *Maritime Strategy* (London, 1965), p. 156.
29. P. W. Gretton, *Former Naval Person* (London, 1968), p. 302.

13 Blockade and the Royal Navy
David Brown

Sir Julian Corbett, in *Some Principles of Maritime Strategy*[1], defined three roles for a fleet off an enemy port: *close blockade* to prevent the enemy's ships from putting to sea; *observation blockade* to induce the enemy to put to sea, with the object of bringing him to decisive action; and *commercial blockade* to prevent trade, or 'economic' shipping, from entering and leaving. The first two were purely military and, involving only the fighting ships of the two sides, they were clear-cut in their interpretation and execution. Commercial blockade would also have been straightforward if only the merchant fleets of the belligerents had been concerned, but this was seldom the case, for an awkward third party – neutral merchant shipping – was usually involved.

The neutrals, when they were genuinely impartial, were motivated by large profit margins to risk interception of their ventures, accepting, if grudgingly, that cargoes intended for an enemy could be regarded as 'lawful prize' by a captor whose right of stop and search was conferred by specific agreement or by common practice. But to be acceptable the risk had to be predictable, which it could not be if the blockading forces were stretched so thin that only a 'paper blockade' – declared but not consistently enforced – was possible or if the belligerents had different interpretations of contraband. Unsurprisingly, Britain and France, the one the principal exponent of blockade and the other the practitioner of a *guerre-de-course*, took diametrically opposed positions on this question. The French, who relied heavily upon neutral bottoms to supply their imports, declared that enemy goods in neutral vessels were not liable to seizure but that neutral goods in enemy vessels were liable to confiscation. The Royal Navy, on station to ensure that the enemy enjoyed neither aid nor comfort, confiscated enemy goods in neutral vessels but respected neutral goods in enemy vessels.

The conduct of blockade had to change with the introduction of new weapons. The range of shore batteries had increased but not beyond visibility distance: the predominantly British squadron in the Baltic in

1855 could still take a station close off Kronstadt – and, because this was now a steam navy, could stay there irrespective of the wind. Until, that is, the *Merlin's* wardroom crockery was broken when she ran into an infernal device planted in the water by the Russians. The mine pushed the blockading forces further out to sea but it could not, unaided, drive them away.

Agreement was eventually reached a year after the first wartime use of the naval mine. The signatories of the 1856 Paris Declaration arrived at a compromise which at last formally codified a common practice: only contraband of war – goods intended to support an enemy's war effort – was liable to seizure, whatever the nationality of the ship carrying it. The Declaration's ban on privateers was even more in Britain's favour, but not at all to her taste was the agreement that *'blockades, to be binding [on neutrals], had to be effective'*. More than once she had announced a 'paper' blockade but now the Royal Navy was bound to ensure that any blockade was *'maintained by a sufficient force really to prevent access to the coast of the enemy'*. The mid-nineteenth century reality was, of course, that only Britain, of all the signatories, did possess the force to mount an effective blockade from a standing start.

The last half century of the singularly ill-named *Pax Britannica* was marked by numerous squabbles and petty wars accompanied by direct and pacific blockades – the latter undertaken by neutrals (including Britain) attempting to subdue or localise a conflict. In the American Civil War the British participated in the unaccustomed role of the injured innocents – persecuted neutrals turning an honest penny running a less than complete blockade imposed by a state which had not signed the Declaration of Paris. On the other hand, the near-simultaneous Allied naval operations against the Shogunate princes scarcely called for blockade, for the last thing the mediaevalists wanted was any non-Japanese visiting their shores.

Numerous gatherings of jurists laid down further rules of blockade which tended to favour Britain. Thus the 1896 adoption by the Institute of International Law of the principles of 'conditional contraband' – ostensibly non-warlike goods which could be used for the benefit of the enemy's war effort, and 'continuous voyage' – the ultimate destination of the cargo, not its stops or trans-shipments en route, governed its status, was to hand in 1900 when, to isolate the Boer Republic, the Royal Navy imposed a blockade on the southern African coasts. Ships proceeding to the Boers' main sources of imports – the ports in the neutral Portuguese and German colonies – were stopped, searched and, when deemed to be carrying either agreed contraband or what the Royal Navy Prize Act described as 'provisional [i.e. conditional] contraband', were sent into a South African port for examination. The German Government protested but to no avail; Britain could legitimately invoke the doctrine of 'continuous voyage'.

The Russo-Japanese War provided more work for the lawyers but it was largely theoretical, for the Russians, who were trying to push the meaning of provisional contraband beyond what even the British would accept, had no way of establishing an effective blockade of Japan. The opening years of the twentieth century were accompanied by a belief, widespread among diplomats, if not more realistic communities, that the effects of wars should not be visited upon non-combatants.[2] The Hague Peace Conferences failed to agree on the principles of blockade but did agree on the need for an international Prize Court. The need to establish accepted rules for the latter led to the last major conference on the subject of blockade, in London in 1908–1909. The ensuing Declaration undermined the strategy which the Royal Navy had been developing to overcome the limits placed on traditional blockade imposed by the mine and the submarine.

Armed with a memorandum by the Secretary of the Imperial Defence Committee,[3] the British Foreign Office delegates had needed little pressure from France and Germany before agreeing to the continental nations' demand for the abolition of a belligerent's right to blockade neutral ports and their insistence on close blockade of enemy ports and coasts, outside which areas neutrals could not be seized even if they were carrying contraband. The Admiralty, having relatively recently identified Germany as the most likely enemy, was extremely displeased that at a stroke it had lost the advantage conferred by the geography of the British Isles, which made possible an effective distant blockade of the entire North Sea, and that although the principle of 'continuous voyage' was preserved, the loss of the right to blockade neutral ports effectively eliminated the prospects of intercepting goods destined for the enemy.[4] The Royal Navy's dissatisfaction was shared by the public and the shipping industry and when, in June 1911, the House of Lords rejected the revised Naval Prize Bill the Government was unable to ratify the 1909 Declaration.

It seemed, then, when the First World War began and Britain, France, and Germany stated their intention to abide by the terms of the London Declaration, even though not all the belligerents had ratified it, that civilisation had prevailed and that legal form would dominate naval warfare. Unfortunately, although the rules were recognised, weapons had evolved even further, inviting transgression or, as it transpired, making it inevitable: close blockade of the enemy's short North Sea coast was not possible, thanks to the risk from mines and submarines, but geography so favoured Britain and France that a manifestly effective blockade could be maintained by closing the Channel and the Shetlands–Norway Gap.

The Western allies therefore immediately imposed the distant blockade which had been outlawed in 1909. Genuine neutral trade was permitted by the device of Navigation Certificates – 'Navicerts' – issued by Allied authorities satisfied at the ports of loading that the cargoes included no contraband bound ultimately for the enemy. In July 1916, the Allied Governments finally abandoned any pretence at observing the Declaration of London, relying thereafter 'on principles underlying the historic and admitted rules of International Law'.[5] The neutrals, and the United States in particular, had been protesting against the allied measures since the outbreak of war but by this date the balance of outrage at violations was definitely against the German anti-shipping campaign.

The German Navy had soon realised that submarines were incapable of imposing a blockade within the bounds of international law or operational reality. Worse, it had a greater problem than the Allies, for the coastlines of Britain and France were far longer, so that total blockade by the smaller surface fleet would have been impossible, even if it had been attempted; as it was, the German capital ships' contribution was limited to a brief series of 'Bomber Command' raids on Hartlepool, Scarborough, and Lowestoft, which inflicted no military damage.

Seen properly, in the long mirrored corridor of maritime history, the 1915–18 U-boat campaign was not a blockade but a *guerre-de-course*. More ships got through than were stopped, even at the height of the unrestricted warfare phase. Stopped is, of course, a euphemism: one of the few real changes in the history of maritime warfare was the adoption of weapons intended to *sink* ships, as opposed to facilitating their capture. That the introduction of the mine and the locomotive torpedo coincided with the iron ship was no more than that – a coincidence: the vulnerability of the uncompartmented iron vessel may have been cruelly exposed by underwater weapons, but the wooden hull was just as certain to go down like a rock. This, of course, washed out at a stroke the jurists' work of the last 60 years, for non-contraband goods in neutral ships were lost with no less finality than were neutral goods lost in enemy ships.

That the German campaign came so close to succeeding in 1917 was due partly to the British Admiralty's reluctance to employ traditional methods against a traditional form of warfare (only the weapon was innovative), but also to a total misreading of the implications of shipping statistics by analysts. Once this was realised, convoy was reintroduced and losses returned to acceptable levels. Germany had no such one-dose remedy to lift the Allied blockade: by the summer of 1918 the population, already war-weary, was beginning to suffer such real privation that, even without the military defeats on the Western Front, collapse was inevitable.

At the end of the First World War, a new concept of institutionalised peacekeeping was adopted by most states. In 1920, the founder members of the League of Nations solemnly agreed, subject to certain qualifications, not to resort to war as a means of solving disputes. The council of the League, in September 1920, extrapolated from this basic agreement the understanding that *'the idea of neutrality of members is not compatible with the other principle that all the members of the League will have to act in common to cause their covenants to be observed'*.[6] This was a bit too extreme for some nations and the implication of obligation to assist in action against an offending state was gradually watered down until, by 1928, it had been generally agreed that while the Covenant of the League entitled members to take non-neutral action, there was no element of duty or obligation to do so.

The Covenant of the League of Nations also introduced the concept of 'sanctions' – coercive economic and financial boycotts – by member states. As conceived, these were obligatory but they could be imposed only after a violation of the Covenant had occurred. Blockade was not mentioned but, in theory at least, the League had established a framework which favoured the blockade of an aggressor. In practice, the system came apart at the first real test, when in October 1935, 50 member states pledged to apply collective sanctions to Italy after Mussolini's invasion of Abyssinia: arms sales were embargoed, as were certain imports and exports, but oil was not included. Everyone shrank from the one step which would have finished the Italian campaign – blockade by closure of the Suez Canal and the Straits of Bab el Mandeb. In June 1936, after less than nine months of ineffectual inaction (as far as the previously sovereign state of Abyssinia was concerned), sanctions were lifted. They had, in fact, cost Italy dearly, halving her exports and reducing her gold reserves by some £20 million; the autocrat was rescued by popular pride sustained by resentment at foreign attempts to interfere with their national destiny, the Italian people supported the war and donated private gold to the state.

A month after the sanctions against Italy were lifted, the Spanish Civil War began. Neither the League of Nations' deliberations nor the successive interwar naval treaties had made provision for civil war and this particular example was further complicated by the scale of foreign intervention. A Non-intervention Committee, representing 27 nations, including all the major interventionists, sought to limit the conflict and ultimately inaugurated a form of blockade to exclude would-be combatants. At the same time, the international community would not recognise the belligerent rights – of blockade, stop and search, or arrest – of either of the rival factions. This, of course, did not stop the Nationalists and

Republicans from instituting blockades which, because they were not recognised, led to the Royal Navy protecting British merchant shipping from interception or arrest by Spanish warships.

The Italian Navy went a step further in 1937, using submarines to reinforce actively the Nationalist blockade of Mediterranean ports; such assistance was, of course, clandestine. In 1930, the Naval Treaty of London had agreed that submarine warfare should be bound by the rules that no merchant ship should be sunk without warning, that crew and passengers should be placed in a place of safety and that an open boat on the high seas did not constitute a place of safety. The Italian submarines, for political and tactical reasons, could not observe the rules and were foolish enough to attack 'genuine' neutrals. This led to a nine-Power conference which, in September 1936, instituted the 'Nyon Patrol', whose coastal zones were allocated to various navies, to prevent outside intervention and to protect neutral shipping – any submarine attacking a neutral was to be regarded as hostile, whatever its nationality. The patrol was credited with suppressing this form of state piracy, but, realistically, it was the grudging Italian participation in the protective patrols which sealed its success.

Notwithstanding the Italian attitude to submarine warfare, the German Navy's U-boat force began the Second World War with a set of Prize Regulations which stated that enemy merchant ships were not to be sunk without warning – provided that they were not armed; this proviso was extended, as the first month of the war went by, to ships that were zigzagging or steaming darkened at night in the eastern Atlantic. No formal blockade could be declared but in the 'War Zones' notified by the German government, neutrals could be stopped and searched, taken in prize or sunk if they were carrying contraband. In October 1939 they were advised not to use French or British ports, tankers became unlimited targets anywhere in the Atlantic in November and from December Greek-flagged ships were deemed to be hostile if encountered in the War Zone around Britain. Sinking on sight at up to 100 miles from the Allied coasts was permitted in January 1940, but wakeless electric torpedoes were to be used if possible, to simulate mine explosions.[7]

This progressive removal of restrictions on the U-boat commanders was in response to the effectiveness of the Allied economic blockade of Germany. As in the First World War, the British and French navies sealed off the Straits of Dover and conducted efficient patrols in the northern approaches to the North Sea, with the cooperation of neutrals who were about their lawful occasions. Close blockade of Germany was not possible, but nor was it really necessary. Unlike the Imperial Navy of the

First World War, the Hitlerian Kriegsmarine was incapable of mounting a realistic surface challenge to the Allies and, beyond coastal waters, the North Sea, which had been a battleground, became a no-man's land in which movement, even by submarines, was limited by minefields and dominated by aircraft.

Merchant ships attempting to return to Germany were snapped up and, as in 1914–15, Allied warships on distant stations conducted what were, in reality, undeclared blockades of concentrations of German merchantmen in neutral ports such as New York, Rio de Janeiro and the harbours of the River Plate. The German surface raiders, whose main contribution should have been to draw off these patrols, never succeeded in breaking the web which ensnared the bulk of the German overseas trading fleet. The loss of certain vital imports from the west was initially offset by supply from the east, from the Soviet Union, and when the latter became an enemy, technology came to the rescue. German industry had developed synthetic substitutes for some essentials, such as oil, rubber, silk and even coffee, and with a centralised war economy even an indefinite blockade might not, alone, cause a collapse.

The immediate objectives of economic blockade had been achieved by the end of March 1940 but Hitler had no intention of confining his armies to theatres which the belligerents' frontiers dictated. Norway was invaded in April 1940 at the urging of the Navy, to outflank the British blockade patrols to the north, and in June 1940 the second phase of the invasion of France left the Biscay ports in German hands and took the French Navy off the board. In two moves, the German position had gone from one of weakness to one of potential supremacy. The British had recognised the peril inherent in the Norwegian campaign and it was they who made the first declaration of an unrestricted submarine operating area, as early as May 1940, in the northern North Sea. The Germans responded on 24 May with their first open announcement of an unrestricted zone around the British Isles and France and by 17 August, with the occupied French Atlantic ports ready to begin U-boat operations, the Germany Navy was ready to declare that Britain was blockaded within a War Zone which extended between the Faeroes and Finisterre, out to 20° West.[8]

This blockade was no more realistic than any Britain could declare against the coastline of occupied Europe. Under modern conditions, there could be no question of maintaining an effective, let alone continuous, presence off all enemy ports, or indeed off any one port, but at the same time no neutral could realistically expect protection from the belligerents' strict observation of long-argued international law (not that they had enjoyed any noticeable degree of protection during the 'Phoney War', when two-thirds of all the independently routed ships sunk by U-boats had been neutral-flagged).

Unable to deny movement, the Royal Navy maintained the observation role, with the help of the Royal Air Force. Submarine and air patrols watched the principal surface ship bases but no attempt was made to engage any sortie until it had reached the open ocean, where the Home Fleet could claim undisputed superiority. Similarly, although Coastal Command flew thousands of missions against U-boats in transit through the Bay of Biscay and the Iceland–UK 'Gap', decision in the battle was reached in mid-Atlantic, where the 'blockade' of Britain was attempted by the German Navy.

RAF Bomber Command's direct contribution to the Battle of the Atlantic was limited to raids on U-boat bases, which devastated the French towns of Brest, Lorient, St Nazaire and La Pallice, but, like the attacks on the U-boat building yards in Germany, were less relevant to the ultimate outcome of the campaign than Drake's attack on Cadiz had been to the Armada. The heavy bombers did, however, make a significant contribution to the campaign against German coast-wise shipping by their minelaying operations in north-west European waters. Seldom was the shipping 'external': inbound blockade-runners were few and most were accounted for by the surface and air patrols long before they came within the range of German protection.

From mid-1941, the British had an additional form of warning of shipping movements – Special Intelligence, or 'Ultra' – decyphered signals betraying preparations for sailing or arrival, including instructions for minesweeping and provision for surface and air escort. Most of the fierce light naval forces and air battles in the English Channel against blockade-runners which were either on the first leg of their outbound voyage or had slipped past the 'Reception Committees' were prompted by this source. This, then, was modern blockade warfare: in the days of sail and uncertain winds, the blockaders had spent months at sea relying upon experience, commonsense and luck to find the enemy – in the twentieth century, they spent longer in harbour, waiting for infrequent but usually well-informed calls for action.

The Second World War differed from all previous wars in its polarisation and in its centralisation. Disregarding the very odd relationship between the Soviet Union and Japan, few genuine neutrals remained after the summer of 1940 and none was a first-rank maritime nation. Merchant shipping was tightly controlled by the belligerent nations and was employed not just for economic sustenance but also for military purposes. Blockade as planned against Britain by the German Navy, and achieved against Japan by the United States, was not intended to stop absolutely the passage of ships, but to inflict heavy attrition by a 'tonnage war' which would leave insufficient cargo capacity for the prosecution of all aspects of the conflict. Only the Royal Navy, in northwest Europe and the Mediterranean, attempted, with fair success, to apply the full stranglehold on surface movement in and out of the German sphere of control.

The war was scarcely over before the Royal Navy was back in the blockade business again. Like the non-intervention patrols of the Spanish Civil War, it was a 'reverse blockade', keeping arms and illegal immigrants out of Palestine, but the international background was quite different and the successes of the Palestine Patrol were usually portrayed by the world's press as excesses. The British Government, in ordering the blockade, was no more than following its obligation under a League of Nations Mandate, endorsed by the newly created United Nations, to restrict Jewish immigration to Palestine to a quota, but it was running against a tidal wave of popular sympathy for the displaced persons involved – refugees whose lives had been broken under German occupation and oppression. Every RN success, and there were many, added to the pressure for the end of British control in Palestine, which finally ended on 15 May 1948: the last overcrowded, unseaworthy blockade-runner was intercepted and taken into Haifa two days earlier, two years to the day after the first had been picked up.

In June 1948, a month after the lifting of the Palestine Patrol and the institution of the West Coast Patrol, the world's greatest non-naval power, the Soviet Union, imposed a total blockade on all surface access to Berlin. Like many naval blockades which had preceded it, this land blockade had unforeseen, wider consequences. For this one act, more than any other, marked a new geopolitical polarisation which was to last for forty years. It accelerated the formation of mutual security pacts and split the world into 'Them and Us'; few genuine neutrals remained. Despite the later proclamation of the 'Third World' most of the 'non-aligned' nations remained to some extent clients of one or other of the Great Powers.

The common meeting-place for all was the United Nations. Its Charter, like the Covenant of the League of Nations, included economic sanctions as a means of preserving peace, but it was potentially more effective than the League's provisions, for no longer did sanctions have to await an aggressive act – Article 39 of Chapter VII permits the Security Council to impose sanctions if it agrees that a threat to the peace exists. Article 41 authorises the imposition of sanctions and Article 42 empowers the use of force.

The key to initiation of such action was, of course, the Security Council's agreement, but this was subject to the absolute power of veto of any Permanent Member of the Council. In the circumstances of the polarised Cold War world, it was almost unthinkable for any Permanent Member to allow a client state to be singled out for sanctions. Only once, indeed, was the unthinkable achieved during the first 20 years of the Security Council's existence – on 27 June 1950, with the Soviet member boycotting the proceedings of the Council, North Korea was formally branded an aggressor and UN member nations were authorised to take action to restore international peace and security.

For three years and eighteen days, the Royal Navy maintained a blockade off the west coast of Korea. United Nations maritime supremacy was complete and it was soon apparent that the Communist armies were almost totally reliant on land means of reinforcement and resupply: the small number of movements by small craft could be adequately detected and interdicted by carrier aircraft, whose main role was support of military operations. The blockade of North Korea played an unquantifiable part in the draw that was eventually achieved, preventing the delivery of bulk cargoes by sea over shorter routes than the road and rail systems leading to North Korea's land frontier, which, once they had crossed the border, were subject to air interdiction.

Ten years after the end of the Korean War, the Royal Navy began another 'reverse blockade', as Indonesia attempted to run weapons and men to foment and sustain insurrection in Borneo and Malaya. This, like many of the minor crises of the 1960s, was a sequel to the decolonisation process, which invited neighbours to settle long-standing (sometimes fanciful) claims with newly sovereign states, who in turn called upon their former oppressors to stand by them. Set fair to run and run, 'Confrontation' ended quite abruptly in 1966, following an equally abrupt change of government in Indonesia.

The reaction of a governing minority to the prospect of decolonisation on unfavourable terms was the occasion for the first exercise of the powers of sanction by the Security Council. The 1965 Rhodesian unilateral declaration of independence from Britain found no supporters in the main power blocs or the Third World to veto a resolution that the continued existence of independence under a white minority government constituted a threat to international peace and security.[9] The British Government, deputed to impose sanctions herself and through the British Commonwealth, imposed a naval blockade on the port of Beira, in Mozambique (then a Portuguese colony), which was the main trans-shipment port for oil destined for Rhodesia. No teeth were given to the blockade for five months, until it was learned that a tanker carrying oil believed to be intended for the 'rebel' state was bound for Beira, and a further Security Council Resolution[10] was passed, authorising the United Kingdom (but no other states) to prevent by force if necessary the arrival of shipping reasonably believed to be carrying oil for Rhodesia; further, it specifically empowered British forces to seize the tanker *Joanna V* at Beira if her cargo was discharged there.

The Beira Patrol lasted for over nine years. Incidents were few as most states respected the UN demand that fuel should not be consigned to Rhodesia and, after the first few tanker boardings, the others were persuaded that the blockade was not merely for form. Alternative routes for imports and exports were found and it cannot be said with any degree of conviction that the long Royal Navy presence made a major contribution to the ultimate acceptance by the self-appointed minority government that its situation was, ultimately, untenable. But it did demonstrate a politically attractive method of implementing sanctions, one which could be imposed at short notice (and withdrawn just as quickly), was cheap, for the international community, in that the ships concerned were already in service and their personnel were being paid from a national budget, and which offered little risk of loss of life to either participant.

The United Nations Security Council did not authorise Britain to use force in 1982 to repossess the Falkland Islands. It did, however, identify Argentina as responsible for the breach of the peace[11] and the British Government thereafter exercised its rights of self-defence. On this occasion, no blockade was imposed: instead, a Maritime Exclusion Zone was first declared around the islands, followed by a Total Exclusion Zone which extended to 200 miles by the time that the 'shooting war' began, and then by a warning that Argentine warships were liable to be sunk on sight outside their own coastal waters. The TEZ was never considered to be a 'sink at sight' zone, other than in the immediate coastal waters of the Falklands. Rather, it served the purpose of clearing the combat area of all ships but those of the Argentinian and British navies: the only innocent caught on passage was a Liberian tanker, bombed by the Argentine Air Force far outside anybody's exclusion zone.

The Iran–Iraq War saw both sides attempting to impose blockades on one another without either possessing the forces needed to make them effective. The United Nations stood back and it was left to national initiatives, primarily by the US Navy and some of the western European navies, to ensure the right of innocent passage to ports in Gulf states not involved in the fighting. Only the US Navy took part in active operations to protect shipping and it was ironic that although its engagements were against

Iranian forces, its most serious casualties were suffered as the result of an indiscriminate Iraqi missile attack.

After two years of relative peace in the Gulf, Iraq invaded and occupied Kuwait. On this occasion the Security Council did not hesitate and on 6 August 1990 adopted a Resolution which condemned the aggression and called upon Iraq to withdraw.[12] Economic sanctions more draconian than any contemplated by the many Declarations of the preceding 130 years were imposed, for only medicines and, in humanitarian circumstances, food, were exempted from the list of contraband.

The announcement by United States and Britain that they would use their naval forces already in the area to enforce the sanctions by sea, was challenged by several states. On 25 August, therefore, a further Resolution was passed, calling upon cooperating maritime forces

> to use such measures commensurate with the specific circumstances as may be necessary... to halt all inward and outward maritime shipping in order to inspect and verify their cargoes and destinations, etc.[13]

Force was not mentioned, but everyone seems to have known that it was authorised.

The Royal Navy was only one of twelve navies to take part in what were called 'embargo operations' but which were straightforward blockade patrols. Old-fashioned they were not, for careful coordination between so many naval forces, and several air forces which backed them up, had never been a feature of previous blockades, and every means possible was used to build up a picture of merchant ship movements to and from the Gulf and the Jordanian port of Aqaba. Royal Navy units challenged over a third of the 9,000 merchant ships sighted – and none were missed – but took part in only 36 of the 1,100 hundred boardings. A number of ships needed a shot across their bows to bring them to, but only 60 were diverted for examination or turned away and a mere handful were seized.

It cannot be claimed that the blockade of Iraq led directly or indirectly to the expulsion of Iraqi forces from Kuwait. That was achieved by far more costly, (in terms of human lives), but much faster direct action. On the basis that the Iraqi régime remains in power nearly four years after the imposition of sanctions, and the country functions after a fashion, it could be asserted with some justification that if blockade had been the only action taken, Kuwait would still be occupied.

The Kuwait crisis and its military sequel can be taken as marking the end of polarised geopolitics. The tension which had bound together the superpower–client state relationships was already beginning to unwind, only to be replaced by a series of Gordian knots, tangled by the nationalism, religious fundamentalism and raw personal ambition which had been held in check by sponsors during the Cold War period and, before that, by colonialism. Even under autocratic governments, peoples have frequently shown that they would prefer to come to terms with acute discomfort rather than accede to foreign demands, such as sanctions; today, the sympathy which they enjoy from co-religionists, those of common ethnic stock, or for reasons of humanity becomes a powerful public relations weapon in the hands of the autocrats. Skilfully deployed, this sympathy waters down the most draconian of sanctions and hampers the maintenance of an effective blockade, whose participants' freedom of action is circumscribed by rules of engagement tailored as much to lower media profile as to implement a Security Council Resolution. Only in Korea and Kuwait has sufficient world opinion been mustered on the side of Alexander, to take a sword to the knot.

Today, ships and carrier aircraft of NATO and WEU are conducting a blockade in the Adriatic on behalf of the United Nations. The identified threat to peace is the state of Serbia, land-locked as far as international recognition of boundaries is concerned, but until recently the actual fighting was taking place outside her borders, waged by war lords with horizons much too limited by time and space to observe the niceties of land war, let alone appreciate the legalistic intricacies of a maritime blockade.

Whether, ultimately, sanctions or blockade will prove to be more effective than they have in the past is a question for crystal-ball gazers, not historians; cynics among the latter may, however, draw the inference that, whatever the result, collective sanctions have at least been shown to promote the 'Feel Good Factor' indispensable to the leaders and media of law-abiding democracies, reminding the law-breakers and their people, and ours, that we are fighting as hard as we can, short of actual war.

NOTES

The views and opinions expressed in this paper are personal to the author and in no way represent those of the Ministry of Defence or the Royal Navy; similarly, all the errors of omission and commission are his own.

1. London (1911), p. 185 *et seq.*
2. PRO: CAB21/307: Hankey–Memorandum on Blockade and the Laws of War (1931); accompanying memorandum by Sir Cecil Hurst.

3. PRO: CAB21/307, CID paper 41-B (December 1904) 'The value to Great Britain... of the right of search and capture of neutral vessels', by Sir G. S. Clarke.
4. Cd. 4554, 'Correspondence and Documents respecting the International Naval Conference held in London December 1908–January 1909', pp. 50–58 (published 1917); CAB 21/307, Hankey, loc. cit.
5. Cd 8293 'Note addressed by HMG to Neutral Representatives in London respecting the Withdrawal of the Declaration of London Orders in Council' (7 July 1916).
6. Covenant of the League of Nations, Article 16.
7. The full sequence of the raising of restrictions on the U-boat fleet is to be found in G. Hessler, *The U-Boat War in the Atlantic* (London, HMSO, 1989), Part I, paras 74–85.
8. Ibid.
9. UN Security Council Resolution 217.
10. UNSCR 221.
11. UNSCR 502.
12. UNSCR 661.
13. UNSCR 665.

14 Decolonisation and Coastal Operations in the East Indies, 1945–50
G. Teitler

From about 1900 the Netherlands Royal Navy (NRN) prepared for war with the Imperial Japanese Navy. In 1942 it lost this war and when it returned to the East Indies in 1945 it was to confront there a totally different opponent. The Indonesian nationalists had established an independent state, directly in the wake of the Japanese surrender. Soon they were fighting the Dutch, with diplomatic means and with guerilla techniques. The Dutch Colonial Army, together with reinforcements sent from the Netherlands, bore the brunt of the counter-guerilla operations. The NRN assisted their efforts, mainly by blockading the enemy-held coasts.

Apart from the operational problems connected with this task, a more fundamental one was worrying the NRN. Just at that time it was in the process of redirecting its strategic focus. Before 1941 it had been tied to the defence of the East Indies and placed under the direct command of the Governor-General in Batavia, the capital of the colony. During the Second World War, however, the NRN proclaimed what it had already felt for a long time: that this arrangement amounted to a strategic mistake. It openly stressed now its 'blue-water' intentions and showed itself quite ready to delegate the immediate security of the East Indies to the care of a separate colonial navy. When this proposal proved impossible to realise in the short run, the NRN set itself to the task at hand – the blockade – but only reluctantly so.

To the majority of its officers this task was too colonial and too restricted to their liking. While not denying the military relevance of a blockade, they were inclined to downplay that aspect. In their view, they were pushed into a policeman's role to which a coastguard-like organisation was more suited. In The Hague, moreover, the Admiralty did not let an opportunity pass to stress the burden this East-Indian commitment placed on the NRN. It was busy formulating plans to finance, build, and man three task forces. Each of these was to comprise a light aircraft carrier, two light cruisers and six to eight destroyers. While the Admiralty was very much in favour of keeping the East-Indies an integral part of the Dutch empire, it feared that the counter-guerilla blockade would play havoc with its task force plans.

This situation placed the flag-officer commanding in the East Indies, Vice Admiral A. S. Pinke, in an unenviable position. On the one hand, he was under an obligation to follow the directions of the colonial government (of which he was a member as head of the naval department in Batavia). This government expected a wholehearted commitment of the NRN to the suppression of Indonesian nationalism. On the other hand, Pinke knew that the Admiralty expected him to sever the bonds of this commitment as quickly as possible. As he was not free to do so, he rapidly learned what it meant to serve two masters. Unable to reconcile their demands, he ended his career a thoroughly frustrated man. In practice he had no choice but to concentrate on the operational task entrusted to him: to fight the guerillas. Inevitably, this choice estranged him from the leadership of his own service. Having been promised to be the next commander-in-chief of the NRN, this post eluded him in the end. The Admiralty, rather unjustly, neither forgot nor forgave him his colonial commitment, thus making him a truly tragic figure.

The nationalists drew their strength from the enthusiasm with which important sections of the Indonesian intellectuals, middle classes, and peasants supported their cause. On this basis they were able to conduct a guerilla war that soon forced the Dutch to strengthen their Colonial Army with units (among them conscripts) from the Netherlands. At sea, however, the nationalists were extremely weak. In fact, a nationalist navy was non-existent. Still the NRN was kept busy till the end of the hostilities in December 1949, because of the activities of thousands of smugglers. Some of these worked directly for the guerillas. The majority, however, was simply after private gain.

Whatever their motivation, all smugglers threatened to undermine the war effort of the Dutch. Through their hands, enormous amounts of plantation and mining products left the archipelago, mainly in the direction of the Singapore market. On their way back, the smugglers loaded their vessels with weapons, munitions, and other items relevant to armed combat. In this way, the NRN saw no reason to differentiate between politically motivated and neutral smugglers. Whoever did the smuggling, the Dutch were hurt militarily, while they lost an important source of income by not being able to levy export dues. The nationalists, on the other hand, controlled and taxed much of the exports. In this way they drew enough income to pay for the weapons and munitions. Worse still, from the

Dutch point of view, this taxation allowed the nationalists to pose as representatives of a regular government. And that, of course, was exactly what the Dutch feared most of all.

In the areas dominated by the Dutch – most of Java, Borneo, and the areas to the East of these island – the NRN was assisted by the civilian Shipping Service (in normal times responsible for coastguard duties, pilotage, etc.). The blockade the NRN tried to uphold, with about fifty rather small vessels, was a double-edged affair. First, the Dutch strove to prevent any ship from leaving the areas controlled by the guerillas. Second, they tried to intercept any ship that approached these parts of the archipelago. To carry out these tasks, the Dutch revived a system of identification, registration, and shipping permits (introduced for the first time during the nineteenth century to fight piracy). Only ships provided with all of the necessary papers were allowed to leave Dutch-controlled harbours. Next, these vessels were ordered to make their voyage along certain well-defined routes across the archipelago.

The NRN, of course, tried to patrol and supervise these 'lanes' by sea and by air. All ships, moreover, had to make calls during their trip on certain islands where the NRN and Dutch Colonial Army had placed small garrisons, equipped with radio sets. Ships found in areas outside the prescribed sea routes or without the necessary papers, were summarily taken and escorted to a Dutch-controlled harbour for investigation and, if found smuggling, for trial. On board the bigger ships, moreover, the Dutch often placed a customs official, demanding from the master and/or shipowner a few hostages in return, to guarantee the safety of this official. In case no Dutch-controlled harbour was available within reasonable distance, the NRN tried to use a landing craft as a substitute.

In this way the Dutch tried to channel all native merchant ships along a few, easily controllable sea routes. To this system was added the reintroduction of maritime exclusion zones. These so called 'maritime circles' had been introduced before the Second World War to keep Japanese fishing vessels – suspected of espionage – at a safe distance from sensitive military areas. Now, these circles were used to tighten the control and registration system. All of these measures called for supervision by NRN ships and aircraft. But these, regrettably, were never available in sufficient numbers, relative to the enormous distances involved. Another problem concerned the relationship between the Dutch and the innocent native traders and fishermen. Permits and passes often meant little to these people, while their means of navigation were sometimes rather primitive. To be caught without a permit or within a maritime circle did not necessarily mean that the seamen concerned were smugglers, assisting directly or not the guerillas. Indiscriminate action by the NRN, or the air arm of the Dutch Colonial Army, would alienate these people and make converts of them for the nationalist cause.

Delicate too was the relationship between the NRN and the Economic Department of the colonial government. This department understandably wanted to stimulate a return to economic normality by all possible means. By working for this it was inclined, however, to accept a certain amount of smuggling as an inevitable aspect of troubled times and as a politically neutral phenomenon. Consequently, it expected the NRN to show a considerable amount of leniency when practising its sea control. The NRN protested. According to its views, under the circumstances prevailing in the East-Indies, no such thing as politically neutral smuggling existed. A smuggler was always harming both the purse and the legitimacy of the colonial government, even if the motive driving him was strictly economic.

These opposing views were never harmonised. The Lieutenant Governor-General hesitated to back up the NRN. First, because his whole pre-war career had been spent within the Economic Department and his postwar policy views were influenced by this experience. Second, because he was afraid that, with an increasing number of Englishmen, Australians and Americans among the smugglers, the line adopted and executed by the NRN would end in so many diplomatic problems, that the Dutch were in danger of losing their last bit of international goodwill. The NRN simply had to content itself with this situation. Vice-Admiral Pinke protested, but in the end went no further than to note in his diary that the Lieutenant Governor-General acted more as the head of the Dutch East-India Company of old, than as a statesman with an eye for the possibilities of military power.

By launching two large-scale military operations in 1947 and 1948 the Dutch succeeded in occupying all of Java and the greater part of Sumatra. Unfortunately, these successes only deepened their counter-guerilla problems. At sea, while now in control of most harbours, the NRN was only marginally better off, as it was ordered to send several of its ships to Europe after each operation. Added to this problem was the fact that the judicial system in the East-Indies was only slowly adapting itself to the new situation. The laxity with which it reacted to the interdiction activities of the NRN brought the latter organisation almost to despair. This feeling was aggravated when the NRN took the discrepancy into account between the sentences passed by the law courts and the profits a smuggler could cash after only a few trips to Singapore. Fortunately, the NRN was better served by the police officers and consular agents sent abroad to gather information about the plans and exploits of the smugglers. More problematic was to find enough competent and incorruptible men to care for the many registration and customs tasks in the harbours of the archipelago. Time and again, the NRN found that its opponents had an excellent intelligence network at their disposal and enough money to bribe local officials, if necessary.

The NRN usually had available for the blockade about three destroyers, eight corvettes, about forty reconnaissance patrol boats (some of which belonged to the civilian Shipping Service) and three to five minelaying and minesweeping vessels. Only half of these ships were employable, however, the rest undergoing repairs that lasted from one to several weeks. On average, a ship was kept at sea for about three to four weeks. Especially on the patrol boats a crew was thoroughly exhausted after such a period, certainly during the monsoon rains. Still, the crews were always ready to return to sea. Disciplinary problems were unheard of, the crews evidently being glad to see some action – if even on a small scale – after having been inactive for years (some of them at least) in German or Japanese prisoner-of-war camps.

For all that, the NRN smarted under the inadequacy of its material. Too few radar sets were available, while not a few smugglers operated with high-speed boats that easily outran the NRN ships, especially on the short track from Singapore to Sumatra. Operationally, the most successful way of dealing with the smugglers in this area was to adopt a 'whalers' system' for exercising sea control. This meant combining a mother ship with a fleet of patrol boats, the latter searching the area for ships suspected of smuggling. Flying boats completed this system, that offered both protection against the sometimes heavily armed opponents and a short reaction time.

Vice-Admiral Pinke never tired of telling the Admiralty that his task, although tactically and operationally of a coastguard type, was an indispensable strategic tool to fight the guerillas. By trying to sever the nationalists' supply lines, Pinke used the NRN in a classic blockading role. Consequently, he was rather touchy about what he perceived as the Admiralty's tendency to downplay the military relevance of this operation and picture him as some kind of police constable. As to the more distant future, Pinke had another axe to grind with his naval superiors. His force of corvettes, patrol boats and destroyers not only suited the small-scale kind of warfare he was waging at that time. In his opinion, this kind of force, supplemented with land-based air, was exactly what the NRN needed for the future defence of the East Indies.

He accused the Admiralty of thinking too big and of building castles in the air with its task force plans. In his view, the American and British navies were fully up to the task of securing Western Europe's sea lines of communication. A Dutch blue-water navy was simply redundant. To an alliance of Western countries, the Dutch could make a no more relevant contribution than to take care of the oil-producing East-Indies. This area was, after the defeat of Japan, relatively safe from external aggression. The danger now threatened to come from within, as the vice admiral saw the Indonesian nationalists as nothing but communists in disguise. That the British government was only lukewarm about a prolonged Dutch presence in the Far East and that the Americans simply were hostile to this prospect, did not deter him. Pinke expected the whole of mainland Asia soon to fall victim to communism. By that time, the British and Americans would realise how important it was to have the Dutch in control of the East-Indian off-shore empire.

Whatever the quality of this long-term view, in the spring of 1949 the Dutch were still far from defeating the guerillas. International support for their stubborn stance was rapidly fading and by the end of that year Indonesian nationalists had won their independence. In the meantime, at sea the military situation was possibly even more hopeless for the Dutch than on land. Whatever the NRN tried to do, its anti-smuggling campaigns had no more effect on the opponent than scratches on a rock. Any other outcome would have come as a surprise indeed. Seldom has it been possible to defeat smugglers, or pirates for that matter, at sea. Truly lasting results have only been obtained when regular forces followed these opponents into their hiding-places and left occupation forces behind in order to prevent the local population from sticking to their nasty habits.

During the seventeenth century the Dutch had already learned this lesson when fighting the Dunkirk privateers. During the nineteenth century they relearned it, while extending their power over the outer islands of the East Indies. In fact, almost every problem the NRN encountered between 1945 and 1949, had been confronted before, on the organisational as well as on the operational level. This point proves how difficult it is to keep memories alive about activities an organisation considers to fall outside its core business. The NRN saw itself primarily as a military organisation, tasked to confront the regular naval forces of a rival empire. Ample experience during the nineteenth century and the 1930s with small-scale actions (against pirates, slave traders, opium smugglers, clandestine fisheries) was not enough to prepare it for its counter-guerilla role directly after the Second World War.

During the nineteenth century the Dutch gradually extended their power over the East-Indian archipelago. To this end they used several kinds of naval organisations. First, of course, the NRN. Second, the Colonial Navy, a force that drew its funds from the colonial government. This Navy's operational area was restricted, but its tasks were many: to suppress piracy, to help the NRN in case of war, and to transport civil servants and troops within the archipelago. This dual arrangement did not work out as expected, problems arising mainly on the side of the Colonial Navy. On a daily basis, this organisation was mainly busy fighting piracy. It soon found out, however, that its ships were too large and slow to be a match for this opponent. This outcome brought the NRN into play against the pirates, but the result of its actions proved that it too was not up to the challenge. Proud, for instance, of its steamships, the NRN soon realised that the superior speed of these vessels was nullified by their smoke, giving away their position hours in advance.

In a reaction to these dismal experiences a third organisation was placed alongside the NRN and Colonial Navy. The 'residents' (the highest-ranking colonial civil servants) were so frustrated with the inability to suppress piracy that they organised their own naval units. These organisations rested on a strictly local footing, their ships being manned by trusted native seamen. The vessels these 'residents' fleets' operated with, closely resembled the praus of the pirates. Too small to accommodate Dutch naval officers, they nevertheless were modestly successful. This performance was small comfort, however, to the Colonial Navy that was unable to compete with the newcomer. In 1836 it was decided to end the life of the Colonial Navy, its officers finding their way into the NRN.

At the end of the nineteenth century the extension of Dutch rule over the outer regions in the archipelago was almost completed. Piracy posed less and less of a problem by now, its place being taken by smuggling, especially of opium. The colonial customs organisation proved unable to stop this lucrative business and the story of the residents' fleets repeated itself. The island of Java, with its many Chinese inhabitants, formed the greatest opium market in the East Indies. The smugglers tried to reach this island mainly by way of its northern coast, and soon several residents organised their own coastguard. Over the years these units transformed themselves into a specialised task force that could, in an emergency, call on the NRN for assistance. Successful as this arrangement was, the residents complained about a lack of cooperation by the law courts. Their ships, being not so particular about the geographical limits of Dutch rule, often caught smugglers beyond the three nautical miles of the territorial sea. Promptly, most of the law courts discharged the culprits, with predictable results. Henceforth the smugglers hovered just outside the three-mile zone and waited till dark or another propitious moment to send their sloops ashore.

Responding to this situation, the colonial government proclaimed in its communal law a customs zone of six nautical miles. In this zone the task force was allowed to stop and search ships with a Dutch or East-Indian registration. By registering their vessels under foreign flags, however, the smugglers could easily evade this measure, leaving the task force as powerless as before. Asked for help, the home government came up with the idea of convening an international conference to decide on a territorial sea of six nautical miles. Apart from its anti-smuggling content, this idea carried additional advantages. The most important one concerned the so-called self-governing areas in the East Indies. The Dutch had left several sultanates here a fair amount of autonomy to regulate their internal affairs. The sultanates' freedom to conduct their own external relations was rather restricted but, at the end of the nineteenth century, not yet formally prescribed in any detail.

In practice this situation seldom gave rise to trouble. It only worried the colonial government when a sultanate bordered the sea and when valuable minerals were found in its domain. Under these circumstances foreign mining companies were in a position to bypass the Dutch and directly contact the sultan or his advisers. A Dutch-controlled territorial sea, preferably of six nautical miles – to separate the sultanate from outside interference – would allay these anxieties. Unfortunately, the international reaction to the Dutch conference proposal proved to be rather mixed. Russia and the United States reacted favourably. Still, the Dutch government backed down when Great Britain announced that it would never approve of a territorial sea of the proposed breadth. Other states had made their reaction dependent on the British point of view and this left the Dutch with no alternative but to withdraw their proposal. Evidently, the international community was not yet in a mood to interfere with what Great Britain cherished as a prime maritime interest.

This episode ended in 1895. Afterwards, the Dutch kept their six-mile belt of territorial sea in the East Indies, but only for ships registered in Holland and its colonies. For the next forty years, the Dutch remained in an ambivalent mood on this subject. On the one hand, their considerable maritime interests made them content with the idea and practice of 'Mare Liberum' and with its corollary – a narrow belt of territorial sea. On the other hand, with only rather weak naval forces at their disposal, they felt rather vulnerable, especially in their overseas possessions. Here they could very well profit from 'Mare Clausum', that is to say from a much broader belt of Dutch control and jurisdiction in the coastal sea. Time and again, the colonial and home governments toyed with the same idea that had led to the ill-fated initiative of 1895. Every time they thought better of it, well aware that Great Britain had not changed its views on the subject and that this country still had the power internationally to veto any Dutch proposal. With an eye to the growing might of Japan in the East, the Dutch had no reason to irritate the British.

After about 1900 the Dutch in the East Indies were finally in a position to differentiate clearly between strictly naval tasks (preparing for a war with Japan) and police duties (keeping smuggling and clandestine fisheries under control). Reflecting this differentiation, the NRN and the Government Navy (the heir to the residents' fleets) grew further apart. Just before the Second World War, however, the line between police and military duties became blurred again. The fishermen who clandestinely operated in the territorial waters of the archipelago were mainly Japanese. Dutch countermeasures, delegated to the Government Navy, sometimes led to Japanese casualties, and the colonial government feared that Tokyo would react by sending naval escorts to the East Indies. To forestall this move, the NRN was ordered to use some of its destroyers in a police role and henceforth keep an eye on the fishermen. The NRN protested, arguing that this task would interfere with its military mission. The colonial government, however, was not impressed. It pointed out that when facing Japan, the East Indies were confronting an integral challenge, making it unwise (for a small country) to differentiate between military duties and police tasks. Such a policy was a luxury a small country could not afford.

In the eyes of the colonial government, the Indonesian nationalists after the Second World War posed a comparable grave and integral challenge. Consequently, the NRN was not for one moment allowed to forget what this judgement meant for its operational employment in the archipelago. Another consequence was that the Dutch again felt an itch to broaden, in the East Indies, the belt of territorial waters. After all, by labelling the counter-guerilla operations an 'internal affair', they deprived themselves of the opportunity to apply the law of naval warfare and uphold the blockade outside these waters. Lengthy deliberations were devoted to this subject, but their outcome in no way differed from the one the Dutch reached fifty years before. Time and again, they found the international diplomatic climate not favourable enough for their plan. What the Dutch were afraid to do before 1950, however, their Indonesian opponent accomplished only seven years later. In 1957 the Indonesian government announced two measures. First, the extension of the territorial sea to twelve nautical miles. Second, the abolishment of the notion of 'open sea' for the waters between the islands of the archipelago. Henceforth these areas would be treated as internal waters, meaning that Indonesian sovereignty there was absolute.

These steps were justified by arguments the Dutch were all too familiar with. First, the protection of indigenous fisheries against foreign (mainly Japanese) encroachments. Second, the necessity to hold the archipelago together, now that its political integrity was threatened by separation movements on several outer islands. This argument too the Dutch could recognize as *déjà vu*. Their policy towards the sultanates during the nineteenth century can be accepted as proof of that. In effect, as late as 1917 the Dutch seriously contemplated exactly the same step as the Indonesians were to take in 1957. The Dutch were only restrained by the negative reaction they thought this unilateral action would draw from the British, By the middle of the 1950s the Indonesians on their part no longer were in a mood to take the reaction of any Western state into account. By 1982, moreover, they had collected enough international support to see their initiative accepted by the United Nations in the Third Convention on the Law of the Sea.

The afore-mentioned facts are not very well known outside the Netherlands, or for that matter, outside the NRN. And even this organisation lost much of its interest when, during the Cold War, it took a dim view of their relevance. Still, it would be interesting to compare these events with the decolonisation experiences of other Western navies. Another reason to take note of them, is because of the transformation Western naval organisations are presently going through now that the Cold War has ended. One of the consequences of this process seems to be that small-scale actions, in brown waters, are operationally coming to the fore again. A parallel trend is that, to a considerable degree, these actions are characterised by coastguard-like elements, as exemplified by the NRN's UN-sanctioned interdiction operations in the Adriatic, and its counter-drugs operations in the Caribbean. At the same time, the NRN tries to preserve the anti-submarine experience it gathered during the Cold War. Confronted with these divergent tendencies, there can be no doubt as to what the NRN, as a military organisation, considers to be its core business, and what not. As this chapter shows, it is not for the first time that the NRN finds itself on the horns of such a dilemma.

Another interesting and connected point concerns the operational implications of the international law of the sea. The Netherlands, as a colonial power, has shown a considerable ambivalence in this regard. Freedom of the sea presented only one side of the coin, as it mainly suited the interests of the mother country. The colonial government, on the other hand, was very much interested in 'Mare Clausum', as it rightly saw this principle as a welcome instrument to extend its control over the waters of the archipelago. Pirates could be fought on the high sea. Smugglers (of opium or weapons) on the other hand could only be brought to bay in the zones directly under Dutch jurisdiction. The broader these zones, the better it suited the colonial authorities. Moreover, to knit an island empire together politically, the idea of 'archipelagic water' was a very tempting one. It should come as no surprise that the Dutch in the East Indies time and again toyed with this notion. In all these respects, the Indonesian Government later on simply followed their track and acted out of roughly the same motivations.

NOTES

G. Teitler, 'Een Vergeten Strijd. Patrouilles, Smokkel, Infiltratie', in: G. Teitler en P. H. M. Groen (red.), *De Politionele Acties* (Amsterdam, 1987).

G. Teitler, *Vlootvoogd in de Knel. Vice-Admiraal A. S. Pinke tussen de Marinestaf, Indië en de Indonesische Revolutie* (Assen, 1990).

G. Teitler, *Ambivalentie en Aarzeling. Het Beleid van Nederland en Nederlands-Indië ten aanzien van hun Kustwateren, 1870–1962* (Amsterdam, 1994).

As regards the Dutch endeavours to keep the smuggling of opium within bounds, an American study is available: J. R. Rush, *Opium to Java. Revenue farming and Chinese enterprise in colonial Indonesia 1860–1910* (Ithaca, NY, 1990).

15 The Canadian Experience of Sea Power
Alec Douglas

Canada, with its huge land mass, is a more likely candidate for Mackinder than Mahan. Immigrants turned away from the sea, as often as not, to settle the country. Railways supplanted ships for moneymakers in the late nineteenth century. The Royal Navy and the Monroe Doctrine together seemed to ensure the protection of the country's seaward flanks. It was soldiers, not sailors, that the Empire asked for in 1914 and again in 1939. Yet so much coastline, such important ocean resources, continually demand attention. 'The wholesome sea', proclaims the motto carved in stone over the entrance to Canada's parliament buildings, 'is at her gates ...'.

Its Atlantic seaboard strategically positioned, close to all the Great Circle routes from North America to northern Europe, the Pacific coast a buffer zone between Alaska and the state of Washington, coveted in the past by Spanish, Russian, and American as well as British interests, Canada owes even more than most former colonies to the exercise of British naval mastery. Indeed, the Canadian experience of sea power, according to some, has been to rely on the strength of powerful friends and maintain the minimum necessary force to avoid loss of national autonomy. Recent scholarship suggests otherwise.

Canadian naval or quasi-naval forces in the nineteenth and early-twentieth centuries sprang out of auxiliary navies to meet needs that were either against British interests, or beyond British naval capacities, or simply of no concern to Britain.[1] And as the Canadian capacity to fill those needs with maritime forces developed, Canada experienced tensions that influenced the shape and role of those forces.[2] The country continues to feel those tensions, exacerbated by financial crisis, and the shape and role of maritime forces continue to evolve accordingly.[3]

It is worth remembering that Canada was far less desirable a region for naval undertakings than the West Indies, until the Seven Years War. It was pressure from west-country merchants (intent on exploiting the Newfoundland and Nova Scotia fisheries), New England colonial agents in

London, and a few naval officers with influence at the Admiralty and personal interest in the northern colonies, that led to the establishment of station ships from the late-seventeenth century, and the so-called Cape Breton squadron in 1744.[4] It was these interests that shaped the Anglo-French struggle for North America, with the naval elements of both powers playing a major part in the contest. Thereafter what was to become Canada became part of British imperial expansion in the last half of the eighteenth century,[5] but both the British and French interest in what was to become British North America was always tempered by competing interests in adjacent regions.

After the War of 1812 British naval forces withdrew from the Canadas as soon as they could. In the period of retrenchment following the Napoleonic Wars a number of half-pay naval officers, and seamen entitled to land grants, settled in British North America. They might have been expected to establish the nucleus of indigenous naval forces, and at periods of crisis some of them did, but their principal aim, like their counterparts in other colonies, was to enjoy the blessings of the land with the often disappointing fruits of their labours. They had, by force of circumstance, 'swallowed the anchor'. The exception that proved the rule was perhaps Henry Bayfield, one of the great nineteenth-century hydrographers, who continued surveying in North America after W. F. W. Owen and the Vidal brothers had either left or settled down to the life of landed gentry.[6] Halifax, only established as a dockyard when in 1757 British dockyards could no longer provide timely support to North American campaigns, was generally secondary to Bermuda. Esquimalt dockyard on the Pacific coast, established in the mid-nineteenth century, also declined in importance. Both Halifax and Esquimalt had been turned over to the Canadian government by 1906.[7]

British attempts to obtain assistance from the self-governing colonies, to cope with new challenges and high costs facing the Royal Navy in the last twenty years of the nineteenth century, met with steadfast resistance. Canada, influenced by the nationalist and imperialist dichotomy that dictated its policy, was more resistant than most. The idea of a Canadian navy was in fact rooting itself in the Canadian mind. Prime Minister John A. Macdonald had not been averse to the idea. Wilfrid Laurier and his Minister of Marine, L. P. Brodeur, had seen the Canadian Government Marine as the embryo of a navy since at least 1903. When the Fisher reforms led to the withdrawal of station ships from the colonies, the British government argued that the Monroe Doctrine shielded Canada from overseas naval attack,[8] but Canada did not react as Britain hoped, by giving all its support to British naval requirements. When as a result of the

Dreadnought scare of 1909 a Conservative member moved that 'Canada should no longer delay in assuming her proper share of the responsibility and financial burden incident to the suitable protection of her exposed coast', there was rare consensus in the House, and the Naval Service Act was passed in 1910. After the election that the Conservative Robert Borden won in 1911, in spite of acrimonious political debate, the Canadian naval idea continued to survive.[9]

Borden adopted a two-track policy to satisfy the sharp differences of opinion in his own party. Debating the Naval Service Bill he had urged a one-time cash gift to Britain for naval construction. That would satisfy the pro-imperialist faction, and assure the nationalists that Canada would not participate in foreign wars. He was also nurturing the concept of a coastal defence navy similar to that proposed by Laurier. The cash gift failed to materialise because the Liberal majority in the Senate defeated Borden's Naval Aid Bill. The coastal defence navy idea languished in the bitter political climate of the day. HMCS *Niobe* and *Rainbow*, the two obsolescent cruisers that sailed so bravely into Halifax and Esquimalt in 1910, experienced high desertion rates and other unhappy setbacks until war broke out in 1914. Borden then took the advice of Winston Churchill, First Lord of the Admiralty, that because of the long time it took to organise naval forces Canada should concentrate on raising troops for the European theatre of war.[10]

The First World War naval experience, somewhat less gratifying to Canadian sensibilities than the noble sacrifice of the Canadian Corps on the Western Front, and the dashing reputation of Canadians in the British flying services, nevertheless set the stage for Canadian naval development in the twentieth century. An unexpected German submarine threat in the western Atlantic turned the RCN from a recruiting agency for the Royal Navy into more or less the kind of small-ship navy that Brodeur, Laurier and Borden had all espoused in their various ways.[11]

The Admiralty's contribution to this development was uneven. Little or no naval force would be needed, said their Lordships, but the senior RN officer on the west coast took over Canadian government resources and personnel without authority and had to be superseded by appointing a retired Canadian RN officer, Rear Admiral W. O. Story, as Rear-Admiral Superintendent of the Esquimalt Dockyard. On the east coast, unable to spare ships from other theatres, the Admiralty reversed its advice when the submarine threat materialised, and again the senior RN officer on the scene, who was found to be 'too advanced in years' to function effectively, acted in high-handed fashion and had to be recalled by the Admiralty. The Commander-in-Chief North America and West Indies

Squadron then began interfering in Canadian matters himself. Consequently, in February 1918 the recently promoted Vice Admiral Story was moved to the east coast as Superintendent of Halifax dockyard. Story now outranked every British officer in the Western Atlantic, and Commodore Walter Hose was free to get the east coast patrols working. Since the Royal Air Force could spare only one or two Canadian organising officers for anti-submarine patrols off Nova Scotia, and no aircraft, Canada formed the short-lived Royal Canadian Naval Air Service. Equipped and manned almost entirely by the United States Navy, it was under the command of Lieutenant Richard E. Byrd, who later won fame as an antarctic explorer.[12] Joined by a small force of 8 USN anti-submarine vessels, the approximately 100 operational Canadian trawlers and drifters based on Halifax and Sydney, Nova Scotia shepherded convoys through the region with remarkable success. U-boats sank a number of unescorted fishing vessels under sail, and were more than a match for any warship the RCN could put up against them in 1918, but located and sank only two large steamers, and one steam fishing trawler.

Captain Herbert Richmond, then on the Admiralty staff, pertinently observed after these events had run their course that it was 'obviously impossible to transplant an ancient growth to new soil as the basis of an entirely new organisation'. Canada needed 'a satisfactory settlement of the question of where Imperial and Canadian Naval responsibility begin and end'.[13] It would take another war to resolve that question, and its resolution would ultimately demonstrate how the aspirations of smaller partners in an alliance will sometimes contribute to the successful prosecution of grand strategy.[14]

The naval staff in 1919, taking their lead from Borden's stand in international negotiations after the First World War, stated the essential requirement of 'nothing more nor less than a separate navy', even though Canada desired 'the closest possible connection with the Royal Navy'.[15] Yet the Admiralty had once again acted without consulting Ottawa, designating Halifax and Esquimalt as the Admiralty's permanent intelligence centres in North America, which threatened to give Bermuda control in the western Atlantic, reminiscent of wartime problems.

The Canadian solution was to make Ottawa the intelligence centre for the whole of Canada and the United States, placing the Halifax and Esquimalt units under that central supervision. The Admiralty agreed, as it was in line with policy recommended by Admiral Lord Jellicoe elsewhere in the empire. This was something that created a link of the first importance between the fledgling Canadian naval service headquarters and the Admiralty's world-wide system of communications and intelligence. The

Director of Naval Intelligence was an officer seconded from the Royal Navy, but the RCN was now directly involved in the whole range of intelligence services and would, for significant periods in wartime, be the lead authority in North America for control of shipping.

The interwar period was one of severe penury for the RCN. The cruiser and two H-Class submarines acquired at the end of the war were paid off in 1922, and the remaining few vessels tended, myth would have it, to go aground on their own gin bottles. When Walter Hose took over from Vice Admiral Sir Charles Kingsmill as Director of the Naval Service he kept the navy idea alive by establishing reserve naval divisions and half-companies in communities across the country, a far-sighted measure that would provide the nucleus for wartime expansion in spite of peacetime retrenchment.[16] The Depression, of course, brought government spending under close scrutiny, so much so that Major-General A. G. L. McNaughton, Chief of General Staff, advocated disbanding the Navy, and the Treasury Board gave brief but serious consideration to reducing the naval estimates from two-and-a-half million dollars to less than five hundred thousand.[17]

When rearmament began in 1936, although the Admiralty would have preferred some cruisers to support RN squadrons, the Canadian naval staff argued successfully for destroyers, which were the most effective anti-submarine vessels and had sufficient fire-power to have a chance of fighting off cruisers. This would reduce the likelihood of Canadian coastal waters becoming hostage to American naval priorities on either coast, and would also reduce the chance that Canadian naval forces would find themselves thrust into operations under direct Admiralty control. Prime Minister Mackenzie King worried especially that Canadian sovereignty would be eroded by relying solely on the United States for local defence. President Roosevelt's repeated observations about American readiness to help Canada, given the weakness of Canadian defences on both coasts, had implications that could not be ignored.[18]

What Canada took into the Second World War was an amalgam of this long and rather complex history of Anglo-Canadian and Canada–US relations. War then exerted its customary influence on affairs. North American supply gave Canadian ports, and Canadian naval and air bases, strategic significance at least equal to that held in any previous war. Even more than in the first U-boat campaign of 1917–18, thanks to improved submarine performance and massive German U-boat construction, the western Atlantic and the eastern seaboard of North America became a target of commerce destruction. Even more than in 1917, Britain hoped for American commitment to the defence of shipping. Roosevelt and

Churchill brought this about through the Atlantic Charter, but Canada played a larger part than anybody, Canadians included, had anticipated.

Naval planners, who have been much maligned in some of the literature, had foreseen a need for expansion, not only in fleet destroyers, but in smaller vessels for anti-submarine defence. The Chief of Naval Staff, Rear Admiral Percy Nelles, was advocating this, but it is not generally realised that Mackenzie King himself, vacationing in Bermuda in 1938, went over war plans for the station with Admiral Sir Sydney Meyrick, the C-in-C, and promised that Canada would fulfil its expected role. The Munich crisis in fact was used as a dress rehearsal for mobilisation, and in January 1939 the Canadian government more than doubled the recruiting ceiling for the naval reserves to nearly 4,000 personnel.[19] The full extent of the need turned out to be much greater than foreseen, and the difficulties of creating a satisfactory naval construction capability in Canadian yards and factories were legion,[20] but with the help of the British Admiralty Technical Mission, Canada produced its quota of corvettes, minesweepers and frigates during the war, and by 1943 Canadian shipyards on the west coast were modifying Auxiliary Aircraft Carriers to Admiralty standards.[21]

Canadian naval operations took place in the context of a society whose experience of war was mostly land-based. Ottawa is 800 miles from Halifax: Halifax is 800 miles from St John's Newfoundland, and communications between operational authorities and Newfoundland, as well as the Gaspé coast, were until at least 1942 primitive in the extreme.[22] Ottawa was often also psychologically remote from the realities of the war at sea. Captain Eric Brand, that estimable and highly effective Director of Trade at Naval Service Headquarters, who had been bred to the sea, is said to have exclaimed with astonishment on seeing a corvette for the first time, 'do you go to sea in that?'[23] As officers with recent operational experience took up appointments in Ottawa the situation improved, but not enough to prevent a major equipment crisis in 1943, nor to prevent shortcomings in training for operational requirements. The removal of the Canadian groups from the Mid-Ocean Escort Force early in 1943 reflected some of this problem; it was not until the summer of 1943 that the RCN arrived at a satisfactory solution. Even then, technological backwardness plagued the fleet. Invariably behind the newest British and American developments, but blessed with some exceptional scientific talent, anxious to use this talent for the stimulation of indigenous production, and not well-informed about every new development elsewhere, the Canadians were slow to acquire reliable centimetric radar, HF/DF and advanced asdic from British and American sources.[24]

Interservice rivalry between the RCN and RCAF, a love-hate relationship between the RCN and RN, and a growing familiarity with the United States Navy, all affected the Canadian naval posture. Wartime employment was seen by certain members of the naval staff as a crucial opportunity to prevent a return to interwar neglect. Enemy activity may have dictated the scope and size of the Canadian naval effort; the determination to take part in fleet operations, not simply to be relegated to convoy escort, led the direction of that effort towards fleet destroyers, cruisers and aircraft carriers.[25]

British manpower shortages helped the RCN achieve this position, when the Cabinet would otherwise have been reluctant to authorise further Canadian naval expansion. Canadian insistence on manning auxiliary aircraft carriers for the RN in 1943, rather than Captain Class frigates, was not entirely welcome to the Admiralty, but for various reasons the RCN prevailed in that case. Since late 1942, led on by the determination of Captain H. N. Lay, Director of Operations at NSHQ, the naval staff had campaigned to get into the naval air business. The urge for cruisers, rejected by the RCN between the wars, came initially in 1940 from a member of the Plans Division, Lieutenant-Commander Geoffrey Todd. This intelligent and articulate officer, an Englishman living in Charleston, S. Carolina at the outbreak of war, argued for cruisers at first within the framework of blockade operations. By 1943, when plans for possible Pacific operations and a postwar navy were underway, he was suggesting that if battle honours were not won by Canadian cruisers and aircraft carriers during the war, it would be difficult to persuade the public after the war that the Navy had any role other than convoy escort. His line of argument sat well with his RCN superiors, and at the Quebec Conference of 1943 the Admiralty delegation happily accepted the offer to man two cruisers. The force planning Todd did for both the Pacific war and the postwar navy remained the basis for all Pacific and postwar fleet compositions put up to the Cabinet until after the war.[26]

The war put the RCN on a relatively secure footing. It had won a measure of public recognition, more it must be said from its record in the Atlantic than from the glamorous fleet operations coveted by the career sailors. It did not emerge as the equivalent of the Canadian Corps in the First World War, which at least one officer thought was the aim. Rapid expansion and equipment problems had caused some embarrassing setbacks in convoy escort operations that were better passed over. The object now was to build on strength, and strength was perceived in 1945 to lie in fleet operations, where the cream of the navy had in official eyes been employed. Korea provided an opportunity for the peacetime navy to prove its skill, and apart from an occasional fall from grace the three Canadian destroyers on station in Korean waters from 1950 to 1955 won a very respectable reputation.[27] The long-term trend, however, was governed by the Soviet submarine fleet, and by 1947 the RCN's most important future role lay in countering that threat, principally in the North Atlantic. This was what governed fleet procurement from 1950 to about 1965.[28]

The Cold War and the weakening of Canada's relationship with the United Kingdom, especially after the Suez crisis, put the RCN more into the American naval orbit than ever before. The Cuban Missile Crisis of 1962 pointed up the situation in dramatic fashion. It also pointed up the ambivalence of the civil–military relationship in Canada. The RCN and RCAF responded to the crisis as they were obliged to respond by alliance commitments. This was splendid, and the Navy's effort received commendation from the USN operational commander. Prime Minister John Diefenbaker, however, deeply suspicious of President Kennedy and attempting to exercise civil control of the military, refused to authorise the Navy's actions. The Defence Minister, Douglas Harkness, with divided loyalties, was left out on a limb. The operational commander, Rear Admiral K. C. Dyer, was forced to act without adequate support from Ottawa. This episode had conflicting implications: the postwar fleet had evidently adapted well to the needs of the time. It proved to be an instrument of both military and diplomatic value, but the diplomatic benefit was lost because the political framework in which the Navy existed was uncertain. Isolated from the society it served, the Navy has been found to be at fault for an unacceptable degree of elitism, and the civil sector for inadequate attention to alliance responsibilities.[29]

The nemesis of the Canadian Navy was believed, and still is believed by a large number of people, to have been Paul Hellyer, Minister of National Defence in Lester Pearson's Liberal government in the mid-60s. Hellyer unified the armed forces, did away with naval uniforms, and fired the admirals who tried to stop him. He never, however, abdicated responsibility for the implications of alliance agreements.[30] Since 1968 the Navy has suffered more from low capital funding than reorganisation, although unification was a painful experience. The end of the Cold War, moreover, effectively put a stop to the procurement pattern that had obtained since 1947, and forced a rethinking of the country's naval *raison d'être*.

The Gulf War, which revealed an astonishing ability to adapt to unexpected and urgent needs, also raises questions about the future. The Navy's monolithic emphasis on combating a Soviet submarine threat had honed its technological capabilities and skills, but had not provided an alternative role for national consumption. Today's Naval Officers'

Association of Canada is doing what the Navy League of Canada tried to do at the turn of the century, publishing pamphlets like *Why Canada Needs Maritime Forces* to educate politicians and the public.

These considerations aside, Canada has not come full circle in the twentieth century, at least not yet. Relegating maritime responsibilities to powerful friends would be a backward step of monumental proportions. The twentieth century may not have fulfilled the expectations of Canadians like Wilfrid Laurier and Robert Borden, but the navy they created has done a great deal to bring Canada to the enviable position it holds in the world today.

NOTES

1. See, for example, Thomas Richard Melville, 'Canada and Sea Power: Canadian Naval Thought and Policy, 1867–1910' unpublished PhD thesis, Duke University, 1981; R. H. Gimblett, 'Tin Pots or Dreadnoughts?: The Evolution of the Naval Policy of the Laurier Administration, 1896–1911', unpublished MA thesis, Trent University, 1981; Roger Sarty & Michael Hadley, *Tin Pots and Pirate Ships: Canadian Naval Forces and German Sea Raiders 1880–1918*, (Montreal, 1991); Roger Sarty, 'The Naval Side of Canadian Sovereignty, 1909–1923' in Fred W. Crickard (ed.), *Oceans Policy in the 1990s: An Atlantic Perspective*, The Niobe Papers, vol. 4, (Naval Officers Association of Canada, 1992), pp. 87–107.
2. W. A. B. Douglas, 'Conflict and Innovation in the Royal Canadian Navy, 1939–1945', in Gerald Jordan (ed.), *Naval Warfare in the Twentieth Century: Essays in Honour of Arthur Marder* (London, 1977).
3. See, for instance, the proceedings of the Maritime Command Historical Conference, October 1993, 'In Quest of a Canadian Naval Identity', Michael Hadley & Fred Crickard (eds), (forthcoming), especially Fred W. Crickard, 'The Strategic Culture of the Canadian Officer Corps', Richard H. Gimblett, 'MIF or MNF?: The Dilemma of the "Lesser" Navies in the Gulf War Coalition', and James D. Kiras, 'Non-traditional roles?: The Past as a Model for the Future'.
4. William T. Baxter, *The House of Hancock: Business in Boston, 1724–1785* (Cambridge, Mass, 1945); Byron Fairchild, *Messrs William Pepperrell: Merchants of Piscataqua* (Ithaca, 1954); Julian Gwyn, *The Enterprising Admiral: The Personal Fortune of Admiral Sir Peter Warren* (Montreal, 1974); James A. Henretta, *'Salutary Neglect': Colonial Administration under the Duke of Newcastle* (Princeton, 1972); Stanley Nider Katz, *Newcastle's New York: Anglo-American Politics, 1732–1733* (Cambridge, Mass, 1968); Michael G. Kammen, *A Rope of Sand: The Colonial Agents, British Politics and the American Revolution* (Ithaca, 1968). See also his 'British and Imperial Interests in the Age of the American Revolution', in

Alison Gilbert Olson & Richard Maxwell Brown, (eds) *Anglo-American Political Relations, 1675–1775* (New Brunswick, New Jersey, 1970).
5. D. K. Fieldhouse, *The Colonial Empires: A Comparative Study from the Eighteenth Century* (London, 1966).
6. W. A. B. Douglas, 'The Blessings of the Land: Naval Officers in Upper Canada, 1815–1841', in Adrian Preston & Peter Dennis (eds), *Swords and Covenants: Essays in Honour of the Centennial of the Royal Military College of Canada* (London, 1976); Robin Harris, 'The Beginnings of the Hydrographic Survey of the Great Lakes and the St Lawrence River', *Historic Kingston*, 14, 1966, 24–39; Paul Cornell, 'William Fitzwilliam Owen, Naval Surveyor, *Collections of the Nova Scotia Historical Society*', XXXII, 1959, 61–82.
7. C. J. Bartlett, *Great Britain and Sea Power, 1815–1853* (Oxford, 1963); Kenneth Bourne, *Britain and the Balance of Power in North America, 1815–1908* (London, 1967); Barry M. Gough, 'The Royal Navy's Legacy to the Royal Canadian Navy in the Pacific, 1880–1914', in James A. Boutilier, (ed.) *The RCN in Retrospect, 1910–1968* (Vancouver, 1982), pp. 1–12; *idem*, 'The End of Pax Britannica and the Origins of the Royal Canadian Navy: Shifting Strategic Demands of an Empire at Sea', in W. A. B. Douglas (ed.) *The RCN in Transition, 1910–1985* (Vancouver, 1988), pp. 90–102; *idem*, *The Royal Navy and the Northwest Coast of North America 1810–1914* (Vancouver, 1971); Gerald Graham, *Empire of the North Atlantic* (Toronto, 1950).
8. Bourne, *Britain and the Balance of Power*, Chaps 9–10.
9. Melville, 'Canada and Seapower', pp. 215, 221; Gimblett, 'Tin Pots or Dreadnoughts?', pp. 235–8; Nigel D. Brodeur, 'L. P. Brodeur and the Origins of the Royal Canadian Navy', in *The RCN in Retrospect*, pp. 13–32; Robert Craig Brown, *Robert Laird Borden: A Biography*, vol. I, Chaps 8 and 11.
10. Borden to McBride, 19 November 1909, file 1/5, Provincial Archives of British Columbia, ADD MSS 347; House of Commons *Debates*, 12 January 1910, 3 February 1910, 15 March 1913 all cited in Roger Sarty, 'The Naval Side of Canadian Sovereignty, 1909–1923'; *idem* 'Silent Sentry: A Military and Political History of Canadian Coast Defence, 1860–1945', unpublished PhD thesis, University of Toronto, 1982, chap. 3; Borden to Sir George Perley, Canadian High Commissioner in London, 7 October 1914; Perley to Borden, 10 October 1914, both printed in G. S. Tucker, *The Naval Service of Canada*, vol. I, *Origins and Early Years* (Ottawa, 1952), pp. 218–9.
11. By far the best account is Sarty & Hadley, *Tin Pots and Pirate Ships*.
12. S. F. Wise, *Canadian Airmen and the First World War: The Official History of the Royal Canadian Airforce*, vol. I (Toronto, 1980), pp. 602–8.
13. Richmond minute of 22 November 1918, ADM 137/1619, cited in Sarty & Hadley, *Tin Pots & Pirate Ships*.
14. David Syrett & W. A. B. Douglas, 'Die Wende in der Schlacht im Atlantik: Die Schliessung des "Grönland-Luftochs", 1942–43', ('The Turning Point in the Battle of the Atlantic: Closing the Greenland Air Gap, 1942–43'), tr. Jürgen Rohwer, *Marine-Rundschau*, vol. 83, Nos I, II and III, pp. 2–11, 70–73, 147–9, 1986.

15. Naval War Staff, 'Occasional paper No. 21, Remarks on Control of the Canadian Navy', 21 October 1919, Desbarats biog file C, Directorate of History, National Defence Headquarters, Ottawa (DHist).
16. James Eayrs, *In Defence of Canada*, vol. I (Toronto, 1964).
17. Gilbert Norman Tucker, *The Naval Service of Canada*, vol I, *Origins and Early Years*, p. 342; see also W. A. B. Douglas *The Creation of a National Airforce*, pp. 125–6.
18. W. L. M. King Diary, 31 July & 9 September 36, 5 March 37, National Archives of Canada ([NAC] MG 26, J13; House of Commons *Debates*, February 19 February 37, 12 November 40; D. Beattie, 'The "Canadian Corollary" to the Monroe Doctrine and the Ogdensburg Agreement of 1940', *The Northern Mariner/Le marin du Nord*, vol. I, No. 1, January 1991, pp. 3–20; W. A. B. Douglas, '"Democratic Spirit and Purpose": Problems in Canadian–American Relations, 1939–1945', in Joel J. Sokolsky & Joseph T. Jockel (eds), *Fifty Years of Canada–U.S. Defence Cooperation: The Road from Ogdensburg* (Lewiston, NY, 1992).
19. Meyrick to 'My dear Roger', 16 October 38, King to Meyrick, 17 October 38, PRO: ADM 116/3802; Admiralty to Cs-in-C, 24 November 38; Meyrick to Secretary of the Admiralty, 31 January 39; Rear Admiral Percy Nelles, CNS, to C-in-C AWI, 24 March 39; CNS to Deputy Minister, 28 October 38; PC 167/26 January 39, NSS 1018-6-2 pt 2, NAC, RG 24, vol. 3852.
20. See for example W. A. B. Douglas and B. Greenhous, *Out of the Shadows: Canada in the Second World War* (2nd edn, Toronto, 1995), pp. 40–61.
21. Tucker, *The Naval Service of Canada*, vol. II, Chaps 2–4; E. R. Forbes, 'Consolidating Disparity: The Maritimes and the Industrialization of Canada during the Second World War', *Acadiensis*, vol. XV, No 2, Spring 1986, 3–27, is an important comment on the competition between naval and mercantile needs, and between regions.
22. Some of the communications difficulties are noted in the official history of the RCAF. See for instance, *The Creation of a National Airforce*, vol. II, p. 495.
23. Interviews.
24. Douglas, 'Conflict and Innovation in the Royal Canadian Navy, 1939–1945'; Marc Milner, *North Atlantic Run: The Royal Canadian Navy and the Battle for the Convoys* (Toronto, 1985); *idem* 'The Implications of Technological Backwardness: The Royal Canadian Navy 1939–1945', *Canadian Defence Quarterly*, vol. 19, No. 3, Winter 1989, 46–53; David Zimmerman, *The Great Naval Battle of Ottawa* (Toronto, 1989).
25. At the QUADRANT meeting in Quebec, on 24 August 1943, John Hingham of the Admiralty delegation noted that the RCN's Director of the Operations Division, Captain H. N. Lay, '. . . intends to recommend a [Fleet Air Arm] as no modern navy, however small, can operate without an air element. He considers that a start should be made now, *while political opportunity offers*, if Canada is to achieve a balanced fleet after the war'. PRO: ADM 1/17498.
26. The substance for this paragraph is to be found in Douglas, 'Conflict and Innovation in the Royal Canadian Navy, 1939–45'; Milner, *North Atlantic Run*, pp. 17–20, 217; Donald Graves & Shawn Cafferky, unpublished narratives on the origins of the naval air branch, DHist. It is remarkable that Joseph Schull's official account of Canadian naval operations, *The Far Distant Ships*, (revised edition, Ottawa, 1952) devotes six of eighteen

chapters to 1944 operations in connection with 'Overlord', and only three to convoy escort operations in the battle of the Atlantic.
27. See for example John Bovey, 'The Destroyers' War in Korea, 1950–53' in *RCN in Retrospect*, pp. 250–270.
28. S. M. Davis, 'The *St. Laurent* decision: Genesis of a Canadian Fleet', in *RCN in Transition*, pp. 187–208; Joel Sokolsky, 'Canada and the Cold War at Sea, 1945–68', *ibid.*, pp. 209–32. The RCN also operated an ice-breaker from 1954 to 1957, to provide a Canadian presence in the Arctic during American supply operations to stations on the so-called Dew Line. In 1957, feeling the strain of NATO commitments, the RCN deliberately relinquished this role to the Coast Guard.
29. Commander Peter Haydon, *The 1962 Cuban Missile Crisis: Canadian Involvement Reconsidered* (Toronto, 1993).
30. Paul Hellyer, *Damn the Torpedoes* (Toronto, 1990); Rear Admiral Jeffry V. Brock, *With Many Voices: Memoirs of a Sailor*, vol. II, *The Thunder and the Sunshine* (Toronto, 1983), self-serving accounts from opposite ends of the spectrum.

16 Imperial Jetsam or National Guardians? The Navies of the Indian Sub-continent 1947–72
James Goldrick

This paper analyses the development of the navies of India and Pakistan in the first twenty-five years after independence. It argues that the two organisations refashioned themselves from their origins in the British Royal Navy into something more distinctly national in character. This change of identity was partly inevitable in itself, partly driven by strategic conditions and, finally, motivated by a developing recognition that survival depended upon each navy gaining external acceptance as a national organisation with a legitimate role in the defence of the state.[1]

The process was not straightforward. In the first decade after independence, both navies utilised the British connection to sustain technical and operational standards which would not otherwise have been possible. The price was that each service became involved in a twilight world of westernised force structures which did not appear relevant. While armies and air forces focussed on the local threat, the Indian Navy (IN) and the Pakistan Navy (PN) became informally part of the Western anti-submarine effort. This dichotomy had internal effects as well. Within both navies, the links with the RN became increasingly uncomfortable as it became obvious that they were not receiving the privileged access to doctrine and equipment enjoyed by other Commonwealth nations. The departure of British loan personnel and the deterioration of relations between India and Pakistan which led to the 1965 conflict marked the beginning of truly national naval thought as each service struggled to prepare itself for war with inadequate resources.

After 1965, both the IN and the PN sought to modernise. Each was forced to compromise on its original conception of a balanced force structure. The PN bought patrol submarines from France and midget craft from Italy, while the IN was able to obtain submarines and missile craft from the USSR. The latter accepted that its plans to expand the Fleet Air Arm would have to wait, while Pakistan could not replace its aged destroyers or frigates. The 1971 War confirmed these trends, although the IN derived the greater relative advantage from its part in the victory over Pakistan, emerging with a more widely accepted role in India's defence. The PN suffered the same partition as Pakistan itself and a nucleus Bangladesh Navy was in being as early as 1972.

The most notable feature of naval development on the sub-continent was the consistency of efforts by local services to maintain or acquire multi-role forces, despite the constraints. Each navy attempted to fuse local requirements with its conception of maritime strategic imperatives. Many of the latter were partially derived from the doctrine of the navies of the West, but such thinking became increasingly national in character. This process of nationalisation was not complete by the end of the 1971 War, but its direction was already well-defined.

Even without partition, the Royal Indian Navy (RIN) was in no condition to embark upon an independent existence in 1947. For over fifty years, sporadic attempts to expand and revitalise the old Royal Indian Marine had foundered on local indifference. Successive Viceroys remained content to entrust the maritime defence of India to the Royal Navy. The RIN was not formally constituted until 1934. Only in 1938 were the funds which had been annually allotted to the RN retained 'for local defence'[2] and a coherent expansion programme was not devised until 1939.[3] In that year the RIN consisted of eight ships and some 1600 officers and men.

This was little enough for wartime expansion, but a key difference between the RIN and the much larger Indian Army was that the former had never employed the 'native officer' system. The marine service only began to recruit Indians for commissioned rank in 1923.[4] By 1944 the RIN unofficially ceased to enter Europeans, but this was too late to ensure that there was any serious possibility three years later of sufficient indigenous expertise to allow it to operate without assistance. Vice-Admiral J. H. Godfrey, who commanded the RIN between 1943 and 1946, estimated that true 'Indianisation' would take between ten and fifteen years.[5]

A second critical element was that the RIN was a small-ship navy. A development programme had been sketched out and discussed with the British Admiralty, but it was no more than a plan.[6] The existing force structure reflected not the needs of an independent state, but piecemeal contributions to Imperial defence. Furthermore, any addition to the fighting strength would have to be made in the face of intense competition for limited funds.

Before 1947 the RIN was subordinate to the Commander-in-Chief of the Army in India and operated as a component of the War Department. There was no tradition of tri-service policy development, nor much experience in its operation when, at independence, all three services were formally placed on an equal footing in each country. The bureaucratic and political weakness which both navies and air forces suffered by comparison to the national armies would prove difficult to remedy. Indoctrination of influential figures and local authorities in naval thought had been attempted as far back as 1923[7], but the process had been fitful over the succeeding decades. Not until J. H. Godfrey's arrival in 1943 was any systematic attempt made to court Indian opinion and even this was hamstrung by political turmoil and the natural tendency of Indian politicians to concentrate on domestic issues.[8] The new regimes were not accustomed to considering the maritime or air context.

Partition destroyed much of the limited foundation which the RIN possessed for coherent expansion. Seagoing units were divided between the rump of the RIN and the new Royal Pakistan Navy (RPN) in the ratio of two to one. India retained the only significant technical support activity, the Bombay dockyard. Most training establishments were in Pakistan, reflecting the pre-war recruiting constituency. The majority of the skilled long service ratings were Punjabi Moslems, most of whom went to the RPN. On the other hand, most of the executive branch officers were Hindus, who remained with the RIN. Pakistan had the dismal prospect of utilising Bombay for maintenance work of any magnitude, which was soon politically impossible, or going as far afield as Malta. Both navies lacked key elements in their logistic and administrative infrastructures.[9]

Even Britain's assistance to the post-independence navies proved a mixed blessing. The extent to which the British senior officers who led the RIN until 1958 and the RPN until 1953 were effective in arguing the naval case is debatable. Debatable that is, with one exception. Even if he never underestimated his own influence in any matter, it is clear that the Earl Mountbatten of Burma capitalised on his relationship with Nehru to secure support for Indian naval projects and his position in the Royal Navy to ensure that the Admiralty did its best to help. Mountbatten also played a key role in bringing the Pakistan Navy's ambitious plans to fruition in the mid-1950s.[10] At a less exalted level, J. W. Jefford, first C-in-C of the RPN (1947–1953) and successive RN Chiefs of the Indian Naval Staff until 1958 enjoyed good relationships with their governments and clearly identified themselves with the services they led, sometimes to the Admiralty's alarm.[11]

Both India and Pakistan drew on the RN for the doctrine, advanced training and deep technical instruction of which they were as yet incapable. British units exercised with the RIN and the RPN in an annual cycle which culminated in the JET (Joint Exercise Trincomalee) series in Ceylonese waters. This access, together with the transfer of refitted craft at preferential prices, allowed India and Pakistan to develop the nucleus of relatively efficient naval forces, equipped for the trade protection and anti-submarine warfare (ASW) role. The Admiralty was careful to ensure that its treatment of the two navies was even-handed and that neither received assistance which would disturb the existing balance, particularly in the form of overtly offensive systems such as submarines.

Herein lay the dichotomy. Unlike many other nations of the British Commonwealth, India would never become a member of the anti-Communist coalition which resulted in the formation of the North Atlantic and South-East Asian Treaty Organisations. Pakistan did join SEATO, largely to strengthen its position in relation to India, but both countries' strategic outlooks were fixed naturally upon defence of land frontiers. Pakistan, with its isolated enclave in East Bengal, endured the prospect of defeat in detail in any conflict with India. The latter had both the threat from Pakistan and a frontier dispute with China to reckon with.

Directing the two navies towards trade protection could not easily be reconciled with local defence needs. This had the effect of placing both navies into the margins of defence policy making. The maritime interests of the two countries were as yet too small to sustain the development of coherent naval strategy on the Anglo-American model. Expansion could only be justified to other national authorities on the basis of an obvious threat. That threat could only be each other.

The British connection was also building up a store of determination for development on indigenous lines. This was more the case for the Indian Navy, which nursed the greater ambitions and which maintained RN personnel on loan for longer than did Pakistan, but it applied to some extent to the latter navy. This was not the result of a clash of cultures or of racism. Indeed, anecdotal evidence is that the experience of Indian and Pakistani officers under training in the United Kingdom was almost uniformly happy.[12]

Indian personnel became acutely irritated by the extent to which the IN's access to the latest developments was confined to what the British thought proper for India to have. This resentment was not wholly reasonable. The British could not be expected to allow access to doctrine or to give financial credits towards creating offensive capabilities for a nation which pursued a non-aligned security policy. It is significant that accounts by Indian naval officers which criticise the Royal Navy's failure to sell ships of the classes and types sought by India make little mention of the fragility of Indian finances.[13] In its negotiations with India and with Pakistan, the British Admiralty sustained a more realistic approach to the budget than did either local service.[14]

Realignment towards local defence requirements did not prove easy for Pakistan, largely because national infrastructure could not support development in the absence of assistance from the UK or the USA. The bulk of the PN's expansion between 1954 and 1958 was financed by the American Military Assistance Program (MAP), which paid for the purchase and modernisation of British ASW escorts and American mine countermeasure craft. If these were not quite what the PN wanted for use against India, they were better than nothing. The only ship bought with national funds was the British light cruiser *Diadem* (renamed *Babur*), ostensibly as a training unit but actually as a counter to the Indian cruiser force.[15] As early as 1957, the Pakistan Navy sought to establish a submarine arm and this step had the backing of both Army and government.[16] Britain and the United States initially refused to support the venture, since it was clearly intended to provide a deterrent against the Indian Navy, rather than training for ASW units.[17] The PN then tried to buy submarines from Sweden, but the cost was such that the Pakistan Finance Ministry would not approve the scheme.[18] This, together with threatened reductions in the surface fleet, brought bitter protests from the naval staff and the resignation of the Navy's C-in-C.[19]

The situation had been confused by Britain's willingness to provide a submarine for exercises, together with the vague promise of a loan in the future. Nevertheless, a key problem became apparent in the affair. The PN had yet to reconcile its concept of operations with either the national defence strategy as envisioned by the Army, or with the realities of the country's economic position. While the Navy agonised over the lines of communication between east and west, the Army concentrated in West Pakistan, hoping that a threat of sufficient magnitude from this direction would deter India from attacking on either side. In the Army's schema, submarines would provide the seaward defence of West Pakistan and the need for surface forces could be discounted. In this context, the Army's strategy was more realistic because the resources to protect both wings of Pakistan simply did not exist. On the other hand, the soldiers were naive to expect that a high technology capability such as submarine force could be created without either the support of a great power or considerable expenditure of hard currency.

The surface forces nevertheless survived. Between 1959 and 1964, the Navy's sustained commitment to Western alliance operations was convenient to the Army because it improved Pakistan's credibility as an alliance partner, keeping open the gates of MAP. For the PN itself, another dividend came in 1964 in the form of an American submarine of the Second World War vintage. Partly demilitarised on arrival, the *Ghazi* was rapidly made fully operational. She was the nucleus of the submarine force which had become the primary goal of the PN.

India's naval ambitions were subject to the steady check of financial reality, which proved more critical than the uncertainty which grew up over the Navy's strategic role. A light cruiser, the *Delhi*, arrived in 1948, but a second could not be made available by the RN until after the end of the Korean War. Lack of refit money then delayed the commissioning of the *Mysore* until 1957. Although six destroyers in all were supplied by the RN between 1949 and 1953, they were not new. Furthermore, despite repeated attempts to secure approval for an aircraft carrier, the Fleet Air Arm expanded only slowly and was operated merely as a fleet requirements force.

Matters improved[20] somewhat when the Indian government approved a relatively large acquisition programme as part of a general expansion in the defence vote. The consistency of the relationship between the IN's achievement of its budget targets and the availability of funds within the wider defence vote was to remain absolute in the years ahead. Provided the Army and Air Force prospered, the Indian Navy would be satisfied, but if economies had to be made, then the IN was vulnerable. For the last time, the programme reflected British thinking rather than Indian. It centred on the creation of an ASW task force for theatre defence of shipping. Apart from a light fleet carrier, no less than twelve ASW and anti-aircraft (AA) frigates were to be built in the United Kingdom, construction made possible by the liberal extension of British credits.

This benign fiscal atmosphere combined with other factors to ensure that the rationale for the new ships was not closely questioned. The first of those factors was Mountbatten, installed as First Sea Lord in 1955. Second, was the expansion programme of the Pakistan Navy. A third consideration was the undeniable old age of the majority of the IN's combatants.

The full programme proved too expensive as India struggled with its balance of payments. Faced with reductions, the IN's priority was clear and four frigates were sacrificed in favour of the carrier. The *Vikrant* would, the IN staff reasoned, restore the operational advantage over the Pakistan Navy with her ASW aircraft and multi-role fighters.

By the time *Vikrant* commissioned in 1961, the Indian Navy's situation had become both uncomfortable and complex, Indonesia, a nation whose Moslem population was naturally sympathetic to Pakistan, was becoming a naval power in its own right, with ambitions to make the region the 'Indonesian Ocean'.[21] Border disputes with China were developing into outright war and this was forcing budgetary priorities away from the IN in favour of the Army and Indian Air Force (IAF). Pakistan's attempts to establish a submarine arm continued and there were indications that the Americans would supply their ally with at least one training unit. Indian attempts to secure British help were rebuffed with the same promise of exercise opportunities as had been made to Pakistan.[22]

Even before the disastrous Sino–Indian border war of 1962, the IN was feeling the pressure. Operating costs were cut, as was expenditure on stores. The loss of sea time not only had a dramatic effect on efficiency, but several newly built ships were immobilised by the lack of spare parts.[23] Some of the IN's problems became obvious during the occupation of Portugese Goa in 1961. The operation was carried out successfully enough, but its execution was marred by a series of mishaps and poor interservice coordination.[24]

The Five Year Defence Plan which the Indian government inaugurated in the wake of the border war provided some relief. The IN took over responsibility for coastal defences and began work on base facilities in the Andaman Islands, a key location for watching the Malacca Straits.[25] The Navy's plans continued to take third place behind the other services, but there were schemes for a modernised destroyer force and a submarine capability, as well as greater emphasis on indigenous shipbuilding.

The Indians lobbied the British hard for assistance, but their demands proved too much even for Mountbatten, now Chief of Defence Staff. Between 1963 and 1965, spurred by the Pakistani acquisition of the *Ghazi*, the IN repeatedly sought the loan of modern surface ships and submarines, as well as assistance with in-country building. Waiting in the wings were the Soviets, who had made overtures as far back as the visit to India of Marshal Zhukov in 1957.[26] The British were willing to subsidise construction of *Leander*-class frigates in Bombay, since this would have obvious dividends for British industry, but the Royal Navy could not spare the units sought by the Indians. Older ships were offered, but the IN proved unwilling to compromise.

The key issue proved to be the submarine requirement. Once Pakistan possessed *Ghazi*, India had to match the capability. Details of the negotiations between Britain and India remain incomplete,[27] but it seems that the latter could not pay the price for modern units that the British required.

In view of the offensive nature of the submarine arm, a credit facility on the lines of that granted for the *Leanders* was not possible. Mountbatten did his best to find a solution, but his proposals came too late; the Soviets had entered the game.[28]

It would be easy to treat the development of the Indo–Soviet naval relationship as inevitable in hindsight, but the truth is otherwise. The USSR did not finally abandon the idea of arms sales to Pakistan until 1968 and the Indian Navy was loath to enter into any agreement, in spite of the wide range of systems offered. Adopting Soviet equipment not only raised the prospect of logistic and personnel problems on the grand scale, it would set the IN apart from the Western navies with which it had operated so comfortably and on whose methods and doctrine, albeit in a restricted sense, it continued to rely.

Indian missions went repeatedly to the USSR in 1964 and 1965, but it took the abortive Indo–Pakistan war of 1965 to force the IN's hand. The latter's role in the short conflict was undistinguished. Caught by surprise, with *Vikrant* in refit and most units returning from ASW exercises in the Bay of Bengal,[29] the IN was hamstrung by restrictive rules of engagement[30] and proved unable to find or attack *Ghazi*. India's lack of offensive maritime activity contrasted with a raid by the Pakistan Navy on the port of Dwarka, which had little strategic value but some moral effect.[31] Of greater concern to India was Indonesia's gesture in despatching submarines and missile boats to Karachi. Had the war continued, it is likely that these vessels would have played some role.[32] The ready availability of such technology gave a clear message to both India and Pakistan.

The Indian Navy was better positioned to meet the challenge. Indeed, its poor performance in the war constituted such an effective argument for modernisation that there is merit in the suggestion that the Dwarka raid proved in the long run to be a strategic disaster for Pakistan. The signing of a naval arms agreement with the Soviets in September 1965 marked the beginning of a much more active period for the IN. The new ships did not come with the benefit of Soviet doctrine. Pre-commissioning training focused wholly upon ship systems, not tactical procedures. The IN had thus to develop not only the technical and logistic infrastructure to support the new submarines, frigates and missile craft it had ordered, but the doctrine required to operate them.

As the Navy grappled with these issues, its strategic thinking became more sophisticated. While the IN sought greater public exposure through fleet reviews and other events, a naval case developed which built upon three basic arguments. The first stressed the vulnerability of India's extended coastline and dispersed island groups.[33] Pakistan aside, the nature of such threats was rarely stated in public, but Indonesia's recent behaviour and Britain's intent to withdraw from East of Suez lent credibility to the concept. The second leg of the naval case was based upon India's own maritime past and the idea that the last and most successful invaders of the sub-continent had come by sea.[34] Thin on detail, this thesis at least provided a useful counterweight to the Army's natural fixation on land frontiers. Finally, the IN pointed to the increasing merchant and fishing fleets and the role which naval and merchant shipbuilding could play in fostering the development of national industry.[35] The campaign eventually developed its own momentum. Whilst the IN's confidence sometimes outran its achieved capability, it was significant that the Indian CNS could claim in 1968 that the departure of the British from the Indian Ocean would leave the IN in complete charge.[36]

The Pakistan Navy was in a difficult position in 1965, with aged ships and no more American and British aid available. In desperation, the PN sought Soviet equipment and protracted negotiations took place from 1965 onwards. In spite of the PN's ardent desire for submarines and missile craft, nothing was ever settled and expectations withered. By 1968 the USSR had determined that its strategic interests lay with India.[37] This meant the end of the PN's hopes for modernising the surface fleet in the near term. While the Navy begged for new construction frigates and even opened talks with British shipbuilders, the Army-led government would only approve funding for submarines or attack craft. Since a renewed conflict with India seemed inevitable, the judgement remained that the priority had to be the defence of the West.

The initiatives adopted were in keeping with this strategy. Three submarines were ordered from France in 1966 and a 'Special Service Group' created around small submersibles, purchased in Italy. The rapid expansion of the submarine force proved possible only with extensive assistance from Turkey, which trained personnel and gave technical assistance for the *Ghazi*, circumventing the American arms embargo.[38] Even then, the trio of French-built *Daphnes* entered service barely in time for the 1971 conflict, while the submersibles' torpedo-tube problems would render them ineffective in the war.[39]

Furthermore, the Pakistan naval staff was acutely aware that even an operational submarine force was not enough to guarantee the seaward defence of West Pakistan. There was little or no cooperation between the services and the PN was not privy to the plans of the Army staff. Although the Navy had repeatedly pressed the case for maritime air forces, it had been unable to obtain any patrol or attack aircraft. The Pakistan Air Force (PAF), hard pressed to match the Indians over the western land frontier, had little interest in providing a maritime strike capability. Matters were not assisted by the steadily widening rift between West and East Pakistan which was to be the primary direct cause of the 1971 war with India. There was little or no evidence of disaffection amongst the Bengali minority within the PN,[40] but the extreme measures taken against East Pakistan made their loyalties uncertain and forced mass internment of the 3,000 personnel involved.

A detailed examination of the 1971 war is outside the scope of this study, but several points must be made. The first was the success of the Indian Navy's operations in the East. After the *Ghazi* came to grief on one of her own mines outside Vishakapatnam, there was no opposition to the *Vikrant*. The ship's air group played a key role in support of the forces which occupied East Pakistan, despite the carrier operating with a defective boiler.[41]

The second feature was the aggressive use of the *Osa*-class missile boats to attack ships and shore facilities around Karachi. The IN's raids were a much more ambitious role for the *Osas* than the coast defence for which the USSR intended the type.[42] The third was the way in which the *Osas'* liberal use of Styx (SS-N-2A) missiles with minimum target classification resulted in the sinking of at least one neutral merchant ship in addition to the Pakistani destroyer *Khaibar* and a minesweeper. The technology had possibly been too new for either naval staff or government to comprehend its implications. By comparison, Indian submarines were under strict orders to attack only visually identified naval targets. With few PN surface ships at sea, they enjoyed no success.

Fourth was the sinking of the Indian frigate *Khukri* by the submarine *Hangor*, an attack conducted with some skill and sophistication.[43] Indian operations in the Arabian Sea were, in the wake of the sinking, rather more cautious than before, providing a clear indication of the deterrent value of the submarines. The PN also remains convinced that a fully operational Special Service Group would have taken a heavy toll of Indian warships in the approaches to Bombay. Fifth, and a point for both navies, was the importance of an all-arms approach to maritime warfare. Pakistan's weaknesses in maritime air contributed considerably to the success of the Indian raids on Karachi.

The sixth event was the ill-judged passage of the *Enterprise* battlegroup into the Bay of Bengal as the Indian campaign in East Pakistan drew to a close. In view of the fact that America's deep involvement in Vietnam meant that there could be no serious prospect of military action over East Pakistan, the decision to despatch the *Enterprise* was egregious in the extreme.[44] Whether or not the deployment was intended as a warning to the Soviet-backed Indians to go no further, it had profound long-term effects. For the first time since independence, the sea had provided the avenue for an external power attempting to thwart what India viewed to be its legitimate goals. From this moment onwards, the IN would argue strongly that it required to maintain force levels sufficient to prevent any great power from intervening in the region again.

There were two contradictory force structure issues which emerged from the 1971 war for the navies of the sub-continent, which soon included a nascent Bangladesh Navy. The first was the clear value of superior technology. The Indians had demonstrated this with their Russian-built Styx missiles, the Pakistanis with the modern *Hangor* and her Type E15 torpedoes.

The second was curiously converse. *Vikrant's* activities, despite her many defects, indicated the merits of even limited capability when facing a limited threat.[45] The Indian Navy confirmed the view that it was better to be able to do something badly than not to be able to do it at all. Neither the Pakistan nor the new Bangladesh Navy would be likely to disagree and their own force structures reflected the same thinking in the years ahead. This is alien to much Western naval doctrine, which has for the last thirty years operated under the influence of systems analysis and the concept of 'cost effectiveness'. The idea is not, however, at all strange to the smaller and poorer navies of the world.

Pakistan's strategic problems had been simplified by the loss of East Pakistan, but the PN's operational conundrums were not solved outright. The mismatch between resources and requirements remained, the more so because any addition to the Indian Navy's capability for long-range operations also improved its potential to interfere with Pakistani shipping. The shared land border with Iran reduced the danger to petroleum supplies, but much vital material could only come by sea. More than ever, the PN would have to define itself almost wholly in terms of its potential to meet the Indians and even this would prove more than the national infrastructure could manage. The dichotomy between the Navy's strategic estimate and that of the still dominant Army remained. The PN refused to abandon its surface fleet outright, but the allocation of resources by the Government would always favour the submarines and Special Service Group.[46]

For its part, access to Soviet technology and a strong national commitment to defence would allow the IN to expand steadily in size and capability in the wake of the 1971 War, while playing an increasingly important role in the exercise of Indian influence in the region. Nevertheless, it too faced perennial difficulties in matching the available resources to its requirements. No supplement to *Vikrant* appeared until the purchase of the elderly British *Hermes* in 1986 and plans for new construction carriers were repeatedly deferred. By the late 1980s, the Soviet connection was increasingly tenuous and the IN would be faced with block obsolescence and inadequate replacement rates within every force element. Despite all this, the intent to maintain a navy which could operate both a strong submarine arm and carrier task groups remained.

The two navies' existence in their second quarter-century would thus continue to display many of the tendencies manifested in their first. A key feature was the struggle to reconcile strategic concepts derived from established maritime powers with the realities of their own situations. Some of that alien doctrine would prove inappropriate, but there was never uncritical acceptance of Anglo-American, Russian or even Chinese thinking. Rather, each service attempted to determine how best such doctrine could serve its vision of the national interest.

If each navy tended to sustain an approach to strategy and force structure not wholly coordinated with other elements of defence policy, or at ease with national perceptions, this was not wholly the result of their origin. Much was due to the environment. Even if naval rhetoric, particularly in Pakistan, sometimes outran the realities of national performance in exploiting the oceans or in developing maritime industries, both services proved reasonably apt in recognising change in the world around them. Both were insistent that national defence had a wider dimension than territorial defence and for this reason, more than any other, they would maintain an allegiance to capabilities which they could maintain only with extreme difficulty.

The problem was to determine where a balance could be struck between the essential and the merely desirable. This is no simple thing within developing countries, in which a navy is not commonly thought of as a first line of national defence and whose requirements can be demanding on limited infrastructure and expensive to meet. From the experience of both India and Pakistan, the solution is likely to be incomplete in nature and erratic in implementation. Yet, on the evidence of the last forty-six years, it may serve.

NOTES

1. This study could not have been written without the benefit of discussions, on and off the record, with a number of senior officers of the navies of India, Pakistan and Bangladesh, both serving and retired. I am extremely

grateful for the assistance they gave, but I must emphasise in fairness to them that the conclusions I have drawn are entirely my own.
2. Vice-Admiral A. E. F. Bedford, 'The Royal Indian Navy', *The Naval Review*, vol. XXVI, No. 2, May 1938, p. 220.
3. Stephen Roskill, *Naval Policy Between the Wars*, Volume II, *The Period of Reluctant Rearmament* (London, 1976), p. 426.
4. Rear Admiral K. Sridharan, *A Maritime History of India* (New Delhi, Government of India, 1982), p. 266.
5. Patrick Beesly, *Very Special Admiral: The Life of Admiral J. H. Godfrey, CB* (London, 1984), p. 293.
6. S. V. Desika Char, 'Planning for the Post-War Defence Forces', Sri Nandam Prasad, *Expansion of the Armed Forces and Defence Organisation 1939–45: Official History of the Indian Armed Forces in the Second World War 1939–45* (Calcutta, 1956), pp. 199–206.
7. Barry D. Hunt, *Sailor-Scholar: Admiral Sir Herbert Richmond 1871–1946* (Waterloo, Ontario, 1982), pp. 144–5.
8. Beesly, *Very Special Admiral*, pp. 260–62.
9. See: Rear Admiral Satyindra Singh, *Under Two Ensigns: The Indian Navy 1945–1950* (Oxford & New Delhi, 1986), pp. 116–26.
10. See correspondence in the papers of Admiral of the Fleet the Earl Mountbatten, Mountbatten Archives, Hartley Library, University of Southampton (hereafter *Mountbatten Papers*) which include extensive correspondence on the acquisition of an aircraft carrier for India and a cruiser for Pakistan. Mountbatten's desire to improve his relationship with Pakistan is particularly evident in the latter case and the internal evidence within the letters exchanged between Mountbatten as First Sea Lord and Rear Admiral M. S. Choudri, Chief of Pakistan Naval Staff, suggests that Choudri was exploiting this for all it was worth. See Mountbatten to Choudri letter of 2 January 1957.
11. Admiral Sir William Parry described Pakistan as 'the enemy' in a visit to the Admiralty in 1949. This was not well received. See: Public Record Office (PRO) ADM 116/5852, Minute M 01679/49 of 19 November 1949.
12. It is not the British which such men complain of in retrospect, it is their weather.
13. See for example: Lieutenant Commander Ravi Kaul, 'India's Russian Navy', *United States Naval Institute Proceedings*, vol. 96, no. 8, August 1970.
14. RIN plans in 1949 for a carrier force which would include two light fleet carriers by 1960 and four fleet carriers by 1968 were reasonably described within the British Admiralty as 'grandiose'. See: PRO:ADM 116/5852 Fifth Sea Lord Minute of 18 January 1950.
15. First Sea Lord Minute of 7 October 1955, *Mountbatten Papers*.
16. Rear Admiral Choudri to Mountbatten letter of 2 November 1957, *Mountbatten Papers*.
17. See: Mountbatten to Admiral Arleigh Burke USN (Chief of Naval Operations) letter of 18 December 1958; and Burke to Mountbatten letter of 6 January 1959, *Mountbatten Papers*. Also: PRO:ADM 205/173 'Sale of Warships to India and Pakistan' Minutes of a meeting held on 2 January 1958.
18. Pakistan Naval History Section, *Story of the Pakistan Navy 1947–1972* (Islamabad, Naval Headquarters, 1991), pp. 199–202.

19. Vice Admiral M. S. Choudri to President Ayub Khan, letter of 26 January 1959. Supplied to the author by Vice Admiral Iqbal F. Qadir.
20. Lorne J. Kavic, *India's Quest for Security: Defence Policies 1947–1965* (Berkeley, 1967), pp. 223–5 (Appendix II, giving statistics on the Indian defence vote).
21. See Ide Anak Agung Gde Agung, *Twenty Years of Indonesian Foreign Policy* (The Hague, 1973), Chap. 16 gives an interesting commentary on Indo-Indonesian relations in this era.
22. PRO:ADM 205/173 'Sale of Warships to India and Pakistan' Minutes of a meeting held on 2 January 1958. Cites First Sea Lord (Mountbatten) to CNS India (Vice Admiral Stephen Carlill) letter of 23 July 1957. See also: First Sea Lord to Vice Chief of Naval Staff Memorandum of 28 May 1957 concerning Krishna Menon's personal request to Mountbatten for the loan of 'one or two' submarines, and an undated letter from Mountbatten to Menon explaining the technical difficulties, *Mountbatten Papers*.
23. Kavic, *India's Quest for Security*, p. 124.
24. Ibid., pp. 62–81; and Sureshwar D. Sinha, *Sailing and Soldiering in Defence of India* (Delhi, 1990), p. 62.
25. Raju G. C. Thomas, 'The Politics of Indian Naval Re-Armament 1962–1974', *Journal of the United Services Institute of India*, October–December 1976, p. 343.
26. Admiral R. D. Katari, *A Sailor Remembers* (New Delhi, 1982), p. 84.
27. Most Admiralty files have yet to be declassified. Rear Admiral Satyindra Singh's *Blueprint to Bluewater: The Indian Navy 1951–65* (New Delhi, 1992), gives an account of the Indian side of the negotiations, pp. 225–44.
28. Philip Ziegler, *Mountbatten* (London, 1985), p. 603.
29. Ravi Kaul, 'The Indo-Pakistani War and the Changing Balance of Power in the Indian Ocean', *United States Naval Institute Proceedings*, 99, 5, (May 1973), p. 186.
30. See Admiral Soman's account in Admiral S. N. Kohli, *We Dared* (New Delhi, 1979), p. 2.
31. Pakistan Navy Historical Section, *Story of the Pakistan Navy*, pp. 219–22.
32. Ibid.
33. Ravindra Tomar *Development of the Indian Navy: An Overstated Case?* (Working Paper No. 26, Strategic and Defence Studies Centre, The Australian National University, Canberra, 1980), p. 4.
34. Thomas, 'The Politics of Indian Naval Re-Armament 1962–1974', p. 344.
35. Vice Admiral A. K. Chatterji (Chief of Naval Staff), 'India and Sea Power' *Hindu*, 11 December 1966.
36. *The Times* (of London), 4 March 1968.
37. Pakistan Navy Historical Section, *Story of the Pakistan Navy*, pp. 283–8.
38. Ibid., pp. 268–70.
39. Ibid., p. 299.
40. The senior Bengali executive branch officer in the PN, the then Commander (later Rear Admiral and CNS of the Bangladesh Navy) M. H. Khan insists that there was no disaffection within the PN before the war. See: Captain A. R. Peters RN letter to the author of 31 August 1992.
41. Vice Admiral N. Krishnan, *No Way But Surrender* (Vikas, New Delhi, 1989), p. 9.

42. See: Kohli, *We Dared* and 'An Interview with Admiral Nanda' in D. Sinha, *Sailing and Soldiering in Defence of India.*
43. Pakistan Navy Historical Section, *Story of the Pakistan Navy*, p. 358.
44. The published accounts indicate considerable confusion in the US decision-making process. See Henry Kissinger, *The White House Years* (Boston, 1979), pp. 842–918; and Elmo R. Zumwalt *On Watch* (New York, 1976), p. 365. The Indian naval commander in the east, Vice Admiral N. Krishnan has suggested in his book, *No Way But Surrender* (p. 57) that 'It was unthinkable that they [the Americans] would commit their aircraft on a ground-support role against our army or air force or wantonly attack our naval forces at sea'.
45. Krishnan, *No Way But Surrender*, pp. 61, 63.
46. For an indication of contemporary problems, see: Lieutenant Commander J. T. Kemper SC, USN (Ret), 'It's More than Ships', *United States Naval Institute Proceedings*, vol. 120, no. 4, (1994), 46–50.

17 British Naval Planning Post-1945
J. R. Hill

Contemporary history is a hard taskmistress. Ruthless with piercing hindsight, relentless with demands for accurate prediction, she is perhaps sternest of all with those who have been near the centre of affairs during the period about which they are writing. Are their personal recollections flawed, incomplete or inaccurate? How much of the inside story did they really know? On the other hand, are official pronouncements to be relied upon, observing their known tendency to the fluffy statement and the weasel word? Are official papers, even classified ones, much better as statements of policy? And finally, how can the planner's individual judgements made at the time not influence his historian's judgement made only a few years later?

This writer served in or around the Ministry of Defence, with occasional remissions, from 1963 to 1980. This paper is therefore subject to all the imperfections implied in the first paragraph. Rather than hedge, it will accept the risks of personal recollection while attempting wherever possible to substantiate its points by reference to published data.

A full statement of the background to naval planning in the post-1945 period would add up to a political, social, and economic history of the time, and that is not the province of this paper. But it is necessary to pick out four elements, themselves interactive, which affected the planning process most profoundly:

The Economic Situation. Britain ended the Second World War in a weak position economically[1] and – not absolutely but relative to other developed economies – hers continued to decline in the next five decades. Resources available for defence were under constant pressure. While this was nothing new in historical terms[2] it was particularly keenly felt by armed services that had been accustomed to priority in defence provision.

Technological Options: The rapid development of military technology during the Second World War laid the foundation for even more swift and diverse development afterwards.[3] A multitude of technical solutions to military problems was available, provided one had the resources. But resources were limited; and this made the planning of naval forces more complex and more dependent on judgement and foresight.

Political Realities. The British Empire still existed in 1945. The USA, then without doubt the world's most powerful nation, was suspicious of empires and would not support its retention; indigenous national movements were widespread; the policing role was increasingly onerous. Retreat from Empire was inevitable, but its timing and implementation were often in doubt and planning had to take account of a plethora of contingencies.

Centralisation of Policy: From 1945 there was a steady trend in British government towards a unified Ministry of Defence with major decisions taken by ministers on the advice of a central defence staff.[4] The two main watersheds in this process were in the early 1960s with the institution of the post of Chief of Defence Staff and the Permanent Under-Secretary's assumption of accounting responsibility for the whole of the defence budget; and in the middle 1980s, with the abolition of single-service Ministers, the strengthening of central staffs and the tightening of control under the Office of Management and Budgets.

The Royal Navy in 1945 had large assets: three-quarters of a million men and women, well over 500 major war vessels, several thousand aircraft and numerous shore-bases at home and abroad. Many elements had had a hard war, but for the most part it was a state-of-the-art force in both material and training, and its very size provided a reservoir of capacity to fill any gaps that appeared. Indeed, there was something of an embarrassment of riches, reflected in both the demobilisation process and the allocation of numerous hulls to the Reserve Fleet.

The Navy was not sorry for this; it was as uncertain of the strategic future as was the government itself, and hedged its bets. Its bid for a Vote A (service personnel) of 150,000 in 1947 was entirely predictable, and was on the same scale as those of the other services. Many proposals for the strength of the fleet, put forward by officers of all seniorities at this time,[5] would have demanded even greater resources. It was unsurprising that the Harwood study of 1949, the first realistic attempt to match strategy, money and force levels with its proposal to reduce the manpower base to under 100,000, was rejected.

The bet-hedgers could point within a very few years to two runners that tended to justify their caution: the Korean War and the Soviet threat. The former was manpower-intensive for the Navy, particularly the Fleet Air Arm which was viewed as the principal instrument of sea power. The latter, recognised by the conclusion of the North Atlantic Treaty in 1949,[6] became eventually, as will be seen, the principal official justification for sizeable and high-quality British maritime forces, but at this time was as much as anything a means of keeping in the mind of public and politicians the need to safeguard the passage of shipping; the very large Soviet submarine force, and the recent experience of the Battle of the Atlantic, were enough to ensure a response, even if on analysis the strategic situation was not parallel with that of the Second World War.

Specifics apart, the Navy and its management had no doubt during this period that it was a national force charged with national tasks. These were acknowledged not always to be predictable, but had to do with preserving the position and influence of Britain wherever the national interest demanded. There was a very strong presumption that Britain might have to act alone in such situations; the Navy thus had to be a balanced force of world-wide reach, and much of the development of the 1950s was directed to this end. The expansion and modernisation of the Royal Fleet Auxiliary, training in replenishment at sea, the introduction of gas-turbine machinery,[7] the continued innovations in carrier technology and the widening of the roles of the Royal Marines along Commando lines were all examples of the implementation of this policy.

Yet however autonomous the Navy might be, it was no longer a powerful enough instrument to enforce the country's will in the face of superpower opposition. Probably the writing had been on the wall since the Abadan crisis of 1951, but it was Suez in 1956 that brought the lesson home. Jackson and Bramall[8] have identified many aspects of misjudgement and poor timing in Britain and France's handling of the affair, but it is doubtful if it could have come off successfully in any event in face of the combined opposition of the USA and USSR (quite apart from the question that exercised so many in Britain at the time: 'What do you do with it when you have got it?').

Nothing would ever be quite the same again. It was not only the assumption that Britain could always undertake unilateral military action that was shaken; the fact that she was so vulnerable to economic pressure (which had been a principal instrument in halting the Suez adventure) was a reminder of the country's worsening relative economic position.

Under the new Macmillan government Duncan Sandys, the Defence Minister, was charged with a thorough review of defence policy taking into account the factors above and, for the first time, a thorough examination of the impact of nuclear weapons (the British thermonuclear weapon was about to be tested). Previously the Royal Navy had rested its case on two foundations: its undoubted flexibility in conventional operations at all levels of conflict; and its claimed ability to conduct a 'broken-backed war' in the wake of a nuclear exchange. Now the latter justification was rudely swept aside; Sandys, a proponent of the massive-retaliation school of deterrence, did not accept it and his judgement was summed up in the famous phrase of his White Paper of April 1957: 'the role of naval forces in total war is uncertain'.[9]

The naval staff, led by Mountbatten, was thrown back on the limited-war role. It was helped by some of the characteristics already mentioned, that had turned it into a balanced and versatile force, and by further emphasis on amphibious warfare as a result of the Suez experience where helicopter-borne assault from carriers had been employed for the first time. There may also have been some perception by the more far-sighted in government that forces of this kind would probably be needed in the next decade (Macmillan's 'Wind of Change' speech was but two years away). In the event, the navy lost only 17% of its manpower, compared with the RAF's 35% and the Army's 45%, and the proportions of the defence budget allocated to each service remained largely unchanged.

The navy was, in structural terms, still a conventional force in the classic mid-century mould. Its main striking power lay in manned aircraft operating from fixed-wing aircraft carriers, its shipping protection capacity in surface units increasingly supplemented by anti-submarine helicopters[10] and helped by cooperation from shore-based maritime patrol aircraft operated by the RAF, and its power projection much enhanced by embarked Royal Marines forces. All these were evolutionary developments from a Second World War base. Two technological developments, one political decision, and increasing financial stringency were conspiring to change that pattern considerably.

The advent of the aerodynamic missile was indeed something the Royal Navy was slow to embrace, compared with some others; this was probably due to the influence of the Fleet Air Arm, who saw in its surface-to-surface application a challenge to their own role, and it was for some years confined to an air defence function. Nevertheless, from the early 1960s onwards the existence of aerodynamic missiles was a factor that entered every aspect of naval planning.

On the other hand, the application of nuclear power to submarine propulsion was, under the influence of Mountbatten, very early embarked upon. By 1962 the *Dreadnought*, her plant acquired with the help of Admiral Rickover USN, with whom Mountbatten had struck up an unlikely friendship,[11] was in the water and the all-British nuclear-powered submarine programme was under way.

It was in good time, for the political decision taken at the Nassau Conference of November 1962, whereby Britain would acquire Polaris ballistic missiles as her strategic deterrent in place of the cancelled

Skybolt, could not possibly have been made without evidence of British expertise in nuclear-powered submarines. The fact that much of the Navy was ambivalent about this novel role was an added twist to the tale. As is known, the brilliantly driven Polaris development programme met all its targets both in the planning stage and operationally; but the cost to other elements of the navy was not negligible.[12]

It was not only the demands of the Polaris programme that caused financial stringency. Indeed this was endemic, and in the mid-1960s matters came to a head with the Healey Defence Review. This coincided with the navy's perceived need for replacement fixed-wing aircraft carriers. The Review indeed revolved around the dispute between the navy and the air force about whether the national interest (it is to be noted that it was still the national interest[13]) in limited conflict would better be served by sea- or land-based air power. The navy's case was weakened by its refusal to accept less costly ships than the proposed 50,000 ton carriers with expensive high-performance aircraft.

The February 1966 decision was traumatic for the navy. Britain would not embark on major operations without allies; the new carriers would not be built. There were two incidental ironies: first, the navy as structured had taken part in the early- and mid-1960s in some of the most successful and economical post-colonial operations ever mounted, notably the confrontation with Indonesia which secured the fledgling state of Malaysia; and second, the overall strategy on which the review was based was still that which some writers[14] have characterised as 'East of Suez', and in the immediate aftermath of the 1966 decision the restructuring of plans by the Future Fleet Working Party continued to use that strategy as its baseline. All that was about to change, and an even more strained period for the naval staff would follow.

While its immediate trigger was an economic crisis, the decision of 15 January 1968 had probably been in Healey's mind for well over a year.[15] By it, the UK commitment to NATO was henceforth to be the justification of the British defence effort; any forces predicated on other than this 'irreducible' task were unlikely to survive. In its effect it stands far and away ahead of any other postwar British strategic decision before or since.

It posed grave problems for the planners on the naval staff. The other two services were well entrenched on the mainland of Europe with relatively well-defined tasks and could with some justification argue that if they gave up some of this commitment NATO's strength and cohesion would be fatally weakened. In the Navy's case the principal ally, the USA, was very powerful at sea and capable in its own view of taking on the

Soviet Navy single-handed. It was happy to accept and acknowledge help from the RN, of course, but the case was not critical as that on the Central Front might be argued to be.

A second problem was the extent of the NATO sea area. Cut off to the south at the Tropic of Cancer, extending only to the Atlantic and Mediterranean, it would if strictly interpreted have limited the Royal Navy to a short reach not imposed upon it since early Tudor times. So far as operations went, Ministers and even civil servants proved flexible about this limitation; and indeed they could hardly have been otherwise in view of the requirements, for example, of the Beira Patrol and the Five-Power Defence Agreement, and Foreign Office pressure to keep up such commitments. But so far as force planning was concerned, the Treasury was always watchful for any development that could not be justified in NATO terms.

Finally, there was a problem concerned with the tempo of operations. One school of Ministers, civil servants and scientists held that any major conflict in Europe was bound to be so short that sea power in any historically recognisable mode would have no effect. Another held that the task of reinforcement across the Atlantic, either during a period of tension or in the early stages of conflict, would be crucial, and in this view were aided by the change in NATO strategy from the tripwire and massive-retaliation of the Military Committee's paper MC 14/2, to the Flexible Response of its successor MC 14/3. But the navy was always on tenterhooks about this aspect of strategy and did not, in my view, sufficiently make the crucial point: that a successful outcome to any major NATO campaign was impossible without continued use of the Atlantic Ocean, and that anyone planning not to ensure such use was planning to lose.[16]

The navy, in any case, never really accepted that British sea power was for NATO purposes only. It had learnt over centuries that the unexpected operation in the unplanned place was quite as likely to happen as the set scenario, and its underlying belief was that it was the Navy's duty – whether so instructed or not – to be ready for such contingencies.

In consequence the naval staff during this period lived a kind of double life. It adopted the single NATO scenario as its justification, particularly the roles of reinforcement of Norway (the Royal Marines had reconstituted themselves as an Arctic force in an astonishingly short space of time) and across the Atlantic, and indeed at one time referred to this as the 'determinant case'; but at the same time it kept firmly in mind the possibility that it might have to cope on a national or *ad hoc* alliance basis with operations, probably of limited scope, further afield, knowing very well that provision for such ventures would have to be justified somehow on a NATO ticket.

So far as force structures and staff requirements were concerned, quality was not difficult to justify. The Soviet Navy was technically advanced and the NATO mandate had to be to match or surpass it, in both material and training. Numbers were a less easy problem; unit costs of ships and aircraft, particularly high-quality ones, were high and subject to escalation beyond normal inflation.[17] Moreover, if British strategy had boiled down to the single phrase 'a contribution to NATO', how big was a contribution? Maintenance of numbers was a constant worry throughout the period.

But the most difficult characteristic of all to justify was reach: the distance from the home base (most foreign bases having gone by now) at which forces could be expected to operate. Operationally, RN ships in the NATO sea area might reasonably be expected to come under the umbrella either of shore-based or USN aircraft, so ship-based air (apart from ASW helicopters, and even they were sometimes challenged by proponents of shore-based ASW aircraft) was arguably a luxury: but the navy knew that beyond the NATO area it was an undoubted necessity. That was a defensive need; it was also highly desirable to have good tactical offensive power, outside the NATO area even more than within it. Logistically, a water-borne supply organisation capable of replenishment at sea was essential for protracted ocean operations.

For the period up to 1980, the naval staff did astonishingly well. It built a case, founded upon the Soviet anti-ship missile threat, for the Sea Harrier VSTOL aircraft which was alleged to be able to shoot down shadowers, probe surface contacts and pose a threat to missile-armed enemy ships. (The air defence role, so prominent later in the very different environment of the South Atlantic, was no doubt in mind, but was not mentioned.)[18] It justified the nuclear-powered submarine programme on ASW grounds; submarine-versus-submarine operations were untried in war (though exercises indicated they could be effective)[19] but at the back of the submariners' minds was the traditional anti-surface ship role. The Royal Fleet Auxiliary was maintained at high standards in numbers and efficiency, justified partly on the low level of afloat support in most Western European fleets. The Royal Marines, as has already been pointed out, were dedicated to the flank role, and Britain's old affinities with Norway were well-deployed in the reasoning.

In this way, aided of course by the material legacy of the previous twenty years when new construction had been predicated – however inarticulately – on a diversity of roles and contingencies, a newly balanced fleet was evolved which was still capable of exercising sea power with a considerable degree of autonomy. But financial stringency, alleviated in the late 1970s by the NATO resolution to increase defence spending by 3% in real terms, was closing in again. The appointment of John Nott as Defence Secretary in 1981 signalled a much sharper attack on naval provision than in any previous review.

The Nott review[20] did not seek to change the strategy set out by Denis Healey in 1968. It was in some ways even more firmly based on 'a contribution to NATO', although it did include an intention 'to exploit the flexibility of our forces beyond the NATO area so far as our resources permit'. Overwhelmingly, however, the new policy was based upon scientific (some in the naval staff might have said pseudo-scientific) advice about the balance of forces needed to fight the NATO-scenario war. There was much discussion of the relative efficacy of 'platforms' and 'weapons', with generalised conclusions in favour of the latter;[21] this inevitably swung the argument away from surface vessels in particular, expensive as they were in both capital and manpower. As was apparent from statements later made by the (by then) ex-Chief Scientific Adviser to the Ministry of Defence,[22] there was decisive rejection of the principle of convoy in the reinforcement role; reliance was placed on the use of shore-based aircraft and submarines in area search and barrier operations, neither of which had been proved anywhere but the computer models of the Defence Operational Analysis Establishment at West Byfleet.[23] The final blow lay in the apparent downgrading of the flanks role; although three Royal Marines Commandos were to be retained, specialist amphibious shipping was to be phased out early.

The effects of the 'Way Forward' document were severe for the navy's plans. In effect, the surface and ship-borne air forces were to be cut by a third, and manpower progressively by almost the same proportion. The balance was to shift even further towards the submarine arm, which already enjoyed greater emphasis than in any other western navy. In summary, the versatility of British sea power, which had been characteristic of our sea forces for several centuries, would be much attenuated.

As everyone knows, the Falklands crisis and subsequent South Atlantic campaign intervened, and the value of balanced naval forces in joint operations was overwhelmingly demonstrated. Nott departed; but the civil servants who had been involved in the 'Way Forward' remained, and so did financial stringency.

Nothing showed the government's unwillingness to change its overall policy better than the loose-leaf Foreword to the 1982 Defence White Paper,[24] dated 18 June, four days after the Argentine forces in Port Stanley had surrendered: 'The events of recent weeks must not, however, obscure the fact that the main threat to the security of the United Kingdom is from the nuclear and conventional forces of the Soviet Union and her Warsaw Pact allies. It was to meet this threat that the defence programme described in Command 8288 was designed. The framework of that programme remains appropriate'.

Thus, although in practice the navy obtained some respite with the retention of the third aircraft carrier and the replacement of war losses of frigates and aircraft, it remained under severe pressure materially and in manpower, where the planned reductions were scarcely abated. Conceptually, however, its position did improve somewhat, for two reasons. First, and not only because of the Falklands conflict, Whitehall was being 'nudged'[25] into a more open acceptance of the out-of-area role. Second, the announcement of the American forward 'Maritime Strategy' in 1986[26] gave the RN a further opportunity to bid for high-quality forces which it exploited to the full. There were dangers in that approach; high-quality forces are expensive, and if the need for them is seen to fall away they are on the priority list for cancellation.

This vulnerability turned out to be less damaging than might have been expected when the Soviet empire collapsed and the Warsaw Pact crumbled in 1989–90. In the turbulent outcome it was clear that the flexibility of naval forces was an important asset, and the strategic aims stated in the Defence White Paper of 1992[27] gave naval forces a sounder policy base than any since 1968. Moreover, it was difficult for detractors to argue that there was serious over-provision of quality in any field except possibly that of anti-submarine warfare, and even there the increasing sophistication and proliferation of submarine forces round the world could be prayed in aid of a continuing high capability.

In consequence, naval planning in 1994 continues to cater for a high-quality, balanced force capable of world-wide operations.[28] The three core capabilities appear to be carriers, nuclear-powered submarines and amphibious forces including specialised shipping with, as supporting units, a reduced destroyer and frigate force, mine countermeasures vessels and the Royal Fleet Auxiliary. Numbers, both of ships and personnel, are probably the matter of greatest concern to the planners; the ability to embark upon an independent operation at any but a strictly limited level, and even more to sustain it once begun, is clearly much strained. Whether, given the modern emphasis on coalition and United Nations operations, the risk is worth taking will be for history (and maybe hindsight) to judge.

This account, personal as some of it is, may give the impression that British naval planners since 1945 were a Macchiavellian lot who subverted government policy in their efforts to preserve an outdated naval capacity. It was much less clear-cut than that. Much of the thinking was inarticulate, reactive, instinctive. It may have been none-the-less correct in its judgement that the nation's needs would best be served by a fleet of high quality and long reach, and that any justification should be employed to achieve that end so far as the Treasury would allow.

The slow gestation and decay of naval forces militated against radical change, and this often helped the navy to hold its position, although when development was very protracted, as it was in the case of all too many British weapon systems, it worked against efficient use of resources.

Finally, though naval planning and its execution put many glosses on government policy, the main lines of that policy were honoured. The Royal Navy was a wholehearted participant in the two greatest developments of post-1945 British military thinking: concentration on alliance operations, including command structures and common procedures; and preparation and training for joint operations, which found its apotheosis (cumbersome command arrangements notwithstanding) in 1982. In a time of Britain's decisive transition to the status of a medium power, naval planning didn't turn out too badly.

NOTES

1. Correlli Barnett, *The Audit of War* (London, 1986), p. 8.
2. David French, *The British Way in Warfare 1688–2000* (London, 1990), pp. 38, 120. D. A. Baugh, quoting B. R. Mitchell's *Abstract of British Historical Statistics* (Cambridge, 1962) derives a 100: 40 mean ratio between wartime and peacetime spending on the navy in the eighteenth century. As Barnett (op. cit., n.1) has shown, in the twentieth century that differential was much greater.
3. Norman Friedman, *The Postwar Naval Revolution* (London, 1986), Chaps 2 and 3.
4. Bill Jackson & Dwin Bramall, *The Chiefs* (London, 1992), pp. xxii, 330–39, 429–31.
5. Eric Grove, *Vanguard to Trident* (London, 1987), pp. 31–3. For unofficial views see 'Nico' , 'The Navy of the Future' , *Naval Review XXXIV* (1946), pp. 147–50, and 'Teaboat' , 'The Shape of Things to Come' in the same, pp. 326–30.
6. Sir Nicholas Henderson, *The Birth of NATO* (London, 1982). In spite of its date of publication this is a contemporary account and all the more valuable. The maritime considerations (pp. 11, 37) are of particular interest in the context of this paper, as is the 'reasoning' for the adoption of the southern boundary of the NATO area (p. 81).
7. Norman Friedman ed., *Navies in the Nuclear Age* (London, 1993) p. 56. Vice Admiral Sir Louis LeBailly in *The Man Around the Engine* (Havant,

1990) regards the gas turbine as an essential innovation in the development of modern fleets.
8. Jackson & Bramall, op. cit., n.4, p. 298.
9. Grove, op. cit., n.5, p. 203.
10. Lieutenant Commander J. M. Milne, *Flashing Blades over the Sea* (Liskeard, 1981) gives one of the best accounts of early shipborne helicopter development and operation.
11. Grove, op. cit., n.5, p. 230. See also P. Nailor, *The Nassau Connection* (London, HMSO, 1988), p. 4.
12. Moreover, the principle that the Navy vote was responsible for the national strategic deterrent was carried on with ever more acute results in the planning for Trident, the successor to Polaris. See Admiral of the Fleet Sir Henry Leach, *Endure No Makeshifts* (London, 1993), p. 198.
13. Even the 1967 Supplementary Statement on Defence, subsequent to the carrier decision, referred to defence in national terms. However far-sighted planners, led by Captain David Williams, the Director of Naval Plans, were already ensuring a NATO footnote to every justification.
14. Grove, op. cit., n.5, p. 245
15. G. Williams & B. Reed, *Denis Healey and the Policies of Power* (London, 1971), pp. 242–5.
16. The only occasion on which, to the writer's knowledge, this point was made openly and directly to H.M. Government was by the Greenwich Forum in 1981, subsequent to the Nott review. Official reaction was very cross indeed, even though the statement received little mention in the press.
17. Sir Frank Cooper, 'Economic Constraints on Britain's Defence Planning', in G. Till ed., *The Future of British Sea Power* (London, 1984), p. 178, and J. R. Hill, 'Apocalypse When?', RUSI *Journal*, June 1981, p. 63, and *Maritime Strategy for Medium Powers* (London, 1986), p. 186, put cost growth for comparable equipments at 6–10% pa and 6% pa respectively.
18. J. R. Hill, *The Royal Navy Today and Tomorrow* (London, 1981), p. 68.
19. For deeper discussion of this vexed question see D. C. F. Daniel, *Anti-Submarine Warfare and Superpower Strategic Stability* (London/IISS, 1986); J. R. Hill, *Anti-Submarine Warfare* (Annapolis, Md., 2nd edn, 1989); Richard Compton-Hall, *Submarine versus Submarine* (Newton Abbot, 1988). All seem to agree that the rate of *effective* encounter (that is, encounters that result in submarine-versus-submarine action) is the most doubtful factor, and likely to be a good deal lower than anything suggested by theoretical models or indeed by works of fiction such as Clancy's *Hunt for Red October* or John Wingate's *Submarine*.
20. HMSO, Cmnd 8288 (1981).
21. Ibid., para 5.
22. Professor Sir Ronald Mason, 'Problems of Fleet Balance' in Till, loc. cit. n.17, pp. 214–15.
23. These were notoriously assumption-sensitive. In one study, which should have become famous, in 1974 it was assumed that whenever opposing forces got within extreme detection range an encounter would ensue. The writer innocently asked the Director, DOAE 'Is it right the sky's always blue over West Byfleet?' He lived to tell the tale, but only just.
24. HMSO, Cmnd 8529-I (1982).

25. Jackson & Bramall, op. cit., n.4, p. 434.
26. Admiral J. D. Watkins USN, *The Maritime Strategy* (Annapolis, Md., 1986).
27. HMSO, Cm 1981 (1992), p. 9.
28. Admiral Sir Benjamin Bathurst, 'View from the First Sea Lord', *RN Broadsheet 93* p. 2. The text is a paraphrase of the First Sea Lord's words but it is believed the sense has been preserved.

18 Partnership Spurned: The Royal Navy's Search for a Joint Maritime-Air Strategy East of Suez, 1961–63

Eric Grove

In the early 1960s the Royal Navy's primary role was power projection in the Indian Ocean and the Far East, 'East of Suez'. It had already been decided in 1957 that here was the area where limited war was most likely, where commitments might have to be discharged without the support of allies and where an 'all purpose fleet' was therefore required.[1] Such was the legacy of Duncan Sandys to his successor as Minister of Defence, Harold Watkinson, who in 1961 asked the Admiralty to consider the shape of Britain's future naval policy for the 1970s. In a major presentation to the minister the Admiralty offered three alternative fleets based on differing assumptions; that things stayed as they were, that Britain withdrew from East of Suez, and that Britain had no bases East of Suez except Australia.

In the first and third of these scenarios carrier-based air power had the central role to play in the support of 'the overseas deployment of our troops against opposition'.[2] The Admiralty was careful to emphasise the complementary nature of carrier and land-based air power. Knowing the Secretary of State's preferences for multi-service projects the Admiralty suggested a common RAF/RN advanced strike aircraft. To operate the new aircraft five new 50,000 ton carriers would be required costing £50–60 million each. If East of Suez was to be sustained with no bases except in Australia, as seemed likely in the 1970s, then the UK's requirement would become 'the ability to deploy our overseas military strength from a Joint Services Seaborne Force', a concept that would require a sixth carrier.[3]

Sir Charles Lambe, the First Sea Lord, was careful to call the suggested JSSF 'much more than a navy', more 'a closely integrated tri-service force'. Lambe argued that it was 'inescapable' that the sea would become

227

more important as the UK was forced out of bases and faced barriers to overflight rights. He made a plea for an investigation on a tri-service basis of a 'world-wide maritime strategy' and 'a truly inter-Service force, which incidentally would do much to bring us together on the battlefield of Whitehall'. Lambe wished, he said, to take carriers

> out of the purely Naval context. I should like to present them as national assets; as mobile self-contained airfields. They are not a naval gimmick. They are in no sense in competition with, nor antagonistic to, our own shore-based air power... It is our belief that if British military power is to continue to be deployed around the world – then mobile airfields in the form of Aircraft Carriers ought positively to be part of this country's armoury. It is sensible for the Navy to own and operate those ships – but we should welcome as much flexibility between seaborne and land-based aircraft squadrons as the Admiralty and the Air Ministry together could devise.[4]

After Lambe's death the policy was continued by his successor Sir Caspar John, the first Fleet Air Arm officer to become First Sea Lord. In Admiralty Board discussions on the draft outline design and proposals of the new 53,000 ton carrier, suggestions that the Navy was being too ambitious were countered by the First Sea Lord who justified the plans on the grounds that 'for some time in the 1970s and onwards, the new carrier force would be the only way to deploy air power flexibly around the world. He expressed hope that the cost would to some extent be offset by reductions elsewhere in the Defence Budget.' The majority of the Board agreed that 'regarding the carriers as floating mobile airfields of national importance, and as the only medium of exercising air power over large areas in the world they should be built so as to be capable of taking a wider range of aircraft types than that used by the RN. A smaller ship might prove to be of no value to the RAF in years to come and would spoil the prospect of a genuine RN/RAF partnership such as was hoped for.' It was decided that the case for the 53,000 ton ship 'should be presented on the broadest interservice basis, and not as a purely naval interest.'[5]

This joint emphasis helped to steer the carrier project through its early stages. The Royal Air Force was forced to come up with a common carrier concept of its own, known colloquially as the 'Pike Ship' after the Chief of the Air Staff, Air Chief Marshal Sir Thomas Pike, a most implacable enemy of the carrier programme. A Joint Planning study resulting from the Admiralty's JSSF concept proposed the concept of a smaller dual-purpose carrier that would 'be basically a commando carrier but capable of the alternative role of acting temporarily as a mobile base for shore-based close support/fighter aircraft'.[6] The Air Ministry argued that operations beyond the range of shore-based transport and strike aircraft would by definition be only of a minor character. This led the airmen to argue that:

> The elimination of the fleet carrier would result in large savings without impairing the ability of British forces to undertake operations likely to be within the scope of their overall resources. For example the estimated cost of a fleet carrier is £50M, by comparison with £5M for an island base, such as Gan, from which a long range air effort could be mounted without dissipating resources on countering the numerous forms of attack to which carriers are vulnerable.'[7]

In reply, the Admiralty emphasised the limitations inherent in relying on shore bases and stressed both the advantages of sealift over the disadvantages of airlift and the ability to poise a seaborne force in an area during a period of tension or negotiation. The most economical and flexible method of ensuring overseas air support for the Army 'would be by the use of fleet carriers operating the Buccaneer or its replacement supported, where security of tenure can be assured, by the Buccaneer or its replacement operating from shore air-bases.'[8]

A joint working party was set up to investigate the issue and the Admiralty seemed to get the best of the argument. John wrote to Pike on 23 November that his ships would not 'ensure safe and timely arrival of a seaborne military force', they could not even provide their own effective fighter defence; they would be strictly an adjunct to an indefinite number of conveniently placed shore bases. 'And when we are talking of a time-scale extending from 1970 to close on 2000 AD, how can we possibly make the assumption that such bases would be available?'[9]

John clearly considered himself to be in a strong position. His confidence was justified in early December 1961 when Lord Mountbatten, the Chief of Defence Staff, gave to the 'neutral' Chief of the Imperial General Staff, Sir Francis Festing, the task of arbitrating between the interested services on the carrier question. Festing produced a paper 'Future Air Strike Policy In Limited War Outside Europe' which came out in favour of a common light bomber/strike fighter for RAF/RN use East of Suez in the 1970s that could 'be used in operations either from shore bases or from carriers according to the requirements of a particular operation'. Festing argued for a fleet of two amphibious task groups with two fleet and two light fleet carriers, although he was willing to accept that it might be more cost-effective to make all the carriers larger types, especially as shore bases declined. Reductions in numbers of aircraft from rationalisation would help pay for a four-carrier force.[10]

Festing's report helped clear the way for Chiefs of Staff approval of further work on the carrier programme. On 5 December the First Sea Lord had submitted a paper that made the case for the carrier as 'a mobile forward base for the operation of manned aircraft' that could 'be deployed at will over wide areas of the world whenever the threat or the active intervention of air power is required in support of U.K. interests.'[11] John called for a ship in the same size category as *Ark Royal* and *Eagle* that would eventually operate aircraft built to common RN/RAF staff requirements; work on a replacement for *Victorious* had to be started immediately for ordering in 1962–63. 'Without replacement carriers', John wrote, 'one could foresee a day when intervention on land by a military force would not be practicable because air support would not be available.'[12]

The question was considered by the Chiefs of Staff on 14 December. It was agreed that

'since the extent to which reliance can be placed in the next ten years or so on fixed bases is at present very uncertain, and we may in this period be faced with having no base between the United Kingdom and Australia, there will be a need for aircraft carriers to provide bases from which British air power can be operated irrespective of whether this power is provided by the Royal Air Force or the Fleet Air Arm.'[13]

It was felt that increasing aircraft size dictated 'carriers which would afford the maximum flexibility and aircraft capacity within the limits of our present docking facilities'.[14] Common VSTOL aircraft were recommended for both the FAA and RAF.[15]

It was agreed that an attempt should be made to combine the TSR2 replacement (OR355) with the Buccaneer replacement (OR346), either in one machine or separate fighter/ground attack and strike/reconnaissance types, both to be used in common and to be available in 1975–77. As a first step the STOV/L P1154 should be procured for both services with an in-service date of 1969–70. This would give the Navy a supersonic fighter – albeit one of limited range – at an earlier date than previously expected. This carefully crafted compromise meant that work on the new carrier could go forward. A meeting of the Chiefs of Staff on 9 January 1962 confirmed the need for a replacement for the carrier *Victorious* but the naval victory was mitigated by the Chief of the Air Staff obtaining agreement that the general question of carrier replacement was still open.[16] The Air Ministry had already unveiled an alternative idea for solving the East of Suez air support problem, one using a network of island bases. This had not received a very favourable initial reaction from the other Chiefs of Staff but Pike was able to keep it on the agenda.[17]

Nevertheless the Air Ministry was not feeling too strong at the beginning of 1962. TSR2 was proving more expensive than expected and the RAF did not want the Navy to question its custody of the strategic deterrent. The air-launched Skybolt missile had been chosen to replace the abortive Blue Streak IRBM but the programme was in doubt and the Air Ministry knew that, if provoked, the Navy might push for Polaris. The Chief of the Air Staff was therefore advised to acquiesce in the Cabinet Defence Committee decision of 31 January 1962 which authorised 'the Minister of Defence and the First Lord of the Admiralty to put in hand the necessary design work for at least one new carrier to replace HMS *Victorious*.'[18] The RAF could console itself that the decision did not commit the Government to an order, let alone a programme.[19] Indeed, the paper on which the Defence Committee's discussions were based made the point that work on the carrier could be stopped if required and that the proposed ship was not 'a 'fleet carrier' in the sense of a capital ship designed for global war. It was to be designed as a floating airfield capable of operating Royal Navy or Royal Air Force aircraft of common types.[20]

This all took place against the background of a major review of Britain's future strategy. The problem was the usual shortfall between existing Defence plans and the Treasury's proposed future allocations. On 23 October 1961 the Prime Minister had ordered the Chiefs of Staff to prepare a new 'strategy for circumstances short of global war' for the 1960s and beyond.[21] The planning assumptions included the following:

> That the circumstances in which our forces might have to intervene could vary from occasions when points of entry, and possibly local facilities, would be available to us to occasions when points of entry would be in hostile hands, requiring us to face opposition to establish ourselves. We do not, however, believe that we would, at least without Allies, attempt to intervene in the face of heavy opposition requiring us to mount full scale assault.[22]

This weakened the long-term case for the carrier but in the meantime the aim was to use seaborne and airborne mobility 'to continue to provide military support for our national policies in spite of diminution of our overseas footholds.'[23] The study therefore called for an extra carrier to be deployed East of Suez as part of a general naval reinforcement of the area, including the provision of new assault ships.[24]

The problem was that the new strategy was still on the margins of affordability. After the 'night of the long knives' of July 1962 when Macmillan drastically reconstructed his Cabinet and brought in both a new Minister of Defence, Peter Thorneycroft and a new Chancellor, Reginald

Maudling, the Defence Committee was hearing that 'the attempt to maintain our role in Europe, our contribution to the deterrent and our worldwide military presence was proving too much for us; and that to try to do all these things upon the scale at present attempted was plainly beyond our resources.'[25] A further review of commitments and forces had therefore to be carried out. Lord Carrington, who had survived as First Lord, sent Thorneycroft a well-argued submission that argued for carriers 'as mobile air bases for RN or RAF aircraft, rather than capital ships for executing purely naval tasks.'[26] It was 'the unique merit of maritime air power ... that the same balanced military capability can be brought to bear in large areas of the world where the changing political scene may require it.'[27]

In September Thorneycroft set up a scientific panel chaired by Sir Solly Zuckerman, the Chief Scientific Adviser, to investigate the circumstances in which the RAF's ideas on a chain of island bases would be effective and those in which a carrier replacement programme would be necessary. This investigation forced both sides to hone their arguments, but especially the RAF who began to develop their island concept into a firm plan.[28] In early October the Air Minister Hugh Fraser provided Thorneycroft with a paper based on the same premises as Carrington's case, the need for flexibility, the restrictions on bases and transit rights, and the desire of the USA to see the UK continuing to play a role East of Suez. It emphasised, however, that an 'Island Stance, ... from which military power could be delivered by air [was] the quickest and cheapest method and the one with maximum potential growth.'[29] The Air Ministry was careful to insist that there was still a need for sea and air power in combination, but what needed to be avoided was 'the present duplication of force, in which we are to maintain two different and costly systems for delivering an assault force and giving it air support.'[30] Strategic airlift was sufficient to move a reinforced brigade group at fighting scales with RAF TSR2s and P1154s in support. The great beauty of the RAF's plan, it claimed, was that it necessitated such a small amount of extra expenditure.

Pike made a similar case 'in a forthright, fearless manner' at a Chiefs of Staff meeting in October, and Mountbatten asked for a written version of the Air Ministry's case.[31] In November the Air Staff produced a brief that was to be the basis of a presentation by Fraser and Pike to Thorneycroft. This was an impressive piece of work, detailing the assets required and the main bases: Masirah, Aldabra (mounting bases), and Ascension and Gan (staging bases). These would cost only £32 million to set up.[32] Pike also submitted a formal paper on carriers to the Chiefs of Staff committee that argued that the UK could not afford weapons systems such as carriers whose cost was 'disproportionate to their effectiveness, or which involve the duplication of effort and expenditure'. The existence or otherwise of carriers had no effect on the size of the RAF; deleting carriers meant no more TSR2s or P1154s, a telling point to cost-conscious planners. Pike's conclusions were as follows:

> It is possible to foresee situations in which carriers would be useful, but we must balance the likelihood and gravity of the risk against the cost of the insurance. In view especially of the advance in the capabilities of aircraft, the risks against which carriers and only carriers can guard seem to me likely to become increasingly remote in the 1970s. For these reasons, and because of their inherent operational limitations and low cost-effectiveness, new carriers seem to me a very poor investment. And even if carriers were operationally more effective and better value for the money spent on them, their cost still seems likely to be unacceptably high. To argue that carriers are essential to our strategy could well precipitate the conclusion that we cannot afford to sustain the commitments for which the carriers would be intended. This would be a pity, since I believe that it should be within our means to do so by other methods which are more effective and very much cheaper.[33]

This was the argument that would have special resonance with Mr Healey three years later.

Caspar John replied on 10 December 1962. He agreed that rising costs were the major problem but staked his case on rationalisation, going back to Lambe's 1961 presentation and the Festing report. He argued that the Island Stance was likely to be both expensive and inflexible and that it could only deal with threats in ways (air strikes) that were politically unacceptable. The First Sea Lord doubted Pike's claims as to cost-effectiveness and argued that, far from being vulnerable, a carrier was 'hard to pinpoint, hard to hit, and even if hit, extremely hard to disable', that its reaction time was better than that of air forces as it could be moved when air movements were inhibited; that it had high endurance; and that carrier aircraft availability was much greater and more flexible than Pike had argued. The First Sea Lord summed up thus:

(a) I have always held that what this country needs is a flexible strategy with versatile forces; and that we should avoid the strait jacket of a wholly land based air strategy.
(b) No valid alternative to aircraft carriers for the flexible deployment of tactical air power world wide has been known to exist, much less costed.

(c) I conclude, therefore that aircraft carriers are, and will continue to be indispensable. Consequently we should not seek economies in the emasculation of the carrier programme.
(d) We should aim instead to affect economies by making sea and land based air power truly complementary. One way to do so would be to pursue the rationalisation of the numbers and types of combat aircraft on the lines recommended by Field Marshal Festing.'[34]

The Admiralty kept up the pressure in January, submitting a point by point refutation of Pike's document to the Chiefs of Staff, and a paper from the First Lord to Thorneycroft. The Island Stance was denounced on both political and military grounds. Bases could not be moved to meet changing threats. Possession of the islands in question was uncertain and the local response to building them up might well be counter-productive strategically. The Island Stance was expensive, offered too few military options to be politically acceptable and would only provide a limited deterrent. The Admiralty stressed its commitment to a balanced strategy.[35]

The context of the dispute changed significantly at the end of 1962, and the stakes became higher, at least for the Air Ministry. Its fears over the future of the nuclear deterrent proved only too well-founded. The Nassau Agreement on Polaris was a major blow to the RAF, whose fundamental *raison d'être* had always been strategic air warfare. A monopoly of other forms of air strike warfare was now essential if the very survival of the service as an institution was to be assured. However much the Admiralty might talk of partnership, a carrier force as the primary mobile limited war air force would look like a naval air arm, beginning a logical process that could well end in the partition of the third service with the Army taking over air transport and close air support. The debate over the creation of the new unified Ministry of Defence was also beginning which meant that bureaucratic structures were unusually fluid. The fact that Mountbatten, who had created much ill-feeling as First Sea Lord by an attempted take-over of Coastal Command, was the primary architect of the new structure did nothing to allay the RAF's fears.[36] In fact, Mountbatten had always trodden very softly on Polaris precisely because he did not want to create an even more aggressive anti-carrier policy on the part of the RAF. A final factor was the French veto on British EEC membership that dashed high hopes of economic expansion at mainland European rates, thus increasing Maudling's desire to assert control over the spiralling defence budget.

Thorneycroft initiated yet another look at long-term strategic planning. Pike argued that his Island Stance remained the cheapest foundation for an intervention capacity East of Suez. The loss of the aircraft carriers was a pity, since carriers could often make a bonus contribution. But they would not enable us to dispense with anything else; they are subject to serious operational limitations; and the risks against which they and they alone can insure us seem to be at best few, marginal, and not among the most likely. We have got to take calculated risks somewhere.[37]

On 21 January a meeting took place in Mountbatten's office at which Pike, perhaps sensing that a more moderate line might make significant inroads into the Admiralty's position and that the Admiralty's partnership proposals had some political attraction, set out the RAF's terms for partnership. He proposed that the Royal Navy reduce rather than abandon its carrier role. This could be achieved by the abandonment of the tactical strike role to avoid 'duplication', abandoning OR346, and moving towards a common fighter/ground attack force of P1154s operating from both ships and shore bases with combined training and logistic support. No take-over bid for the Fleet Air Arm was intended.[38]

John was encouraged by these apparent concessions as he made clear to Pike in a letter of the following day. He foresaw no difficulty in FAA aircraft operating ashore under RAF command and welcomed Pike's views on the maintenance of the Fleet Air Arm. It was important to the First Sea Lord to have this firmly established 'because I strongly feel that there are the seeds of great danger for our successors, if the Navy were once again in the fatuous position of providing mobile airfields for the RAF without the knowledge and experience to make sense of them.'[39] John however still asserted the Royal Navy's desire to retain the tactical strike role, and the need for a special version of the P1154 with two seats and a radar which would be catapulted off the carrier in order to optimise its range and make it a suitable successor to the Sea Vixen.[40]

The new more conciliatory RAF line began to bear fruit. On Saturday 9 February important meetings of the Cabinet Defence Committee were held at Chequers to decide on major questions of strategy and force posture.[41] At Chequers Caspar John made the case for the carriers in terms of the need to protect British shipping and make armed interventions on a global basis. He specifically denied the validity of the NATO Striking Fleet concept, an interesting volte-face compared to the carrier controversy of a decade before.[42] Thorneycroft supported the First Sea Lord on completing design work on the new carrier and ordering long-lead items – but at a price. The Navy was indeed to lose the long-range strike role and OR346. Instead, a 'thorough study of alternative methods whereby the navy and air force could combine in support of the army at less cost than by the provision of a carrier fleet' would be carried out.[43]

This was a significant reverse for the Admiralty but the outlook did not remain bleak for long. In late April the Zuckerman Report was circulated. It concluded that the most likely form of intervention was at the invitation of a threatened regime for internal security purposes. This would require neither carriers nor the Island Stance. In the less likely event of intervention against low or moderate opposition, carriers, because of their proximity, could provide more effective air defence and more flexible air support than aircraft flying from distant islands. The panel's last paragraph was remarkably prescient:

> Failing the provision of an effective carrier task force or conceivably of an air task force considerably strengthened above present Air Ministry estimates – and both these would be very expensive – it seems to us that Her Majesty's Government will be committed to a policy of using the carrier forces and bases which we now have, and to use these as long as possible, cutting political commitments accordingly and recognising that in the future they will be more and more limited militarily in the interventions which they can make.[44]

At the 1963 Admiralty this was interpreted to mean that carriers were essential for an effective overseas strategy. Later governments would take a different view.

A few days later the Board of Admiralty met to take two papers prepared in accordance with the Chequers directive. The first concluded that air support for army intervention could be provided by 'offshore support ships' operating RAF VSTOL aircraft but that the ships would be quite expensive, £39–45 million each, and they would be unusable without carrier support. The second paper considered a small 15,000 ton P1154 carrier but concluded that for the operation of sufficient fixed-wing aircraft even in the bare minimum of roles, 'aircraft carriers as we know them are essential'.[45] The Admiralty made clear its continued commitment to partnership in a third paper. 'Aircraft Carrier Replacement'. On current plans there were to be based East of Suez a total of ninety RAF combat aircraft and 60 Royal Navy. This total could be reduced to 100 if the Services adopted a common inter-operable tactical aircraft and two carriers were kept East of Suez to give 'full mutual reinforcement'. RN squadrons would normally be embarked in the ships but the mix of aircraft would be varied according to operational considerations. In the spirit of coming unification the Admiralty was proposing a unified Tactical Air Command for logistics and training. The Admiralty asserted that until a common multi-purpose aircraft could be developed the plan could be implemented with Buccaneers and P1154s. Rather optimistically, in the context of the RAF's historic hostility to the type, it suggested that the RAF adopt the Buccaneer for East of Suez operations. If this was too difficult then a start on rationalisation could be made when the P1154 came into service. The aim was 20 fighter and strike aircraft in each carrier with 60 more distributed between Aden and Singapore.[46]

The Admiralty was continuing its old strategy of trying to get the Air Ministry to support the 53,000 ton ship as a joint air base. A larger 53,000 tonner would make its group up to strength with RAF aircraft, ten visiting RAF aircraft to 20 resident Fleet Air Arm. The Navy was also turning the cancellation of OR346 to advantage by arguing that *Eagle* and *Hermes* be kept longer, until about 1980, operating Buccaneer/P1154 groups. The new carrier programme could thus be slowed down from four ships in the period 1964–75 to two in 1964–75 and two more in 1975–80. The bill between 1963 and 1975 would be reduced to about £436 million.[47]

There were some doubts on the Board that the Admiralty was making too many concessions but in the end it was decided to push the paper forward as it was urgent to obtain a decision on the first carrier order. On 6 May 1963 John wrote a conciliatory note summarising the new policy to Pike. It concluded:

> You and I have spoken in the past and in general terms of the desirability of flexibility of air squadrons between ship and shore. There is nothing new in the idea but I thought I'd let you know in advance that we have now made a positive suggestion on paper. By it, we hope to put forward a realistic approach to the problem of duplication, on which I know you yourself feel strongly.[48]

The Air Ministry was in no mood to accept the olive branch. It was angry at what it felt was the Admiralty's perversion of the Pike Ship into a smaller kind of carrier and was still convinced that a simple support vessel would be adequate, integrated into the overall 'Island Stance'.[49] It had a strong ally in the Treasury, which was horrified at the increase in defence expenditure in comparison with previously agreed ceilings.[50] On 19 June the Cabinet Defence Committee met to discuss the problem of which hard choices to take. The carrier looked vulnerable as it was agreed to plan on the assumption 'that by 1970 we should not undertake by ourselves to mount assault operations against entrenched opposition and that any operations of this kind would be undertaken, if at all, as part of an allied campaign'. But this did not necessarily spell its doom. As the minutes of the discussion went on:

It had sometimes been assumed that the abandonment of a requirement to make opposed landings in the face of entrenched opposition would remove the need for a replacement carrier programme. This was at once an oversimplification and a misunderstanding of the true position. Present naval plans required the maintenance of a carrier fleet not solely for assault purposes, but for the conduct of naval operations of any kind.... The problem of maintaining the air power of the United Kingdom should not be looked at in terms of a sea-based and a land-based element; there were important possibilities of closer integration between the Air Force and the Navy which could lead to a more rational organisation and to substantial economy.[51]

Thorneycroft was sent away to draw up compromise proposals based on that day's rather inconclusive discussion. His paper showed that the Navy had at least one buyer for the carrier case. The Defence Minister argued that carriers were an integral part of Britain's ocean-going navy, they provided necessary flexibility in an uncertain world, their abandonment would mean the 'virtual dissolution of the Royal Navy' or its expensive conversion into a missile-armed fleet, either outcome being 'a serious political decision which I am sure my colleagues would wish to weigh most carefully'. This meant that a minimum carrier force of three ships had to be maintained with one new ship to be ordered to replace both *Victorious* and *Ark Royal*; the question of further ships was to be kept open. The Buccaneer 3 was to be abandoned and a study made of replacing the proposed fully navalised P1154B with a version of the RAF's P1154A. Such an aircraft might replace the Lightning interceptor as well as the Sea Vixen and it would be followed by a common variable-geometry fighter for both services. The Admiralty's partnership concept was the key to Thorneycroft's thinking:

An important aim of these proposals would be that an aircraft carrier would be regarded as a floating air base available for use by both the Fleet Air Arm and the Royal Air Force and that many fewer aircraft would be required. A preliminary study by the Admiralty and the Air Ministry suggests that it might be possible to save 38 aircraft from the planned RN and RAF front-line strengths of 108 P1154 aircraft East of Suez, which would reduce the total number of aircraft by some 80 or more.

He put the estimated savings to be obtained from this policy over ten years at over £225 million in 1963 costings prices.[52]

The Treasury refused to accept this compromise at the meeting of the Defence Committee on 10 July and Macmillan decided he had to take the decision to full Cabinet.[53] A last-minute meeting of the Defence Committee on the 24th only succeeded in bringing the Air Ministry out in support of the Chancellor.[54] The matter went before the Cabinet on Thursday 25 July. It was a straight confrontation between the Treasury and Air Ministry on the one hand and the Ministry of Defence and Admiralty on the other.[55] The arguments were evenly balanced, the need for a carrier East of Suez being countered by its opponents casting doubts both on the technical viability and the affordability of Thorneycroft's compromise. The decision was deferred for another week.

When the Cabinet reconvened on Tuesday 30 July it had before it a final paper by Thorneycroft and Carrington.[56] This emphasised the inadequacy of a two-carrier force and the impossibility of running *Victorious* and *Ark Royal* beyond 1971–72. It spelled out the savings obtained by not building three more new carriers and by aircraft rationalisation. It quoted both the Zuckerman and Festing reports to counter the accusation of carrier vulnerability and it pointed to the problems of converting the fleet to an alternative structure. It stressed the need for a decision and the extent of the studies undertaken. It concluded 'that the Cabinet are not now being asked to consider a "carrier-replacement programme". The proposal is that we should decide now, and announce our decision to build this one ship'.[57]

On this condition, the Treasury reluctantly gave in and it was accepted that a new carrier could be built to replace *Ark Royal*, thus allowing a three-carrier force to be maintained during the 1970s; the decision was to be announced to Parliament that afternoon.[58] The Admiralty's partnership strategy seemed to have worked, in the way which had always been intended to sell the carrier programme (albeit reduced) to a reluctant Government. Despite the clear emphasis on only one new carrier, the Admiralty was convinced that the government had effectively committed itself by the order to a full carrier programme of at least two more ships and was not too worried about the concessions on P1154. It was already showing interest in the American Phantom as a more realistic Sea Vixen replacement.[59]

Overall, by using the partnership gambit to demonstrate sweet reasonableness and good intentions to Watkinson and Thorneycroft the Naval Staff had apparently scored a significant victory over Pike and the Air Staff. On 6 August 1963 the last First Sea Lord to sit for his entire period in office on the Board of Admiralty handed over the torch to his successor Sir David Luce with the carrier programme apparently finally in place. Or so it seemed. Within less than three years it would all turn to ashes, but that is another, if not too dissimilar story.

NOTES

1. 'Role and composition of the Navy', memorandum by Minister of Defence, 14 November 1957, copy in PRO:CAB 131/18.
2. PRO:ADM 205/192.
3. Ibid. folio 36.
4. Ibid. folio 43.
5. Board Minute 5535, 20 June 1962, PRO:ADM 167/160
6. 'Future Carrier Policy', note by the Air Ministry, PRO:AIR 8/2328.
7. Ibid.
8. Admiralty comments on the Air Ministry note: 'Future Carrier Policy', PRO:AIR 8/2328.
9. Sir Caspar John to Sir Thomas Pike, 23/11/61, PRO:AIR 8/2328.
10. Copy of the Report in PRO:AIR 8/2328.
11. C.O.S. (61) 475, PRO:DEFE 5/121; copy in AIR 8/2328.
12. Ibid.
13. CDS/P(61) 12th Meeting, copy in PRO:AIR 8/2354.
14. Ibid.
15. Ibid.
16. Minutes of meetings in PRO:AIR 8/2354.
17. The first exposition of what became known as 'The Island stance' seems to have been in COS(61) 358.
18. PRO:CAB 131/17.
19. Ibid.
20. Aircraft Carriers, D(62)6, PRO:CAB 131/27.
21. Files on this study have only recently been released. This and following quotations come from PRO:DEFE 7/2235.
22. Annex to COS(61)499, ibid.
23. Ibid.
24. D(62) 1st Meeting, PRO:CAB 131/27.
25. D(62) 43 quoted in First Lord's memo of 21 August 1962, PRO:AIR 8/2354.
26. Memo of 21 August, PRO:AIR 8/2354.
27. Ibid.
28. Report of enquiry into Carrier Task Forces, 22 April 1963, copy in PRO:AIR 8/2354.
29. 'The Island Strategy', 18 October 1962, PRO:AIR 8/2354.
30. Ibid.
31. Copy in PRO:AIR 8/2354.
32. 'An Island Stance', PRO:AIR 8/2354.
33. COS(62) 497, PRO:AIR 8/2354.
34. COS(62) 476 plus annex, copy in PRO:AIR 8/2354.

35. 'The Island Strategy', 9 January 1963, PRO:AIR 8/2354.
36. For Mountbatten's campaign to absorb Coastal Command, see Geoffrey Till's chapter on him in Malcolm Murfett's forthcoming *The First Sea Lords, From Fisher to Mountbatten* (Liverpool and London, 1995).
37. Ibid.
38. Report of the meeting in a letter of First Sea Lord to CAS, 22 January 1963, PRO:AIR 8/2354.
39. Ibid.
40. Ibid.
41. D(63) 3rd and 4th Meeting, PRO:CAB 131/28.
42. 4th meeting, ibid. For the earlier controversy see my *Vanguard to Trident*, chap. 3.
43. Ibid.
44. Copy of the report in PRO:AIR 8/2354.
45. Paper B in Board Memo B1451, PRO:ADM 167/162.
46. Paper C in ibid.
47. Ibid.
48. 'Secret and Personal' letter from First Sea Lord to CAS, copy in PRO:AIR 8/2354.
49. D.A.S.B. 2 document 'Off Shore Support Ships', 14 May 1963, PRO:AIR 8/2354.
50. 'Strategic Options and Costs'. Memo by the Chancellor of the Exchequer to the Cabinet Defence Committee, 17 June 1963, PRO:CAB 131/8.
51. D(63) 8th Meeting, 19 June 1963, PRO:CAB 131/28.
52. 'Future Defence Policy'. Memo by the Minister of Defence, D(63) 23, PRO:CAB 131/28.
53. D(63) 9th Meeting, PRO:CAB 131/28.
54. D(63) 11th Meeting, PRO:CAB 131/28.
55. CC(63) 48th Conclusions, PRO:CAB 128/37; the position papers are C(63) 128, 132, 133 and 139 in CAB 128/37.
56. 'Defence Programme:Aircraft Carrier Replacement', C(63) 141, PRO:CAB 128/114.
57. Ibid.
58. CC(63), 50th Conclusion, PRO:CAB 128/37.
59. Information from J. D. Brown, head of Naval Historical Branch.

19 American Naval Strategy in the Era of the Third World War: An Inquiry into the Structure and Process of General War at Sea, 1945-90
David Alan Rosenberg

The end of the Cold War marked the end of an era in twentieth-century naval history. Although competition between the navies of the United States and the Soviet Union never resulted in open conflict, the prospect of confrontation fuelled the development of plans and programmes on both sides for more than four decades. The global war which was feared and anticipated was the subject of endless study and analysis. How might it begin? How would it be fought? Which side was in the stronger position? What strategic and technical innovations might shift the military balance? The plans, strategies, and weapons ultimately went untested, but the story of their creation constitutes an important chapter in twentieth-century naval history.

This essay surveys the development of American naval strategy during the era of planning for the Third World War, identifying factors which must be taken into account, and laying out its general stages of development. It proposes a framework for analysis which consists of five contentions about the nature of the Soviet–American naval arms competition and the strategies developed by the United States and the United States Navy during the Cold War.[1]

The first contention is that the concept of the Third World War, as it changed and evolved over five decades, provides a useful, unifying analytical tool for assessing Cold War military and naval history. There is a widespread popular belief that any global war during the Cold War would have inevitably escalated to a nuclear Armageddon. The reality is far more complex. Nuclear weapons may have revolutionised warfare, but the nature of global war at any given time in the period 1945–90 would have depended on a great many factors, some easily identified, and some extremely difficult to assess. As a result of generational change, both political and technological, and the changing geopolitical context, strategic planning passed through four distinct periods between 1945 and 1990, each characterised by different perceptions and plans for the Third World War. Both the Soviet Union and the United States experienced this progression, within roughly the same time-frames, although not along strictly parallel lines.

The four periods of Third World War planning can be described as follows. The first was an era envisioning a third world war as a protracted, multi-phase conflict, where use of nuclear weapons would be increasingly important but not clearly decisive in determining the ultimate outcome. This period lasted from the late 1940s through the early 1950s. It was followed by the thermonuclear and ballistic-missile revolutions of the mid-1950s, which ushered in an era of preparation for all-out nuclear war, identified with the Eisenhower doctrine of 'massive retaliation'. The incoming Kennedy administration in 1961 launched a period of re-evaluation and retrenchment which lasted through the late-1970s. It involved a not always fruitful search for military options, establishing progressive levels of 'flexible' response to Soviet challenges. Finally, the 1980s witnessed a period of American resurgence, during which new approaches were developed based on the concept of attacking Soviet military strategies and operational practices, as perceived and understood by military planners in the West, rather than just Soviet forces.

The first three of these periods proved difficult for the US Navy. During the 1950s and 1960s, Navy uniformed and civilian leaders often found themselves at odds with the strategic concepts or operational and analytical assumptions which underlay US national strategy, and fought an uphill battle for recognition of their minority views. Arguably it was not until the 1980s that Navy strategic concepts achieved some degree of general acceptance in US and NATO defence planning as a cutting-edge component of overall deterrent and war-fighting strategy.

The second contention is that institutions, rather than ideas or individuals, make naval strategy and policy, and that navies in general, and the US Navy in the Cold War in particular, were affected by a wide array of internal and external influences. Elsewhere Jon Sumida and I have argued that historians must set the study of naval history firmly within the context of machines, men, manufacturing, management, and money. In addition, it is necessary to understand how naval culture and traditions shape strategy-making.

Briefly, their impact might be outlined as follows:

Machines. The US Navy in the postwar era may well have actively promoted and managed a wider array of technology than any other single institution in a comparable period of time in world history. Technological innovation and strategy were intrinsically intertwined throughout all the dimensions of naval planning, programming and operations throughout the period.

Men. US Cold War naval strategy was made by at least four generations of leaders, with views shaped by very different experiences and systems of education and training. Sources of commissioning changed, for example, from exclusively Naval Academy, to substantially Reserve Officers Training Corps and Officers Candidate Schools. Nuclear submariners, highly disciplined technical and operational specialists who had a much narrower base of experience in strategic and politico–military matters than many of their aviator and surface-warfare contemporaries, became increasingly prominent in leadership positions by the 1980s.

Manufacturing. The dramatic decline of the US maritime and shipbuilding industrial base – and its impact on the flexibility of American shipbuilding and conversion, as well as on the increasing cost of warships – was one of the fundamental constraints on US naval strategy in the Cold War era. The dozens of shipyards that existed in 1945 gave way ultimately to only four major building yards by the 1990s. Similar reduction, merger, and consolidation occurred in the aircraft industry. The electronics industry is a new frontier deserving increased attention.

Management. The strategy-making process in the US Navy might be said to involve four levels of discourse: what the admirals said to Congress and the public; what the admirals said to the Office of the Secretary of Defence (OSD) and Joint Chiefs of Staff (JCS); what the admirals said to their action officers; and what the admirals said to each other. It is the historian's job to sort this process out, and place it within the context of an evolving national system of policy and decision making. The postwar period was marked by tremendous managerial change sparked by the 1947 unification of the armed forces and its subsequent amendments to the National Security Act that increasingly bounded naval leaders' strategic and operational freedom of action.

Money. Finance and budgeting is an integral part of strategy making. Particular issues for the Cold War era are the impact of unification and Defense Department reform on programming; competition between the

Navy and the other services for funding; and the impact of the national economy, and inflation in particular in the 1970s, on spending and force levels.

The US Navy's unique 'traditions and culture' profoundly influenced its strategic thinking and strategy making. There are four points which must be given due regard. First is the profound importance of *operational experience*. A strong operational orientation during the Second World War and into the 1950s led the US Navy to emphasise deploying its forces at sea, and developing strategies based on current capabilities and actual operational experience.

Second, the US Navy's concepts of leadership and systems for decision-making were grounded in the common experience of its leadership experienced in *command at sea* which was central to its systems of training and promotion. Operations at sea required pragmatism, flexibility, individual initiative, and individual responsibility. Decision-making was remarkably decentralised, with each commander exercising both individual initiative, and total responsibility. Coordination was achieved not by careful pre-planning and the hierarchical delegation of authority, but by cooperation on the basis of common knowledge and experience.

Third, the strategy built on this foundation was deliberately ambiguous, open-ended, and flexible. The Navy had *no written strategic doctrine* equivalent to those that were regularly reassessed and rewritten in the US Army and US Air Force. Such an approach to strategy-making ran strongly counter to the rigid strategic plans being adopted by the American JCS and the Strategic Air Command (SAC) in the 1950s.

Finally, it is important to note the influence of this Navy culture on force structure. The US Navy sought to maintain *internally balanced, multi-purpose forces* capable of pursuing a wide variety of objectives. The air, surface, and submarine communities within the Navy increasingly competed with each other for funding and prominence, but without the expectation that any branch of the service was expendable, or that one branch could completely dominate the others.

The third contention of this paper is that between 1948 and 1961, the US Navy developed a mature, broad and flexible strategy for guiding operations in peace and war. It was in many respects a significant departure from what had come before in US naval history. This strategy rested on four main pillars:

The first pillar was a *Peacetime Strategy of Forward Deployment*. Prior to the Second World War, between 1922 and 1941, there had been a single US Fleet based on the continental United States, with only small, generally ill-equipped forces deployed overseas in Europe, Asia, and the

Caribbean. The Fleet came together annually for fleet exercises. The postwar US Navy, by contrast, was organised into two geographic fleets and four major striking fleets, two of which were permanently deployed overseas (although the forces rotated at six-month intervals). Carrier task forces, not the traditional battle line, determined much of the task organisation. Forward deployment focused on countering the Soviet submarine threat to allied Sea Lines of Communication (SLOCs), and on the newly formed land-based Soviet Naval Aviation (SNA). It aimed both at deterring the USSR and at expanding US influence overseas with allies and neutral states. Missions for the forward deployed fleets shifted in emphasis in line with changing national policy. During the 1950s they served as nuclear alert forces as well as first response forces in local crises.

The second pillar was a *Wartime Strategy of Forward Defence*. Built on the nuclear and conventional capabilities of the forward-deployed strike fleets, this strategy provided for power projection into Europe and Asia at the outset of a global conflict, and envisioned the forward deployment of additional naval forces around the periphery of the USSR as the conflict developed. Plans were made for attacks on 'targets of naval interest', including naval bases, port facilities, naval airfields and associated industries, in order to destroy, if possible, Soviet submarine and naval air forces before they could threaten the SLOCs. The strategy also provided for defensive and offensive anti-submarine barriers in the north Atlantic and Norwegian Sea, along with hunter-killer groups and convoy escorts to defend the SLOCs. Although some early advocates of naval air power envisioned a leading role for the Navy in the strategic nuclear offensive, most naval leaders rejected that option, preferring to concentrate on maritime objectives and the supplementary use of naval air power in support of ground forces.

The third pillar of US postwar naval strategy was an 'Alternative Nuclear Strategy' which came into focus in the mid- to late-1950s. As noted above, during the first decade of the Cold War, the United States increasingly emphasised the full-scale nuclear air offensive as its primary attack option in a general war. The Navy's alternative strategy, as enunciated by Chief of Naval Operations, Admiral Arleigh Burke, in 1956, grew out of Burke's commitment to reducing reliance on strategic nuclear warfare and its vulnerable land-based delivery forces. In pursuit of this objective he promoted rapid development of submarine-based ballistic-missile technology. Best described by the terms 'Finite Deterrence, Controlled Retaliation, Secure Basing', the alternative nuclear strategy envisioned a force of forty-five nuclear-powered ballistic-missile submarines (SSBNs) that would target a finite, rather than constantly expanding, number of Soviet military and civilian targets. It would provide for controlled, incremental attacks on those targets in the event of war, so as to exercise coercive leverage against the Soviet leadership while reducing potential casualties. Sea-basing made such withholding feasible: Polaris submarines at sea were not readily targetable by the Soviets when submerged, and thus avoided the 'use it or lose it' dynamic of land-based forces on airfields, 'soft' missile bases and even hardened missile silos. Burke argued that as the nation moved into the missile age in the 1960s, such a strategy and its attendant weapons systems should replace the nation's reliance on SAC as its first line of nuclear defence.

The fourth pillar of postwar Navy strategy was the emphasis placed on preparations for *Limited War*. Doubts about orienting national strategy primarily toward general war had been voiced in the Navy in the 1940s, and these were consolidated by the experience of the Korean War. In 1954–55, the Navy's first full postwar long-range shipbuilding plan postulated that limited rather than general war would be the nation's and the Navy's primary national security challenge in the future, a posture which was reaffirmed in 1957–58 and after. While limited war planning initially focused primarily on Asia (Korea, Taiwan, and Vietnam) and the Middle East, Nikita Khrushchev's threat of a confrontation over Berlin in 1958–59 sparked the development of US and NATO Maritime Contingency (MARCON) planning for potential crises in Europe. After the Castro takeover of Cuba in 1959, and the failure of the Central Intelligence Agency's Bay of Pigs operation in 1961, plans were also drawn up for blockading, striking, or invading Cuba as well.

The fourth contention of this paper is that the larger context of national politics, defence policy, foreign affairs, and economics and finance within which the Navy functioned, effectively prevented full implementation of its four-pillared strategy during the two decades from the early 1960s to the late 1970s.

During the Eisenhower years, the Navy had worked at cross purposes with a national policy dominated by a strategic nuclear fixation which undermined mobilisation, naval industrial infrastructure, and the maintenance of any capability to fight a protracted conventional war. Adoption in 1960 of the first Single Integrated Operational Plan (SIOP) for general nuclear war, which called for a single, massive coordinated strike against all targets, involved an explicit rejection of the Navy's strategy of finite deterrence/controlled retaliation.

The incoming Kennedy administration shared many of the Navy's reservations about massive retaliation, but failed to understand or pursue the alternative strategy the Navy had developed. The problem was

Secretary of Defence Robert McNamara's Planning, Programming and Budgeting System, which relied heavily on quantitative and systems analysis, tools generally unsuited to evaluating the flexible, organic Navy approach to planning, or the warfare capabilities inherent in its multi-purpose warships. The failure of McNamara's defence team to build on the Navy's strategic pillars appears to have been an important missed opportunity in American national defence planning.

The Vietnam war brought new problems, including the rapid degrading of the Navy's supply of ships and aircraft as a result of heavy operational demands, and a general decline in military morale and confidence. The inflation and economic weakness of the late-1970s made it impossible for the Navy to rebuild the fleet to anything approaching the 700 to 900 ships it had planned for in the 1960s, or even the 600 it hoped to have by 1980. As a result of the pressures of these two difficult decades, the Navy of the late 1970s was seriously diminished in capabilities, lacking confidence in its own strategies, divided internally, and profoundly concerned that it would be unable to counter the expanding Soviet maritime threat. The spectre of a powerful Soviet Navy leaving home waters, overwhelming US and allied defensive chokepoints and barriers, and proceeding into the open oceans to disrupt the SLOCs grew to near-crisis proportions from the late-1960s through the mid-1970s.

The final contention is that the US Navy's Maritime Strategy, as it evolved in the 1980s, was a culmination and fulfilment of the postwar strategy which for so many years had appeared doomed to irrelevance. It involved a multi-faceted approach to the maritime dimensions of the military and diplomatic problems facing the United States and the NATO alliance, and served as a vehicle for rebuilding morale and consensus within the Navy community. The beating heart of the Maritime Strategy was the exploitation of both existing forces and technological innovation in an operational context, informed by a new understanding of the nature of Soviet naval strategy in war. The main objective of the strategy was to enhance deterrence by attacking the Soviet strategic mindset before war began.

The Maritime Strategy grew out of a variety of dynamics. Among the most important were challenges posed by the international environment of the late-1970s. The continuing strategic arms competition between the US and USSR, and the questions it raised about Soviet intentions, as addressed by the 1976–77 Team A/Team B intelligence analyses, was one spur. So too was the end of detente, signalled by increased Soviet support of insurgent movements in Africa and military client states in the Middle East and south-west Asia, and most significantly the 1979 invasion of Afghanistan.

Geopolitics also played a role. The People's Republic of China, formerly a favourite target of Navy general and limited war planning, was now a potential ally against the USSR, while Japan's economic miracle made it not just a mutual defence-treaty partner but also a potential 'arsenal of high-tech democracy'. The growing importance of China and Japan led to a reassessment during the Carter administration of the traditional 'swing' strategy, which called for US forces in Asia and the Pacific to swing to Europe in event of a major crisis. Finally, the continuing growth and modernisation of the Soviet Navy, including its greatly strengthened capacity for global operations, created a maritime challenge that was hard for even the most continental-minded defence intellectual to ignore.

The national political climate within the United States also contributed to support for a naval strategic initiative. In particular, the election of Ronald Reagan to the presidency in 1980 signalled a full-scale political commitment to reversing downward defence-funding trends and an increase in rhetorical challenges to the USSR. Reagan had been elected on a platform that resurrected a national requirement for a 600-ship Navy, and the author of that particular platform plank, John F. Lehman, Jr., was appointed Navy Secretary in 1981. In his first few years in office, Lehman was allowed enormous leeway by Congress and OSD in seeking to recast the Navy and its leadership in the image he thought appropriate to an aggressive American maritime resurgence in a renewed Cold War. Furthermore, in 1982 the Reagan administration issued a National Security Decision Directive that mandated development of the capability for fighting a protracted (time-frame unspecified) conventional war with the USSR and its allies, looking to sequential rather than simultaneous military options to provide leverage. Such a policy, however difficult to implement, reversed the assumption, almost universally accepted from the 1950s on, that a quick, decisive and disastrous nuclear conflict would be the inevitable outcome of global war.

Finally, the Maritime Strategy grew out of the Navy as an institution. Some of the root causes of change were technical and operational while others related to conceptual innovation and strategic process. With respect to technology and operations, three developments stand out. The first was the progress made in the gathering, analysing and disseminating of operational intelligence on the Soviet Navy. In the early 1970s, the Ocean Surveillance Information System (OSIS) was established in a cluster of national and fleet operational intelligence centres. By the 1980s, this system and its associated intelligence sensors provided Navy operational commanders and strategic planners with an unprecedented picture of the capabilities and disposition of current Soviet maritime forces.

The second development involved putting to sea a collection of high-technology sensors, command, control and communications systems, and accurate long-range conventional weapons systems that would enable naval operational commanders to operate forward in a hostile environment more effectively than ever before. The Aegis cruisers, armed with long-range land-attack cruise missiles, surface-to-air defences, anti-ship missiles, and a long-range command, control and warning system, first deployed in the early 1980s, in particular, represented a quantum leap over prior capabilities.

Thirdly, the late-1970s and early-1980s saw a rebirth of tactical planning in the US Navy, built on both the information OSIS provided about the Soviet air, surface and sub-surface threats, and the new technology finally being brought into the fleet. The Composite Warfare Commander (CWC) system, with its associated command and control systems and tactical command procedures and applications, was designed to take carrier battle-groups into enemy waters, and fight and defeat the attacking air, surface, and submarine threats. This forward defence would serve both to defend the SLOCs and position the Navy to provide air support for the land battle in Northern and Central Europe.

Strategic and programme planning initiatives played an important role in furthering the process of strategic innovation in Washington and in fleet headquarters. The 1978 Navy force planning study, SEA PLAN 2000, argued for a 14-carrier, 28-Aegis cruiser, 98-nuclear attack submarine (SSN) 'lower risk' (*vis-a-vis* the Soviet maritime threat) navy, one that required a funding level of sustained four per cent 'real growth.' Based conservatively on available technology, not proposed future developments, it presaged Lehman's subsequent proposal for a 15-carrier, 100-SSN, 600-ship fleet, despite contemporary analyses which showed these to be economically and financially unattainable or at least unsustainable force goals.

Among the important strategic planning initiatives was a series of exercises conducted by Admiral Thomas B. Hayward as Commander-in-Chief of the Pacific Fleet in the late-1970s, codenamed 'Seastrike'. Designed to use carrier battle-forces to draw out and neutralise the Soviet Navy in the event of war, these became the basis for much of Hayward's offensive thinking and planning for naval strategy in a 'come as you are global war' when he served as Chief of Naval Operations in 1978–82.

A final critical factor was an emerging intelligence consensus on the strategic concepts that would most likely govern Soviet initiatives in the event of war. Such analyses were developed, based in part on Soviet military writings and doctrine, beginning in the late-1970s, and resulted in such initiatives as the so-called 'countervailing strategy' for nuclear war, the US Army's AirLand Battle Doctrine and NATO's strategy of Follow-On-Forces-Attack to counter Soviet deep penetration tactics in Europe. Naval analysts concluded, as presented in the 1982 National Intelligence Estimate, that the Soviet Navy would follow a largely defensive strategy, placing highest priority on defending the Soviet homeland from sea-borne attack out to a range of some 2,000 to 3,000 kilometres, within reach of the US SLOCs to Europe and East Asia. Its SSBN forces would be deployed not into the open oceans, but into heavily defended maritime bastions near Soviet home waters.

Based on this intelligence consensus, the Navy settled on an avowedly offensive strategy toward the USSR, as a key component of the Maritime Strategy. If the USSR was predisposed to use large portions of its naval air and submarine forces to defend the approaches to the motherland, and to shelter its SSBNs in home waters, navy strategists argued, it was clearly in the American interest to reinforce such an inclination. An offensive posture would serve, it was hoped, as an active deterrent to an actual outbreak of hostilities during a crisis, and if hostilities broke out, would help to keep the Soviet Navy on the defensive and in a position of relative vulnerability.

The Maritime Strategy was the first explicit revision of the phasing of US strategy since US joint war plans in the 1950s moved from a multi-phase protracted war to a two-phase nuclear conflict. The strategy's three phases, Transition to War, Seizing the Initiative, and Carrying the Fight to the Enemy were ambiguous by design, but they clearly indicated that the US was once again preparing to defend the seas in a protracted, conventional campaign of forward defence. Moreover, there was more than one campaign. The Maritime Strategy involved multiple theatres of operations, each with its own set of campaign objectives to be run by on-scene commanders in keeping with the service's long-held strategic traditions and operational practice.

After two decades of decline and doubt, the US Navy's strategies developed in the 1950s seemed to be coming into their own. Forward deployment and forward defence were intrinsic aspects of the Maritime Strategy, enhanced by new understanding of Soviet naval strategy, and new technologies and techniques, that enabled ships and submarines to undertake operations much farther forward than had been envisioned in the 1950s. The third pillar of Navy strategic thinking, the alternate nuclear strategy, was not adopted as such, but the nation was moving toward greater reliance on secure sea basing as evidenced in deployment of a second generation of Trident SSBNs beginning in the early 1980s, and decisively rejecting the 1950s concept, to which the Navy had so strongly objected, that global war would automatically escalate to strategic nuclear conflict. Finally, throughout the 1980s, the US Navy found itself employed in crisis and contingency operations around the globe which did not involve a confrontation with the Soviet Union: off Grenada, Lebanon, and Libya, and in the Persian Gulf. Such operations verified the need for a fleet flexible enough to function effectively not just in global conflict, but in limited war.

What impact did forty-five years of preparing for a Third World War have on the United States Navy? The answer seems to be that the Navy came out stronger for the experience. The many and rapid changes in national and alliance policy and strategy, the intense interservice disagreements over policy guidance, strategic plans, programme/priorities and budget allocations, and the changing internal administrative structures and processes of the Navy itself – particularly those designed to develop and field high technology – were challenges successfully met.

The US Navy of the 1980s proved itself to be an institution of remarkable political proficiency, technical genius and professional flexibility, capable not only of adapting to changes mandated by policy fiat, but also of generating such changes based on its own unique professional mindset. One observer described that peculiar Navy mindset as 'arrogant in victory, surly in defeat, and difficult at all points in between', much to the delight of numerous senior naval officers proud of their independent ways. The upshot of four decades of Navy recalcitrance and cross-grained analysis of national defence policy was a remarkably capable force structure and strategy designed to deal with a wide array of potential threats from the USSR. The remarkable shift within a two-year period from a Cold War strategy for fighting the Third World War on the open ocean to a post-Cold War strategy that emphasised a violent peace and littoral warfare, both exploiting existing capabilities, testifies to the inherent flexibility and adaptability of the Navy's approach to strategy-making.

External criticism of the Navy in recent decades has usually focused on the problem of force composition, particularly the numbers of existing forces, rather than on prospective technological developments. The large aircraft carrier has attracted by far the most criticism. In the 1940s, the Air Force, planning primarily for a nuclear war, argued that most if not all large carriers should be decommissioned, a course of action that would have proved disastrous when the Korean War began. The 1950s and 1960s saw a debate on numbers of active large carriers: the Navy generally arguing for 15 or 16; the other services and the Office of the Secretary of Defense advocating 10 to 12. The 600-ship navy envisioned 15 carriers for the 1980s and beyond. Significantly, this number represented a comfortable force-level for peacetime and crisis operations rather than for a general war with the USSR.

Recently declassified documents indicate that the Navy considered an adequate carrier force-level for a non-nuclear war with the USSR to be 24, indicating that preparation for a conventional Third World War was never seriously considered. The costs would have been prohibitive. In fact, while naval planners generally 'kept their eye on the big red bear', the force-levels they advocated related primarily to forward presence and crisis response missions, based on political realism and immediate operational requirements. The one area where this approach may have proved in error relates to nuclear attack submarine force-levels. By the 1980s, SSNs had become the capital ships of the Third World War, and the 100-SSN force-level established for the 600-ship navy might have proved inadequate against the submarine-dominated Soviet fleet.

In the end, there is another question that must be asked: what impact did the US Navy have on the Soviet Union, both in its plans to fight a Third World War, and in deterring any opportunistic adventures that might have led to such a confrontation? The answer to that question must await the opening of the Soviet naval and general staff archives. It should be pointed out, however, that it was not until the 1980s, with the advent of the Maritime Strategy, that the US Navy was able to fully engage its strategy with that of its greatest adversary. The Maritime Strategy attempted to do more than counter the Soviet Navy by taking into account its geographic position and its estimated technical capabilities. It was clearly aimed at influencing the Soviet naval and military mindset and dealing with a perceived defensive strategy designed to protect the Soviet homeland and the strategic submarine force deployed in defensive 'bastions'. The attempt to engage Soviet naval strategy as well as capabilities represents the high point in the development of post-Second World War American naval strategy and provides important lessons as to how concepts for the use of naval power may mature over time.

Postscript
Arleigh Burke to Robert Dennison, 6 August 1952: The Navy is very much in the same position with regard to public relations as a virtuous woman. Virtue seldom is spectacular and less often causes long editorials. Naval philosophy and maritime strategy are not spectacular. They offer no panaceas. Their success depends upon long, dull hours of hard work in which no one action is clearly decisive by itself. Its final success depends upon a series of small successes.

NOTES

1. This essay is built on four of the author's recently completed essays: 'Process: The Reality of Formulating Modern Naval Strategy' in James Goldrick & John B. Hattendorf, eds, *Mahan is Not Enough: The Proceedings of a Conference on the Works of Sir Julian Corbett and Admiral Sir Herbert Richmond* (Newport, R.I., 1993); 'Nuclear War Planning' in Michael Howard, George Andreopoulos & Mark Russell Shulman, eds, *The Laws of War: Constraints on Warfare in the Western World* (New Haven, Ct., 1994); 'The History of World War Three, 1945–1990: A Conceptual Framework' in Robert David Johnson, ed., *On Cultural Ground: Essays in International History in Honor of Akira Iriye* (Chicago, Ill., 1994); and 'Machines, Men, Manufacturing, Management and Money: The Study of Navies as Complex Organizations and the Transformation of Twentieth Century Naval History' co-authored with Jon Tetsuro Sumida to be published in John B. Hattendorf, ed., *Doing Naval History: Essays Towards Improvement* (Newport, RI., forthcoming).

Index

Abadan crisis (1951), 217
abbreviations, list of, vii–viii
Abnour, Rear Admiral R., 55 (n.35)
Abyssinia, *see* Ethiopia
Aconit (French frigate), 63
Aden:
   British presence, 124
   French evacuation, 64
Adriatic Sea:
   blockade of former Yugoslavia, xi, 64, 175, 186
   Italian bases, 69
   Italian fleet, 67, 68, 71
Aegis cruisers, 250
Africa:
   British presence, 124
   French presence, 45
   German policy, 28, 94
   Italian presence, 69, 71
   Soviet policy, 248
Agosta, battle of (1676), 60
Agung, Ide Anak Agung Gde, 213 (n.21)
aircraft carriers:
   British, 129, 137–9, 141, 146, 154–60, 219, 223, 228–40
   French, 63
   Japanese, 84
   super-carriers, xiii
   US, 4–12, 253
   WWII, 4
Akagi (Japanese battle-cruiser), 81
Alanbrooke, Field-Marshal Sir Alan Brooke, Lord, 125
Alatri, Paolo, 74 (n.18)
Albania, 22, 68
Aldabra Islands (Indian Ocean), 232
Alexandria, 76 (n.37), 134, 135, 142, 143
Alnwick Castle (British corvette), 158
Amagi (Japanese battle-cruiser), 81
American Civil War (1861–65), 164
amphibious warfare:
   British capability, 223
   US strategy, 8, 11
   WWII, 4
Andaman Islands (Bay of Bengal), 206
Andrei Pervozvanni (Soviet battleship), 18
Andrew, Christopher, 54 (n.32), 55 (n.51)
Anglo-French Entente (1904), 44
Anglo-German Naval Agreement (1935), 90
Anglo-Japanese naval treaty (1902), 42, 44, 48, 57 (n.72)
anti-submarine warfare (ASW):
   British strategies, 130, 221, 223
   Cold War, 7, 8–9, 10–11, 186, 246
   Indian Navy, 200, 203, 205
   Pakistan Navy, 200, 203, 204
   US Navy, 7, 8–9, 10–11, 246
   WWII, 130, 137–8, 151–3
Aoki, Eiichi, 78
Arctic:
   convoys (1944–45), 151–61
   Soviet submarines, 16
Aréthuse-class submarines, 63
Ark Royal (British aircraft carrier 1937–41), 137–8, 145
Ark Royal (British aircraft carrier 1958–80), 230, 238, 239
Armstrong of Pozzuoli, 70
Arnold-Foster, H.O., 53 (n.16)
Arrighi, Giorgio, 76 (n.34)
artillery, coastal, 1, 20
Asada, Sadao, 85, 86 (n.8)
Ascension Island (Atlantic Ocean), 232
Asquith, Herbert, 50–1
Assmann, Vice Admiral Kurt, 100 (n.24)
Atlantic:
   Barthélémy-Smith agreement (1964), 63
   National Security Zone, 63
   NATO limits, 220
   South, 221
   US Cold War strategy, 246
   WWII, 95–7, 124, 127–8

Atlantic, Battle of the (1942–43):
  defensive/offensive strategies, xi
  German strategy, xi, 94–7, 151
  influence, 151–2, 160, 217
  RAF role, 127–8, 170
  RN role, 128, 131, 152, 160
Atlantic Charter, 193
atomic bomb, *see* nuclear arms
Aube, Vice Admiral Hyacinthe
  Laurent Théophile, 61
Auckland (New Zealand), 50
Auphan, Rear Admiral Paul Gabriel,
  62
Aurora (Russian cruiser), 18
Australia:
  British bases, 120, 227
  defence, 48, 51, 122, 123
  docks, 50
  naval preparations, 51
  WWII, 131
Austrian Navy, 67, 68, 73 (n.10)
Avice, J., 55 (n.43)

Bab el Mandeb, Straits of (Red Sea),
  167
Babur (Pakistani cruiser), 204
Baer, George W., xxiii (n.7), 75 (n.29)
Bagnasco, Erminio, 76 (n.34)
Balfour, Arthur, 117 (n.15)
Balliano, Adolfo, 67
Baltic:
  British fleet (1855), 163–4
  German withdrawal (1945), 16
  Soviet fleet, 20–1
  War of Intervention, 18–19
  WWI, 34, 89
Bangladesh Navy, 201, 210
Barents Sea, 156, 157
Barham (British battleship), 127
Barnett, Correlli, 116 (n.10), 117
  (nn.13, 21, 25), 133 (nn.4, 5, 6, 8,
  9, 10, 13–16), 161 (n.1), 224
  (nn.1, 2)
Barros, James, 74 (n.13)
Barthélémy-Smith agreement (1964),
  63
Barthélémy-Woods agreement (1965),
  63
Bartlett, C.J., 26 (nn.5, 6), 197 (n.7)

Barzini, Luigi, 75 (n.27)
Bathurst, Admiral Sir Benjamin, 226
  (n.28)
Battenberg, Admiral Prince Louis of,
  56 (n.62)
battle-cruisers, 42, 122
battleships:
  British, 42, 48, 123, 127
  German, 32, 91, 127, 152, 155, 156
  Italian, 139
  Japanese, 81, 84
  Soviet, 18
Baugh, Daniel A., 116 (n.6), 117 (n.14)
Baxter, William T., 196 (n.4)
Bayfield, Henry, 189
Beachy Head, battle of (1690), 60
Bear Island, 22, 153, 155, 157, 159
Beattie, D., 198 (n.18)
Beatty, Admiral David, 19, 117 (nn.15,
  16)
Bedford, Vice Admiral A.E.F., 212
  (n.2)
Beesly, Patrick, 212 (nn.5, 8)
Behrens, C.B.A., 133 (n.11)
Beira Patrol, 172–3, 220
Belli, Vladimir, 20, 22
Berghahn, Volker R., 38 (nn.1, 13, 14),
  39 (nn.20, 24, 26, 27, 32, 34), 98
  (n.3)
Berlin:
  blockade (1948), 171
  confrontation (1958–59), 247
Berliner Tageblatt, 35
Bermuda, 189, 191
Bernardi, Giovanni, 75 (n.25)
Bernotti, Romeo, 75 (n.29), 76 (n.39)
Bethell, Rear Admiral Alexander, 50,
  58 (nn.76, 79)
Bethmann Hollweg, Theodor von, 34
Bialer, Uri, 118 (n.27)
Bidwell, Shelford, 133 (n.7)
Bigelow, Poultney, 39 (n.18)
Bigot de Morogues, Sébastien
  François, 61
Bismarck, Otto von, Prince, 28
Bismarck (German battleship), 127
Black Prince (British cruiser), 154
Black Sea, 20, 75 (n.23), 158
Bletchley Park (Bucks), 153, 158

Index

blockade, naval:
  conduct of, 163–4
  Falklands Exclusion Zones, 173
  French Navy, 64, 163
  German Navy, 169, 170–1
  Indonesia, 172
  Iraq 174
  Italian Navy, 70–1, 168
  Korean War, 172
  London Conference (1908–9), 165
  Navigation Certificates, 166
  Netherlands Royal Navy, 177–85
  Palestine, 171
  Rhodesia, 172–3
  Royal Navy, 34–5, 88, 163–75
  Spanish Civil War, 70–1, 167–8
  US Navy, 170–1
  Venezuela (1902), 2
  WWI, xviii, 34, 165–7
  WWII, 4, 168–71
  Yugoslavia (former), 64, 175
Blue Streak, 231
Bluebell (British corvette), 158
Boer War (1899–1902), 164–5
Bombay (India), 50, 202, 206, 209
Borden, Robert, 190, 191, 196
Borghese, Junio Valerio, Prince, 76 (n.37)
Borkum Island (E. Friesland) proposed attack (1914), 126
Borneo, 172, 179
Bouet-Willaumez, Vice Admiral Louis Edouard, 61
Bourdé de la Villehuet, Jacques Pierre 61
Bourne, Kenneth, 197 (nn.7, 8)
Bovey, John, 199 (n.27)
Bradley, General Omar, 7
Bragadin, Marc' Antonio, 76 (n.39)
Braisted, William, 56 (n.64)
Bramall, Field Marshal Sir Edwin, 217, 224 (n.4), 226 (n.25)
Brand, Captain Eric, 193
Bravetta, Ettore, 67, 68
Brest (France), 60
Brezhnev, Leonid, 23
Britain:
  Admiralty, 41–4, 50–1, 106–7, 128, 155, 165, 227, 229, 234, 236–9

Admiralty Technical Mission, 193
Air Ministry, 229, 231, 237, 239
Anglo-French Entente (1904), 44
Anglo-German Naval Agreement (1935), 90
blockades (WWII), 169–70
Defence Operational Analysis Establishment, 222
defence planning (1919–39), 101–15
Defence Requirements Committee, 111
defence reviews, 219, 222
Defence White Paper (1982), 222
Defence White Paper (1992), 223
East Indies naval policy (1895), 184–5
East of Suez policy (1961–63), 227–40
economy and sea power, xviii–xix
Empire-Commonwealth, 105–6, 121–4, 126, 216
Five-Power Defence Agreement, 220
Foreign Office, 165, 220
Home Defence Air Force, 107
industrial base, 129–30
Japanese alliance (1902), 42–3, 44, 48, 57 (n.72)
Liberal government (1905), 50–1
merchant fleet, 49
Ministry of Defence, 215, 216
NATO commitment, 219–22
naval planning (post-1945), 215–24
naval policy (before WWI), 41–52
naval strategy (German perception of), 88–9
Pacific policy (1905–9), 43–4, 48–52
shipbuilding, 33, 111, 112, 122, 129
shipyards, 79, 129
Suez crisis (1956), 217
Ten-Year Rule, 107
US relationship, 105, 109, 110, 131
see also Royal Air Force, Royal Navy
Britain, Battle of (1940–41), 135
British Army, 131
Brock, Rear Admiral Jeffry V., 199 (n.30)

Brodeur, L. P., 189, 190
Brodeur, Nigel D., 197 (n.9)
Brogan, Patrick, xi
Brown, Harold, 10
Brown, J. D., 241 (n.59)
Brown, Robert Craig, 197 (n.9)
Buccaneer aircraft, 229, 230, 237, 238
Bülow, Bernhard von, 30–1
Burke, Admiral Arleigh, 7, 8, 212 (n.17), 246–7, 253
Burma, 122
Butman, Boris S., 26 (n.11)
Byrd, Lieutenant Richard E., 191

Cafferky, Shawn, 198 (n.26)
Cain, P. J., 116 (n.8)
Caix, Robert de, 54 (n.31)
Calabria (1940), 138
Canada:
　history of sea power, 188–96
　Naval Service Act (1910), 190
　Navy League, 196
　Pacific fleet plan, 51
　shipyards, 193
　WWI, 190–1
　WWII, 192–4
　see also Royal Canadian Navy
Caprivi, General Georg, Count von, 28
Caribbean:
　NRN counter-drugs operations, 186
　Soviet presence, 24
　US defence, 1, 49, 246
Carlill, Vice Admiral Stephen, 213 (n.22)
Carls, Admiral Rolf, 91
Carlton, David, 117 (n.19)
Carrington, Peter, Lord, 232, 239
Carter, Jimmy, 249
Cecil, Lamar, 57 (n.67)
Ceva, Lucio, 76 (n.33)
Chad crisis (1984), 64
Chalmers, W. S., 162 (n.9)
Chamberlain, Austen, 56 (n.55)
Chamberlain, Neville, 111, 116 (n.9), 118 (n.25), 123–4
Channel, Barthélémy-Woods agreement (1965), 63
Char, S. V. Desika, 212 (n.6)

Chateaubriand, François René, vicomte de, 59
Chatfield, Admiral of the Fleet Alfred, Lord, 123
Chatterji, Vice Admiral A. K., 213 (n.35)
Cherbourg (France), 60
Chernavin, Admiral Viktor, 17
Chesapeake, battle of the (1780), 60
Chichester, Commander Michael, 162 (n.12)
China:
　Empire, 31
　German presence, 79
　Indian border dispute, 203, 206
　Japanese trade, 77
　US policy, 249
　war with Japan (1894–95), 78
　war with Japan (1937–45), 84, 85
China squadron, 43, 44, 48, 51
Choiseul, Étienne François, duc de, 60
Choudri, Rear Admiral M. S., 212 (nn.10, 16), 213 (n.19)
Churchill, Winston:
　Arctic convoys, 156, 158
　Atlantic Charter, 193
　Dardanelles expedition (1915–16), 126
　defence cuts (1920s), 109
　Greek campaign (1941), 125, 126, 127
　influence on WWII strategy, 126–7, 131
　Mediterranean strategy (WWII), 124–7, 137, 140
　rearmament (1935), 112
　WWI, 126, 190
Ciano, Costanzo, 73 (n.9)
Ciasca, Rafaele, 74 (n.19), 75 (n.30)
Clancy, Tom, 225 (n.19)
Clarke, Sir G. S., 176 (n.3)
Clausewitz, General Karl von, 29
Claytor, W. Graham, 10
coal supplies, 49, 56 (nn.63, 66)
coastal defence vessels, 1
Cold War:
　end, xi, 12, 24, 25, 186, 195, 242, 252

Index

era, xiii, 16, 17, 21, 175, 195, 242–3
Soviet Navy's mission structure, 21 (Table 2.1)
US strategy, 242–53
Colletta, Paolo E., 13 (n.8)
Colomb, Vice Admiral P. H., xvii
Colonial Conference (1907), 51
Composite Warfare Commander (CWC) system, 250
Compton-Hall, Richard, 225 (n.19)
Conolly, Admiral Richard L., 7
Conte-Helm, Marie, 86 (n.4)
convoys:
  WWI, 2, 80, 89, 191
  WWII Arctic, 151–61
  WWII Atlantic, 96–7, 124, 194
  WWII Mediterranean, 136 (Map 11.1), 143, 144, 146
Cooper, Sir Frank, 225 (n.17)
Corbett, Sir Julian, xvii, 163
Corfu, occupation (1923), 68
Cornell, Paul, 197 (n.6)
Coronel, battle of (1914), 34
Corradini, Enrico, 74 (n.17)
Cortada, James W., 76 (n.31)
Coverdale, John F., 75 (n.31)
Cowie, Paymaster-General T. J., 56 (n.66)
Crete, campaign (1941), 126, 139, 140–1, 143, 145, 146
Crickard, Fred W., 196 (n.3)
Crimean War (1853–56), 15, 163–4
cruisers:
  armoured, 42, 43–4, 50, 51
  British, 44, 50, 51, 110, 111, 154, 156
  Canadian, 190, 194
  French, 43–4, 45
  German, 89, 90
  Indian, 205
  Japanese, 82, 83, 110
  Pakistani, 204
  Russian, 18
  Soviet, 22
  US, 1, 250
Cuba:
  Bay of Pigs (1961), 247
  Missile Crisis (1962), 195

Cunningham, Admiral of the Fleet Andrew, 127, 134–5, 137–47, 158–9
Cunninghame-Graham, Rear Admiral A. E. M. B., 159
Cyprus, 124, 141
Cyrenaica (Libya), 141, 143, 146

Da Zara, Alberto, 67
Dakar (West Africa):
  expedition (1940), 127, 138
  French base, 45
Dalrymple-Hamilton, Rear Admiral Sir Frederick, 155, 156
Daniel, D. C. F., 225 (n.19)
Daphné-class submarines, 63, 208
Dardanelles expedition (1915–16), 126
Darrieus, Georges, 61
Daveluy, René, 55 (n.35), 61, 90
Davis, S. M., 199 (n.28)
De Felice, Renzo, 75 (n.31)
de Gaulle, Charles, 62, 63
Defence Operational Analysis Establishment, West Byfleet, 222
Deist, Wilhelm, 39 (n.20), 99 (nn.14, 19, 20)
Delcassé, Théophile, 45
Delhi (Indian cruiser), 205
Dennison, Robert, 253
Derna (Libya), 143
destroyers:
  British, 111, 140, 153–5
  French, 63, 64
Di Sambuy, Vittorio, 76 (n.41)
Diadem (British cruiser), 155, 204
Diefenbaker, John, 195
Diego Suarez (Madagascar), 45
Dingman, Roger, 86 (n.8)
disarmament:
  Geneva Conference (1932–37), 111
  Geneva Naval Conference (1927), 82–3
  League of Nations role, 81, 110
  London Naval Conferences (1930, 1936), 83, 110
Djibouti (East Africa), French support, 64

Dodecanese Islands:
  British attempt (1943), 127
  Italian base, 70, 71, 139
  Italian seizure (1911–12), 68
Dönitz, Grand Admiral Karl, 95–6,
  151–2, 153–4, 156–7, 161
Donnelly, Christopher, 26 (n.21)
Douglas, W. A. B., 196 (n.2), 197
  (nn.6, 14), 198 (nn.17, 18, 24, 26)
Drax, Rear Admiral Reginald, 119
  (n.36)
Dreadnought (British submarine),
  218
Dülffer, Jost, 98 (n.12)
Dunkirk, (1940), 134, 141
Duppler, Host, 38 (n.7)
Durand de la Penne, Luigi, 76 (n.37)
Duroché, J., 55 (n.34)
Dutch Navy, *see* Netherlands Royal
  Navy
Dwarka, Pakistani raid (1965), 207
Dyer, Rear Admiral K.C., 195

Eagle (British aircraft carrier
  1918–42), 138
Eagle (British aircraft carrier
  1946–78), 230, 237
Earle, Edward Mead, 76 (n.40)
East Indies:
  nationalist movement, xxi–xxii,
    177–8
  NRN coastal operations (1945–50),
    177–87
  smuggling, 179–81, 183
Eayrs, James, 198 (n.16)
Edwards, Kenneth, 69, 73 (n.3), 75
  (nn.21, 26), 76 (n.35)
Egypt, 124, 125, 141, 143
  see also Alexandria, Suez
Eisenhower, Dwight D., 243, 247
Enigma, 157, 160
Enock, Artur Guy, 73 (n.4)
Enterprise (US aircraft carrier), 209
Epkenhans, Michael, 38 (nn.14, 16), 39
  (nn.26, 27, 34, 35), 40 (nn.42, 43,
  46)
Eritrea, Italian base, 70
Esquimalt (British Columbia), 189,
  190

Ethiopia (Abyssinia):
  Djibouti, 64
  Italian conquest, 70, 167
Etzold, Thomas H., 13 (n.15)
European Community, British
  membership, 234
Ewe, Loch, 153, 154, 156, 157

Fairchild, Byron, 196 (n.4)
Falkland Islands:
  campaign (1982), 222, 223
  Maritime Exclusion Zone, 173
Fashoda Incident (1898), 44
Fencer (British aircraft carrier), 156
Ferrante, Ezio, 72 (n.2), 74 (n.15)
Ferrari, Paolo, 75 (n.24)
Ferris, John Robert, 116 (nn.11, 12),
  117 (nn.18, 20, 22)
Festing, Sir Francis, 229–30, 233–4,
  239
Fieldhouse, D. K., 197 (n.5)
Fioravanzo, Giuseppe, 68, 69, 74
  (nn.11, 15, 18, 20), 75 (n.21), 76
  (n.39)
First World War (1914–18):
  Anglo-German naval conflict, 34–7
  blockade, xviii, 34, 165–7
  Canadian role, 190–2
  convoys, 2, 80, 89, 191
  German Navy, 34–7, 89–90, 97,
    165–6
  Italian Navy, 67–70
  Japanese Navy, 79–81
  Mahanian position, xviii
  merchant shipping, 89, 169
  mines, 2, 67, 89
  naval blockade, xviii, 34, 165–7
  RN role, 34–7, 106
  submarines, 2, 67, 89, 92
  USN role, 2
Fisher, Sir John, xxii, 42–4, 48, 50–1,
  78, 189
Fiume:
  Italian annexation, 68
  torpedo works, 69
Five-Power Defence Agreement, 220
Fleet Air Arm (FAA):
  John's role, 228, 235
  Korean War, 216

Index

missiles, 218
RAF relationship, 114, 235, 237, 238
RN control, 114, 129
VSTOL aircraft, 230
WWII (Mediterranean), 137–9, 143, 146
Forbes, E. R., 198 (n.21)
Ford, Admiral Wilbraham, 142
Formidable (British aircraft carrier), 139, 140, 141, 146
Forstmeier, Friedrich, 40 (n.46)
Fournier, François, 54 (n.22)
Fraccaroli, Aldo, 76 (n.39)
France:
  Anglo-French Entente (1904), 44
  Conseil Supérieur de la Marine, 47
  German invasion (1940), 169
  Indo-China, 44, 45, 46–7
  NATO, 62–3
  naval history, 59–64
  naval strategy, xxi
  Pacific strategy, 43–8
  Revolution, 60
  Russian alliance, 44, 45
  Suez crisis (1956), 217
  WWII defeat, 103, 104, 115, 123, 124, 132
  see also French Navy
Franco, General Francisco, 71
Frank, Willard C. Jr, 76 (n.31)
Franks, 60
Fraser, Admiral Sir Bruce, 153–5
Fraser, Hugh, 232
Fremantle (Western Australia), 50
French, David, 224 (n.2)
French Air Force, 107
French Navy:
  blockades, 163
  cruisers, 43–4, 45
  history, 59–64
  jeune école, 32, 59, 61
  Mediterranean fleet, 45
  Oceanic Strategic Force, 63
  Pacific strength, 45
  Plan Bleu, 60, 63
  side-armoured cruisers, 43
  size, 63

  status, xxi
  submarines, 45, 46, 47–8, 63, 64
Fricke, Vice Admiral Kurt, 95
Friedberg, Aaron, 52 (n.1), 53 (n.11), 56 (n.58)
Friedman, Norman, 6, 224 (n.3)
frigates:
  British, 157, 159, 194
  French, 63
  Indian, 206–7, 209
Friz, Giuliano, 66, 74 (nn.14, 16, 17)
Frothingham, Thomas G., 73 (n.10)
Frunze, Mikhail, 19
Fuller, General J. F. C. ('Boney'), 124
Fuller, William C., 26 (n.7)
Fulmar aircraft, 137, 138

Gabriele, Mariano, 66, 74 (nn.14, 16, 17)
Gaeta, Franco, 74 (n.17)
Gallery, Rear Admiral Daniel, 6
Gallipoli campaign (1915–16), 126
Galster, Vice Admiral Karl, 33
Gan Island (Indian Ocean), 232
Gatti, Angelo, 73 (n.8)
Geneva Naval Conference (1927), 3, 82–3
Genoa (Italy), 146
German Navy, 27–37, 88–98
  battleships, 32, 91
  cruisers, 89, 90
  High Seas Fleet, 2, 30, 32–3, 34, 35, 41, 89–90, 97
  inter-war, 90–1
  Mediterranean Division (WWI), 89
  Prize Regulations, 168
  Schnorchel, 152, 153, 156, 157, 159–60
  size, 32
  U-boats, 32, 34, 36, 91–7, 124, 128, 130, 147, 151–61, 166, 168, 170, 191, 192
  WWI, 34–7, 89–90, 97, 166
  WWII, 91–7
German Navy League, 30
Germany:
  Anglo-German Naval Agreement (1935), 90
  blockade (WWI), 166

Germany *continued*
  blockade (WWII), 168–70
  Federal Republic, 98
  Luftwaffe, 125, 139–41, 142, 145, 147, 153, 159
  merchant shipping, 169
  naval power (WWI and WWII), 88–98
  Navy Law, 36
  shipbuilding, xxi, 32
  Tirpitz-Plan, 31–3, 36
Gervaise, Professor B. B., 19–20
Ghazi (Pakistani submarine), 205, 206, 207, 209
Gibbs, Norman, 117 (n.24), 118 (n.25)
Gibraltar:
  British base, 27, 48, 120
  WWII, 95, 135, 143, 144
Gilbert, Martin, 148 (n.18), 149 (n.38)
Gimblett, R. H., 196 (nn.1, 3, 9)
Giorgerini, Giorgio, 72 (n.1), 76 (n.36)
Glennie, Vice Admiral I. G., 154
Glete, Jan, 118 (n.33)
Gnat torpedoes, 153, 154, 156, 157, 160
Godfrey, Vice Admiral J. H., 201, 202
Goering, Hermann, 156
Goglia, Luigi, 74 (n.19)
Goodall (British frigate), 159
Gorbachev, Mikhail, 24–5
Gordon, G. A. H., 117 (n.24)
Gorshkov, Admiral Sergei, 14, 16, 17–18, 20, 21, 23
Goschen, George, Lord, 53 (n.14), 54 (n.25), 57 (n.73)
Gough, Barry M., 197 (n.7)
Graham, Dominick, 133 (n.7)
Graham, Gerald, 197 (n.7)
Grand Fleet, xviii
Grand Port, battle of (1810), 62
Grandi, Dino, 75 (n.25), 76 (n.32)
Grasse, François Joseph Paul, comte de, xii
Graves, Donald, 198 (n.26)
Gray, Colin S., xix
Great East Asia Co-Prosperity Sphere, 84–5
Great Patriotic War (1941–45), 16, 17, 20–1,
  see also Second World War

Great White Fleet, 2, 48, 49
Greece, campaign (1941), 125, 126, 127, 139–40, 145
Grenier, Jacques, vicomte, 61
Gretton, Admiral Sir Peter, 161
Grivel, Vice Admiral Louis Antoine Richild, baron, 61
Grove, Eric, 224 (nn.5, 7), 225 (nn.9, 11, 14)
Gulf War (1991), xii, 64, 174–5, 195
Gwyn, Julian, 196 (n.4)

Hadley, Michael, 196 (n.1), 197 (n.11)
Hague Peace Conferences (1899, 1907), 165
Haiti embargo, 64
Halifax (Nova Scotia), 58 (n.78), 189, 190, 191, 193
Halpern, Paul G., 73 (nn.3, 7), 74 (nn.13, 18)
Hangor (Pakistani submarine), 209, 210
Hankey, Sir Maurice, 113
Harding, Warren, 81
Hardy (British destroyer), 153
Harkness, Douglas, 195
Harkort, Friedrich, 28
Harris, Sir Arthur, 127, 129
Harris, Robin, 197 (n.6)
Harwood study (1949), 216
Hawaii, US base, 3
Hawke, Admiral of the Fleet Edward, Lord, xii
Haydon, Commander Peter, 199 (n.29)
Hayward, Admiral Thomas B., 13 (n.12), 250
Healey, Denis, 219, 222, 233
Heeringen, August von, 39 (n.36)
helicopters, 218, 221
Hellyer, Paul, 195
Henderson, Sir Nicholas, 224 (n.6)
Henretta, James A., 196 (n.4)
Hermes (British aircraft carrier, *later* Indian), 211, 237
Herwig, Holger H., 40 (nn.48, 49, 50)
Hessler, Günther, 99 (n.23), 161 (n.4), 162 (n.5), 176 (n.7)
Heye, Commander Hellmuth, 99 (nn.20, 21)

Index

Hicks-Beach, Sir Michael, 53 (n.14), 54 (n.25), 57 (n.73)
Hideyoshi, Toyotomi, 77
Hill, J. R., 225 (nn.17, 18, 19)
Hillgruber, Andreas, 100 (nn.26, 28, 29)
Hingham, John, 198 (n.25)
Hinsley, F. H., 162 (n.6)
Hirama, Yoichi, 80
Hitler, Adolf, 90–1, 93–7, 113, 123–4, 169
Holland, *see* Netherlands
Holland, John Philip, 78
Hong Kong, 50, 51
Hood, Ronald Chalmers, 59
Hood (British battle-cruiser), 122
Hopkins, A. G., 116 (n.8)
Hopman, Captain Albert, 33
Horton, Admiral Sir Max, 152, 153–4, 155, 159, 160
Hose, Commodore Walter, 191, 192
Hoste, Fr Paul, SJ, 61
Hough, Richard, 73 (n.6), 98 (n.7)
Howard, Michael, 116 (n.10), 117 (n.25), 118 (n.34), 162 (n.15)
Humble, Richard, 162 (n.10)
Hunt, Barry D., 212 (n.7)
Hurd, Archibald, 54 (n.33), 73 (n.10), 74 (n.18)
Hurst, Sir Cecil, 175 (n.2)
Hussein, Saddam, xii

Ikeda, Kiyoshi, 86 (nn.5, 9, 10)
Illustrious (British aircraft carrier), 137, 138, 139, 141
Imperial Conference (1909), 51
Inchon landing (1950), 8
India:
  defence, 122, 123, 124
  Five Year Defence Plan, 206
  war with China (1962), 206
  war with Pakistan (1965), 207
  war with Pakistan (1971), 208, 209–10
  WWII, 70
Indian Air Force, 206
Indian Navy (IN), 63, 200–11
Indian Ocean, 24, 69
Indo-China, French defence, 44, 45, 46–7

Indomitable (British aircraft carrier), 141
Indonesia:
  blockade, 172
  British relations, 208, 219
  Indo-Pakistan War (1965), 207
  nationalist movement, 177, 178, 185
  naval power, 206
  territorial waters, 185–6
Inskip, Sir Thomas, 113
Institute of International Law, 164
Iran–Iraq War (1980–88), 64, 173–4
Iraq, blockade (1990), 174
Ishii, Count Kikujiro, 81
Italian Naval League, 67–8, 69
Italian Navy:
  size, 63
  Spanish Civil War, 70–1, 168
  status (1911–43), 66–72
  WWI, 67–9
  WWII, xxi, 71–2, 138, 144
Italy:
  invasion of Abyssinia, 70, 167
  League of Nations sanctions, 167
  Regia Aeronautica, 134–5, 137, 146
  WWII, 123, 134–47

Jackson, Bill, 217, 224 (n.4), 226 (n.25)
Jaffe, Lorna S., 116 (n.5)
Jane, Fred T., 14, 54 (n.27), 86 (n.4)
Jansen, Marius, 86 (n.2)
Japan:
  British alliance (1902), 42–3, 44, 48, 57 (n.72)
  East Indies naval policy, 185, 186
  Guards mutiny (1936), 84
  Manchurian crisis (1931–33), 83
  National Defence Policy, 82, 84
  naval strategy, xxi
  oil supplies, 85
  sea power, 77–86
  Twenty-one Demands on China, 80
  US relationship, 82–5, 249
  war with China (1894–95), 78
  war with China (1937–45), 84, 85
  war with Russia (1904–5), xviii, 15, 44, 45–6, 49, 78, 79, 165
  Washington naval treaty, 81–2

Japan *continued*
  WWI, 79–81
  WWII, 4, 177
Japanese Navy, 77–86
  air force, 84
  aircraft carriers, 84
  coal supplies, 49, 56 (n.66), 57 (n.68)
  cruisers, 82, 83, 110
  East Indies presence, 185
  8–8 fleet, 80, 81
  Replenishment Programmes, 84
  shipbuilding, 79, 84, 85
  size, 81–2
  status, 78, 79
  WWI, 79–81
  WWII, 84–5, 177
Java, 179, 180, 183
Jefford, J. W., 202
Jellicoe, Admiral of the Fleet John Rushworth, Lord, 191
Jenkins, E. H., 59–60
Joanna V (tanker), 173
John, Sir Caspar, 228, 229–30, 233–5, 237, 239
Johnson, Louis A., 7
Joint Exercise Trincomalee (JET), 203
Joint Services Seaborne Force (JSSF), 227–8
Jutland, battle of (1916), 19, 34, 89

Kahn, David, 162 (n.21)
Kammen, Michael G., 196 (n.4)
Kanya-Forstner, A. S., 55 (n.51)
Kashmir (British destroyer) 140
Katari, Admiral R. D., 213 (n.26)
Kato, Admiral Tomosaburo, 81, 82
Katz, Stanley Nider, 196 (n.4)
Kaul, Lieutenant Commander Ravi, 212 (n.13), 213 (n.29)
Kavic, Lorne J., 213 (nn.20, 23)
Kelso, Frank B. II, 13 (n.16)
Kemper, Lieutenant Commander J. T., 214 (n.46)
Kennedy, Floyd D., 13 (n.7)
Kennedy, John F., 195, 243, 247
Kennedy, Paul M., xix, xx, 26 (n.5), 39 (nn.17, 32), 52 (n.1), 53 (n.11), 57 (n.73), 98 (nn.5, 6), 115 (n.1)

Keppel (British destroyer), 154
Kerr, Admiral Lord Walter, 43, 54 (nn.17, 29), 55 (n.34)
Key West Agreement (1948), 6
Khaibar (Pakistani destroyer), 209
Khan, Ayub, 213 (n.19)
Khan, Rear Admiral M. H., 213 (n.40)
Khrushchev, Nikita, 22, 23, 247
Khukri (Indian frigate), 209
Kidd, Admiral Isaac C. Jr, 9
King, Mackenzie, 192, 193
King, W. L. M., 198 (n.18)
Kingsmill, Admiral Sir Charles, 192
Kipling (British destroyer), 140
Kiras, James D., 196 (n.3)
Kissinger, Henry, 214 (n.44)
Kitchener, Horatio Herbert, Lord, xviii, 125
Kite (British sloop), 156
Klado, Admiral Nikolai, 16, 19, 22
Kobe (Japan), 49
Koh Chang, battle of (1941), 62
Kohli, Admiral S. N., 213 (n.30), 214 (n.42)
Kola Inlet, 156, 157, 158, 159
Korb, Lawrence J., 13 (n.13)
Korea, Japanese invasions, 77, 79
Korean War (1950–53), 8, 172, 194–5, 216, 247, 252
Kornilov, General Lavr, 18
Krishnan, Vice Admiral N., 213 (n.41), 214 (nn.44, 45)
Kronstadt:
  British attack (1919), 18
  British blockade (1855), 164
  mutiny (1921), 18, 19
Krupp, Friedrich A., 30
Kuropatkin, General A. N., 15, 25
Kuwait crisis (1990), 174
Kuznetsov, Admiral Nikolai, 20

La Hogue, battle of (1692), 59, 60
Lacy, James L., 13 (nn.7, 14)
Lambe, Sir Charles, 227–8, 233
Lambert, A. D., 162 (n.20)
Lambert, Nicholas, 53 (nn.3, 5, 6, 7, 8), 54 (nn.19, 28), 56 (nn.57, 62), 58 (nn.81, 84, 91)

Index

Lambi, Ivo N., 38 (nn.2, 5, 9), 39 (nn.29, 34), 98 (n.3)
Lapwing (British sloop), 159
Lark (British sloop), 158
Laubeuf, Maxime, 47, 48
Laughton, Sir John, xvii
Laurier, Wilfrid, 189, 190, 196
Lay, Captain H. N., 194
Le Masson, Henri, 55 (nn.41, 44, 46)
Leach, Admiral of the Fleet Sir Henry, 225 (n.12)
League of Nations:
 collective security scheme, 104
 Covenant, 167
 disarmament meetings (1920), 81
 German exit, 111
 naval cutbacks, 122
 Non-intervention Committee, 167
 Palestine mandate, 171
 sanctions, 110, 167
Leander-class frigates, 206–7
Leatham, Admiral Sir Ralph, 143
Lebanon conflict, 8, 64, 252
Lehman, John F. Jr, 249, 250
Lend-Lease Act (1941), 131
Leningrad, siege (1941–44), 20
Libya:
 British action (WWII), 127
 Italian base, 70
 Italian traffic (WWII), 135, 143
 Senussi revolt, 71
 Soviet plan, 22
 Tunisian conflict, 64
 USN role, 252
Liddell-Hart, Basil, 124
Lie, Trygve, 22
Lightning aircraft, 238
Lissa, battle of (1866), 67, 72
Locarno Pact (1925), 110
Lockroy, Edouard, 54 (n.22)
London Declaration (1909), 165, 166
London Naval Conferences (1930, 1936), 3, 83
London Naval Treaty (1930), 110, 168
Longmore, Air Marshal Sir Arthur, 145
Louis XIV, King, 59, 60, 62
Louis XV, King, 59, 60
Luce, Admiral Sir David, 239
Lyon, Hugh, 117

McConnel, J. M., 26 (n.20)
Macdonald, John A., 189
MacDonald, Ramsay, 110, 111
McGrigor of McGrigor, Rear Admiral Rhoderick, 155, 158
MacIntyre, David, 162 (n.17)
Mackay, Ruddock F., 53 (n.6), 56 (nn.55, 56)
Mackinder, Sir Halford, xix, 16–17, 18, 24, 25, 35, 188
Macmillan, Harold, 217, 218, 231–2, 239
McNamara, Robert, 248
McNaughton, Major-General A. G. L., 192
Mahan, Alfred Thayer:
 Canadian position, 188
 influence, xvii–xx
 influence on Britain, 44, 51
 influence on France, 61
 influence on Germany, 29–30, 32, 35, 36, 37, 88
 influence on Japan, 87 (n.16)
 influence on US, 1–6, 10–12
 Japanese comparison, 78
 on French Navy, 59
 on RN, 120–2
 Russian position, 14, 15, 17, 25
Maigret, Vice Admiral Marie Edgard, comte de, 55
Makarov, Vice Admiral Stepan Osipovich, 78
Malaya, 122, 129, 172
Mallman-Showell, J., 161 (n.4)
Malta:
 British base, 50, 71, 120, 124
 dockyard, 202
 WWII, 125, 134, 135, 139, 140–4, 146
Manchester, William, 117 (n.17)
Manfroni, Camillo, 73 (n.7)
Manila (Philippines), 44
Manzini, E., 74 (n.11), 76 (n.34)
Marder, A. J., 26 (n.5), 52 (n.1), 54 (n.23)
Marine Française, *see* French Navy
Maritime Contingency (MARCON), 247

Index

Masirah Island (Muscat and Oman), 232
Mason, Sir Ronald, 225 (n.22)
Masson, Philippe, 65 (n.10)
Matabele (British destroyer), 154
Matapan (Cape), battle (1941), 115, 139, 144, 146
Matsu Island (China Sea), 8
Mattesini, Francesco, 76 (nn.38, 39)
Maudling, Reginald, 231–2, 234
Maurer, J. H., 56 (n.65)
Mazzei, Jacopo, 74 (nn.17, 19)
Mazzetti, Massimo, 75 (n.29)
Meaney, Neville, 56 (n.59), 58 (nn.86, 87)
Mediterranean:
  British convoy route, 136 (Map 11.1)
  British fleet, 50, 124–5, 134–47, 145, 152
  French fleet, 45
  German fleet, 89, 95, 96
  Italian role, 70
  Japanese role (1918), 80
  Maritime Interest Zone, 63
  Soviet presence, 9, 24
  Tardi–Turner agreement (1977), 63
  WWII, 71, 95, 96, 124–6, 134–47
Meiji Restoration (1868), 77–8
Melville, Thomas Richard, 196 (nn.1, 9)
Menon, Krishna, 213 (n.22)
merchant shipping:
  coal supplies, 49
  East Indies, 179
  London Naval Treaty, 168
  WWI, 89, 169
  WWII, 94, 168–9, 170–1
  see also convoys
Merlin (British paddle survey ship), 164
Mersa Matruh (Egypt), 142
Meyer, Jean, 65 (n.7)
Meyrick, Admiral Sir Sydney, 193
Mid-Ocean Escort Force, 193
Miller, Edward, 56 (n.66)
Millo, Enrico, 69
Milne, Lieutenant Commander J. M., 225 (n.10)

Milner, Marc, 4, 198 (nn.24, 26)
mines:
  blockade role, 165
  countermeasures, 223
  effectiveness, xiii
  first wartime use, 164, 166
  WWI, 2, 67, 89
  WWII, 147, 157, 159, 169
missiles:
  British, 218–19, 231, 234
  cruise, xii, 250
  development (1950s), 22–3, 243
  Osa-class boats, 209
  Polaris, 8, 218–19, 231, 234, 247
  Soviet, 9
  Styx, 209, 210
  US, 8, 243, 246–7, 250, 251
Mitchell, B. R., 224 (n.2)
Molotov, Vyacheslav, 20, 22
Monfalcone, shipyard, 69
Monger, George, 53 (n.1)
Monroe Doctrine, 188, 189
Monterisi, M., 74 (n.11), 76 (n.34)
Moore, Admiral Sir Henry, 156, 157
Morse, Philip M., 13 (n.2)
motor torpedo-boats:
  Italian (MAS), 67, 69
  Soviet, 20
Mottez, Captain Lucien, 47–8
Mounsey (British frigate), 157
Mountbatten of Burma, Admiral of the Fleet Louis:
  Air Ministry relations, 229, 232, 234–5
  dive-bombing victim, 141
  India and Pakistan navies, 202, 205, 206–7
  nuclear-powered submarine programme 218
Mundy, Carl E. Jr, 13 (n.16)
Munich agreement (1938), 123, 193
Murmansk convoys, 153
Murray, Williamson, 116 (n.7)
Mussolini, Benito, 68, 69, 70–1, 125, 167
Mutsu (Japanese battleship), 81
Mutual Assured Destruction, 12
Mysore (Indian cruiser), 205

Index

Nagato (Japanese battleship), 81
Nailor, Peter, 225 (n.11)
Napoleon Bonaparte, 60
Nassau Conference (1962), 218–19, 234
National Security Act (1947), 6
NATO (North Atlantic Treaty Organisation):
  Adriatic blockade, xi, 175
  Atlantic limits, 220
  British commitment, 219–22
  Cold War, 17
  defence spending, 222
  Follow-On-Forces-Attack strategy, 251
  formation, 203
  French role, 62–3
  German role, 98
  Maritime Contingency (MARCON), 247
  name, 5, 216
  naval strategy, 243, 248
  sea area, 220
  Striking Fleet concept, 235
  USN role, 10
Navigation Certificates, 166
Naylor, John F., 117 (n.21)
Nehru, Jawaharlal, 202
Neilson, Keith, 53 (n.2), 54 (n.34), 58 (n.83)
Nelles, Rear Admiral Percy, 193
Nelson, Admiral Horatio, Lord, xii, 34
Netherlands, Far East naval strategy, xxi–xxii, 177–87
Netherlands Royal Navy (NRN), xxi–xxii, 177–87
New Zealand:
  coal supplies, 49
  defence, 122, 123
  docks, 50
  WWII, 131
Nimitz, Admiral Chester W., 6
Niobe (Canadian cruiser), 190
Nipperdey, Thomas, 38 (n.15)
Nish, Ian, 53 (nn.9, 10, 13), 54 (n.29)
Normandy landings (1944), 132, 156
North Atlantic Treaty (1949), 5, 216
  see also NATO

North Korea, 172
North Sea:
  British strategy, 42, 50, 165
  French history, 60
  German fleet, 32, 34, 35, 89, 90
  WWI, 89, 90
  WWII, 169
Norway:
  campaign (1940), 127, 134, 169
  German forces, 151, 152, 153, 160
  German invasion (1940), 115, 169
  NATO, 220, 221
  WWI, 36
Norwegian Sea, 246
Nott, John, 222
nuclear arms:
  British, 217, 218–19
  Cold War, 243, 246
  deterrence, xii
  Soviet Navy, 21, 22–4
  US strategy, 6–7, 243, 246, 249
nuclear-powered submarines, 218, 221, 223
Nyon Patrol, 168

Oba, Osamu, 86 (n.2)
Ocean Surveillance Information System (OSIS), 249, 250
O'Connor, General Sir Richard, 127
Odell, Captain Paul, 13 (n.1)
Ogarkov, Marshal, 24
oil supplies, 80–1, 85
Okabe, Count Nagakage, 85
Okada, Admiral Teisuke, 83
O'Keefe, Sean, 13 (n.16)
Oleg (Soviet cruiser), 18
Operation Catherine (1939), 126–7
Operation Fortitude (North), 156
Operation Neptune (1944), 132
Operation Overlord (1944), 132, 151, 152, 155, 160
OR346, 230, 235
Osa-class missile boats, 209
Otranto barrage (1918), 67
Ottley, Captain Charles, 56 (n.61)
Overy, R. J., 118 (n.28)
Owen, Captain W. F. W., 189

Index

P1154 aircraft, 230, 232–3, 235, 237, 238, 239
Pacific:
  British fleet, 48, 51, 129
  British policy (1905–9), 43–4, 48–52
  French policy (1905–9), 43–8
  Japanese fleet, 44
  US bases, 2, 3
  US strategy, 1, 3
Padfield, Peter, 162 (n.5)
Paixhans, General Henri Joseph, 61
Pakistan:
  war with India (1965), 207
  war with India (1971), 208, 209–10
Pakistan Air Force, 208
Pakistan Navy (PN), 200–11
Palermo, battle of (1676), 60
Palestine Patrol, 171
Palmer, Michael A., 13 (n.6)
Pantellaria plan (1940–41), 127
Paris Peace Declaration (1856), 164
Parry, Admiral Sir William, 212 (n.11)
Pearl Harbor, 4, 139
Pearson, Lester, 195
Peden, G. C., 116 (n.10), 117 (n.24), 118 (n.32)
Pelz, Stephen E., 87 (n.14)
Perry, Commodore Matthew Galbraith, 77, 78, 79
Persian Gulf, 124, 252
Peters, Captain A. R., 213 (n.40)
Petropavlovsk (Soviet battleship), 18
Petrov, Professor M. A., 19–20
Petter, Wolfgang, 38 (nn.2, 3)
Phantom aircraft, 239
Philibert, Rear Admiral Joseph-Alphonse, 46, 55 (n.35)
Philip Augustus, King, 59
Philip II, King of Spain, 131
Phillips, Admiral Sir Tom, 129
Pietromarchi, Luca, 75 (n.25)
Pike, Air Chief Marshal Sir Thomas, 228–30, 232–5, 237–9
Pinke, Vice Admiral A. S., 178, 180, 181–2
Pizzigallo, Matteo, 74 (nn.12, 13)
Pluviôse-class submarines, 47–8
Pola (Italian heavy cruiser), 139

Polaris, 8, 218–19, 231, 234, 247
Pompidou, Georges, 60
Port Arthur, 43, 46
Port Courbet, 45
Portal, Air Marshal Sir Charles, 127
Porter, A. N., 54
Post, Gaines Jr, 75 (n.28)
Pound, Admiral of the Fleet Sir Dudley, 124, 127, 128, 134–5, 141, 142
Pratt, Lawrence R., 75 (n.30)
Pridham-Wippell, Admiral Sir Henry, 146
Prince of Wales (British battleship), 123, 127
Prize Regulations, 89, 165, 168
Pusan defence (1950), 8
Quartararo, Rosaria, 75 (n.30)
Quebec Conference (1943), 194
Quemoy Island (China Sea), 8

radar:
  British, 130, 235
  Canadian Navy, 193
  Netherlands Royal Navy, 181
  WWII (Arctic convoys), 157
  WWII (Mediterranean), 134, 135, 137, 139, 142, 146
Radford, Vice Admiral Arthur, 6
Raeder, Grand Admiral Erich, 36, 90–2, 93–4
Rahn, Werner, 38 (nn.2, 14), 39 (n.38), 40 (n.41), 98 (nn.1, 8, 9, 10, 11)
railways, xviii, 188
Rainbow (Canadian cruiser), 190
Ramsay, Admiral Sir Bertram, 132
Reagan, Ronald, 24, 249
Reed, B., 225 (n.15)
Repulse (British battle-cruiser), 123, 127
Rhodes, 139
Rhodesia, blockade, 172–3
Riccardi, Arturo, 73 (n.8)
Richardson, Admiral James O., 4
Richelieu, Cardinal, 60
Richmond, Admiral Sir Herbert, xvii, 15, 191
Rickover, Admiral Hyman G., 10, 218
Rizzo, Luigi, 73 (n.9)

Index

Robbins, Keith, 115 (n.2)
Robertson, Esmonde M., 75 (n.29)
Rochat, Giorgio, 74 (n.19)
Rommel, Erwin, 127
Roosevelt, Franklin D., 3–4, 162 (n.16), 192–3
Ropp, Theodore, 54 (nn.22, 33)
Rosenberg, David A., 13 (nn.7, 11), 53 (n.7)
Roskill, Captain Stephen, 117 (n.17), 156, 160, 162 (nn.12, 14), 212 (n.3)
Rosyth (Fife), 50
Royal Air Force (RAF):
   Arctic convoys, 156
   blockade, 163–75
   Bomber Command, 128, 130, 131, 170
   bombing strategy, 107–8, 112–13, 127, 131
   Coastal Command, 127, 128, 129, 130, 144, 156, 170, 234
   creation, 129
   cuts, 218
   government expenditure, 111, 113–14
   Home Defence Air Force, 107
   joint RN strategy, 227–40
   Joint Services Seaborne Force, 227–8
   Mediterranean role (1940–42), 134–47
   shore-based patrols, 218, 222
   status (post-WWI), 106
   Unity of the Air, 115
Royal Canadian Naval Air Service, 191
Royal Canadian Navy (RCN), xxi, 130, 190–6
Royal Fleet Auxiliary, 217, 221, 223
Royal Indian Marine, 201
Royal Indian Navy (RIN), 201–2
Royal Marines, 217, 218, 220, 221, 222
Royal Naval Air Service, 129
Royal Navy:
   aircraft carriers, 129, 137–9, 141, 146, 154–60, 219, 223, 228–40
   Arctic convoys, 151–61

Beira Patrol, 172–3, 220
Canadian defences, 188
China battle-squadron, 43, 44, 48, 51
coal supplies, 49
cruisers, 44, 50, 51, 110, 111, 154, 156
destroyers, 111, 140, 153–5
Dreadnought revolution, 42
East of Suez strategy (1961–63), 227–40
Fleet Air Arm (FAA), see Fleet Air Arm
Future Fleet Working Party, 219
Home Fleet, 152, 155, 156, 157
human skills, 114
Intelligence Department, 49
joint RAF strategy (1961–63), 227–40
Joint Services Seaborne Force, 227–8
Korean War, 172
Mediterranean role (WWII), 123–6, 134–47, 152
missiles, 218–19
NATO, 219–22
overseas bases, 50
Pacific Fleet (1945), 129
Palestine Patrol, 171
Polaris, 218–19
RAF relationship (1961–63), 227–40
Reserve Fleet, 216
shipbuilding, 33, 111, 112, 122
size, 121, 122, 216
submarines, 42, 50, 131, 143, 170, 218–19, 221–3
technology, 130
West Coast Patrol, 171
Western Approaches Command, 152–5
WWI, 34–7, 106
WWII, 122, 124–32, 134–47, 151–61, 168–71
WWII losses, 71, 125, 141
Royal Navy Prize Act, 164
Royal Pakistan Navy (RPN), 202
Rozhestvensky, Admiral Zinovi Petrovich, 49
Ruge, F., 162 (n.24)

Rules of Engagement, xii
Rush, J. R., 187
Russia:
  British relations, 41, 43
  French alliance, 44, 45
  Revolution, 18
  see also Soviet Union
Russian Imperial Navy:
  coal supplies, 49
  Fortress Fleet, 15
  nineteenth century, 15
  Pacific presence, 43
  Second Pacific Squadron, 45–6
  status, 15–16
  WWI, 34
Russo-Japanese War (1904–5), xviii, 15, 44, 45–6, 49, 78, 79, 165
Rwanda, French intervention, 64

Sadkovich, James, 72 (n.1), 74 (n.11), 75 (nn.22, 24), 76 (nn.36, 38)
Saigon (Vietnam), 45, 46
Saionji cabinet, Japan, 79
Saito, Admiral Makoto, 79, 82
Salewski, Michael, 99 (nn.13, 16, 20, 23), 100 (nn.29, 30, 31, 32)
Sandys, Duncan, 217–18, 227
Santiago de Cuba, battle of (1898), 2
Santoni, Alberto, 76 (nn.37, 39)
Sarty, Roger, 196 (n.1), 197 (n.11)
Satsuma naval clan, 77, 78, 79
Scapa Flow, 156
Schanzer, Carlo, 68
Scharnhorst (German battleship), 152
Scheer, Admiral Reinhard, 34
Schmidt, Gustav, 116 (n.3), 118 (nn.26, 27)
Schnorchel, 152, 153, 156, 157, 159–60
Schröder, Klaus, 99 (nn.15, 16)
Schull, Joseph, 198 (n.26)
Sea Gladiator aircraft, 138
Sea Harrier VSTOL aircraft, 221
Sea Lines of Communication (SLOCs), 246, 248, 250, 251
Sea Vixen, 235, 238, 239
SEATO (South-East Asia Treaty Organisation), 203

Second World War (1939–45):
  Atlantic, 95–7, 124, 127–8
  anti-submarine warfare, 130, 137–8, 151–3
  Arctic convoys, 151–61
  blockade, 4, 168–71
  Canadian Navy, 192–4
  convoys, 96–7, 124, 136
    (Map 11.1), 143, 144, 146, 151–61, 194
  French defeat, 103, 104, 115, 123, 124, 132
  German Navy, 91–8, 169
  Italian Navy, xxi, 71–2, 138, 144
  Japanese Navy, 84–5, 177
  Mahanian position, xviii
  Mediterranean, 71, 95, 96, 124–6, 134–47
  merchant shipping, 94, 168–9, 170–1
  mines, 147, 157, 159, 169
  Phoney War, 169
  RN role, 120–32, 134–47, 151–61, 168–71
  submarine warfare, 4, 92–7, 152, 161, 169
  US role, 3–5, 93, 95, 124, 131
  see also Great Patriotic War
Segrè, Claudio, 75 (n.20)
Selborne, William Waldegrave Palmer, Lord, 53 (n.16), 54 (nn.17, 23, 24, 29), 55 (n.34), 56 (n.62)
Semenoff, V., 26 (n.4)
Serbia, 67, 175
Settsu (Japanese battleship), 81
Sherman, Vice Admiral Frederick C., 6–7
Shimonoseki, treaty of (1895), 78
Siam, Gulf of, 46, 47
Sicily, 70, 125, 139, 144
Siegfried, Jules, 61
Siemens bribery scandal, Japan, 79
Silva, Pietro, 67
Simonstown (South Africa), 50
Singapore:
  docks, 50
  mutiny (1915), 80
  RAF, 237

smuggling trade, 178, 181
WWII, 115, 123, 127, 129
Singh, Rear Admiral Satyindra, 212 (n.9), 213 (n.27)
Sinha, Sureshwar D., 213 (n.24)
Sino-Indian border war (1962), 206
SIOPS (Single Integrated Operational Plan), 8, 247
Skua aircraft, 137, 138
Skybolt, 219, 231
Smith, Adam, 72
Smith, Malcolm, 118 (nn.31, 32, 34)
Soavi, Giuseppe, 67
Somalia, 64, 70
Soman, Admiral, 213 (n.30)
Somerville, Admiral Sir James, 134–5, 137–8, 141, 143–6, 147
Somerville, Lieutenant Mark, 148 (n.20)
Sondhaus, Lawrence, 73 (n.7)
South China Sea, 46, 50
Soviet Naval Aviation, 246
Soviet Navy, 14, 16–25
  Arctic convoys, 156
  Fortress Fleet, 18, 20
  Northern Fleet, 20
  Pacific Fleet, 20
  size, 22
  SSBNs, 8–9, 11, 251
  status, xxi, 16
  submarines, 5, 8–9, 11, 16–17, 20, 22–4, 195, 217, 246, 253
  technology, 221
Soviet Union:
  Arctic convoys, 151, 159
  Berlin blockade, 171
  détente, end of, 248
  Great Patriotic War, 16
  Indian Navy relationship, 206–7, 208, 210
  interwar policy, 102
  naval strategy, xxi
  Red Army, 125
  shipbuilding, 17, 19
  Spanish Civil War, 70, 71
  Suez crisis (1956), 217
  threat (British perception), 216, 223
  War of Intervention, 18–19
  see also Russia

Spain:
  Civil War (1936–39), 70–1, 167–8
  Empire, 121
  war with US (1898), 2, 46
Spee, Admiral Maximilian, Count von, 19
Spigai, Virgilio, 76 (n.37)
Sridharan, Rear Admiral K., 212 (n.4)
Stalin, Joseph, 16, 20, 21–2
Steinberg, Jonathan, 98 (n.4)
Stimson, Henry, xviii
Story, Rear Admiral W. O., 190–1
Stosch, General Albrecht von, 28
Striker (British cruiser), 156
submarines and U-boats:
  blockade role, 165, 166
  British, 42, 50, 131, 143, 170, 218–19, 221–3
  conventional, xiii
  French, 45, 46, 47–8, 63–4
  Indian Navy, 200, 203, 206, 207
  Italian, 67, 70–1
  German U-boats, 32, 34, 36, 89, 91–7, 124, 128, 130, 147, 151–61, 166, 168, 170, 191, 192
  London Naval Treaty, 83
  midget, 152
  nuclear-powered, 218, 221, 223
  Pakistan Navy, 200, 203–10
  Polaris, 8, 218–19, 231, 234, 247
  Soviet, 5, 8–9, 11, 16–17, 20, 22–4, 195, 217, 246, 253
  SSBNs, 8–9, 11, 246, 251
  US, 4, 9, 11, 12, 246, 250, 253
  WWI, 2, 67, 89, 92
  WWII, 4, 92–7, 152, 161, 169
  see also anti-submarine warfare
Suez:
  Canal, 142, 143, 146, 167
  crisis (1956), 8, 195, 217, 218
Suffren-class destroyers, 63, 64
Suffren de Saint Tropez, Pierre André de, 62
Sullivan, Brian, 72 (n.1), 74 (n.20)
Sumida, Jon T., 53 (nn.3, 4, 7), 54 (nn.18, 20, 26), 56 (n.55), 117 (n.23), 119 (n.36), 243, 254 (n.1)
Sverdlov-class cruisers, 22

Sweden, 15, 126–7, 204
Swordfish aircraft, 138, 146, 156, 157
Sydney (Cape Breton Island), 191
Sydney (New South Wales), 50
Syrett, David, 162 (n.26), 197 (n.14)

Taiwan, 8, 247
Takahashi, Korekiyo, 84
Takarabe, Admiral Takeshi, 79
Taranto attack (1940), 138, 144, 146
Tardi-Turner agreement (1977), 63
Tedder, Air Chief Marshal Sir Arthur, 144, 145
Terni steelworks, 70
Terraine, John, 133 (n.12)
Third World War, concept of, 242–3
Thomas, Hugh, 76 (n.76)
Thomas, Raju G. C., 213 (nn.25, 34)
Thompson, Gaston, 46
Thorneycroft, Peter, 231, 232, 234, 238, 239
Till, Geoffrey, 119 (nn.35, 37), 241 (n.36)
Tirpitz, Admiral Alfred von, 15, 27, 29, 31–7, 78, 88, 91
Tirpitz (German battleship), 127, 152, 155, 156
Tobruk, 139, 142
Toby, Ronald, 86 (n.2)
Todd, Lieutenant-Commander Geoffrey, 194
Togo, Admiral Heihachiro, Count, 80
Tokugawa shogunate, 77
Tomar, Ravindra, 213 (n.33)
torpedoes:
  electric, 168
  Gnat, 153, 154, 156, 157, 160
  human, 147
  introduction, 166
  Pakistan Navy, 208, 210
  WWII (Mediterranean), 138
Touchard, Vice Admiral Philippe, 46
Toulon:
  fleet scuttled (1942), 60, 62
  port, 60
Tourville, Admiral Anne Hilarion de Cotentin, comte de, 62
Trafalgar, battle of (1805), 34, 62
Treitschke, Heinrich von, 28

Trenchard, Air Marshal Sir Hugh, 106, 107
Tress, Harvey B., 118 (nn.31, 34)
Trident, 225 (n.12), 251
Trieste, shipyard, 69
Tripartite Alliance, 84, 85
Tripoli (Libya), 127, 142, 143, 145, 146
Tromp, Maarten van, xii
Trotha, Admiral Adolf von, 35
Trumpener, Ulrich, 98 (n.7)
TSR2, 230, 231, 232–3
Tsushima, battle of (1905), 44, 46, 79
Tucker, Gilbert Norman, 198 (nn.17, 21)
Tunisia:
  French control, 71
  French support, 64
Turkey, 15, 22, 69, 89, 208
Tweedmouth, Edward Marjoribanks, Lord, 57 (n.75), 58 (n.83)

U-boats, *see* submarines
Ultra, 130, 153, 154, 156–8, 170
United Kingdom (UK), *see* Britain
United Nations, 64, 171–4, 186, 223
United States:
  British relationship (interwar), 105
  Civil War (1861–65), 164
  Congress, 3, 5, 10, 244
  Defense Department, 8, 244
  Eighth Army, 125
  India–Pakistan war (1971), 209–10
  Lend-Lease Act (1941), 131
  Maritime Strategy, 223
  Military Assistance Program (MAP), 204, 205
  National Security Act (1947), 6
  National Security Decision Directive (1982), 249
  naval power, 219–20
  naval strategy (1945–90), 242–53
  Suez crisis (1956), 217
  war with Spain (1898), 2, 46
  WWII, 93, 95, 131
United States Air Force, 5, 6–8
United States Marine Corps, 5, 7, 12
United States Navy (USN), 1–12

Index

aircraft carriers, 4–12, 253
anti-submarine warfare, 7, 8–9,
    10–11, 246
Cold War strategy, 22, 243–53
Composite Warfare Commander
    (CWC) system, 250
cruisers, 1, 250
government attitude, xxi
Great White Fleet, 2, 48, 49
Iran–Iraq War, 173–4
Mahan's work, xvii, xviii
Maritime Strategy, 10–12, 24, 223,
    248–53
Ocean Surveillance Information
    System (OSIS), 249, 250
offensive sea control, 1–6, 7, 8, 12
Pacific presence, 3–4, 44, 49
reduction in strength (1975), 10
SEA PLAN 2000, 250
shipbuilding programme, 81, 106
SSBNs, 9, 246–7, 251
strength, 219–20
submarines, 4, 9, 11, 12, 246, 250,
    253
technology, 130
Third World role, 9, 11
War Plan Orange, 2, 3, 49
WWI role, 2
WWII role, 3–5, 124
USSR, *see* Soviet Union

Valori, Aldo, 66, 74 (n.17), 75 (n.23)
Vansittart, Robert, Lord, 70
Varè, Daniele, 75 (n.27)
Varillon, Pietro, 75 (n.27)
Vauban, Sébastien le Prestre de, 60
Venetae, 60
Venezuela, blockade (1902), 2
Verdun (French aircraft carrier), 63
Vernet, Joseph, 59
Versailles Peace Treaty (1919), 90
Victorious (British aircraft carrier),
    230–1, 238, 239
Vidal brothers, 189
Vietnam War (1956–75), 8, 209, 247,
    248
Vikrant (Indian aircraft carrier), 205–6,
    207, 209, 210
Vindex (British aircraft carrier), 156

Viti, Guido, 74 (n.18)
Vittorio Veneto (Italian battleship), 139
VSTOL aircraft, 221, 230, 236

Wark, Wesley K., 118 (nn.28, 30)
Warner, Oliver, 149 (nn.38, 39)
Warsaw Pact, 223
Washington Naval Conference
    (1921–22), 3, 68, 81–2, 117 (n.15)
Washington Naval Treaty (1922), 82,
    105, 110, 122
Wasp (US aircraft carrier), 143
Watkins, Admiral J. D., 226 (n.26)
Watkinson, Harold, 227, 239
Watt, D. C., 116 (nn.3, 9), 118 (n.31)
Wegener, Edward, 40 (n.47), 98 (n.5)
Wegener, Lieutenant-Commander
    Wolfgang, 36
Weir, Gary E., 73 (n.3)
West Coast Patrol, 171
Western Approaches, xxii, 152–3,
    154–5, 157
Western European Union (WEU), 175
Wilhelm II, Kaiser, xxi, 28–32, 35
Williams, Captain David, 225 (n.13)
Williams, G., 225 (n.15)
Wilson, Woodrow, 2
Wingate, John, 225 (n.19)
Winzen, Peter, 38 (nn.6, 10)
Wise, S. F., 197 (n.12)
Wittelsbach (German pre-
    dreadnought), 30
Wolff, Eugen, 38 (n.8)

Yamamoto, Admiral Gombei, 78, 79
Yamato-class battleships, 84
Yap Island (South Pacific), 81
Yawata steelworks strike (1920), 80
Yugoslavia, blockade of former, xi, 64,
    175, 186

Zaghi, Carlo, 74 (n.19)
Zeigler, Philip, 213 (n.28)
Zhukov, Marshal Georgi, 206
Zimmerman, David, 198 (n.24)
Zof, Admiral V. I., 19
Zuckerman, Sir Solly, 232, 236, 239
Zumwalt, Admiral Elmo R. Jr, 9, 10,
    214 (n.44)